D1145753

Revolution and Counterrevolution

Revolution and Counterrevolution
Change and Persistence in Social Structures

Seymour Martin Lipset

Revised, with a new introduction
by the Author

JA
76
₀L55
1988

Transaction Books
New Brunswick (U.S.A.) and Oxford (U.K.)

New material this edition copyright © 1988 by Seymour Martin Lipset. Original Edition © 1970 by Seymour Martin Lipset.

All rights reserved under International and Pan-American Copyright Conventions. No part of this book may be reproduced or transmitted in any form or by any means, electronic or mechanical, including photocopy, recording, or any information storage and retrieval system, without prior permission in writing from the publisher. All inquiries should be addressed to Transaction Books, Rutgers—The State University, New Brunswick, New Jersey 08903.

Library of Congress Catalog Number: 87-30215
ISBN: 0-88738-694-6
Printed in the United States of America

Library of Congress Cataloging in Publication Data

Lipset, Seymour Martin
    Revolution and counterrevolution: change and persistence in social structures / Seymour Martin Lipset.—Rev. with a new introduction / by the author.
        p.   cm.
    Includes bibliographical references and index.
    ISBN 0-88738-694-6 (pbk.)
    1. Political sociology.   I. Title.
JA76.L55   1988
306′.2—dc 19   87-30215

To Bob, Paul, and Bob
for origins and encouragement

Introduction to the Transaction Edition

Revolution and Counterrevolution was published in 1968 and revised in 1970. In many ways it is a sequel to two earlier works, *Political Man* and *The First New Nation*.[1] Like these two books, it has a strong comparative emphasis, seeking to explain variations in political outcomes by reference to differences in the history and social structure of nations, both industrialized and less developed. The title, *Revolution and Counterrevolution*, refers to the fact that the United States is the country descendant from the revolution triumphant, while Canada is formed from the parts of British North America in which the revolution failed.

Political Man tended deliberately to emphasize the role of economic and class factors in political development, and political cleavage in democratic states—voting behavior and political participation, for example. In this book, more stress is laid on the role of factors that generally go under the rubric of values. Thus chapters 2 and 3, which bear on aspects of the development process, focus on values, while the equivalent chapters of *Political Man* dealt with political development, emphasized the role of structural factors, largely aspects of the level of economic development.

The shift in emphasis from the specification of the way in which structural factors limit behavior to a concern with the way in which varying historical events determine future political choices by affecting national values, does not represent a rejection of the approach followed in *Political Man*, but rather an effort to highlight the analysis of similar matters from different perspectives. *The First New Nation*, which followed *Political*

vii

Man, sought to point up the way in which the formation of national values affected both the development process in different nations, and the types of political cleavages that evolved within them.

The First New Nation focused on the ways variations in basic national values, particularly those of the United States, are linked to differences in contemporary structures and behaviors. To account for American behavior, I also dealt with the other major predominantly English speaking countries, Australia, Canada and Great Britain. These comparative analyses are elaborated in Parts I and II of *Revolution and Counterrevolution*, which discuss the relationships in the context of comparisons within the Americas, Canada with the United States, and Latin America, including Quebec, with Anglophone North America. The sections also contain an analysis of the Jewish communities in comparative perspective.

Political Man sought to elaborate on the conditions of the democratic order, first by specifying factors relevant to the presence of democracy, and second, through a detailed analysis of the sources of electoral diversity, of the way social cleavages are institutionalized in the support base of democratic parties. It treated at some length social class as a major source of political alignment, but did not seek to generalize on a theoretical level about class analysis in politics and sociology. Part III of this book seeks to remedy that deficiency, first by analyzing in Chapter 5 how the different approaches to social class of Karl Marx, Max Weber, and the sociological functionalists who derived from Emile Durkheim, can be used to account for varying aspects of political behavior; then, in Chapter 6, by looking at the role of class-relevant "interest" factors on a more concrete level, and that of value-generating institutions, particularly religion, in determining the nature of the political participation of different groups.

Parts IV and V, which are more empirical in character, constitute an effort to show how the interplay of factors that can be related to class and religion help to account for various forms of specific political choice or group behavior in different countries. Part IV does this on a comparative level, while Part V contains an analysis of American politics.

The core chapters of this book, those which define the theoretical and methodological orientations, are the first two, which deal with history and sociology and with the United States and Canada. These present the arguments and evidence for the thesis that any effort to understand the contemporary behavior, institutions and values of a country, in particular my own, the United States, requires historical and comparative analysis. Since my graduate student days, I have had a deep interest in Canada. That interest was inspired, however, by questions about the United States, in particular why it is the only highly industrialized democratic country which does not have an electorally viable socialist, social democratic, or labor party. Since Canada has had such a party since the 1930s, one that is now known as the New Democratic Party (NDP), which has been first or second in national election surveys for 1986 to the present (1988), the question I have sought to answer in one book and many articles from the late forties through to today is, why does Canada have a socialist party and, it may also be noted as of the eighties, a far stronger trade union movement?[2]

When the social scientist seeks to explain a particular difference among a limited number of cases—for instance, the prevailing political values in two countries—the problem of "too few cases, too many variables" can be mitigated somewhat by the selection of countries for analysis. That is, by choosing countries for comparison so that the range of variables on which the chosen cases are similar is maximized, the researcher can increase the certainty with which the variation in the phenomenon being studied can be attributed to those variables on which the two cases differ from each other. While obviously not as stringent as laboratory procedures, a careful selection of cases can allow the investigator to control for a large number of variables, and hence greatly enhance the analytic rigor of the research. The set of considerations renders Canada and the United States a promising combination for the purposes of comparative analysis.

It is important to note that any effort to specify the values, ethos, or national character of nations confronts the problem that such statements are necessarily made in a comparative context. Thus the assertions that the United States is a materialistic nation, that it is egalitarian, that its family system is unstable, obviously do not refer to these characteristics in any absolute sense. The statement that a national value system is egalitarian clearly does not imply the absence of severe differences in power, income, wealth or status. Generally this means that from a comparative perspective, nations classified as egalitarian tend to place more emphasis on universalistic criteria in judging others, and tend to de-emphasize the institutionalization of hierarchical differences.

The key words here are "tend," "more than" and "comparative." No one suggests that any given complex social structure is in fact egalitarian in any absolute sense. Macroscopic sociology employs polarity concepts when it compares core aspects of societies—*Gemeinschaft-Gesellschaft*, organized solidarity-mechanical solidarity, inner directed-other directed, diffuseness-specificity, achievement-ascription, traditional-modern, and this approach purposely exaggerates such differences for analytic purposes.

Related to this point is a second one concerning the frame of reference within which specific comparisons are made. It may seem a truism, but is nonetheless worth stating, that what appear as significant differences when viewed through one lens may seem to be minor variations seen through another. The issue of whether a given difference is great or not may be exemplified by reference to comparative analyses of Canada and the United States.

CANADA AND THE UNITED STATES

Analysts of the continent-spanning North American democracies have differed with respect to whether they stress the similarities or differences between them. For example, an American political scientist, Louis Hartz, has emphasized the comparabilities, arguing that Canada, the United States and other countries settled by groups emigrating from Europe are all "fragment cultures" formed by the middle class, since the upper and lower strata did not move. Hence, for Hartz the American Revolution is not, and cannot be seen as, a watershed event signalling a radical distinction between the value system developing in post-revolutionary America and that emerging in counter-revolutionary Canada.[3] The minor differences between the two are of far less significance than the traits they share in common, which sharply set them off from European societies.[4] By contrast, the perspective that I have emphasized in Chapter 2 of this book and other writings on the two nations sees a greater degree of continuity between the communitarian and elitist aspects of Imperial Britain and the character of Canadian value orientations than Hartz assumes. My analysis indicates that the survival of these attitudes in Canada and their relative absence in the United States is an important distinction between the two countries that has led to many important variations, resulting initially from the success of the Revolution south of the border and its rejection to the north.

One aspect of this distinction is a greater conservatism in Canada—in the European sense of the word—than in the United States, where eighteenth century *laissez-faire* liberalism became the national tradition. The content of Canadian conservatism, its emphasis on the values of *noblesse oblige* and state responsibility, has meant, ironically, that Canada has provided a more favorable political and social climate for the development of welfare state policies than is found south of the border. The values inherent in a monarchically rooted conservatism such as those which developed in Canada and much of Europe have given rise in the modern world to support for social democratic redistributive and welfare policies. Conversely a dominant *laissez-faire* Lockean tradition which has been characteristic of the United States for much of its history is antithetical to such programs. Hence, it may be argued the greater strength of socialism and trade unions in Canada as compared to the U.S. is to a considerable degree a function of the fact that the counter-revolution triumphed north of the border, resulting in among other things a legitimation there of Tory statist values and policies, while the success of the American Revolution made the United States the prototypical classically liberal anti-statist bourgeois society. Northrop Frye, Canada's leading literary critic, called attention to this alliance of opposites when he stated in 1952: "The Canadian point of view is at once more conservative and more radical than Whiggery [the liberal ideology of the American Revolution], closer both to aristocracy and to democracy [equality]. . . ."[5] Canada's greatest novelist,

Robertson Davies, a committed Tory (a political point of view defined by Harold Macmillan as "paternalistic socialism"), points up the continuing impact of the Tory tradition in Canada. "When you visit us, you may not immediately sense that you are in a socialist country. . . . But . . . we are a people firmly set in the socialist pattern. . . ."[6]

The attitudes and values characteristic of a people do not exist in a vacuum. It is important to recognize that one of the major factors explaining the persistence of particular orientations is that they become embodied in institutions which help perpetuate them. An illustration of this interaction between values and institutions can be found by comparing religious institutions and attitudes in Canada and the United States, which have consistently differed.[7] The American tradition and law have placed much more emphasis on separation of church and state than has the Canadian. A large majority of Americans have adhered to the Protestant sects, mainly the Methodists and Baptists, which had formed in opposition to the established state Church in England. These largely have a congregational structure and foster the idea of an individual relationship with God. The smaller Protestant sects, many of them founded in the United States, have proportionately many fewer adherents in Canada. Most Canadians belong to either the Roman Catholic or the Anglican churches, both of which have been hierarchically organized state religions in Britain and Europe. While efforts to sustain church establishment ultimately failed in Canada, state support of religious institutions, particularly schools, has continued into the present. Hence religious institutions have both reflected and contributed to anti-elitist, individualist, and anti-statist orientations in the United States and countered them in Canada.

It should be noted that a great deal of debate has been generated over the question of the relative significance of Canadian-American value differences. The argument essentially has been between those like myself, who emphasize the distinctiveness of the *values* of the two countries and the ways these in turn affect behavior, beliefs and institutional arrangements, and those who place primary importance on various *structural* differences, particularly geographic, economic, and political factors. It should be stressed, however, that a concern with the influence of economic, ecological, or value elements in determining given national developments or traits is not a matter of dealing with alternative mutually exclusive hypotheses. Rather, as in the case of Max Weber's discussion of the relative contribution of economic and value factors in the rise of capitalism, one may conclude that different variables are each necessary but not sufficient to produce the results sometimes credited to one of them alone.

And, in fact, when the arguments of those identified as adhering to one or the other approach to the sources of Canadian-American differences (values or structure) are carefully examined, it becomes apparent that most of the distinctions really are ones of emphasis. For example, my own analysis takes into account that the two nations do vary in their ecology, demography and economy, and that these differences have exerted an important influence on the development of values and attitudes on both sides of the border. Canada controls an area which, while larger than her southern neighbor's, is much less hospitable to human habitation in terms of climate and resources. Her geographical extent and weaker population base have contributed to an emphasis on direct government involvement in the economy to provide various services, for which sufficient private capital or a profitable market has not been available.[8] South of the border, the anti-statist emphasis subsumed in the revolutionary ideology was not challenged by the need to call upon the state to intervene economically to protect the nation's independence against a powerful neighbor.[9]

In a similar way, those whose analyses emphasize the significance of structural factors also acknowledge the role that values play in affecting the development of political and economic differences across the border. A good example can be found in the writing of Friedrich Engels, the co-founder of the most influential structural approach of all. He was one of the first analysts to contend that Canada's economic backwardness compared to the United States is primarily a function of her value system. Following a visit to both countries in 1888, he wrote in deprecating terms concerning Canadian economic development as compared to American, and argued that these differences demonstrated "how necessary the *feverish speculative spirit* of the Americans is for the rapid development of a new country" and looked forward to the abolition of "this ridiculous boundary line" separating the two countries.[10] More recently, Harold Innis, Canada's preeminent economic historian, who has strongly emphasized structural factors, such as the "hard" character of the Canadian frontier, in affecting national orientations, has also noted the importance of "the essentially counterrevolutionary traditions, represented by the United Empire Loyalists and by the Church in French Canada, which escaped the influences of the French Revolution"[11] For more on these themes, I would refer the reader to Chapter 2, as well as my more recent analyses, cited earlier.

OLD AND NEW POLITICAL CLEAVAGES

Parts III and IV of *Revolution and Counterrevolution* are concerned with the topic of political conflict. The connection between social class analysis and the study of political cleavages is clear. In *Political Man* I summarized it thusly: "The most important single fact about political party support is that in virtually every economically developed country the lower income groups vote mainly for the parties of the Left, while the higher income groups vote mainly for the parties of the Right."[12] This conclusion was congruent with the basic anticipation of Karl Marx, who emphasized that economic development under capitalism would result in a situation in which employed workers would form a majority of the labor force and that as a result of economic constraints and industrial environments workers would organize economically (unions) and politically (a revolutionary socialist party). They would give the organizations majority support, enabling them to take power and create a socialist society.

The era immediately following World War II seemingly validated a major element of Marxist analysis in that left parties held office in most of the advanced industrial states of northern and central Europe and Australasia. But even then, the contradictions between political realities and Marxist predictions were much greater than the agreements. The most industrialized and pure bourgeois society, the United States, has never had an electorally viable socialist or labor party and continues to exhibit one of the lowest correlations between class position and party choice, facts which explicitly negate the Marxist dictum in *Capital* that "the country that is more developed industrially only shows, to the less developed, the image of its own future."[13] In any case, in the highly developed countries in which social democrats then held office, Scandinavia, Australasia, Britain, Austria, etc., the parties were not revolutionary, sought to make a multi-class appeal, and clearly had no intention of trying to eliminate capitalism. A comparative study of party platforms from 1910 to 1960 (later extended to 1970) by John Thomas indicated that the differences between the platforms of bourgeois and socialist parties had narrowed over time.[14] Ironically, revolutionary movements still had strength in the then less industrialized European countries in the Latin and southern tier, Spain, France and Italy, as well as in Finland. But, whatever the form or intensity, class conflict was a reality everywhere and it was reflected in election contests which I described in *Political Man* as the "democratic class struggle."

An emphasis on class as the only important determinant of political cleavage past, present and future is, of course, wrong. However class is defined, it has never accounted for more than part of the causal mechanisms involved in political differentiation. Recognizing this, Stein Rokkan and I tried to systematize the structural factors underlying the diverse character of European party systems. In *Party Systems and Voter Alignments*, we analyzed modern political cleavages as the outgrowth of two revolutions, the National Revolution and the Industrial Revolution.[15]

These transformations produced various social cleavages which became linked to party divisions and voting behavior. The first political revolution resulted in a *center–periphery* conflict between the national culture and assorted subordinate ones, for example, ethnic, linguistic, or religious groups often located in the peripheries, the outlying regions, and *church–state* tension between the state, which sought to dominate, and the church, which tried to maintain its historic corporate rights. The economic revolution gave rise to *land–industry* cleavage between the landed elite and the growing bourgeois class. This was followed by the cleavage Marx focused on, that between *capitalist and workers*.

These four sources of cleavage, each of which has continued to some extent into the contemporary world, have provided a framework for the party systems of the democratic polities. But as Rokkan and I noted, class became the most salient source of conflict and voting, particularly after the extension of the suffrage to all adult males. The partisan expressions of the four cleavage models obviously have varied greatly internationally. They have been most fully expressed in multi-party systems and condensed into broad coalitions in two-party ones like those of the United States or Australia. Given all the transformations in western society over the first half of the twentieth century, it is noteworthy how little the formal party systems changed.[16] Essentially the cleavages had become industrialized, and the party systems of the 1960s closely resembled those of pre World War I Europe. The main changes related to the rise and disappearance of fascist movements, and to the division of the working-class parties into two major ones in some countries. The latter parties, of course, were much stronger in the post World War II political arenas than earlier, attesting to the increased salience of class.

Some critics of the four cleavage model have argued that it assumes too much rigidity, and largely derives party systems from structure. But as a discussion by Russell Dalton, Scott Flanagan and Paul Beck notes,

> Although the Lipset-Rokkan model emphasized the institutionalization and freezing of cleavage alignments, the model also has dynamic properties. It views social alignments as emerging from the historical process of social and economic developments. New alignments develop in response to major social transformations such as the National and Industrial revolutions. While the structure of cleavages is considered to be relatively fixed, the political salience of the various cleavages and patterns of party coalitions may fluctuate in reaction to contemporary events.[17]

The western world appears to have entered a new political phase which roughly dates from the mid 1960s with the rise of so-called "post-materialistic issues, a clean environment, use of nuclear power, a better culture, equal status for women and minorities, the quality of education, international relations, greater democratization, and a more permissive morality, particularly as affecting familial and sexual issues."[18] These have been perceived by some social analysts as the social consequences of an emerging third "revolution," the Post-Industrial, which is introducing new bases of social and political cleavage. The underlying economic analysis has been associated with the work of Daniel Bell,[19] while the emphasis on the emergence of new political cleavages is linked to the work of Ronald Inglehart.[20] Essentially Bell and others have sought to document the effects on the culture of structural shifts which have sharply increased the importance of occupations linked to high-tech, informational, knowledge and public service industries, and require greater reliance on universities and research and development centers, while the production focused positions—farm and manual work—have been declining.[21] Inglehart and others have pointed to new lines of cleavage between the adherents of the industrial society's emphasis on production and of conservative positions on social issues, and those who espouse the post-industrial stress on the quality of life and liberal social views when dealing with ecology, feminism, and nuclear energy.[22] Life concerns are difficult to formulate as party issues, but groups such as the Green parties and the New Left or New Politics educated middle class tendencies within the traditional left parties have sought to foster them.

Issues and cleavages derivative from those of industrial society, however, remain a more important source of policy division and electoral choice, since the more materialistically oriented workers and self-employed constitute much larger strata than the intelligentsia. The perceived failure of the social democratic welfare state to solve key issues has, however, resulted in a renewal of the appeal of classic liberal (free market) approaches, sometimes presented in the context of solutions to quality of life concerns as well.

The effects of the recent changes, whether they deserve the term "revolution" or not, may be seen in the reduction of the correlation between class and voting which has occurred in many countries, in the decline in commitment to traditional parties, a phenomenon which often presages alignment or the rise of new parties, and in the increased volatility among the electorate from one election to another. It is too early to anticipate whether these recent developments will produce a new party system. But as Rokkan and I stressed, it is difficult to break the attachments to the established parties. What is more likely is a reorganization of their programs and social base.

THE END OF IDEOLOGY

Another concept dealt with in *Political Man*, which is further explicated in Chapter 8 of this book, is the "end of ideology." This concept describes the results of a situation in which the intensity of political conflict among citizens of industrialized countries has declined, resulting in the cross-party agreement in a broad range of ideas and policies documented by Thomas. This approach has been subjected to severe criticisms, particularly by left oriented scholars who identify it with a preference for consensus rather than conflict in the polity.[23]

Without going into further detail on the subject, I would note that I have replied in depth to much of that criticism in a more recent work, particularly to critics who see in the proliferation from the mid sixties of mass single issue movements and the emergence of assorted New Lefts evidence that ideology is far from dead.[24] But as I have noted, neither I nor others who wrote on the subject in the 1950s and early sixties assumed that ideology or political conflict was over in any sense. Raymond Aron, Daniel Bell, Edward Shils, and myself had anticipated that political protest would continue and that it would largely be supported by the very strata so involved in the New Left revolt of the 1960s; students, excluded minorities and the intelligentsia. We never forecast the end of ideological orientations, protest or social reform efforts, but rather stated that there was and would continue to be a decline in the appeal of total ideologies for those segments of society integrated into the system, increasingly including the working class. Thus in my original discussion I specifically excluded "ethnic, racial, or religious groups, like American blacks or Ulster Catholics, who are still deprived in citizenship terms," from the groups for whom total ideologies would have less appeal. The continuing and inherently adversarial relationship of American intellectuals to their society was the theme of Chapter 10 in the 1960 edition of *Political Man.* The history and development of the concept is analyzed in depth in *Conflict and Consensus* and I will not, therefore, go into further detail here.

SOME LARGE SCALE GENERALIZATIONS

Finally, I would note one of the reviewers of the first edition, Robert L. Heilbroner, did me the rare courtesy of summarizing my work in this book in terms of a number of "large-scale generalizations," which strike me at least as accurate. They are as follows:

The essential building blocks of political stability are social rather than economic.

This does not deny the enormous moving force of economic change. Rather it implies that economic changes operate through social motivations. Thus poverty in itself does not lead to social restlessness any more than affluence alone leads to social harmony. The existence, or the narrowing, of economic gaps does not necessarily offset motivations born of status, tradition, ethnicity, etc. Hence the search for the causes of social stability or change must always include matters of status and value as well as questions of economics: "The prolonged intensity of class conflict in many continental nations," Lipset writes, "was owing to the overlap of economic class conflict with 'moral' issues of religion, aristocracy, and status. Because moral issues involve basic concepts of right and wrong, they are more likely than economic matters to result in civil war or at least class cleavage."

The basic movement of Western society is toward industrial bureaucratic societies in which traditional class conflicts are lessened.

Social unrest, as Lipset sees it, is primarily a product of social change. Hence we must expect to find it in its most exacerbated form when change is most acute as in the case of the Third World or in the West, in those nations and eras when the industrial transformation was most rapid. Conversely, the gradual surmounting of the dislocation of industrialization opens the way for the emergence of a pragmatic rather than polarized politics.

This is not to maintain that conflict ceases in such an environment. As Lipset notes, "All democratic countries, from the lands of the Mediterranean basin to Sweded, Australia, or the United States, remain highly stratified societies in which access to education, economic opportunity, culture, and consumption goods is grossly unequal." Hence conflict necessarily continues, even in the most advanced nations. But the conflict becomes institutionalized and muted, as the values of industrial society triumph over those of the pre-industrial.

A new ideological consensus begins to unite the formerly opposed classes, but fails to include all elements or to bridge the gap between the industrialized and nonindustrialized world.

As bureaucratization softens the views of the upper class vis-a-vis the lower, and the slow rise in living standards lessens the gap between the lower and the upper, a consensus begins to emerge around a view that Lipset calls "conservative socialism." This clearly heightens the change of social peace insofar as this is threatened by economic conflict. Yet the new ideology fails to include both the extreme Right and the far Left, including the student body, and it fails as well to seem relevant to the leaders of the underdeveloped world. Thus, as so often before, this generation finds that it has achieved extraordinary social progress by comparison with the last—and yet discovers to its discomfiture that social harmony is no nearer. Like preceding generations, it fails to perceive that the very act of raising standards also changes them. The old frictions are lessened, but new ones arise. The acceptance of industrialism brings a new ideological center, but not an end to ideological or economic conflict.[25]

    The essays in this book largely represent work of the early 1960s, prior to the rise of massive protest movements in America and Europe. Since then, I have written extensively on student protest, the politics of the professoriate, right wing movements in the United States, the factors relevant to the weakness of socialist movements in the U.S., the decline of American trade unions, the impact of a changing occupational structure on class conflict and values, the fall off in confidence in American institutions, the conditions for democracy, and Canadian and American culture and institutions.[26] As far as I can judge, my writings since 1965 follow the same methodological and theoretical orientations as in the previous period. I believe the analyses in *Revolution and Counterrevolution* continue to hold up, but these judgements are not for me to make. I welcome this new edition as an opportunity for readers to see the corpus of my work through the prespective of time.

Seymour Martin Lipset
Stanford, California
February 1988

NOTES

1. S.M. Lipset, *Political Man: The Social Bases of Politics* (New York: Doubleday-Anchor Books, 1960), revised and updated paperback edition (Baltimore: John Hopkins University Press, 1981); *The First New Nation: The United States in Comparative and Historical Perspective* (New York: Basic Books, 1963), expanded paperback edition (New York: Norton Library, 1979).
2. S.M. Lipset, *Agrarian Socialism* (Berkeley: University of California Press, 1950), revised and expanded paperback edition (Berkeley: University of California Press, 1968); "Radicalism in North America: A Comparative View of the Party System in Canada and the United States," *Transactions of the Royal Society of Canada*, Series IV, 14 (1976), pp. 19–55; "American Exceptionalism in North American Perspective," in E.M. Adams, ed. *The Idea of America* (Cambridge, Mass: Ballinger, 1977), pp. 107–161; "North American Labor Movements: A Comparative Perspective," in S.M. Lipset, ed., *Unions in Transition: Entering the Second Century* (San Francisco: ICS Press, 1986), pp. 421–452.
3. Hartz, however, does note that English Canada is "etched with a Tory streak coming out of the American Revolution," Louis Hartz, *The Founding of New Societies* (New York: Harcourt, Brace and World, 1964), p. 34.
4. For a recent work which emphasizes the similarities between Anglophone Canada and the U.S., see Peter Brimelow, *The Patriot Game* (Toronto: Key Porter Books, 1986).
5. Northrup Frye, "Letters in Canada: 1952. Part I: Publications in English," *The University of Toronto Quarterly* 22 (April 1953), pp. 269–80.
6. Robertson Davies, *One Half of Robertson Davies* (New York: Penguin Books, 1978), pp. 274–275.
7. S.M. Lipset, "Canada and the United States: The Cultural Dimension," in Charles F. Doran and John H. Sigler, eds., *Canada and the United States: Enduring Friendship, Persistent Stress* (Englewood Cliffs, NJ: Prentice-Hall, Inc. 1985), pp. 109–160; S.D. Clark, *Church and Sect in Canada* (Toronto: University of Toronto Press, 1948).
8. James Bryce, *Modern Democracies*, vol. 1 (New York: Macmillan, 1921), p. 471.

9. The so-called Laurentian thesis advanced by some economic historians suggests that without state intervention and economic links in Europe, Canada could not have survived as a separate country. See Harold A. Innis, *Essays in Canadian Economic History* (Toronto: University of Toronto Press, 1956).

10. Friedrich Engels, "Engels to Sorge," September 10, 1888, in Karl Marx and Friedrich Engels, *Letters to Americans* (New York: International Publishers, 1953), pp. 203–204, emphasis mine.

11. Innis, *Essays in Canadian Economic History*, p. 406.

12. Lipset, *Political Man*, pp. 223–224.

13. Karl Marx, *Capital*, vol. I (Moscow: Foreign Language Publishing House, 1958), pp. 8–9.

14. John Thomas, *The Decline of Ideology in Western Parties: A Study of Changing Policy Orientations* (London and Beverly Hills: Sage, 1974); "The Changing Nature of Partisan Divisions in the West," *European Journal of Political Research* 7 (1979), pp. 403–5.

15. S.M. Lipset and Stein Rokkan, "Cleavage Structures, Party Systems and Voter Alignments," in Lipset and Rokkan, eds., *Party Systems and Voter Alignments* (New York: The Free Press, 1967), pp. 1–64; also included in S.M. Lipset, *Consensus and Conflict: Essays in Political Sociology* (New Brunswick, NJ: Transaction Books, 1985), pp. 113–185.

16. Richard Rose, "Persistence and Change in Western Party Systems Since 1945," *Political Studies* 18 (1970), pp. 287–319.

17. Russell J. Dalton, Scott Flanagan, and Paul Beck, *Electoral Change in Advanced Democracies* (Princeton: Princeton University Press, 1984), p. 455.

18. S.M. Lipset. *Political Man* (expanded and updated edition), pp. 503–521.

19. Daniel Bell, *The Coming of Post-Industrial Society* (New York: Basic Books, 1973).

20. Ronald Inglehart, "The Silent Revolution in Europe: Intergenerational Change in Post-Industrial Societies, *American Political Science Review* 65 (1971), pp. 991–1017; *The Silent Revolution: Changing Values and Political Styles Among Western Publics* (Princeton: Princeton University Press, 1971); and Dalton, et al., *Electoral Change*.

21. For a detailed analysis similar to Bell's by Czech scholars, see Radovan Richta, et al., *Civilization at the Crossroads*, (White Plains, NY: International Arts and Science Press, 1969).

22. Russell Dalton, et al., *Electoral Change*; Max Kaase and Sam Barnes, eds., *Political Action* (Beverly Hills: Sage, 1979); Everett C. Ladd, Jr., *Transformations of the American Party System*, (New York: W.W. Norton, 1975); Lipset, *Consensus and Conflict*, pp. 187–217.

23. For a discussion of the intellectual problems inherent in efforts to classify scholarship as consensus or conflict, see Lipset, *Consensus and Conflict*, especially pp. 1–79.

24. Ibid., pp. 81–109.

25. Robert L. Heilbroner, "Societies and Change," The New Republic 159 (July 13, 1968), pp. 27–28.

26. Some of this work not previously cited here is contained in S.M. Lipset, *Rebellion in the University* (Chicago: University of Chicago Press, 1976); (with Everett Ladd) *The Divided Academy: Professors*

and *Politics* (New York: Norton Library, 1967); (with Earl Raab), *The Politics of Unreason: Right-Wing Extremism in America 1790-1977* (Chicago: University of Chicago Press, 1978); (with William Schneider), *The Confidence Gap: Business, Labor and Government in the Public Mind* (Baltimore: Johns Hopkins University Press, 1987); "Why No Socialism in the United States?" in S. Bialer and S. Sluzar, eds., *Sources of Contemporary Radicalism*, vol. I (Boulder, Colo: Westview Press, 1977), pp. 31–149 and 346–363; and (with Larry Diamond and Juan Linz), "Building and Sustaining Democratic Government in Developing Countries: Some Tentative Findings," *World Affairs* 150 (Summer 1987), pp. 5–19. The latter article is a summary of materials in a forthcoming book by the same authors, *Democracy in Developing Countries,, Persistence, Failure and Renewal*, Vol. 1 (Boulder, Colo: Lynne Rienner Publishers, 1989).

Contents

PART I

INTRODUCTION: COMPARATIVE SOCIOLOGY AND HISTORY

CHAPTER 1

History and Sociology:
Some Methodological Considerations

American sociology has been criticized for having departed from the historical concerns of its nineteenth-century European founders. This departure was characterized by a shift from a macroscopic to a more microscopic focus on society, from studies of social change and aspects of total societies, viewed in a historical and comparative perspective, to the study of interpersonal relations, the structure of small groups, and the analysis of the decision-making process, accompanied by an emphasis on improving the quantitative methodology appropriate to these topics. This change suggested to its critics that modern sociology had lost contact with its original intellectual traditions. The writings of men such as Alexis de Tocqueville, Max Weber, Robert Michels, and Vilfredo Pareto were apparently of contemporary interest only insofar as they had attempted to specify functional relationships and social psychological processes of the type that interested latter-day sociologists.

There are many examples which indicate ways in which sociological research has made major errors by ignoring historical evidence. Oscar Handlin and Stephan Thernstrom have given us an illustration of the weakness of an ahistorical

sociology when they demonstrate how W. Lloyd Warner mis-
interpreted a number of patterns in his Yankee City series
of studies of a New England community by relying on contemporary reports concerning past patterns and ignoring the
actual history of the community as available in documentary
sources.[1] Thernstrom has also pointed out the weakness of
many assumptions made about rates of social mobility. He
indicates that both sociologists and historians have erred in
their interpretations concerning the extent of social mobility
in mid-nineteenth-century America by relying either on impressionistic accounts by contemporaries concerning the presumed high rates of upward movement, or on logical deduc-
tions concerning an inherent need for a high mobility rate
in a rapidly expanding economic system. His detailed
quantitative analysis of the actual movement of unskilled
workers in Newburyport, Massachusetts, a century ago, suggests a rate of mobility that is lower than has been found in
studies of contemporary communities.

THE REVIVAL OF HISTORICAL AND COMPARATIVE SOCIOLOGY

In the last decade, the situation with respect to sociological
concern with historical topics has begun to change. There
has been a significant revival of historical and comparative
sociology. This revival has taken many forms, including interest in the sociology of science, concern with the determinants of change in intellectual life, interest in the evolution
of national values, study of past patterns of electoral behavior, analysis of changes in religious life, and the like. The
growth of interest in such problems is so recent that many
with an interest in sociology, including some in the profes-
sion itself, are unaware of the extent to which leading sociologists have become involved in these fields of inquiry.

---

[1] See Handlin's reviews of two books of W. L. Warner and associates,
"The Social Life of a Modern Community" in *New England Quarterly*,
15 (1942), 556, and "The Social System of the Modern Factory" in
Journal of Economic History, 7 (1947), 277; and Stephan Thernstrom,
Poverty and Progress. Social Mobility in a Nineteenth Century City
(Cambridge: Harvard University Press, 1964).

A significant source of the renewed interest in historical and comparative sociology has been the emergence of the body of inquiry which has been called the sociology of development. This term refers to interest in the processes which affect propensities to "modernize" total societies. As a field of research, it parallels the work of economists on problems of economic development. And just as economists concerned with economic development have recognized that much of what is conventionally termed economic history is actually the study of economic development, and that generalizations concerning economic development which are relevant to contemporary "developing economies" can be tested by reference to the past history of developed economies, so sociologists interested in problems of societal modernization and nation building in Africa and Asia have come to understand that the "old states" of the world have much to tell us about these problems. In sociology, as in economics, interest in comparative development has involved a renewed concern with historical analysis.[2]

The re-emergence of historical and comparative sociology does not reflect any general feeling on the part of sociologists that the emphases on quantitative techniques, rigorous methodology, and systematic theory, which have characterized the work of the discipline in recent decades, were misguided. If there is any criticism of these efforts, it is only that they had the temporary effect of narrowing the focus of concern from the macroscopic (total society) to microscopic (small-unit) problems, and from concern with patterns of social change to the analysis of the processes determining group behavior, regardless of time or place. In a sense the swing back to the macroscopic and the historical involves an effort to relate the new methodological and theoretical developments to the analysis of total social systems and social change. Much of the logic of inquiry developed and tested with respect to experimental and microscopic sociology and to analysis of current contemporary processes has proven applicable to macroscopic research, including comparative and historical.

[2] See, for example, T. H. Marshall, *Class, Citizenship, and Social Development* (Garden City: Doubleday, 1964).

SOCIOLOGICAL APPROACHES

If the sociologist has erred in the past by ignoring historical data, the historian has erred in the eyes of the sociologists by ignoring concepts and methods which are as available and useful to the historian as to the sociologist. This does not mean that sociologists seek to turn historians into historical sociologists. From an ideal-typical point of view, the task of the sociologist is to formulate general hypotheses, hopefully set within a larger theoretical framework, and to test them. His interest in the way in which a nation such as the United States formulated a national identity is to specify propositions about the general processes involved in the creation of national identities in new nations. Similarly, his concern with changes in the patterns of American religious participation is to formulate and test hypotheses about the function of religion for other institutions and the social system as a whole. The sociologist of religion seeks to locate the conditions under which chiliastic religion occurs, what kinds of people are attracted to it, what happens to the sects and their adherents under various conditions, and so on. These are clearly not the problems of the historian. History must be concerned with the analysis of the particular set of events or processes. Where the sociologist looks for concepts which subsume a variety of particular descriptive categories, the historian must remain close to the actual happenings and avoid statements which, though linking behavior at one time or place to that elsewhere, lead to a distortion in the description of what occurred in the set of circumstances being analyzed. As Lewis Namier has put it:

> The subject matter of history is human affairs, men in action, things which have happened and how they happened; concrete events fixed in time and space, and their grounding in the thoughts and feelings of men—not things universal and generalized; events as complex and diversified as the men who wrought them, those rational beings whose knowledge is

seldom sufficient, whose ideas are but distantly related to reality, and who are never moved by reason alone.[3]

To use concepts and methods developed in sociology or in the other social sciences, however, does not turn the historian into a systematizing social scientist. Rather, these offer him sets of categories with which to order historical materials, and possibly enhance the power of his interpretive or causal explanations. Thus, looking at the findings of social science may give a particular historian certain ideas as to types of data to collect which may be pertinent to his problem. For example, in recent years students of stratification have formulated the concept of status discrepancy as an explanatory variable. Status discrepancy refers to situations in which individuals or groups are ranked at different levels of prestige or reward on various dimensions of stratification. A college graduate who is a manual worker is high on one dimension, education, but low on the other, occupation. A political boss may be much higher on the power dimension than he is on prestige. College professors may be higher in prestige than they are in income, and so on.

The students of status discrepancy have postulated that those who are in discrepant positions will behave differently in specific ways from those whose statuses are congruent, i.e., all relatively on the same level. It has been suggested, for example, that individuals subject to status discrepancies are likely to be more liberal politically than others who are in the same income, occupational, or other stratification category as themselves. They are also more likely to react in extreme fashion with respect to political and religious behavior. Clearly, a concept such as this may be of use to the historian. It indicates the need to consider the possibility that the varying status positions might explain the deviation from expected behavior of some individuals or groups in the past. I do not suggest that the sociologist can furnish the historian with certain definite facts to incorporate into his analysis; just the opposite is true—the sociologist is complicating the work of the historian by indicating that he ought to examine even

[3] Lewis Namier, "History and Political Culture," in Fritz Stern (ed.), *The Varieties of History* (New York: Meridian Books, 1956), p. 372.

more factors because evidence drawn from sociological studies suggests that these may be relevant.

To take another example, work in sociology and social psychology on attitudes has indicated that the conventional contemporary American definition of liberalism which assumes that to be liberal means to support socioeconomic policies which involve redistribution of community resources in favor of the underprivileged, the welfare state, trade unions, civil rights for Negroes and other minority groups, civil liberties for unpopular minorities, internationalism, liberal immigration policies, and so forth, turns out to create major analytical problems when the actual attitudes of samples of the general population are examined. Opinion studies suggest that there are at least two dimensions of liberalism: economic and noneconomic. The first refers to support for welfare state reforms, trade unions, planning, redistributive tax policies; the second includes backing for civil rights, civil liberties, internationalism, and similar issues.[4] Moreover, the evidence indicates that the less income people have, the more likely they are to be liberal on economic issues; while higher education is closely correlated with noneconomic liberalism. Since the better educated are generally more well to do than those with less education, one finds that poor and less educated people are liberal on economic issues and illiberal on noneconomic ones, while well-educated and well-to-do people tend to be liberal on noneconomic measures and illiberal on economic ones.[5] There are, of course, many who are liberal on both; such a position characterizes the intellectual community and is the policy fostered by the liberal wing of the Democratic party and organizations which support the liberal coalition, such as trade unions and civil rights groups. There are those who are illiberal on both dimensions; these include Southern conservatives, lower-class Republicans, and many right-wing organizations and political leaders.

[4] See G. H. Smith, "Liberalism and Level of Information," *Journal of Educational Psychology*, 39 (1948), 65–81, and "The Relationship of 'Enlightenment' to Liberal-Conservative Opinions," *Journal of Social Psychology*, 28 (1948), 3–17; Herbert H. Hyman and Paul Sheatsley, "Trends in Public Opinion on Civil Liberties," *Journal of Social Issues*, 9, No. 3 (1953), 6–17.
[5] See S. M. Lipset, *Political Man* (Garden City: Doubleday, 1960), pp. 96–130.

The significance of this distinction for the historian is fairly obvious. It should be possible to discover to what extent similar variations existed in the past. As one illustration, this distinction may be reflected in the fact that in debates over the suffrage in New York State, Federalists and Whigs fa- vored equal suffrage rights for Negroes and whites (non-economic liberalism), but the Federalists sought to preserve a property franchise (economic class illiberalism). The Demo-crats, on the other hand, opposed a property requirement, but showed little interest in Negro suffrage.[6] The hypothesis would suggest that xenophobia, nativism, anti-Catholicism, had a strong appeal to less educated lower-class persons all during the nineteenth century. Thus, the Whig and Repub-lican alliances with nativist and Know-Nothing elements may have been their primary means of securing lower-class sup-port away from the Democrats.[7] Such hypotheses might be tested by analyses of the various referenda conducted before, as well as after, the Civil War, which dealt with issues of Negro rights as well as with suffrage rights for the foreign-born, prohibition, and other noneconomic issues.

In urging that historians apply generalizations developed in contemporary analysis to the past, I am not suggesting that they should assume that such propositions have always been valid, or even that the same relationships among different factors will probably help account for given past events. It is quite possible that under the different conditions of pre-Civil War America, anti-Catholic or anti-foreign prejudices were not located preponderantly among the lower strata. How-ever, the hypothesis does suggest the need to investigate the relationship between class and prejudice during that period.

Another group of concepts which may be useful for his-torians is that subsumed in the terms "frame of reference" and "reference group." These concepts involve the assump-tion that, to understand the behavior of individuals or groups, it is necessary to locate the framework within which they evaluate or compare stimuli. Implicit here is the assumption that two events or measures which are objectively similar

[6] Marvin Meyers, *The Jacksonian Persuasion: Politics and Belief* (Stanford: Stanford University Press, 1957), pp. 189–190.
[7] See Lipset and Raab, *op. cit.*, chapter 2.

when judged against an absolute standard may have quite varying consequences when viewed from different frames of reference. Thus, an income or occupation which places a man close to the top of the stratification system in a small community may locate him in the lower-middle class in a large city or in the nation as a whole. To specify social location in relative rather than absolute terms may enhance explanatory analysis. To cite an example from my own work, a study of voting patterns in the elections of 1860 indicated that the extent of slavery in Southern counties correlated with the way in which they voted in the presidential race and the subsequent secession referenda. However, if counties are classified in terms of whether they ranked high or low in proportion of slaves in the South as a whole, the correlation is quite low. If the classification of high or low is made within state lines, then the correlation is much higher. High slave counties within state boundaries behaved similarly politically, even though the statistical meaning of high proportion of slaves varied greatly from states with many slaves to those with few.[8] Thus, it would appear that the relative position of areas within the frame of reference of state politics strongly affected their reaction to the secession question.

The concept of reference group has, of course, emerged largely within social psychology as a way of conceptualizing the group authorities from which individuals derive their standards of judgment. To understand the behavior of historically relevant actors, it may often be necessary to locate or impute their reference group, e.g., to determine whether a given political leader judges his actions by comparison with his estimate of those of his noteworthy predecessors, whether a man relates his present behavior to those standards held by his peers when he was young, and the like. Such guides to action may not be located by examining the immediate external pressures on a decision maker, but require detailed biographical knowledge which permits imputations concerning an individual's reference group. As Thomas Cochran, however, points out: "In many cases empirical evidence short of

---

[8] Lipset, *op. cit.*, pp. 344–354. I did not report the methodological analysis in this discussion.

that from interviews by skilled psychologists will not suffice to establish a reference group. Occasionally such information is plausibly given in autobiographies."[9] There are, of course, many examples of the fruitful use of sociological concepts and hypotheses by historians. Stanley Elkins and Eric McKitrick applied concepts developed in the context of a sociological study of political participation in a contemporary New Jersey housing project to an analysis of the nineteenth-century frontier. Robert Merton has demonstrated the way in which new communities with a homogeneous population faced with a period of problem solving involved a very large proportion of citizens in politically relevant community activities. And Elkins and McKitrick were able to locate comparable processes and factors in new prairie frontier settlements, thus using Merton's propositions to locate the processes underlying many of Turner's assumptions about frontier democracy.[10]

In his study of the formation of political parties in early American history, William Chambers used Max Weber's analysis of the role of charismatic leaders in post-revolutionary situations to interpret George Washington's role in encouraging the trend toward a rational legal basis of authority.[11] He also examined some of the sociological propositions that have been advanced in a comparative context concerning the social requisites for democracy, and related these to the social structure of the early United States. Thus, the explanation for the success of early American democracy is linked to generalizations about factors associated with democratic institutions on a world-wide scale.[12]

Robert Lamb's interest in explaining some of the factors involved in American economic development, particularly in

[9] Thomas C. Cochran, "The Historian's Use of Social Role," in Louis Gottschalk (ed.), *Generalization in the Writing of History* (Chicago: University of Chicago Press, 1963), pp. 107–108.
[10] Stanley Elkins and Eric McKitrick, "A Meaning for Turner's Frontier," in Richard Hofstadter and S. M. Lipset (eds.), *Turner and the Sociology of the Frontier* (New York: Basic Books, Inc., 1968), pp. 120–151.
[11] William Nisbet Chambers, *Political Parties in a New Nation* (New York: Oxford University Press, 1963), pp. 36, 42, 95.
[12] *Ibid.*, pp. 99–101.

the cotton textile industry, between 1787 and 1816, was explicitly premised on the application of systematic social science approaches to a particular set of events. As Lamb described his method:

> [W]e need models descriptive of the structures and functions of national and international communities at moments of time, and of their changes through time. These models should be made by students of entrepreneurship, working with political, social and economic historians. To build such models we need, for example, to trace the pattern of a given social structure such as an extended-kinship system at a moment of time, study its connections with the surrounding community, and follow its changes over time.[13]

In addition, Lamb argued, the weakness of efforts to analyze early American economic development lay in large part in the lack of experience by entrepreneurial historians in dealing with such models. One needed a model with its subsumed hypotheses to indicate the kinds of data to collect, the relationships which needed tracing, and so on. He developed his own research within the context of a model of community decision making. His concern with the decision-making process led him to look for the effective basis of the influence by the successful entrepreneurs on their communities and regions, which he traced to the extended kinship system and family connections.

The efforts of sociologists to differentiate a number of stratification dimensions and to suggest that incongruent positions, high in one, low in another, would affect behavior in determined ways have been applied in various analyses of different events in American history. Thus, the emergence of the temperance movement and the various stages it has taken since the early nineteenth century have been explained in terms of reactions of groups to the tensions inherent in conflicting stratification positions.[14] A number of writers have dis-

[13] Robert Lamb, "The Entrepreneur and the Community," in William Miller (ed.), *Men in Business* (Cambridge: Harvard University Press, 1952), p. 93.

[14] Joseph Gusfield, *Symbolic Crusade: Status Politics and the American Temperance Movement* (Urbana: University of Illinois Press, 1963).

cussed status tensions as a source of support and leadership for the abolitionist movement.[15] Stanley Elkins applied the analysis of the French sociologist, Émile Durkheim, of the social conditions which result in *anomie,* a social state in which individuals feel disoriented, unrelated to strong norms —and hence are more available to be recruited to new movements—to an understanding of the emergence of the abolitionist movement. He suggests the intense economic expansion of the 1830's resulted in a situation "in which limits were being broken everywhere, in which traditional expectations were disrupted profoundly."[16]

The study of ethnic prejudice and nativist social movements is clearly one in which the substantive interests of historians and sociologists overlap. And here again, propositions concerning status tensions have informed the analysis of historians. John Higham has pointed to status rivalries occasioned by upward mobility as the basic set of processes that underlies the conflicts of different ethnic and religious groups. He has applied on the level of broad historical events the same sort of analysis of these tensions that one may find in the detailed community studies by sociologists of the frictions fostered by ethnic and religious status conflicts.[17]

A comprehensive discussion of the application of the concepts of social science to the work of the historian may be found in the report of the Committee on Historical Analysis of the Social Science Research Council. It is interesting to note that the one sociological concept discussed in any detail there is that of social role. The interest in this concept seems to reflect a concern with the need clearly to specify the expectations held by a group or society concerning behavior associated with a given status or position. As Thomas Cochran put it: "Much of the value of history, whether viewed aesthetically or scientifically, depends on assumptions or generalizations regarding anticipated uniformities in role-playing. . . . Knowledge of the intricacy of role analysis can also

[15] David Donald, *Lincoln Reconsidered* (New York: Vintage Books, 1961), pp. 19–36; Stanley Elkins, *Slavery* (Chicago: University of Chicago Press, 1959), pp. 165–167.

[16] *Ibid.,* pp. 165–166.

[17] John Higham, "Another Look at Nativism," *Catholic Historical Review,* 44 (1958), 148–158.

guard the historian against over-simplified views of the pattern of social interaction."[18]

Perhaps as significant as the interchange of concepts between sociology and history is the transference of methods. Lee Benson has pointed to the failings in much of American political history occasioned by the fact that many historians have attempted to explain political shifts without doing the necessary research on easily available voting statistics.[19] Much as the sociologist prefers to deal with quantitative data drawn from interviews, the historian seems to prefer qualitative materials drawn from printed matter, diaries, and letters. The "reasons" often given by historians for the defeat of a particular party may be tested through a simple statistical analysis of voting returns. We can find out, for example, how many of the gains made by the Republicans between 1856 and 1860 occurred in areas which were sharply affected by the depression of the late 1850's, or were shifts to the Republicans of Know-Nothing votes, as contrasted with increases from districts which had shown concern with the slavery issue. Research on the election of 1860 in the South indicates that the division between Breckenridge and Bell, the two candidates who secured most of the votes in that region, correlated greatly with the lines of electoral division which formed around the Jacksonian Democrats three decades earlier. Specifically, Breckenridge, the secessionist Democrat, secured the bulk of his votes from the traditionally Democratic poor white areas where there were relatively few slaves; while Bell, the anti-secessionist Constitutional Union candidate, received most of his votes from areas characterized by plantation agriculture, a high ratio of slaves, and a past tradition of voting Whig. In subsequent referenda and convention delegate elections in late 1860 and early 1861—held not on party lines but on the issue of union or secession—the majority of the plantation areas which voted for the Constitutional Unionists opted for secession, while the majority

[18] See Cochran, *op. cit.*, see also Walter Metzger, "Generalizations about National Character: An Analytical Essay," in Gottschalk, *op. cit.*, pp. 90–94.

[19] Lee Benson, "Research Problems in American Political Historiography," in Mirra Komarovsky (ed.), *Common Frontiers of the Social Sciences* (Glencoe: The Free Press, 1957), esp. pp. 114–115.

of the low slavery counties, which had backed the secessionist Democrats in the presidential election, voted for the Union. Analysis of shifts of sentiments and behavior of this kind provides firm evidence regarding the trends and processes at work in the American population during the crucial years before the Civil War, and raises questions concerning assumptions of a consistent relationship between party policies and opinions of party supporters.[20]

In his effort to spell out ways in which historians may verify generalizations about national character differences, Walter Metzger has detailed the way in which sociologists handle multivariate analysis in survey research. As he points out one of the major problems in drawing conclusions about national character is to distinguish among attributes of societies which are properly characteristic of the culture and those which result from the fact that societies vary in their internal composition, containing more of certain groups or strata than another. Thus, the question may arise as to whether society A differs from B because it is predominantly rural, or Catholic, or has a much higher level of education rather than because basic values or "character" vary. To test out these possibilities he suggests a "simple trick of the sociological trade (one familiar in this discipline but surprisingly little appreciated by historians)," namely, to hold factors constant as is done in intranational opinion research. One may compare Catholic Canadians with Catholic Americans, or college-educated Canadians with Americans of comparable education.[21]

In yet another area of political history, the sociologist Sidney Aronson has tested the various assumptions made by historians concerning the supposed introduction of the spoils system by Andrew Jackson. Aronson carefully coded the social background characteristics of the higher civil servants in the administrations of John Adams and Thomas Jefferson, and of John Quincy Adams and Andrew Jackson, much as one does with interview data. He is able to show that the overwhelming majority in all four administrations came from

[20] Lipset, *Political Man,* pp. 344–354.
[21] Metzger, *op. cit.,* pp. 99–100.

the socioeconomic elite.[22] This study offers another example
of the way in which contemporary observers may be deceived
about what is happening around them, particularly when
they are making statistical guesses about facts which actually
are unavailable to them. The ideology of a group may lead
it to claim to be doing things which in fact it is not doing.
Thus, Jackson sought to appeal to a mass electorate, and the
claim that he was throwing old Federalists from office and
replacing them by good plebeian Democrats may have been
good politics. Both friend and foe alike may have agreed in
print concerning his actions, and thus not only misled contemporaries but future historians.

Paul Lazarsfeld[23] has pointed out the utility for historical
research of the opinion survey, a method long used by sociologists. He has called the attention of historians to the
enormous quantities of information on a multitude of issues which have been gathered by commercial and academic
polling organizations over the past three decades. Unlike historians dealing with pre-New Deal events, the contemporary
historians of the New Deal period, or those in later decades
or centuries who will study the twentieth century, will have
available to them fairly reliable data about the state of public
opinion, voting behavior, and various other activities such as
church attendance, membership in voluntary organizations,
drinking and gambling habits, and much more. In evaluating
Roosevelt's or Eisenhower's role in a foreign policy crisis they
will be able to know what the American people thought on
the issues. They will be able to differentiate as to the characteristics of those who attended church regularly, as to shifts
in sentiments toward McCarthy or racial integration, and
so on.

To do this, however, the historian will have to take courses
in survey analysis; he may want to learn certain statistical
techniques so as to know how to make up various attitude
scales, or to evaluate the validity and reliability of his results.

[22] Sidney Aronson, *Status and Kinship in the Higher Civil Service*
(Cambridge: Harvard University Press, 1964), p. 32.
[23] Paul F. Lazarsfeld, "The Historian and the Pollster," in S. M.
Lipset and Richard Hofstadter (eds.), *Sociology and History: Methods*
(New York: Basic Books, Inc., 1968), pp. 386–407.

And to maximize the use of survey data for future historians, those of the present may want to dictate some of the questions which are asked by contemporary pollsters. For the sake of future generations of historians, it may be useful to repeat the identical questions about certain attitudes and behaviors every few years, so that a reliable estimate of changes may be made.

Until very recently, few historians, including those dealing with the modern period of American history, seem to have been aware of the uses of survey data for their problems. One may point to books on the 1930's which make inferences concerning the social base of the Coughlin movement, of isolationism, of popular attitudes toward the third term or to Roosevelt's proposal to enlarge the Supreme Court, which were written in apparent ignorance of the body of opinion data dealing with these matters. And in a number of cases, historians relying on their interpretation of election results, or assuming that congressional or press reaction reflected predominant trends among the public, have been quite wrong in their conclusions. Such mistakes are not likely to recur since many younger historians have now begun to apply quantitative techniques to the study of political history.

While the sociologist believes that he might help the historian methodologically, he would like assistance from the historian to test some of his generalizations about changes in social structure. Many social scientists have presented hypotheses concerning the relationship of changes in the occupational and class structures to other institutions. It has been suggested, for example, that the development of a predominantly bureaucratic and tertiary economy oriented around leisure and consumption has led to a change in many fundamental patterns such as child-rearing practices, the content of American religion, or the modal personality structure. In *The First New Nation*[24] I have questioned the validity of some of these propositions concerning fundamental changes in American values and behavior, but for the most part, I, too, relied heavily on extant reports of subjective observations. The techniques of content analysis, which involve the coding

[24] Seymour Martin Lipset, *The First New Nation* (New York: Basic Books, 1963).

of qualitative documents so as to permit quantification, have obvious applicability to efforts to verify assumptions concerning the direction and extent of such changes. Analyses of diaries and other autobiographical materials, coding of the themes of ministers' sermons, and examination of newspaper discussions of how to raise children could undoubtedly tell us a great deal about social changes.[25]

Some indication of the utility of content analysis applied to a historical issue may be found in a study dealing with the extent to which consciousness of being Americans rather than British colonials, overseas Englishmen, or residents of a particular colony, existed among the inhabitants of the colonies prior to the Revolution. Richard Merritt analyzed the symbols in newspapers from Massachusetts, New York, Pennsylvania, and Virginia from 1735 to 1775. And he found a sharp increase in reference to American rather than English events, and in the use of the term Americans.[26]

It is important to recognize that values expressed in the mass media at any given time may not be a good indicator of popular attitudes. Thus a recent analysis by Fred Greenstein which compares a "forgotten body of survey data" from the late nineteenth and early twentieth centuries, questionnaire studies of school children's ideals and occupational aspirations, with comparable ones from recent years, reports little change over a sixty-year period. His results contradict the assumptions of writers such as William Whyte, Erich Fromm, and others, that the achievement goal or "Protestant ethic" has been declining in American life. The one major change which seems to have occurred is a decline in references to national heroes, particularly to Washington. Since some studies of the themes of children's textbooks or of popular fiction do indicate changes in "achievement orientation," and of the occupations of fictional idols, these findings argue for the

[25] An example of such research may be found in Clark E. Vincent, "Trends in Infant Care Ideas," *Child Development,* 22 (September 1951), 199–209. In this study Vincent analyzed the literature of infant care from 1890 to 1949 dealing with "breast versus artificial feeding," and tight versus loose feeding schedules.

[26] Richard L. Merritt, "The Emergence of American Nationalism: A Quantitative Approach," in Lipset and Hofstadter (eds.), *op. cit.,* pp. 138–158.

thesis that changes in social ideology as expressed by popular or textbook writers need have little relationship to variations in the underlying popular values. And latter-day intellectuals who conclude that intellectual consensus equals popular agreement may be confounding "rationalization with reality."[27]

COMPARATIVE HISTORY

Basically, all social science is comparative. Social scientists, sociologists included, seek to formulate generalizations which apply to all human behavior; to do this, of course, involves specifying the conditions under which a given relationship among two or more variables holds true. And it may be that these conditions make a given proposition unique, it may only occur under conditions which rarely happen. The fact, however, that a combination of circumstances occurs uniquely or rarely does not mean that its conditions cannot be presented in terms of general concepts or categories. The test, of course, of any proposition is the analysis of varying conditions in which it should predict behavior.

In attempting to account for a specific pattern of behavior which has occurred in a given part of the world, as, for example, the causal relationship, if any, between the emergence of Protestantism and the rise of capitalism, it is clearly necessary to engage in comparative research. Without examining social relations in different nations, it is impossible to know to what extent a given factor actually has its suggested effect. Some important problems which have been raised by this type of analysis are treated at some length in Chapters 2 and 3 of this book, and hopefully illustrate the utility of such research for both disciplines. For example, if it is true that the German *Standesstaat* (rigid status system) has played an important role in determining the authoritarian pattern of German politics, how does it happen that a similar structure in Sweden is associated with a very different political culture?

[27] See Fred I. Greenstein, "New Light on Changing American Values: A Forgotten Body of Survey Data," *Social Forces*, 42 (1964), 441–450. Greenstein cites a number of studies of changes in values as measured by content analyses, and also many studies of *children's beliefs* and values made since the 1890's.

Or, the fact that American rates of mobility are not uniquely greater than in countries with class-conscious politics obviously raises a number of questions: Why has there been consensus concerning the relative openness of American society; perhaps the emphasis placed in the value system on equality of opportunity or on social equality in interaction is more important than the "invisible" rate of mobility; or is the image of a uniquely open society fostered by the American standard of living, higher than that of any other country for many generations, which has permitted the large majority of the population greatly to improve their living standards from one generation to the next, and has narrowed the gap in consumption standards among the classes more than in other countries?

Questions such as these are as important to historians as to sociologists. Many historians have long recognized that the study of national behavior is enhanced by comparisons of similar developments in different countries. Such comparisons can provide the historian with some controls for evaluating the significance of the factors which he uses for interpretive purposes. Perhaps the most systematic efforts to account for structural differences between countries by comparative historical analysis have been done by Canadian scholars. Canadians are forced to learn almost as much about the United States as Americans do, and they know their own country as well. Thus, many of them continually raise questions as to why various differences between the two countries have occurred or exist. S. D. Clark, a former historian turned sociologist, and various Canadian historians such as Frank Underhill, A. R. M. Lower, and Harold Innis, have suggested that Canada is a more conservative or traditional country culturally because it is a nation which has emerged out of a successful "counterrevolution," while the United States represents the outcome of a successful revolution.[28] They have urged that if one looks at developments north *and* south of the American border after 1783, it is clear that the

[28] This thesis is elaborated in Frank Underhill, *In Search of Canadian Liberalism* (Toronto: Macmillan, 1960); A. R. M. Lower, *From Colony to Nation* (Toronto: Longmans, Green and Company, 1946); J. M. S. Careless, *Canada. A Story of Challenge* (Cambridge: Cambridge University Press, 1963).

success or failure of the Revolution had major consequences on the core national values which have informed behavior, on the nature of class relations, on the extent of education, on the type of religious organization, and so on, points which will be elaborated in Chapter 2.

The effort to relate variations in the value system and institutions of nations to the differences in their key formative experiences provides a good illustration of Max Weber's methodological dictum that current differences among social structures may often be linked to specific historical events which set one process in motion in one nation or unit and a different one in a second. Historical events establish values and predispositions, and these in turn affect later events.[29]

The general thesis laid down by Frederick Jackson Turner concerning the impact of the frontier on various characteristics of American society has led to a number of efforts to test it in the context of other frontier societies such as Canada, parts of Latin America, and Australia.[30] Although frontier geographic conditions in the two North American states were quite comparable, these frontiers also differed greatly in large part for reasons derivative from their varying political histories, which are discussed in detail in Chapter 2. Inasmuch as Canada had to be on constant guard against the expansionist tendencies of the United States, it could not leave its frontier communities unprotected or autonomous.[31]

The development of the Canadian frontier, in fact, did not simply follow on population movements impelled by natural social pressures, as occurred in the United States. Rather, the Canadian government felt the need deliberately to plan for the settlement of the West. As the Canadian sociologist S. D. Clark has put it:

[29] Max Weber, *The Methodology of the Social Sciences* (Glencoe, Ill.: The Free Press, 1949), pp. 182–185.

[30] See F. J. Turner, *The Frontier in American History* (New York: Holt, Rinehart and Winston, 1962). For a collection of some of the American literature discussing and evaluating Turner's theses, together with a detailed bibliography on the subject, see George R. Taylor, *The Turner Thesis* (Boston: D. C. Heath, 1949). See also Hofstadter and Lipset (eds.), *op. cit.*

[31] Edgar W. McInnis, *The Unguarded Frontier* (Garden City: Doubleday, 1942), pp. 306–307.

Canada maintained her separate political existence but only by resisting any movement on the part of her population which had the effect of weakening the controls of central political authority. The claims to the interior of the continent were staked not by advancing frontiersmen, acting on their own, but by advancing armies and police forces, large corporate enterprises and ecclesiastical organizations, supported by the state. The Canadian political temper, as a result, has run sharply counter to the American. Those creeds of American political life—individual rights, local autonomy, and limitation of executive power—which have contributed so much to the political strength of the American community have found less strong support within the Canadian political system.[32]

A recent effort to explain why Brazil, the largest, most populous, and best endowed of the Latin American states, has done so much more poorly than the United States also emphasizes the varying nature of frontier settlement in the Americas. Vianna Moog points to the differences between "Bandeirantes" and "pioneers" as a key source of the varying patterns of development in his native Brazil and the United States. As Adolf Berle summarizes his thesis:

"Bandeirantes" ("flag-bearers") were the explorers and settlers of the interior of Brazil, as "pioneers" were the conquerors and colonizers of the great unoccupied heartland of the United States. The difference lies in their motives and ideals. The Brazilian bandeirantes were perhaps the last wave of colonial conquistadores. The American pioneers, though of all kinds, were predominantly Reformation settlers. The resulting civilizations set up by the two groups of wilderness-conquerors were therefore quite different, despite many elements common to both.[33]

Moog relates the varying nature of the Brazilian and United States frontiers to the fact that for three centuries in Brazil the main motive for going to the frontier was to get rich quickly, to find gold or other precious minerals, that

[32] S. D. Clark, *The Canadian Community* (Toronto: University of Toronto Press, 1962), p. 214.

[33] Adolf A. Berle, "Introduction," to Vianna Moog, *Bandeirantes and Pioneers* (New York: Braziller, 1964), p. 9; see also Charles Wagley, *An Introduction to Brazil* (New York: Columbia University Press, 1963), pp. 74–75.

labor whether in urban or rural occupations was denigrated as fit only for slaves; while the English and later American settlers looked for new homes based on their own work.[34] These differences are linked to varying cultural traits and motives for seeking new opportunity on the frontier. In Brazil the *bandeirante* is credited with the geographic enlargement of the country, much as the pioneer is in the United States. "In the United States a thing, to be capable of arousing enthusiasm, must bear the label of pioneer; in Brazil . . . it must merit the epithet of *bandeirante.*"[35]

The history of Argentina offers yet another example of the way in which the social structure of an American frontier was determined by the predominant structures and values established in colonial times. Values and structures endemic in the settlement of an open frontier neither served to influence the social organization of the rural community nor helped shape a national democratic outlook. Argentine agriculture developed much like that of Australia, with large cattle and sheep ranches which used many workers either as hired help or as tenants, and preserved a hierarchical status system. Various efforts to encourage small landholding after Independence failed because of the power of the large landowners. And subsequently, in the latter part of the nineteenth century, it proved to be impossible to apply meaningful homestead legislation to Argentina, although there was a general belief among Argentine experts that United States' prosperity and development was attributable to its policy of encouraging land settlement in the form of family homesteads. The Argentine pampas, which closely resembled the prairies of the United States and Canada, remained in the hands of a small class of large landowners. "Churches, schools, and clubs did not develop in rural Argentina for the simple reason that settlement was dispersed and often temporary."[36] And as in Australia, the urban centers of Argentina, particularly Buenos Aires, became the focus for im-

[34] *Ibid.,* pp. 119–121.
[35] Moog, *op. cit.,* p. 171.
[36] James R. Scobie, *Argentina* (New York: Oxford University Press, 1964), p. 124. For a discussion of the way in which efforts to encourage farming on the North American pattern were defeated see pp. 78–81, 121–130.

migrant settlement. "Rather than a frontier, Argentina had a city."[37]

The argument that the varying characters of the Brazilian, Argentine, Canadian, and American frontiers flow from differences in their early values assumes the perspective taken by Max Weber which stresses the role of core values in influencing the institutional structure of a nation. As applied here, it suggests the need to modify the assumptions of many historians who accept variants of the Turner thesis that the frontier experience was a major, if not the major, determinant of American egalitarian values. Rather, the comparisons with Brazil, Argentina, and Canada would suggest that the egalitarian character of the American frontier was in some part determined by the values derived from the revolutionary political origins and the Calvinist work ethos. The thesis that basic social values shaped the frontier society has, of course, been advanced by a number of historians.[38]

It should be clear that a concern with the influence of economic, ecological, and value elements in determining given national developments or traits is not a matter of dealing with alternative mutually exclusive hypotheses. Rather, as in the case of Weber's discussion of the relative contribution of economic and value factors in the rise of capitalism, one may conclude that different variables are each necessary but not sufficient to produce the results sometimes credited to one of them alone. Thus, as will be discussed in Chapter 2, the comparative data for the two North American countries indicate that an open unsettled rural frontier need not result

[37] *Ibid.*, p. 130. The impetus for the "growth of cities, which would eventually make the Argentines Latin America's most urbanized people . . . came from [the extensive] agricultural exploitation of the pampas. The immigrants who were drawn to Argentina in the late nineteenth century found the land already controlled by *estancieros* [large landlords] and speculators. With the ownership of land largely beyond their reach, the newcomers accumulated in Argentina's port cities, especially in Buenos Aires."

[38] Henry Nash Smith, *Virgin Land: The American West as Symbol and Myth* (Cambridge: Harvard University Press, 1950), p. 124. For similar points of view see George W. Pierson, "The Frontier and American Institutions," *New England Quarterly*, 15 (1942), 253, and W. W. Rostow, "The National Style," in E. E. Morison (ed.), *The American Style: Essays in Value and Performance* (New York: Harper, 1958), pp. 247, 259.

in egalitarian, individualistic, and democratic institutions and values. On the other hand, political movements which stress such values have found great difficulty in institutionalizing them in the countries whose ancient structures have been able to resist political efforts to change values. The American and French revolutions espoused similar ideologies and societal outlooks. The American, developing in a new society with an open frontier, could impose its values on the culture. The French failed to do so; the rightist culture supporting throne and altar has remained a powerful force in France to the present day.[39] Thus it may be argued with Weber that the appropriate structural environment for a given development requires the emergence of facilitating values, or that necessary values will not result in the anticipated changes unless the structural conditions are propitious.

If much of comparative history and sociology seeks to point out, and account for, variations among nations, this emphasis also may lead to highlighting the effects of common experiences or factors. Thus, in recent years, a number of studies have sought to specify the conditions facing new nations or other post-revolutionary societies which seek to establish legitimacy, to find a basis for national linguistic and value consensus, so as to have a stable national society which does not rest on force, or which will not come apart during the strains of major crises. Most of this literature deals with the contemporary new nations or with Latin America. Some, however, have included the United States in this category and have sought to re-examine early post-Revolutionary American history with a view to learning how the United States dealt with these problems. Methodologically these studies have taken various forms. Karl Deutsch and a group

[39] See John Sawyer, "The Entrepreneur and the Social Order. France and the United States," in William Miller, *op. cit.*, pp. 7–22. "The French case offers striking testimony to the tenacity of inherited patterns. Here the old institutional structure was most violently assaulted; here more than anywhere else in Europe new ideas and institutions emerged triumphant in the Revolution and the Republic. . . . Yet France . . . carried forward elements of the European past that have remained widely diffused to this day. Over the centuries when commercial capitalism was enlarging its place in the national life, a series of historical turnings kept peculiarly alive aristocratic values and patterns . . . (p. 13).

of historians spent some considerable time working over the histories of a number of nations, including the United States, which were successfully created out of independent subunits, so as to formulate propositions which held true in most of these occurrences.[40] On the other hand, Chambers and I have sought to specify propositions about the requirements for stable new nationhood from the literature of latter-day new nations, and to re-examine American history to see to what extent such propositions could inform historical inquiry, and conversely, to develop propositions from a detailed historical case study which might be useful in analyzing contemporary events occurring under relatively comparable conditions.[41]

Concern with the social requisites of new nationhood also inspired the work of Robert Lamb and Richard Merritt dealing with pre-Revolutionary America. Both recognized that the creation of a new nation, or even united colonies in rebellion, required as Lamb put it a new *national* elite which had to be in communication with each other, and which had a consciousness of kind. As noted earlier, he traced through the interconnections which emerged in terms of personal, family, and business ties among members of the elite in Virginia, Pennsylvania, New York, and Massachusetts.[42]

Merritt, discussed above in a slightly different context, sought to demonstrate that a national consciousness had emerged before the Revolution through an analysis of the symbols in the colonial press which showed a steady increase in use of the term "Americans" and a decline of words which

[40] See Karl W. Deutsch, S. A. Burrell, R. A. Kann, M. Lee, Jr., M. Lichterman, R. E. Lindgren, F. L. Loewenheim, R. W. Van Wagenen, *Political Community and the North Atlantic Area* (Princeton: Princeton University Press, 1957).

[41] Chambers, *op. cit.*, S. M. Lipset, *The First New Nation*. R. R. Palmer also points to the "typical problem of a new nation" which faced the United States in very similar terms. See *The Age of the Democratic Revolution: The Struggle* (Princeton: Princeton University Press, 1964), pp. 518–522.

[42] See memorandum by Robert K. Lamb presented in Karl W. Deutsch, *Nationalism and Social Communication* (New York: John Wiley, 1953), pp. 18–20. See also Robert K. Lamb, "The Entrepreneur and the Community," *op. cit.*, for another report on the same research presented in the context of analyzing the conditions for economic development.

in any way pictured the colonists as transplanted English-men.[43] Both studies, it should be noted, were consciously concerned with general processes of national development, and refer their work to those interested in these larger issues. Thus Lamb addressed himself, in part, to "those interested in the role of elites in the formation of new nation-states," and Merritt suggested that "the evidence provided by the American experience is useful in testing current ideas about nation-building. . . ."[44]

Most recently, Louis Hartz and a group of historians have introduced the concept of the "fragment" society or culture to characterize those *new societies* which were formed out of the overseas nations settled by Europeans—the nations of the Americas, Australasia, and South Africa. The concept of the fragment refers to groups which emigrated from European countries to settle abroad as coming from parts or fragments of the mother culture. Despite all their variations they represent for Hartz a common body of experiences in being "fragments" of Europe which developed very differently from the mother cultures since they did not embody the European "whole." Many important European strata, values and institutions, usually those associated with the privileged classes, never reached the "new societies." All of these societies, "in the midst of the variations they contain, are governed by the ultimate experience of the American liberal tradition."[45] Each left behind in Europe an ancient source of conservative ideology in the form of the traditional class structure. Hence in British Canada, the United States, and Dutch South Africa, particularly, enlightenment doctrines could dominate. In Australia, created by a fragment of nineteenth-century Britain, radical principles carried by working-class immigrants could form the national tradition unhampered by the need to compromise with powerful Tory values and supporters. But over time, the very absence of a traditional

---

[43] Merritt, *op. cit.*

[44] Lamb's memorandum in Deutsch, *op. cit.*, p. 19, and Merritt, *op. cit.*

[45] Louis Hartz, *The Founding of New Societies; Studies in the History of the United States, Latin America, South Africa, Canada and Australia,* with contributions by Kenneth D. McRae and others (New York: Harcourt, Brace and World, 1964), p. 4.

right transmutes the liberal or radical doctrines into conservative dogmas of the "fragment." It is impossible to build
an ideological left in the fragment cultures because there is no
hereditary aristocracy against whom to rebel, and because the
philosophical bases on which an ideological left might be
founded are already institutionalized as part of the received
liberal and radical tradition of the society.

In stressing similarities among these nations, Hartz is, of
course, sensitive to the many differences among them. Thus,
he relates the varying attitudes toward race relations in these
societies to the strength or weakness of feudal remnants.
Feudalism as a system of defined statuses may more easily
accommodate hierarchical race differences, as may be exemplified by the situation in Brazil. Enlightenment or radical
values which have predominated in the United States, South
Africa, and Australia find it more difficult to encompass
such differences, and foster policies of complete separation,
such as "white Australia," South African apartheid, the
"separate but equal" doctrine of the American South, or a
massive moral struggle for real equality and integration as in
the United States as a whole.

There can be little doubt that the concept of the fragment,
like those employed in the comparisons among new nations,
points out interesting hypotheses about sources of similarities
among the societies they subsume. At the moment, however,
comparative analysis is faced with the difficulty that many
of its most illuminating ideas are used by their proponents as
literary devices, as ways of organizing a mass of information,
not as means of testing specific alternative hypotheses. One
may point to contradictory propositions advanced by different exponents of the comparative method which are not
explored. Thus, Louis Hartz contends that the major factors
forming the American liberal ethos derive from the fact that
it is a fragment culture, a new society. The assumption demands that he find that the American Revolution was a relatively moderate revolt, that it was not a basic source of the
American institutional system, and in line with this thesis,
the chapter on Canada (written by Kenneth McRae) treats
English Canada as a liberal Enlightenment society, not very
different from the United States. Hartz and McRae argue that

the two English-speaking American nations never had an aristocracy, a fount of conservative elitist anti-Enlightenment values. But Robert Palmer in his treatment of the late eighteenth-century revolutions in America and Britain assumes that the American Revolution was a major dynamic event which not only greatly changed the course of American society, but was a major force affecting the character of the subsequent revolutions in Europe. He traces strong similarities among the American, French, and other revolutions. To do this, he postulates that

> "Aristocracy" [is] characteristic about 1760 of the society established in all countries, including the Anglo-American colonies. . . . Family self-perpetuation, inter-marriage, inheritance of position, and privileged or special access to government and to its emoluments or profits are found to have been common phenomena over a wide range of institutions—the governors' councils in the British American colonies, the two houses of parliaments of Great Britain and Ireland, the *parlements* and provincial estates of France, the town councils and estates of Belgium, Holland, Switzerland, Italy and Germany, the diets of Hungary, Bohemia, Poland and Sweden.[46]

These were in his language "constituted bodies."

Palmer attempts to show that in many of these countries movements based on Enlightenment ideas emerged, directed against the power of the "constituted bodies." These advocated equality as a reaction to the fact that an "aristocratic resurgence" was occurring in which "exclusiveness, aristocratic class-consciousness, and emphasis on inheritance were increasing. . . ."[47] And he contends that the revolution succeeded in the two countries in which the agricultural population collaborated with urban middle-class leaders, France and the United States, but failed in other countries of Europe because of the political apathy or weakness of their agrarian populations.

[46] R. R. Palmer, "Generalizations about Revolution: A Case Study," in Gottschalk (ed.), *op. cit.*, pp. 69–70. Here Palmer summarizes the second and third chapters of his book, *The Age of the Democratic Revolution*.
[47] *Ibid.*

It would not be appropriate to evaluate the head-on controversy between Palmer and Hartz here. In comparing Canada and the United States in the following chapter I argue that the American Revolution was a major revolution, which had enormous consequences in forming American values, political system, and general institutional structure. One must face up to the issue, however, as to whether it is possible to evaluate the utility or validity of different comparative concepts such as "fragment," "new society," "new nation," "aristocracy," and "revolution."

To a considerable degree, the issue in comparative analysis often involves evaluating the same fact as meaning "as much as," or "as little as." Thus one way to judge how "revolutionary" the American Revolution was is to see how many were removed by the upheaval. Palmer attempts to deal with this problem by comparing the number of emigrés who left the United States and France after the two revolutions. If we accept the French Revolution as a standard for a "real revolution," then the fact that there "were 24 emigrés per thousand of population in the American Revolution, and only 5 emigrés per thousand of population in the French Revolution," argues that "there was a real revolution in America."[48]

Hartz also compares the American and French revolutions as evidence for his opposite thesis that the American Revolution had *relatively* little effect. He points out that contemporary American conservatives hail the Revolutionary heroes, while in France "the royalist still curses the Jacobin."[49] Palmer would reply (in fact the two ignore each other) that the French emigrés returned to France after the Restoration while the American emigrés did not come back and that this fact made for great differences between the two countries, that the American Loyalists are forgotten. "The sense in which there was no conflict in the American Revolution is the sense in which the loyalists are forgotten. The 'American consensus' rests in some degree on the elimination

[48] R. R. Palmer, *The Age*, p. 188. He also compares the compensation paid for confiscation of the property of counterrevolutionaries by the British government and the French Bourbon restoration. The sums were similar, holding population size constant.
[49] Hartz, *op. cit.*, p. 82.

from the national consciousness, as well as from the country, of a once important and relatively numerous element of dissent."[50]

Clearly the issues posed here concerning different macroscopic judgments can rarely be resolved by empirical tests. The way in which one looks at data depends in large measure on the questions asked, the theory employed, and the classifications used. It is obvious that in dealing with complex alternative interpretations, no matter how rigorous the methodology employed, most historians and sociologists basically present an argument which they then "validate" by showing that there are more positive than negative data available. Most of the concepts used, however, such as revolution, class, aristocracy, are necessarily very imprecise. They leave a great deal of room for the analyst, willingly or not, to find reasons for selecting those indicators of a concept which best fit the over-all conceptual framework he is using. And when existing data are confirmatory, most of us are not motivated to look further. It is only when data are in conflict with our theory, hunches, or prejudices that most social scientists decide there must be something wrong with the data, or with the concepts underlying the selection of the data, and look further. In reading the work of others, we are normally inclined to accept their findings as both valid and reliable, as long as they agree with our predispositions. Disagreement, however, results in efforts to reanalyze the evidence and to demonstrate that previous work has drastically oversimplified, or simply ignored, many data.

It is important to recognize that by looking at the same problem from different theoretical perspectives, we increase knowledge even if the conclusions seem contradictory. Different conceptual frameworks lead one man to highlight certain aspects which another ignores. Often findings which are not congruent with one another merely reflect the fact that different scholars have used different concepts. Thus Hartz in stressing the differences between pre-Revolutionary America and Europe emphasizes in his conception of the European

[50] Palmer, *The Age*, pp. 189–190. On the meaning of the elimination of the Tories and their outlook from American life see William H. Nelson, *The American Tory* (Oxford: The Clarendon Press, 1961).

class structure the notion of a feudal rigid status system. Palmer, on the other hand, has a very different conception of aristocracy on both sides of the ocean, which basically sees the late eighteenth-century societies as governed by small oligarchies, whose members are closely related to one another.

Historians and social scientists should not feel inhibited to admit that one of their main analytical procedures is, what I have called elsewhere, the "method of the dialogue." In large measure the very meaning of scholarly verification in history has been the re-examination of the same problem by different scholars operating with alternative approaches. As long as men agree concerning the meaning of hypotheses and the nature of evidence, the dialogue can result in replication and the growth of knowledge. The sociologist can and has contributed to the dialogues in historical analysis by introducing concepts and methods which expand the possibilities available to the historian.

Many scholars, both historians and sociologists, despair of the value of introducing the methodological approaches of sociology or the other social sciences into historical work. They point to the fact that given historical situations are determined by a multitude of factors and that it is impossible to perform the methodological operation of holding other factors constant, or randomizing them, as can often be done when studying large numbers of individuals. The social psychologist or sociologist dealing with a sample of 2,000 people may compare the consequence of a factor being present or not among people who are comparable on a variety of other variables. The historian or the historical sociologist cannot do so. This does not rule out the utility of applying sociological generalizations to historical events. The sociologist engaged in a historical case study uses it to draw out generalizations that can apply to all similar cases, say of post-revolutionary officeholders, of reactions to authority in systems in which public offices are directly responsible to the people, and so forth. One may compare reactions to events within the same larger national system, e.g., regional differences, in which many over-all factors are obviously being held constant. There is no necessary clash between developing general sociological hypotheses and taking historical specificity into account. T. H. Marshall argues that sociologists must accept historians as experts and rely on their accounts of events:

> [S]ociologists must inevitably rely extensively on secondary authorities, without going back to the original sources. They do this partly because life is too short to do anything else when using the comparative method, and they need data assembled from a wide historical field, and partly because original sources are very tricky things to use. . . . It is the business of the historians to sift this miscellaneous collection of dubious authorities and to give to others the results of their careful professional assessment. And surely they will not rebuke the sociologists for putting faith in what historians write.[51]

Clearly we may apply the logic of science to the study of social systems with as much justification as we apply it to the analysis of individuals and institutions. Despite the fact that two individuals have the same growth pattern or history, experts from varied fields continue to make generalizations about individual behavior by comparing instances in which the circumstances of development have been similar. It is true that there are fewer societies than there are individuals to compare and that hypotheses about the operation of a specific variable in the evolution of the former are, therefore, less subject to explicit verification than are generalizations about the operation of variables in individual development. It is for this reason that we will always have to rely on historical case studies as one of our basic sociological methods.

The use of historical case studies and a comparative analytic approach have made it possible for sociological investigations to be internationalized. Instead of studying exclusively the culture of his own interest, the sociologist would do well to study several cultures with reference to the same analytic questions for which comparative facts can be collected and examined. Few historians or sociologists have taken advantage of the magnificent laboratory for comparative analysis offered by the almost thirty independent states of the Americas. These nations vary considerably with respect to the stability and nature of political institutions and rates of economic development. To account for such differences among

[51] Marshall, *op. cit.,* p. 38.

any two or more of them some have pointed to variations in their religious ethos, to differences in their pattern of frontier settlement, to varying constitutional arrangements, to differences in their systems of class and ethnic relationships, and so on. In the following two chapters this kind of comparative analysis is used to illuminate the differences between Canada and the United States and among some of the Latin American countries.

PART II

VALUE DIFFERENCES: HISTORICALLY
AND COMPARATIVELY

CHAPTER 2

Revolution and Counterrevolution:
The United States and Canada

I

The strong cultural similarity between English-speaking Canada and the United States has often led citizens of the latter to wonder why the two remain in separate polities. Yet, although these two peoples probably resemble each other more than any other two nations on earth, there are consistent patterns of difference between them. To discover and analyze the factors which perpetuate such differences among nations is one of the more intriguing and difficult tasks in comparative study.

Any effort to specify the values, ethos, or national character of nations confronts the problem that such statements are necessarily made in a comparative context. Thus the assertion that the United States or Canada is a materialistic nation, that it is egalitarian, that its family system is unstable, obviously does not refer to these characteristics in any absolute sense. The statement that a national value system is egalitarian clearly does not imply the absence of severe differences in power, income, wealth, or status. Generally this statement means that from a comparative perspective, nations defined as egalitarian tend to place more emphasis on universalistic criteria in judging others, and tend to de-emphasize the institutionalization of hierarchical differences. The key word here is "comparative." No one suggests that any given complex social structure is in fact egalitarian in any absolute sense. The same may be said about the terms "aristocratic" and "ascriptive" when applied to complex modern societies. No society is in fact ascriptive in any total sense; all systems about which we have systematic empirical data reveal considerable social mobility, both up and down. What we are speaking of here are relative differences. Macroscopic sociology employs polarity concepts when it compares core aspects of societies—*Gemeinschaft–Gesellschaft*, organic solidarity–mechanical solidarity, inner-directed–other-directed, diffuseness–specificity, achievement–ascription, traditional–modern—and this approach purposely exaggerates such differences for analytic purposes.

One particularly effective schema for systematically classifying the central values of social systems is the pattern-variables as originally set forth by Talcott Parsons. These are dichotomous categories of modes of interaction. Those distinctions which seem particularly suitable for the analysis of the United States and Canada are achievement–ascription, universalism–particularism, self-orientation–collectivity-orientation, and egalitarianism–elitism. (The latter is not one of Parsons' distinctions, but one added here.) A society's value system may emphasize that a person in his orientation to others: (1) treats them in terms of their abilities and performances or in terms of inherited qualities (achievement–ascription); (2) applies a general standard or responds to some personal attribute or relationship (universalism–particularism); (3) perceives the separate needs of others or subordinates the individual's needs to the interests of the larger group (self-orientation–collectivity-orientation); and (4) stresses that all persons must be respected because they are human beings or emphasizes the general superiority of those who hold elite positions (egalitarianism–elitism).[1]

The great mass of literature on these two North American democracies suggests the United States is more achievement-

---

[1] Because of the absence of clear indicators and the overlap with the egalitarian–elitist dimensions, the specificity–diffuseness pattern variable is not discussed in this chapter which compares only Canada and the United States. For reasons of parsimony, I ignore Parsons' other pattern variables—affectivity–affective neutrality and instrumental–consummatory distinctions. See Talcott Parsons, *The Social System* (Glencoe: The Free Press, 1951), pp. 58–67. See also Parsons' more recent elaboration of the pattern variables in "Pattern Variables Revisited," *American Sociological Review*, 25 (1960), 467–483.

oriented, universalistic, egalitarian, and self-oriented than Canada. Previous tentative evaluations of all the major English-speaking nations indicated that Canada is very much like the United States on these value dimensions, that both lie somewhere between the other two major English-speaking societies, Great Britain and Australia.[2] Since the value differences between Canada and the United States are not great, we expect to find strong similarities in many social characteristics, such as the demographic profile, occupational structures, and various institutional arrangements, e.g., labor-management relationships. The test of the utility of the comparative approach to the two North American societies so similar in value orientations depends upon specifying the special differences that *do* exist and identifying the historic issues and problems which sustain the near differences between them.

Although many factors in the history of these nations have determined the current variations between them, three particular factors may be singled out: the varying origins of their political systems and national identities, varying religious traditions, and different frontier experiences. In general terms, the value orientations in English-speaking Canada stem from a counterrevolutionary past, a continuing need to differentiate itself from the United States, the influence of monarchical institutions, a dominant Anglican religious tradition, and a less individualistic and more governmentally controlled frontier expansion than was present on the American frontier.

II

Both nations are largely urbanized, heavily industrialized, and politically stable. They share many of the same ecological and demographic conditions, approximately the same

[2] S. M. Lipset, "The Value Patterns of Democracy: A Case Study in Comparative Analysis," *American Sociological Review*, 28 (1963), 515–531. See also my comparison of the four English-speaking democracies in *The First New Nation* (New York: Basic Books, 1963), esp. pp. 248–273 and in "Anglo-American Society," *International Encyclopedia of the Social Sciences* (New York: Macmillan and Free Press, 1968), vol. 1, 289–302.

level of economic development, and similar rates of upward and downward social mobility. To a very great extent Canada and the United States share the same values, but, as Kaspar Naegele has pointed out, in Canada these values are held much more tentatively.[3] Both are new peoples and new states, but Canada's relationship to Britain has helped perpetuate in a North American nation elements of a set of values having Old World origins and a more conservative character. Thus, while equality and achievement are values emphasized in both North American societies, in Canada the emphasis is somewhat less, and therefore the contrast between the nations remains one of degree.

Perhaps no other value emphases are as paramount in American life as the twin values of egalitarianism and achievement. Both have been strongest in the school system where the principles of the "common school" and "equal opportunity for success" remain viable educational ideals. In the United States the effective emphasis on achievement and on equality of opportunity is reflected by the demands of lower-status individuals for access to education as a means to success, and the recognition by the privileged that education as a means to success must be given to all who are qualified. By contrast, in Canada education has had a more elitist and ascriptive import. These value differences are indicated by a comparison of college enrollment figures. In Canada only 9.2 per cent of the 20- to 24-year-old age group compared to 30.2 per cent in the United States were enrolled in institutions of higher learning in 1960. Even on the secondary school level, the United States showed a higher level of enrollment (76 per cent) than Canada (64 per cent).[4]

It has been suggested that elitist tendencies among Canadians account for the education of a limited few at the college

[3] Kaspar D. Naegele, "Canadian Society: Some Reflections," in Bernard Blishen and others (eds.), *Canadian Society* (Toronto: Macmillan, 1961), p. 27. A journalistic account of Canada written by an English novelist makes and illustrates many of the same points about Canadian institutions as I have tried to suggest here. See V. S. Pritchett, "Across the Vast Land," *Holiday*, 35 (April 1964), 52–68, 184–189.

[4] UNESCO, *Basic Facts and Figures*, 1962 (Paris, 1963), p. 54; United Nations, *Demographic Yearbook*, 1960 (New York), pp. 182, 191–192; United Nations, *Compendium of Social Statistics*, Statistical Papers, Series K, No. 2 (New York, 1963), pp. 324–325, 329.

level. Some Canadian writers have pointed out that until very recently education in their country was designed to train an ecclesiastical and political elite much in the British tradition.[5] In Canada "only a small part of the youth was expected to attend the university; higher education was reserved for an intellectual elite—and for the children of the well-to-do."[6] The content of the education curricula also appears to reflect value differences. In the United States, where status differences are seemingly less emphasized than in Canada, education curricula include more vocational, technical, and professional courses in "academic" type schools and colleges. This reflects the American view that education should not only be concerned with the transmission of intellectual and purely academic skills, but should also provide practical knowledge that is directly applicable to an occupational situation.[7]

Canadian educators have shown resistance to the inclusion of purely vocational and professional curricula, especially in institutions of higher learning. Technical training has been viewed as corrupting the "aristocracy of intellect," those being educated for political and social leadership. Canadians, therefore, differ from Americans in being more eager to maintain the humanist emphasis in the curricula, a point of view which seems to accompany ascriptive values in other societies as well. So we find that Latin is still taught in most Canadian secondary schools.[8] The humanist tradition in Canadian education may be related also to the greater strength of traditional religion in Canada. But, as S. D. Clark notes, "the strength of the puritan tradition in Canadian society has not been unrelated to the strength of the aristocratic tradition. . . ."[9]

[5] Dennis Wrong, *American and Canadian Viewpoints* (Washington: American Council on Education, 1955), p. 20; Wilson Woodside, *The University Question* (Toronto: Ryerson Press, 1958), pp. 21–22.

[6] Woodside, *loc. cit.*

[7] James Bryant Conant is one of the best-known advocates of the thesis that technical high schools are necessary in the United States; see Conant's *Slum and Suburbs* (New York: McGraw-Hill, 1961); also, "A Hard Look at Our High Schools," in C. Winfield Scott and others (eds.), *The Great Debate* (Englewood Cliffs, N. J.: Prentice-Hall, 1959), pp. 165–171.

[8] Woodside, *op. cit.*, p. 19.

[9] S. D. Clark, "The Canadian Community," in G. Brown (ed.), *Canada* (Berkeley: University of California Press, 1950), pp. 386–387.

Education is one area in which there is some systematic comparative evidence concerning the varying opinions of Canadians and Americans. A survey of the attitudes of samples of educators and citizens sought to assess public perceptions of the task of education, and to discover the extent to which perceptions of Canadians and Americans diverge. Sixteen basic elements, synthesized from some of the most notable statements of school functions, made from the time of Horace Mann on, were classified into four mutually exclusive categories: intellectual dimensions, social dimensions, personal dimensions, and productive dimensions. The results point up the validity of many of the impressionistic generalizations such as those cited above concerning differences in national orientations. "The analysis of regional differences demonstrated that there were greater differences between Canada and any single American region than there were between any two American regions. Comparisons between all [English-speaking] Canadians and all Americans revealed even greater differences."[10]

The data indicate that "Canadians, as a group, assigned considerably higher priority than did Americans to knowledge, scholarly attitudes, creative skills, aesthetic appreciation and morality, as outcomes of schooling. Americans emphasized physical development, citizenship, patriotism, social skills and family living much more than did Canadians."[11] These findings that Americans are more likely than Canadians to view education as a means of gaining facilities in interpersonal skills, while Canadians tend more to see schooling as a way of training youth in the traditional values and high culture of the society, are congruent with the assumption that Canada is more elitist than its neighbor. Elsewhere I have elaborated the thesis that the great concern of Americans with

---

Clark adds: "Canada shared with the United States in the great democratic movement, with its almost fanatical emphasis upon the principle that all men are equal. The frontier provided favorable ground on which to build an elaborate structure of social classes, which broke down under the influence of the common experience of frontier life. . . . Yet in spite of the strength of such forces, the aristocratic principle has persisted as an important organizing principle in Canadian society."

[10] Lawrence W. Downey, *The Task of Public Education* (Chicago: Midwest Administration Center, 1960), p. 42.

[11] *Ibid.*, p. 44.

getting along with others, as reported by many European observers over the past century and a half, is closely linked to its strong emphasis on egalitarianism. The very fact that claims to higher status are less stable in the United States than in countries with more elitist orientations has made Americans more sensitive to the opinions of others and seemingly more concerned with imparting social adjustment skills to their children.[12]

The results of this opinion survey support the idea presented in many analyses of Canadian education that the country is caught in a dilemma between European and American orientations.[13] There are many in Canada today who see a clash between quantity and quality, and who choose quality by explicitly defending an elitist national policy. One critic of the emphasis on equality in education writes that "In Canada . . . there seems no valid reason . . . why our educational aims should be cluttered with this awkward word [democracy]. We should stop being concerned about the common man and instead turn our attention to the aristocratic elite upon whom the quality of our civilization depends."[14] Conversely, Canadian educators who favor egalitarianism complain that Canadians are too traditional, that they see amount of knowledge gained and intellectual discipline as the only measures of education.[15]

Status distinctions, which exist in all nations, have less legitimacy in the United States than they do in Canada. The Canadian sociologist Kaspar Naegele concluded that the evidence on the subject indicates there is "less emphasis in Canada on equality than there is in the United States" and "a greater acceptance of *limitation,* of hierarchical patterns."[16] For example, the greater strength of elitist and ascriptive value emphases in Canada would seem to be reflected in a paternalistic organization of the family, in the reverence

[12] Lipset, *The First New Nation,* pp. 114–117.
[13] Paul Nash, "Quality and Equality in Canadian Education," *Comparative Education Review,* 5 (1961), 118–129.
[14] Hilda Neatby, *So Little for the Mind* (Toronto: Clarke, Irwin, 1953), pp. 36, 46–47. See also Hilda Neatby, *A Temperate Dispute* (Toronto: Clarke, Irwin, 1954).
[15] W. H. Swift, *Trends in Canadian Education* (Toronto: Gage, 1958), p. 62.
[16] Naegele, *op. cit.,* p. 27.

paid to the clergy by the laity, in the diffuse deference granted the old by the young, men by women, teachers by students, and politicians by electorate.[17] From James Bryce to S. D. Clark, sociologically oriented observers have stressed the greater respect for political leaders in Canada than in the United States, symbolized in part by Canadian loyalty to monarchical institutions. W. L. Morton has pointed out that among the institutions and norms linked to monarchy and cabinet government has been

> the limited franchise and the idea that the franchise was a trust. Another was the British system of justice, challenged at the time by the principle of election applied to the selection of judges by the Jacksonian Democrats across the border. Yet another was the sense of public rank and personal honor. . . . The monarchy, in short, subsumed a heterogeneous and conservative society governed in freedom under law, law upheld by monarchy, where the republic would have levelled the diversities and made uniform the various groups by breaking them down into individuals, free indeed, but bound by social conformity and regimented by an inherent social intolerance.[18]

It is significant that Canadian political debates concerning the suffrage in the late nineteenth century still involved discussions of how much property a man should have to qualify to vote. Manhood suffrage was not enacted federally until 1898.[19] In the United States, the egalitarian emphasis facilitated the extension of male suffrage among whites almost everywhere by 1845.[20]

The American populist and egalitarian ethos also "leads

[17] One of the more subtle signs of certain status distinctions was noted by A. R. M. Lower, *Canadians in the Making* (Toronto: Longmans, Green, 1958), p. 446, n. 11, who observed that, to his astonishment, in one Midwestern university in the United States known to him, students and faculty actually share the same lavatory. Dennis Wrong points out that "with respect to the position of women, greater conservatism exists in Canada than in the United States . . . relatively fewer women have achieved prominence as public figures." Wrong, *op. cit.*, p. 11.

[18] W. L. Morton, *The Canadian Identity* (Madison: University of Wisconsin Press, 1961), pp. 105–106.

[19] Norman Ward, *The Canadian House of Commons: Representation* (Toronto: University of Toronto Press, 1950), pp. 216–225.

[20] Robert Lane, *Political Life* (Glencoe: The Free Press, 1959), p. 11.

to certain impatience with legal process and, occasionally, to outright disrespect for law."[21] There are several indicators of the differences in Canadian and American respect for public authority. Where diffuse respect for public authority exists, we should expect to find greater reliance on informal social controls based on traditional obligations. One indicator of the relative strength of the informal normative mechanisms of social control as compared with the restrictive emphases of legal sanctions may be the extent to which a nation requires police protection or lawyers. The data in Table 2–1 indicate that the United States ratio of police to population

Table 2–1.

NUMBER AND RATES OF POLICE PROTECTION IN CANADA AND THE UNITED STATES

Country	Number of police personnel	Ratio per 100,000 population
Canada (1961)	26,189	143.2
United States (1962)	360,000	193.8

Source: Canada: Dominion Bureau of Statistics, *Police Administration Statistics*, 1961, p. 18; United States: U. S. Department of Commerce, Bureau of the Census, *Statistical Abstract of the United States*, 1963, p. 436.

is more than one-third greater than that of Canada, a difference that holds for communities of the same size. The proportionately fewer lawyers in private practice in Canada (one for 1,630 people) as compared to the United States (one for 868) points to the much lower propensity of Canadians to rely on the law, even for civil matters.[22]

[21] Wrong, *op. cit.*, pp. 36–37.

[22] Lipset, *The First New Nation*, pp. 264–265. Dennis Wrong notes that "one finds less of the frequent American distrust of lawyers as 'shysters' or as ambitious politicians, in English-speaking Canada and a greater sense of remoteness and majesty of the law." Wrong argues that the contrast between the popular culture heroes of American and Canadian westward expansion indicates the respect among Canadians for the law and the converse for Americans: ". . . in the United States it is the cowboy, a rugged individualist whose relationship to the forces of law and order was at least ambiguous, who has come to symbolize the frontier, while in Canada the 'mountie,' a policeman who clearly stands for law and order and traditional institutional authority, is the corresponding symbol of Canadian westward expansion." Wrong, *op. cit.*, p. 38.

The greater obedience to the law by Canadians may be reflected also in varying crime rates in the two countries. Though data on crime rates are far from amenable to accurate cross-national comparisons, both countries offer the same definition and report statistics for several major criminal offenses. Perhaps the most dramatic such difference is that only one police officer in Canada was killed by criminal action while on duty, compared to 37 killed in the United States in 1961. By 1963, the United States figure had risen to 55 police officers killed in a single year, while the figure in Canada remained at one.[23] (The United States has about ten times the population of Canada.) The data in Table 2–2 indicate that United States crime rates for various offenses are substantially higher than Canadian rates for the same offenses.

It is therefore not at all surprising, as one writer has remarked, that "Canadians are today perhaps more aware of the differences in their attitudes toward the law than anything else distinguishing them from Americans."[24] Half a century ago, James Bryce suggested that this habit of obedience to the law among Canadians "was formed under governments that were in those days monarchical in fact as well as in name, and it has persisted. . . . The sentiment of deference to legal authority, planted deep in days when that authority was regarded with awe as having an almost sacred sanction, has lived on into a time when the awe and sacredness have departed. . . ."[25]

Many have argued that the more widespread deferential respect for the elite in Canada as compared with the United States, rather than a more libertarian popular opinion, underlies the freedom of political dissent and guaranteed civil liberties so characteristic of English-speaking Canada. The emphasis on diffuseness and elitism in the Canadian system is reflected in the ability of the more unified and influential elites to control the system so as to inhibit the emergence of

[23] Dominion Bureau of Statistics, *Police Administration Statistics,* 1961, p. 19; U. S. Federal Bureau of Investigation, *Uniform Crime Report—1961,* pp. 20, 110, Table 36, and *Uniform Crime Report—1963,* pp. 33–34.

[24] Wrong, *op. cit.,* p. 38.

[25] James Bryce, *Modern Democracies,* I (London: Macmillan, 1921), pp. 501–502.

Table 2-2.

ADULTS CHARGED ON SELECTED INDICTABLE OFFENSES, BY CLASS OF
OFFENSE, 1960, FOR CANADA AND THE UNITED STATES

| | CANADA | | UNITED STATES* | |
	Number	Rate per 100,000 pop.	Number	Rate per 100,000 pop.
Criminal Homicide	207	1.2	7,956	7.3
Burglary	8,267	46.4	137,800	126.7
Forgery and Counterfeiting	1,158	6.4	25,244	23.2
Fraud and Embezzlement	2,414	13.5	42,189	38.8
Theft-Larceny	15,545	87.2	237,193	218.1

Source: Canada: Dominion Bureau of Statistics, *Canada Year Book,*
1962, p. 356; United States: U. S. Bureau of Census, *Statistical
Abstracts of the United States,* 1962, p. 152.
* The rates for the United States were computed from a total population
base of 108,779,000; for Canada's rates, the population base used was
17,814,000. The weaker authority of the American federal government as compared to the Canadian over local policing makes it
more difficult for the former to collect reliable crime statistics;
hence the discrepancy in the proportion of the total population for
whom data exist.

populist movements, such as McCarthyism, which express
political intolerance. However, as S. D. Clark warns, Mc-
Carthyism (like Coughlinism and the Ku Klux Klan) does
not indicate greater intolerance in the United States as compared to Canada so much as it reflects the strength of populist, anti-elitist values:

> The attack of Joseph McCarthy upon Communist influ-
> ences in the government of the United States is a clear and
> genuine expression of the American frontier, isolationist
> spirit. . . . In Canada it would be hard to conceive of a
> state of political freedom great enough to permit the kind of
> attacks upon responsible leaders of the government which
> have been carried out in the United States. More careful
> examination of the American community in general, and
> perhaps of the academic community in particular, would
> probably reveal that, in spite of the witch hunts in that
> country, the people of the United States enjoy in fact a much
> greater degree of freedom than do the people of Canada.[26]

[26] S. D. Clark, "The Frontier and Democratic Theory," *Transactions of the Royal Society of Canada,* 48 (1954), 72; see also Morton,
op. cit., pp. 105–106.

Ironically, civil liberties for unpopular groups would seem to be stronger in elitist democracies than in egalitarian ones. The lesser respect for public authorities in the United States than in Canada may also be indicated by the considerable variation in the extent to which the public has insisted on the right to elect officials or to change them with the fortunes of elections.[27] In Canada legal officers tend to have life tenure, and are not directly involved in politics. Judges in Canada at every level are appointed for life by the federal authorities. Crown attorneys are designated by the provincial governments for indefinite terms, and are rarely terminated before retirement. They are not fired when a new party comes to power, and since prohibited from political activity, they are never under pressure to handle cases in a way that might facilitate their re-election or attainment of higher electoral office.[28]

In the United States not only are more legal offices open to election, but elections are more frequent than in any other modern society. In a discussion of American urban politics, Edward Banfield and James Wilson point out that

> our government [in the United States] is permeated with politics. This is because our constitutional structure and our traditions afford individuals manifold opportunities not only to bring their special interests to the attention of public officials but also—and this is the important thing—to compel officials to bargain and to make compromises . . . there is virtually no sphere of "administration" apart from politics.[29]

Such a comment underlies the populist sentiments and structures that pervade the American polity. The strong egalitarian emphasis in the United States which presses for expression in the *vox populi* makes Americans more derisive and critical of their politicians and government bureaucrats.

The same differentiating factors seemingly are reflected in

[27] As early as 1921 Bryce had noted that "The respect felt for the judiciary contributes to that strict ministration of the civil law which are honourable characteristics of Canada." Bryce, *op. cit.*, p. 486.

[28] Henry H. Bull, "The Career Prosecutor of Canada," *The Journal of Criminal Law, Criminology, and Police Science,* 53 (1962), 89–96.

[29] Edward C. Banfield and James Q. Wilson, *City Politics* (Cambridge: Harvard University Press and M.I.T. Press, 1963), p. 1.

varying administrative practices at the national government level. Alexander Brady, a prominent Canadian student of comparative political institutions, has strongly emphasized these differences:

> In Ottawa, no less than in London, the dividing line between the politician craving publicity and the permanent official cherishing anonymity is drawn higher in the administrative hierarchy than in Washington. A political party replacing another in power does not, as in the United States, introduce to public office a new and large retinue of top advisors and administrators. It assumes that in the civil service it will find a reliable and competent corps of officials to supplement its thinking and implement its decisions. The deputy-minister as the permanent chief of a department is a non-political figure who normally brings to the aid of his minister the resources of seasoned experience and knowledge.[30]

The lesser respect for the law, for the "rules of the game" in the United States, may be viewed as inherent in a system in which egalitarianism is strongly valued and in which diffuse elitism is lacking. Generalized deference is not accorded to those at the top; therefore, in the United States there is a greater propensity to redefine the rules or to ignore them. The legitimacy and decisions of the leadership are constantly being questioned. While Canadians incline toward the use of "lawful" and traditionally institutionalized means for altering regulations which they believe are unjust, Americans seem more disposed to employ informal and often extralegal means to correct what they perceive as wrong.

The greater lawlessness and corruption in the United States may be attributed in part to the greater strength of the achievement and self-orientation values in the more populous nation. As Robert Merton has pointed out, a strong emphasis on achievement means that "the moral mandate to achieve success thus exerts pressure to succeed, by fair means if possible and by foul means if necessary."[31] Merton accounts for the greater adherence to approved means of behavior in much of

[30] Alexander Brady, "Canada and the Model of Westminster," in William B. Hamilton (ed.), *The Transfer of Institutions* (Durham: Duke University Press, 1964), p. 77.

[31] Robert K. Merton, *Social Theory and Social Structure* (Glencoe: The Free Press, 1957), p. 169.

Europe compared to the United States as derivative from variations in the emphasis on achievement for all. And the same logic implies that since Americans are more likely than their Canadian neighbors to be concerned with the achievement of ends—particularly pecuniary success—they will be less concerned with the use of the socially appropriate *means;* hence we should expect a higher incidence of deviations from conventional norms in politics and other aspects of life south of the forty-ninth parallel.[32]

The variations in the legal status of labor conflict and the behavior of the trade unions in the two countries illustrate both the greater willingness of Americans to accept conflict as a "normal" method of resolving disputes and to violate rules and laws to attain desired ends. Thus in Canada a union's right to strike must be earned through a process of legal certification of majority backing (a restriction which does not exist in the United States where any group of workers may employ the strike weapon in order to resolve a dispute).[33] And where labor conflicts have occurred,

> there has generally been less violent conflict between workers and employers [in Canada than in the United States]. The use of professional strike breakers, labor spies, "goon squads," "vigilante" groups, armed militia, and other spectacular features of industrial warfare in the United States in previous decades have been absent from the Canadian scene—again with several notable exceptions.[34]

[32] See Bryce, *op. cit.,* p. 501, for a discussion of the greater propensity of Americans as compared to Canadians to engage in corrupt practices and demagoguery in politics.

[33] A restraint exercised over Canadian labor groups and not over American ones is found in the "certification" policy which demands that "a union must claim a 50% membership in the proposed bargaining unit to be eligible to apply for certification, and must be supported by at least half the unit members in a vote if one is taken by the appropriate board. Again there are variations across the country, but the fact remains that a union which is a minority can neither be certified nor can it use its collective power to force recognition. In other words, where no majority can be established the employer is protected by law from collective bargaining, and those employees who do wish to be represented by a union are denied such representation." H. D. Woods, "Labor Law and Unionization in the U.S. and Canada," a paper presented at the meeting of the American Sociological Association, September 3, 1964.

[34] Stuart Jamieson, *Industrial Relations in Canada* (Ithaca: Cornell University Press, 1957), p. 7.

The greater diffidence of Canadians with respect to their adherence to achievement and self-orientation values may also be reflected in their reluctance to be overoptimistic, assertive, or experimentally inclined in economic affairs. This Canadian caution manifests itself in several ways: one is

> that Canadians take out more insurance *per capita* than any other race in the world. Another is that they buy considerably less on hire-purchase [installment plan] than the Americans. . . . The average Canadian is also cautious about his savings, favouring Government bonds and savings banks. Whereas over the years the American big investor has tended to take a risk on the future of Canada and invest heavily in more speculative Canadian enterprises, the wealthy Canadian cautiously puts his money into Standard Oil of New Jersey.[35]

The earliest empirical efforts to determine Canadian self-perceptions, made in the thirties, indicate that Canadians of that period thought of themselves as "quieter, slower in tempo, and saner in quality" than Americans, saw Americans as loud, shrewd, less honest, and more anxious to get rich quickly.[36] Clearly, as Canadian sociologists Kaspar Naegele and Dennis Wrong have argued, the Horatio Alger

[35] Alistair Horne, *Canada and the Canadians* (London: Macmillan, 1961), p. 245.

[36] See S. D. Clark, "The Importance of Anti-Americanism in Canadian National Feeling," in H. F. Angus (ed.), *Canada and Her Great Neighbor* (Toronto: The Ryerson Press, 1938), pp. 392–438. These differences are frequently cited as typical of Canadians today also. See, for example, Horne, *op. cit.*, p. 9, "[P]erhaps the most universally valid quality about Canadian speech is its *quietness*. And this quietness points to a general dislike of noise, to a distrust of ostentation, and to a tendency towards conservatism that is distinctly more British than American. . . ."; G. V. Ferguson, "The English-Canadian Outlook," in Mason Wade (ed.), *Canadian Dualism* (Toronto: University of Toronto Press, 1960), p. 5: "A stranger on brief passage might mistake Vancouver for Seattle, Winnipeg for Des Moines, Toronto for Buffalo or Cleveland. It would be only on closer examination that the marked differences would become manifest: the slightly slower tempo of life, the less volatile reaction to events, the more sober, more conservative attitudes of mind, the higher degree of sabbatarianism, the greater gift for compromise and the middle way, the stricter disciplines of a parliamentary as against a congressional democracy, the respect for law and for order, the modesty which flows as much from a long history of colonial dependence as from a realistic sense of the place of a small nation in a big power world."

success story has never taken hold in Canadian society, perhaps because of Canadian resistance to economic aggressiveness, social informality, and unabashed materialism.[37] Canadian historian Arthur Lower has even argued that

> Henry Ford was a figure who could hardly have been other
> than American. Canada did not provide a stage for such as
> he. Yet this was not on account of lack of opportunities here
> [in Canada] for accumulating wealth, but rather because
> that process called for more betting on the sure thing than
> was necessary across the border.[38]

The variation in the strength of the achievement and self-orientation values in the United States and Canada may account for another political difference—the fact that "free enterprise" ideology, though accepted in Canada, has never been the source of as violent political conflicts there as in the United States. The greater respect for government and political leaders, derived in part from elitism and in part from the need dictated by special historic circumstances (see below) requiring that the central government intervene repeatedly in economic and local political matters to assure national survival, has inhibited the development of strong economic individualism as a dominant political virtue. As James Bryce remarked some decades ago,

> the policy of *laissez-faire* has few adherents in a country
> which finds in governmental action or financial support to
> private enterprise the quickest means of carrying out every
> promising project. So when party conflicts arise over these
> matters, it is not the principle that is contested . . . but the
> plan advocated by the Government or the Opposition as the
> case may be.[39]

Canada has clearly been much more collectivity oriented than the United States. In recent years, proposals for medicare, grants for large families, government intervention in the economy, and public ownership of major enterprises have

[37] Naegele, *op. cit.*, pp. 29–30, Wrong, *op. cit.*, p. 30.
[38] Lower, *op. cit.*, p. 426. For a discussion in support of this same thesis, see Horne, *op. cit.*, p. 9.
[39] Bryce, *op. cit.*, p. 471.

encountered much less opposition north of the border than south of it. "The extreme economic individualism expressed by such slogans as 'the best government is the one that governs least' does not have such deep roots in Canada" as it has in the United States.[40] As one English writer notes:

> One of the strange contradictions of Canada is that although it has never had anything resembling a Socialist Government in Ottawa, the list of its "nationalized" industries is almost as imposing as Britain's: more than half the railways; the principal airline; most of radio and television; the Atomic Energy Corporation and one of the biggest uranium producers; a big plastics industry; many of the power utilities [and telephone and telegraph]; and the entire liquor retailing business.[41]

And as a Canadian points out, "it is interesting to note that at a time when the *laissez-faire* philosophy was prevailing in the rest of the Western World, there was no protest in Canada against government intervention and interference, not even from business circles."[42] Far from turning to McCarthyism or Goldwaterism, Canadian conservatives responded to years of political defeat by renaming their party the *Progressive* Conservatives.

The emphases on achievement and self-orientation in the United States are strongly linked to universalism. In the United States there is a proclaimed need to treat everyone according to the same standard. This universalistic objective underlies the concept of the "melting pot" which holds that no one should be disqualified from full participation on the grounds of ethnic origin or other social distinctions. The melting-pot concept is the achievement orientation applied to

[40] Wrong, *op. cit.*, p. 29.

[41] Horne, *op. cit.*, pp. 248–249. It might be added that hotels are owned by the CNR, and now all provinces except Quebec have Hospitalization Insurance Plans; Canada also has Family Allowances of $6 a month for every child under 10, and $8 for those between 10 and 15. See *ibid.*, p. 250. See also Lloyd D. Musolf, "Canadian Public Enterprise: A Character Study," *American Political Science Review*, 50 (1956), 405–421.

[42] Maurice Lamontagne, "The Role of Government," in G. P. Gilmour (ed.), *Canada's Tomorrow* (Toronto: Macmillan, 1954), p. 125. See also Bryce's discussion of Canada's resistance to *laissez-faire*, *op. cit.*, p. 471.

entire ethnic groups.[43] In contradistinction to the melting pot of the United States, Canadians speak of their society as a "mosaic," a concept which enunciates in theory the "right to sustained collective individuality."[44] As Canadian sociologist John Porter points out, the difference between the ideas of the *melting pot* and the *mosaic* is one of the principal distinguishing features of United States and Canadian society at the level of social psychology as well as that of social structure."[45] Vincent Massey, former governor general, has expressed the Canadian stress on the preservation of particularistic values:

> We have been successful in our manner of adjusting the relations of the varied communities making Canada their home. About one out of three speaks French as his mother tongue. He is no minority assimilated within a common Canadianism, but rather a partner sharing equally in the joint project of Confederation. Then there are the "new Canadians" of whom two million from Great Britain and from Europe have reached our shores since 1945. . . . We try to fit in the newcomers much as they are, as pieces in the Canadian mosaic.[46]

Canadians emphasize the contribution which diverse ethnic and linguistic groups bring to Canadian life in the form of cultural heritage. "New Canadians have been encouraged to maintain many of their distinctive folk traditions, and their songs, dress, and folklore," and they "are often publicized as indications of the richness and diversity of Canadian life —an approach to ethnic differences that is much less common in the United States. . . ."[47]

[43] "In the United States the Briton hastened to become a good American; in Canada he has been encouraged to remain a good Briton. Nor has any vigorous effort been made to assimilate continental European peoples in Canada, except through the public schools; as with the French Canadians, the break of continental Europeans from their cultural past has tended to expose them to European influences." Clark, "The Canadian Community," pp. 386–387.

[44] Naegele, *op. cit.*, p. 44.

[45] John Porter, *The Vertical Mosaic: An Analysis of Social Class and Power in Canada* (Toronto: University of Toronto Press, 1965), pp. 70–72.

[46] Vincent Massey, *Canadians and Their Commonwealth* (Oxford: The Clarendon Press, 1961), pp. 5–6.

[47] Naegele, *op. cit.*, p. 49: "In public discussions of New Canadians the emphasis tends to be on the contribution which the diverse cultural

Canadian particularism has been demonstrated also in the requirement, in existence until recently, that Canadian passports indicate ethnic origin, e.g., a Canadian of German origin, even though the German origin may go back more than a century. The Canadian census not only differs from the American in that it records religious data gathered from each individual, but it also reports on the national origins of every Canadian, except Jews. The latter, regardless of country of paternal ancestry, are classified as Jews in the category of national origin as well as religion.

Canada's political party system has witnessed the rise of a number of "particularistic" third parties, various French-Canadian nationalist or separatist movements, plus the Progressives, Social Credit, and the Cooperative Commonwealth Federation (CCF). The last, a socialist party, joined in 1961 with the Canadian Labor Congress to form the trade-union based New Democratic party (NDP) the largest contemporary "third" party. This pattern of Canadian politics —i.e., the continued presence of strong particularistic third parties—is consistent with the assumption that Canada is more particularistic (group-attribute conscious) than the seemingly more universalistic United States.

III

Many writers seeking to account for value differences between the United States and Canada suggest that they stem in large part from the revolutionary origins of the United States and the counterrevolutionary history of Canada, from two disparate founding ethos. The Loyalist emigrés from the American Revolution and Canada's subsequent repeatedly aroused fears of United States encroachment fostered the institutionalization of a counterrevolutionary or conservative ethos.[48]

heritages they bring with them will make to Canadian life rather than, as is commonly the case in the United States, on their expectation of life in the New World."

[48] See J. M. S. Careless, *Canada: A Story of Challenge* (Cambridge: Cambridge University Press, 1963), pp. 111, 112, 113. Even since World War II, as Careless argues, Canada has remained more conservative than the United States: "In comparison with the rich and restless republic [the United States], Canada was a cautious and conservative

By contrast the core values of the United States, linked to the utopian ideology which emerged during the Revolution, were codified in the Declaration of Independence and elaborated in the principles successfully pressed by the Jeffersonian Democrats in the formative post-Revolutionary decades.

In these counterrevolutionary beginnings of Canada, we find the clue to the continuance of British ascriptive and elitist value patterns. The Canadian historian Arthur Lower has pointed out that "in its new wilderness home and its new aspect of British North Americanism, colonial Toryism made its second attempt to erect on American soil a copy of the English social edifice. From one point of view this is the most significant thing about the Loyalist movement; it withdrew a class concept of life from the south, moved it up north and gave it a second chance."[49]

During the American Revolution, Nova Scotia had a population of 17,000; almost double that number of Loyalists entered it afterward, "swallowing the older 'neutral Yankee' elements in an ardently Loyalist mass." New Brunswick was set up as a separate province in 1784, largely because of the great Loyalist influx. The Loyalist settlers in Upper Canada (now Ontario)

> would form the backbone of western resistance in a second war with the United States, the War of 1812. They were the original founders of the present province of Ontario, and did much to mould its character. On one hand, they brought to Canada a conservative outlook, a quick distrust of any new idea that might be called republican, and a readiness to make loyalty the test for almost everything. On the other, they themselves represented a declaration of independence against the United States, a determination to live apart from that country in North America.[50]

Thus Tory conservatism and anti-Americanism affected "not only the St. John Valley where the Loyalists were a majority,

country: cautious because her path was harder, more conservative because of her closer bonds with the Old World, and the stronger power of traditions brought from Britain and France." Careless, *op. cit.*, p. 405.

[49] A. R. M. Lower, *From Colony to Nation* (Toronto: Longmans, Green, 1946), p. 114.

[50] Careless, *op. cit.*, pp. 111–113.

but other regions where they were a minority." These "interlocked neatly with the prevalent conceptions of oligarchy and privilege."[51]

After the Revolution, undisguised efforts were made to check American influences. The first governors, Simcoe and Carleton, of what is now Ontario and Quebec were men who had played a leading role in fighting the Revolution. To them republican principles were anathema.[52] The antirevolutionary and anti-American character of Canada's political and social development helped strengthen ethnic particularism and ecclesiasticism. The English Protestant rulers of French Canada opposed assimilation and weakening of the semi-Establishment status of the Catholic church in Quebec as a means of resisting Americanization. Sir Robert Falconer says that "as late as 1822 Lord Dalhousie favored the French Canadians of the lower province as a means of make-weight against Americanizing tendencies which he discerned in Upper Canada."[53] Support for the hierarchically organized churches, Anglican and Roman, served to reinforce hierarchical, anti-democratic tendencies. As the famed Canadian historian Harold Innis noted, a "counterrevolutionary tradition implies an emphasis on ecclesiasticism."[54]

Continued Canadian allegiance to the British monarchy undoubtedly has also contributed to the greater sense of legiti-

[51] J. Bartlett Brebner, *Canada* (Ann Arbor: University of Michigan Press, 1960), p. 107. See on this point Careless, *op. cit.*, p. 150: "The English influence also tended to work in this direction. English gentlemen who entered the government service or the dominant Church of England brought a decided belief in class distinctions with them and a dislike of 'levelling' democracy." Frank Underhill, *In Search of Canadian Liberalism* (Toronto: Macmillan, 1960), esp. p. 12, notes that "the mental climate of English Canada in its early formative years was determined by men who were fleeing from the practical application of the doctrines that all men are born equal and are endowed by their creator with certain inalienable rights. . . ."

[52] See George M. Wrong, *The United States and Canada* (Nashville: Abingdon Press, 1921), pp. 54–55, 57, 63.

[53] Sir Robert Falconer, *The United States as Neighbour* (Cambridge: Cambridge University Press, 1925), p. 23. Or as Brady has put it, "To remain British the colony must remain French." See his "Canada and the Model of Westminster," p. 61.

[54] Harold Innis, *Essays in Canadian Economic History* (Toronto: University of Toronto Press, 1956), p. 385.

macy for hierarchical distinctions characteristic of the northern nation. In the early history of Canada, the public authorities tried consciously to foster such values as a barrier to
American influences.[55] Clark says:

> Efforts to strengthen the political ties of Empire or of nation
> led to deliberate attempts, through land grants and political
> preferments, to create and strengthen an aristocracy in the
> colonies . . . and later in a less obvious fashion, in the
> Canadian nation. The democratic movement it was felt was
> liable to draw Canadian people closer to their neighbors to
> the south; and a privileged upper class was a bulwark of
> loyalty and conservatism.[56]

The unification of the British North American colonies into
a federal union was procured by Empire-oriented Canadian
Conservatives who feared United States expansion across the
border, and the growth in influence within Canada of reform-
minded "pro-American" frontier settlers who favored local
autonomy. The decision to provide Canada with a strong
central government, which unlike that of the United States
would be able to veto or "disallow" provincial laws, was designed to resist the democratic threat within and across the
border.[57] According to W. L. Morton,

> With the Reformers committed to local democracy, and the
> Conservatives to continental expansionism, it is not surpris-
> ing that Confederation was, by and large, a Conservative

[55] Clark, *The Developing Canadian Community* (Toronto: University of Toronto Press, 1962), p. 192. See also Bruce Dunlop, "The Law
of Torts," in Edward McWhinney (ed.), *Canadian Jurisprudence* (Toronto: Carswell, 1958), p. 145. "In Canada, as in the United States,
legal institutions began simply as offshoots of the parent organ in the
mother country. In the United States, however, there was a revolution
and reaction to everything British. The Americans retained the Common Law but acquired an independence of approach. Canadians, on
the other hand, continued to look to England as the fountain-head. In
fact, the revolution that set American jurisprudence free may have
heightened the tendency of Canadian courts to use the English line.
What was being done by the Americans was revolutionary, radical, not
to be trusted."
[56] Clark, *The Developing Canadian Community*, p. 194.
[57] W. L. Morton, "The Extension of the Franchise in Canada," *Report of the Canadian Historical Association* (Toronto: University of
Toronto Press, 1943), p. 76.

party measure, and also a measure conservative in tone and substance. A striking venture in federalism, it neither, except in establishing representation by population, widened the basis of self-government nor altered the depository of sovereignty.[58]

In contrast to Canada, the United States is the result of a successful revolution and prolonged war of independence organized around the ideology embodied in the Declaration of Independence, which proclaimed the validity of egalitarian and universalistic social relations. Out of a sort of Utopian conception of men's egalitarian and universalistic relations with one another a national consciousness arose which infused men with a new awareness and new confidence in what they were and in their own kind.[59] The new value consensus and normative prescriptions of the American people were sustained by at least two major conditions: territorial expansion and nonalignment with European nations.

In newly independent societies there has often been a transition from a system dominated by traditionalist, usually aristocratic, values to one characterized by egalitarian concepts. Consequently, most struggles for independence have employed leftist ideologies—socialism today, and equality in revolutionary America—in which man's status is to depend not upon inherited but achieved qualities. Thus the system in

---

[58] *Ibid.*

[59] "Behind the spreading of national consciousness there was at work perhaps a deeper change—a new *value* assigned to people *as they are,* or as they can become, with as much diversity of interlocking roles as will not destroy or stifle any of their personalities. After 1750 we find new and higher values assigned in certain advanced countries to children and women; to the poor and the sick; to slaves and peasants; to colored races and submerged nationalities. . . ." Karl Deutsch, *Nationalism and Social Communication* (New York: John Wiley, 1953), pp. 153–155. A study of American Tories in the Revolution concludes: "If there were any serious consequences to America from the silencing and expulsion of the Loyalists, they were certainly not social or, in the narrow sense, political consequences. Rather they were philosophical consequences: the Tories' organic conservatism represented a current of thought that failed to reappear in America after the revolution. A substantial part of the whole spectrum of European social and political philosophy seemed to slip outside the American perspective." William H. Nelson, *The American Tory* (New York: Oxford University Press, 1961), pp. 189–190.

America was geared to abolish all forms of privilege and primogeniture and to reward achievement.

Despite the conviction of many revolutionary leaders that the struggle for independence was primarily an issue of political and national independence, large segments of the American people organized against the emergence of any ruling oligarchical forces. Many insisted that the franchise be extended to everyone, that the people be regarded as the source of power and authority. The very early arguments for the extension of the suffrage to all were "based on the rights of man given special impetus by the Declaration of Independence and the terms of conflict of the American Revolution."[60] The demands on American politicians to be competent and to deliver some rewards to the people were as natural in the Revolutionary era as they are today. Although the Federalists attempted to preserve some elements of elitist values and resisted populist reforms, there is general agreement among historians that a major cause of their decline was the refusal to accommodate themselves to the strength of egalitarian sentiments. All succeeding parties were to be egalitarian in ideology and populist in spirit.[61]

The significance of the "leftist" egalitarian populist character of core values in the American political tradition may best be perceived from the vantage point of comparative North American history. For although American historians and political philosophers may debate the extent of radicalism, liberalism, leftism, or even conservatism, in Revolutionary and post-colonial American politics, there is little doubt in the mind of most Canadian historians. Looking at the divergent political history north and south of the border, they see the continued politics of their nation as reflecting the fact that it is a descendant of a counterrevolution, while the United States is a product of a successful revolution. Once these events had formed the structure of the two nations, their institutional characters were set. Subsequent events tended to enforce "leftist" values in the south and "rightist" ones in the north. The success of the Revolutionary ideology, the defeat of the Tories, and the emigration of many of them

[60] Lane, *op. cit.*, p. 12.
[61] Lipset, *The First New Nation*, pp. 82–90.

north to Canada or across the ocean to Britain—all served to enhance the strength of the forces favoring egalitarian democratic principles in the new nation and to weaken conservative tendencies. On the other hand, the failure of Canada to have a revolution of its own, the immigration of conservative elements, and the emigration of radical ones—all contributed to making Canada a more conservative and more rigidly stratified society. This does not mean, as S. D. Clark has pointed out, "that revolutionary forces developed no strength in Canada. We have had our revolutions but they have been largely unsuccessful, and being unsuccessful we try to forget them. Thus we have tended to dismiss our rebels of the past as misguided individuals out of accord with their fellow Canadians. . . ."[62]

American Democratic party reformers from Jackson to Bryan to Wilson to the leaders of the modern New Deal–Fair Deal–New Frontier–Great Society party have presented their programs as means of implementing the egalitarian ideals of the Revolution. In Canada, which not only emerged out of a defeated democratic revolution, but has a history of defeated nineteenth-century reformist movements, advocates of progressive reforms cannot link these to historic national movements. Of course,

> as in other industrial societies, there has been some extension of social rights . . . [but] their haphazard development has come about more by the "demonstration effect" of their existence in other countries, than because they have formed the social philosophy of either of the two parties which have been in power at the federal level.[63]

In addition to fostering politically relevant norms, American values have encouraged egalitarian social relations by contributing to the enormous increase in national wealth, an increase which made it possible to assure the lower classes a standard of living which would support their claim for equal treatment by those who excelled them in economic and politi-

[62] S. D. Clark, *Movements of Political Protest in Canada* (Toronto: University of Toronto Press, 1959), p. 3; see also Underhill, *op. cit.*, p. 12; Lower, *From Colony to Nation*, pp. 84–85.
[63] Porter, *op. cit.*, p. 370.

cal power. American values have engendered strong positive orientations toward hard work and economic development. The emphasis on equality and achievement reinforced the belief that one could and should get ahead by hard, continuous work, frugality, self-discipline, and individual initiative. The absence of an aristocratic stratum following the Revolution left the United States free to develop a socially as well as economically dominant class of merchants and manufacturers whose desire for wealth was uninhibited by norms denigrating hard work and the accumulation of capital. Such norms were present in much of Europe, and to some extent even in Canada, although more among the French than the English. Thus the rapidity of American economic growth must be credited, in some degree, to a symbiotic relationship between economic motivation and the system of general values.

IV

The differences between American and Canadian religion have been of considerable significance in producing the admittedly small differences between the values of the two countries, as well as affecting national differences in political and economic development. Denominational religion, often evangelistic, secular, and voluntary in character, has contributed to the American emphases on self-orientation, egalitarianism, universalism, and achievement. Conversely, religion in Canada retained its ecclesiastic character and its strong relationship to the state with the consequence that religious organization in Canada, emphasizing elitism and particularism, acted as a counterforce inhibiting excessive individualism (self-orientation) and egalitarianism.

In the first half century of the American Republic, the champions of religious traditionalism were seriously weakened, as the various state churches—Anglican in the South and Congregationalist in New England—were gradually disestablished. From the beginning, the United States was heir to a Calvinistic Puritanism which was stronger in the colonies than in the mother country, and it was congenial to modernity in a sense that the Anglican Church in English Canada and the Gallican Church in Quebec were not. The two denominations, Methodist and Baptist, which became dominant in the early nineteenth century, stressed religious doctrines that supported "anti-aristocratic tendencies."[64] After the Revolution, the Calvinist doctrine with its belief in innate predestination was gradually supplanted by Arminian religious beliefs, not only as an evangelical revivalistic religion, but as a reflection of the fact that

> in a period when the special privileges of individuals were being called into question or destroyed, there would naturally be less favor for that form of theology which was dominated by the doctrine of the especial election of a part of mankind, a growing favor for those forms which seemed more distinctly to be based upon the idea of the natural equality of all men.[65]

The Arminian emphasis on the personal attainment of grace, embodied in "doctrines of free will, free grace, and unlimited hope for the conversion of all men," even more than Calvinism, served as a religious counterpart to the democratic goals of equality and achievement.[66] A devout man was an ambitious man, and as Philip Schaff, a Swiss theologian who eventually emigrated to America, reported, the "acquisition of riches is to them [the Americans] only a help toward higher spiritual and moral ends."[67] Righteousness was to be rewarded both in this life and in the hereafter.

The abolition of established religion in the United States fostered a strong commitment to voluntarism. This commitment, together with the considerable strength of the dissenting and anti-statist Methodist and Baptist denominations, meant that religion not only contributed to the economic orientations

[64] Timothy L. Smith, *Revivalism and Social Reform in Mid-Nineteenth Century America* (New York: Abingdon Press, 1957), pp. 24–25.

[65] J. Franklin Jameson, *The American Revolution Considered as a Social Movement* (Princeton, N. J.: Princeton University Press, 1926), p. 157.

[66] Smith, *op. cit.*, pp. 88–89. Smith concludes that the Calvinist belief in predestination "could hardly survive amidst the evangelists' earnest entreaties to 'come to Jesus.'"

[67] Philip Schaff, *America: A Sketch of the Political, Social, and Religious Character of the United States of North America* (New York: Scribner, 1855), p. 259.

of the people, but also reinforced the egalitarian and democratic social ethos. Tocqueville pointed out that all American
denominations were minorities and hence had an interest in
liberty and a weak state. As he put it in discussing Catholics:
"They constitute a minority, and all rights must be respected
in order to assure to them the free exercise of their own
privileges. These . . . causes induce them, even unconsciously,
to adopt political doctrines which they would perhaps support
with less zeal if they were preponderant."[68] Denominational
voluntaristic religion not only reinforced the support for
minority rights in the religious sphere, but also found deeply
religious men in government arguing strongly that the rights
of the irreligious and of Jews must be the same as those of
Christians.[69]

In Canada state-related religion has provided that country
with a hierarchical and traditionally rooted control mechanism that is largely lacking in United States history. Because
of the strong tie between church and state in Canada, religious development there, in contrast to religious movements in
the United States, has been less prone to both fundamental-
ism and experimentalism.

Both the Church of England and the Roman Catholic
Church, which were hierarchically organized and received
overt governmental support, gave strong support to the established political and social order. Hence one found mutually
reinforcing conservative forces at the summits of the class,
church, and political structures.[70]

The interlocking character of political and religious conservatism may be seen in the extent to which patterns of
marriage and divorce have been affected by religious practices. As recently as World War II, the law of most provinces,
including Ontario, did not provide for civil marriage.[71] The
extent to which Canadian religion has been more successful
than American in maintaining traditional and conservative
principles may be seen in the much lower divorce rate in Can-

[68] Alexis de Tocqueville, *Democracy in America*, II (New York:
Vintage Books, 1954), p. 312.
[69] Lipset, *The First New Nation*, pp. 164–166.
[70] Clark, "The Canadian Community," p. 388.
[71] Dennis Wrong, *op. cit.*, p. 10.

ada as compared with the United States, as shown in Table 2–3. The greater moral conservatism of English Canada is

Table 2–3.

DIVORCES PER 1,000 MARRIAGES FOR SPECIFIED YEARS IN CANADA AND THE UNITED STATES

Year	Canada	United States
1891	less than 1	60.0
1911	less than 1	93.4
1941	29.3	168.5
1951	41.0	230.4
1956	45.2	233.0
1960	53.5	257.3

Source: Canada: Dominion Bureau of Statistics, *Canada Year Book*, 1962, pp. 209, 211; United States: U. S. Department of Commerce, Bureau of the Census, *Statistical Abstracts of the United States*, 1962, p. 52, and United Nations, *Demographic Yearbook*, 1960 (New York), p. 607. See also Lincoln Day, "Patterns of Divorce in Australia and the United States," *American Sociological Review*, 29 (August 1964), 509–522, esp. Table 2.

also revealed in the fact that many "blue laws" and Sunday observance regulations remained in force much longer in the north than the south, and, in fact, a number of such restrictions on behavior still exist in many Canadian cities.

The ecclesiastical character of the predominant Canadian religions has also greatly inhibited the development of egalitarian and achievement emphases comparable to those fostered by anti-elitist sects and denominations in the United States. American Protestantism, with its emphasis on the personal attainment of grace, reinforced the stress on personal achievement dominant in the secular value system. Both sets of values stressed individual responsibility, both rejected hereditary status. The Methodists and Baptists, who together contained the great majority of American Protestants, stressed religious doctrines that reinforced "anti-aristocratic tendencies."[72] In English Canada, the Anglican Church "set a standard of dignity for all the leading denominations which was absent in the United States."[73]

And while the dominant Arminian denominations have fos-

[72] Smith, *op. cit.*, pp. 88–89.
[73] A. R. M. Lower, "Religion and Religious Institutions," in Brown, *op. cit.*, p. 465.

tered economic ambition in the United States, Canadian
ecclesiasticism has been less able to provide a stimulus for
new forms of economic enterprise.

> Religion has given support to an attitude of mind, and a
> governmental policy, which has placed a check upon that
> kind of economic and social mobility conducive to the de-
> velopment of capitalism. Churches are essentially status
> institutions, and this has meant that the organization of re-
> ligion has served to maintain status distinctions that have had
> no meaning in terms of economic endeavor. The strength of
> the aristocratic tradition in Canada owes much to the influ-
> ence of religion. . . . In English-speaking Canada . . .
> Church establishment in colonial times placed a considerable
> dependence upon a close alliance with a privileged upper
> class that lacked the imagination or inclination to take any
> sort of lead in the economic development of the country, and,
> although the formal disestablishment of the Church weakened
> the religious support of such a class system, the organization
> of religion has continued to be sufficiently powerful to main-
> tain to some degree the status distinctions of a religiously
> oriented rather than economically oriented society.[74]

Religious sects have, of course, developed in Canada,
facilitated by much the same social conditions inherent in
rapid social change as in the United States, i.e., the heavy
shift of population to the frontier or the growing cities and
the related social mobility, which have torn individuals from
their traditional ties and made them available for recruitment
to new loyalties. However, the fact that religion is less explicitly separated from the "national community" in Canada has meant that sects have been less able to survive there
than in the United States. In Canada: "Political pressures,"
says Clark,

> have forced the community to come to the support of or-
> ganized religion and such support has placed a definite limita-
> tion upon sectarian activity. With the collective weight of the
> community brought to bear upon them, the sects have been
> forced to retreat behind a wall of isolation or build them-
> selves into an integral part of the community, or else to seek
> denominational support by aligning themselves with the state
> and with the traditional institutions of the community.[75]

[74] Clark, *The Developing Canadian Community*, pp. 173–174.
[75] *Ibid.*, p. 178.

Once the historic sects allied themselves with the established institutions in the community, their differences became less important and they found it easier to forget about sectarian beliefs and unite. As a result the union of the major "nonconformist" Protestant denominations proceeded much more rapidly in Canada than in the United States. The United Church of Canada was formed in 1925 out of a merger of Methodist, Presbyterian, and Congregationalist denominations. In many parts of English Canada, it now shares an unofficial but real "establishment" status with the Anglican church.[76]

V

Some of the flavor of the social distinctions in Canada and the United States which reflect the greater strength of traditionalist and conservative values in the former may be traced also to a Canadian frontier fashioned in a spirit of cautious defensiveness against American absorptionist tendencies. For this reason, "It was the established tradition of British North America that the power of the civil authority should operate well in advance of the spread of settlement."[77] Law and order in the form of the centrally controlled Northwest Mounted Police moved into the frontier settlements before and along with the settlers. This contributed to the establishment of a greater tradition of respect for institutions of law and order on the Canadian frontier as compared with the American.

[76] C. E. Silcox, *Church Union in Canada* (New York: Institute of Social and Religious Research, 1933).

[77] Edgar W. McInnis, *The Unguarded Frontier* (Garden City: Doubleday, 1942), p. 307. The lawlessness that overflowed into Canada was quickly wiped out by the Northwest Mounted Police: "'An imaginary line,' wrote a later Westerner, 'separated Canada from the United States for a distance of 800 miles. South of that line strategic points were garrisoned by thousands of United States soldiers; an almost continuous condition of Indian warfare prevailed, and the white population in large measure ran free of the restraints of established authority. There had been an overflow of "bad men" from Montana into what is now southern Alberta and southwestern Saskatchewan, who repeated in Canada the exploits by which they had made Montana infamous. In large measure the world took it for granted that lawlessness must accompany pioneer conditions. Canada's Mounted Police was the challenge to that idea.'"

> This famous force [Mounted Police] was organized in
> 1874. To the 300 men who composed it was given the task
> of seeing that the law was obeyed from Manitoba to the
> Rockies and from the forty-ninth parallel to the Arctic
> Circle. . . . Organized whiskey traffic with the Indians was
> broken up within a year. Horse stealing was made so pre-
> carious that there was seldom need for the drastic commu-
> nity action which was the normal procedure in many parts of
> the American West. Perhaps most important of all, Canada
> was enabled to avoid the series of desperate conflicts with
> the Indians which was necessary to clear the way for the
> final advance of settlement in the United States.[78]

The Canadians, being more prone to identify liberty and
democracy with legal traditions and procedures than with
populism, the right of the people to rule, or with the freedom
of business and enterprise, have given equal juridical rights
to minority and ethnic groups, while in the United States
debates over the position of minority groups have been at the
root of Indian wars and of the Civil War. On the American
frontier the quality of law enforcement was often dependent
on local policy authority which reflected the values of the
frontiersmen, including their prejudices against Indians and
their lack of understanding for legal procedures incorporat-
ing the guarantee of due process. In Canada, Indian chiefs
"were impressed by the fact that, if Indians were punished
for crimes against the whites, the whites were equally punished for outrages against the Indians. Their previous experience [with American whites] had taught them to appreciate
such impartial justice."[79] The Queen's peace was maintained
even in the mining camps, which were characteristically un-
disciplined in the United States. Conditions during the gold
rush in British Columbia differed greatly from those in the
American Western mining frontier. There were no vigilantes
or massacres of Indians.[80]

The presence of national governmental controls weakened
the development of excessive individualism which expresses

[78] *Ibid.*, pp. 307–308.
[79] *Loc. cit.*
[80] Brebner, *op. cit.*, p. 255; Bryce, *op. cit.*, pp. 486–487. Paul F.
Sharp, "Three Frontiers: Some Comparative Studies of Canadian,
American and Australian Settlement," *Pacific Historical Review*, 24
(1955), 373–374.

itself south of the border in a greater faith in the future and a greater willingness to risk capital, personal security, or reputation. The Canadian frontier experience did not undermine the traditional bases of authority; Canadians even on the frontier retained a more deeply internalized sense of obligation, of the need to conform to the rules even when there was no visible threat of coercion. As the Canadian historian Arthur Lower has put it:

> We have always carried authority and a code along with us, no matter how far from "the law" we have happened momentarily to be. . . . The result has been less non-conformity in Canadian life than in America, less experimentation, more acceptance of standards built up in the long history of the English-speaking race.[81]

The frontier settlers in both North American nations spawned important reformist movements. They tended to see themselves as exploited by the dominant economic and political power centered in the Eastern cities. To a considerable extent, those located at the farther reaches of the nation sought to free themselves from this control. "It was this insistence upon local autonomy, this separatist spirit, which was the dominant characteristic of those revolutionary or reform movements which grew up in the interior parts of the continent."[82] For Canada, frontier separatism was always a threat to the integrity of the nation, and often constituted a pro-American liberal response. The Canadian government consequently engaged in systematic actions to reduce frontier autonomy, to guarantee that national institutions and values would dominate on the frontier.[83] The American government, however, had no reason to fear that frontier movements would be a source of secessionism, or would lead to demands for incorporation by a foreign neighbor.

In the United States, frontier agricultural, ranching, and mining areas, uncontrolled for long periods by any central government or policing system, provided unlimited opportuni-

---

[81] A. R. M. Lower, "Education in a Growing Canada," in Joseph Katz (ed.), *Canadian Education* (Toronto: McGraw-Hill, 1956), p. 8.
[82] Clark, "The Frontier and Democratic Theory," p. 66.
[83] *Ibid.*, p. 68.

ties, and disposed settlers to use their own resources as they saw fit. And these rugged individualists, the cowboy, the frontiersman, and even the vigilante, not the uniformed disciplined Mountie, are the heroes of American Western settlement. The frontiersman, on the other hand, has never been a figure for special glorification in Canadian literature as he has been in American. "Canadian writers and critics drew back in well-bred horror from the distasteful crudities of the frontier, and looked, more resolutely than ever, eastward across the Atlantic to the source of all good things."[84]

Geography also served to reinforce social factors in reducing the influence of the more democratic and egalitarian practices of the frontier on the rest of the country. The Canadian prairies, the provinces of Manitoba, Saskatchewan, and Alberta, were separated from the populous East by the Great Lakes and a one-thousand-mile, almost uninhabitable, rock shield which ran north of the lakes. These "provided an effective barrier to close and constant intercourse."[85] And these same geographic factors reinforced the need for systematic government intervention to assure communications, since private enterprise could not afford the great cost of bridging the gap between East and West.

> [T]he colonization of the West, in Canada, was to a large extent a government enterprise and not a purely private venture as in the United States. . . . The central government owned the land, brought the people, mainly immigrants, provided directly or indirectly the transport system and made sure that wheat would move within Canada at low rates.[86]

The considerable involvement of the Canadian government in fostering economic development enhanced the emphasis on collectivity as distinct from self-orientation values discussed earlier. Whether Conservative or Liberal, leftist or rightist, Canadian political leaders have recognized that a

---

[84] John Pengwerne Matthews, *Tradition in Exile* (Toronto: University of Toronto Press, 1962), p. 38; see also Claude T. Bissell, "A Common Ancestry: Literature in Australia and Canada," *University of Toronto Quarterly*, 25 (1956), 133–134.

[85] Clark, *The Developing Canadian Community*, p. 103.

[86] Lamontagne, *op. cit.*, p. 124.

sparsely settled country bordering on a wealthy, powerful, and attractive neighbor must supply many services through governmental agencies which could be furnished by private enterprise in nations with more densely settled populations.[87]

VI

Born in a prolonged struggle for independence, the United States defined itself from its beginning in ideological terms. As many writers have noted, Americanism is an ideology, a set of integrated beliefs defining the good society. Property relations apart, the social aspects of the doctrine of Americanism have a close resemblance to those advocated by socialists. Both urge that men should treat one another as equals regardless of their differences in ability or position, and that all should have an equal opportunity to succeed. With these social concepts has gone a belief in populist democracy, in the right of the people to govern, and in the assumption that sovereignty rests in the people. For much of American history, autocratic and highly stratified societies have constituted a negative reference image. From its founding until World War I, the United States saw itself politically to the left of, and in opposition to, European monarchical and aristocratic reactionary regimes. Americans sympathized with democratic revolutionaries and nationalists fighting reactionaries and foreign rulers. Following World War I, the United States increasingly took on the role of the most powerful Western *capitalist* nation, a role which led the left, Communist, socialist, and the nationalist movements of the underdeveloped and then largely colonial nations, to see the United States as the principal center of conservatism and the source of support for conservatism, traditionalism, and imperialism. The United States, however, has rejected a conception of itself as a conservative power. It still tries to see itself as a supporter of the struggle against reactionary tyranny in the Communist countries, and a proponent of progressive democratic and egalitarian reforms in the underdeveloped nations of Africa, Asia,

[87] Dennis Wrong, *op. cit.,* p. 29; Horne, *op. cit.,* pp. 239–240; Edgar McInnis, "The People," in Brown, *op. cit.,* pp. 30–31; Lamontagne, *op. cit.,* p. 125.

and Latin America. There can be little doubt, however, that America's world activities as supporter of existing regimes against Communist and sometimes non-Communist revolutionary movements has undermined much of this image, even within its own borders.

Canadian national identity is clearly not bound up with the ideology of a successful revolution or a dramatic political movement. Rather, as we have seen, Canadian identity is the product of a victorious counterrevolution, and in a sense must justify its *raison d'être* by emphasizing the virtues of being separate from the United States. Frank Underhill has pointed out that Canadians are the world's oldest and continuing anti-Americans.[88] The Canadian sense of nationality has always felt itself threatened by the United States, physically in earlier days, and culturally and economically in more recent years. As S. D. Clark has put it: "Canadian national life can almost be said to take its rise in the negative will to resist absorption in the American Republic. It is largely about the United States as an object that the consciousness of Canadian national unity has grown up. . . ."[89]

From Confederation in 1867 on, Canadian political leaders and intellectuals have sought to locate Canadian superiority over the United States in its rejection of the crudities of a populist democracy and culture. As against the powerful American model, Canada has always emphasized its connection with and resemblance to Britain.[90] "[I]n the field of literature, one could argue that Canadian writers have been less responsive than the Australian to American influences. As between English and American influences, they have preferred the English. . . ."[91] Loyalty to the British Crown has been one effective means of arousing sentiment against American intervention and control. The social consequence of Canadian allegiance to a British monarch has been the acceptance of a national purpose based on the principle of

---

[88] Frank H. Underhill, "The Image of Canada," address given at the University of New Brunswick Founders' Day, March 8, 1962.

[89] Clark, "The Importance of Anti-Americanism in Canadian National Feeling," p. 243.

[90] On the identification of Canadian writers with British models see Matthews, *op. cit.*, pp. 40, 58–59.

[91] Bissell, *op. cit.*, pp. 133–134.

the "indivisibility of the Commonwealth." As Vincent Massey has put it,

> There are some people in Canada with strong nationalist feelings who think that their end could only be achieved through a republican form of government. There are, happily, very few persons with such views, and they are profoundly misguided in labouring under the delusion that as a republic we could remain an independent nation. We could not. The Crown-in-Parliament is the supreme symbol of our nationhood and our greatest defense against absorption into a continental state.[92]

There is at present extensive United States capital investment in Canada, high consumption of American goods, and wide circulation of American communication media. Many have rebelled against this penetration into Canadian life.[93] The Canadian nationalist points to such facts as proof of "domination" by the United States.[94]

Nationalism in English Canada has undergone some curious changes from the time when it represented a left-wing, often pro-United States protest against the Imperial connection, and the closed economic-political-ecclesiastical system sustained by this connection. Today it is often the left-winger who is most anti-American and pro-British. The more traditional form of Canadian nationalism would seem to continue in the French-Canadian protest movements with their anti-English and anti-establishment overtones directed at those within Canadian borders who represent English cultural, political, and economic domination. As English Canadians seek to isolate Canada from the United States, French Canadians look for means to assure the safety of their culture surrounded by 200 million English speakers. In a sense both English and French Canadians have similar objectives, to

[92] Massey, *op. cit.*, p. 19.
[93] The concern of Canadians with the large amount of American investment is based not only on the historical insecurity of Canada vis-à-vis its more powerful neighbor. It is interesting to note that Americans owned 44 percent of Canadian manufacturing industry in 1959 and that America has more money invested in Canada than in any other world area. See Norman L. Nicholson, *Canada in the American Community* (Princeton, N. J.: Van Nostrand Company, 1963), p. 119.
[94] Harry G. Johnson, "Problems of Canadian Nationalism," *International Journal*, 16 (Summer 1961), 238–249.

protect two tiny minority cultures from being absorbed by
more powerful neighbors.[95]

The problem of changing Canadian and American identities
is clearly linked to the broad topic of this chapter, the nature and sources of the differences in values and institutions
of the two North American democracies. In the past decades
the world image of the United States has changed drastically.
Relatively few in the rest of the world still see the United
States in the idealistic terms with which it views itself. To the
leaders of the underdeveloped and the Communist world, and
to many in the developed world, including Canada as well,
the United States is now the leading defender of conservative
traditional social forms, and is governed from within by an
oligarchy or power elite. Many Canadians now seek to defend
the integrity of Canada against the United States by defining
their own country as more humane, more egalitarian, more
democratic, and more anti-imperialist than the United States.
Many Canadians now view their country as more "leftist" or
liberal in its institutions and international objectives than the
United States. Whether this shift in the definition of the character of Canada's chief reference group, the United States,
will also affect Canadian values, remains to be seen. Canada's
"swinging" Prime Minister, Pierre Elliot Trudeau, fits the
"new" Canadian image better than any previous political
leader in both ideology and personal style. Ironically, the
shift symbolized by Trudeau in Canada's self-image from
that of a nation to the right of the United States to one on its
left may in the long run contribute strongly to eliminating
the relatively small differences between the values of the two
countries. For a democratic leftist ideology is synonymous
with the social content of Americanism. As Frank Underhill
has pointed out to his fellow Canadians: "If we are eventually
to satisfy ourselves that we have at last achieved a Canadian
identity, it will be only when we are satisfied that we have
arrived at a better American way of life than the Americans
have."[96]

[95] S. D. Clark, "Canada and Her Great Neighbour," *Canadian Review of Anthropology and Sociology*, 1 (1964), 193–201.
[96] Frank Underhill, *The Image of Confederation* (Toronto: Canadian Broadcasting Corporation, 1964), p. 69.

The comparison between the United States and English Canada illustrates the fact that structure and values are clearly interrelated. But any value system derivative from given sets of historical experience, institutionalized in religious systems, family structures, class relations, and education will affect the pace and even the direction and content of social and economic change. In comparing the United States and Canada the emphasis has been more on the effect of values on political development than on economics. In the next chapter the focus is on the effect of values on Latin American economic development. It examines the changes in the value system which may foster emergence of an entrepreneurial elite.

CHAPTER 3

Values and Entrepreneurship in the Americas

The approach used to account for variations in patterns of national development which has been elaborated to analyze the relatively slight (on an international comparative scale) differences between English-speaking Canada and the United States may also be employed in an effort to understand the variations between Latin America and Anglo-Saxon America. Perhaps the most striking differences between the two cultural areas have been the variations in level of economic development. Hence, much of this chapter will focus on the sources of such differences.

Discussions of the requisites of economic development have been concerned with the relative importance of the appropriate economic conditions, rather than the presumed effects on varying rates of economic growth of diverse value systems. Much of the analysis which stems from economic thought has tended to see value orientations as derivative from economic factors. Most sociological analysts, on the other hand, following in the tradition of Max Weber, have placed a major independent role on the effect of values in fostering economic development.[1]

[1] For an excellent general discussion of the relationships between val-

Although the evaluation of the causal significance of economic factors and value orientations has often taken the form of a debate pitting one against the other, increasingly more people have come to accept the premise that both sets of variables are relevant. Many economists now discuss the role of "noneconomic" factors in economic growth, and some have attempted to include concepts developed in sociology and psychology into their over-all frame of analysis. Sociologists, from Weber on, have rarely argued that value analysis could account for economic growth. Rather the thesis suggested by Weber is that, given the economic conditions for the emergence of a system of rational capital accumulation, whether or not such growth occurred in a systematic fashion would be determined by the values present. Structural conditions make development possible; cultural factors determine whether the possibility becomes an actuality. And Weber sought to prove that capitalism and industrialization emerged in Western Europe and North America because value elements inherent in or derivative from the "Protestant Ethic" fostered the necessary kinds of behavior by those who had access to capital; while conversely during other periods in other cultures, the social and religious "ethics" inhibited a systematic rational emphasis on growth.[2]

The general Weberian approach has been applied to many of the contemporary underdeveloped countries. It has been argued that these countries not only lack the economic prerequisites for growth, but that many of them preserve values which foster behavior antithetical to the systematic accumulation of capital. The relative failure of Latin American countries to develop on a scale comparable to those of North America or Australasia has been seen, in some part, as a consequence of variations in value systems dominating these two areas. The overseas offspring of Great Britain seem-

---

ues and economic behavior written in a Latin-American context see Thomas C. Cochran, "Cultural Factors in Economic Growth," *Journal of Economic History,* 20 (1960), 515–530; see also John Gillin, "Ethos Components in Modern Latin American Culture," *American Anthropologist,* 57 (1955), 488–500.

[2] Max Weber, *The Protestant Ethic and the Spirit of Capitalism* (New York: Scribner, 1935).

ingly had the advantage of values derivative in part from the Protestant Ethic and from the formation of "New Societies" in which feudal ascriptive elements were missing.[3] Latin America, on the other hand, is Catholic, and has been dominated for long centuries by ruling elites who created a social structure more congruent with ascriptive social values.

Perhaps the most impressive comparative evidence bearing on the significance of value orientations for economic development may be found in the work of David McClelland and his colleagues, who have undertaken detailed content analyses of folk tales in primitive cultures and of children's storybooks in literate ones, seeking to correlate degrees of emphasis on achievement values in these books with rates of economic development.[4]

Among the primitive tribes, those which were classified as high in achievement orientation on the basis of the content of their folk tales were much more likely to contain full-time "business entrepreneurs" (persons engaged in a market economy) than those which were low. To measure the relationships in literate societies, McClelland and his coworkers analyzed the content of children's stories read by early primary school children during two time periods, 1925 and 1950, in many nations. Statistically significant correlations were found between this measure of achievement level for 1925 and the extent to which the increase in use of electrical energy (a measure of development) was higher or lower than the expected rate of growth for the period from 1925 to 1950, for a group of twenty-three countries. Similar findings are reported for forty countries for the period 1952 to 1958. As McClelland comments, the latter

> finding is more striking than the earlier one, because many Communist and underdeveloped countries are included in the sample. Apparently N Achievement [his term for the

[3] See Louis Hartz, *The Founding of New Societies. Studies in the History of the United States, Latin America, South Africa, Canada, and Australia* (New York: Harcourt, Brace, & World, 1964).

[4] David C. McClelland, *The Achieving Society* (Princeton: Van Nostrand, 1961), pp. 70–79; McClelland, "The Achievement Motive in Economic Growth," in Bert F. Hoselitz and Wilbert E. Moore (eds.), *Industrialization and Society* (Paris: UNESCO-Mouton, 1963), pp. 79–81.

achievement orientation] is a precursor of economic growth—
and not only in the Western style type of capitalism . . .
but also in economies controlled and fostered largely by the
state.[5]

These findings are reinforced by two historical studies of the
thematic content of various types of literature in England
between 1400 and 1800, and in Spain between 1200 and 1700.
In both countries, the "quantitative evidence is clear cut and
a rise and fall of the *n* Ach level *preceded in time* the rise and
fall of economic development."[6]

Striking differences have been found by McClelland and
his collaborators in the value orientations of comparable samples of populations in less developed as compared with more
developed countries. Thus, research in Brazil and the United
States analyzing the achievement motivations of students aged
nine to twelve, with the Brazilian sample drawn from São
Paulo and Rio Claro, and the North American one from four
northeastern states, reports that

> Brazilian boys on the average have lower achievement mo-
> tivation than their American peers . . . [that] upper, middle,
> and lower class Brazilians tend to have lower achievement
> motivation scores than Americans of a comparable class.
> *What is more startling is the finding that the mean score of
> Brazilian boys in any social class is lower than the motivation
> score of the Americans . . . whatever their class may be.*[7]

On a theoretical level, the systematic analysis of the relations of value systems to the conditions for economic development requires concepts which permit one to contrast the
relative strength of different values. Thus far, the most useful
concepts for this purpose are Talcott Parsons', which were
elaborated on more fully in Chapter 2. These refer to basic

[5] McClelland, "The Achievement Motive in Economic Growth," p.
79.

[6] Juan B. Cortés, "The Achievement Motive in the Spanish Economy
between the 13th and 18th Centuries," *Economic Development and Cultural Change*, 9 (1961), 159, 144–163; Norman N. Bradburn and David E. Berlew, "Need for Achievement and English Industrial Growth,"
Economic Development and Cultural Change, 10 (1961), 8–20.

[7] Bernard Rosen, "The Achievement Syndrome and Economic
Growth in Brazil," *Social Forces*, 42 (1964), 345–346 (emphasis in
original).

orientations toward human action and are sufficiently comprehensive to encompass the norms affecting behavior within all social systems, both total societies and their subsystems, such as the family or the university.[8]

In his original presentation of the pattern variables, Parsons linked combinations of two of them: achievement-ascription and universalism-particularism to different forms of existing societies. Thus the combination of universalism-achievement may be exemplified by the United States. It is the combination most favorable to the emergence of an industrial society since it encourages respect or deference toward others on the basis of merit and places an emphasis on achievement. It is typically linked with a stress on specificity, the judging of individuals and institutions in terms of their individual roles, rather than generally.[9] The Soviet system expresses many of the same values as the United States. One important difference, of course, is in the position of the Communist party. Membership in the party conveys particularistic rights and obligations. Otherwise both systems resemble each other in "value" terms with reference to the original pattern variables. Both denigrate extended kinship ties, view ethnic subdivisions as a strain, emphasize individual success, but at the same time insist that inequality should be reduced and that the norms inherent in egalitarianism should govern social relationships. The two systems, North American and Communist, diverge, however, with respect to another key pattern-variable polarity, self-orientation vs. collectivity-orientation—the emphasis that a collectivity has a claim on its individual units to conform to the defined interests of the larger group, as opposed to the legitimacy of actions reflecting the perceived needs of the individual unit.

Conceptualization at such an abstract level is not very use-

[8] See Talcott Parsons, *The Social System* (Glencoe: The Free Press, 1951), pp. 58–67 and *passim;* "Pattern Variables Revisited," *American Sociological Review,* 25 (1960), 58–67; and "The Point of View of the Author," in Max Black (ed.), *The Social Theories of Talcott Parsons* (Englewood Cliffs, N. J.: Prentice-Hall, 1961), pp. 319–320, 329–336. I have discussed the pattern variables and attempted to use them in an analysis of differences among the four major English-speaking nations. See S. M. Lipset, *The First New Nation* (New York: Basic Books, 1963), pp. 207–273.

[9] See Parsons, *The Social System,* pp. 182–191.

ful unless it serves to specify hypotheses about the differences in norms and behavior inherent in different value emphases.[10] Such work would clearly have utility for the effort to understand the varying relationships between levels of economic development and social values.[11]

The Latin American system has been identified by Parsons as an example of the particularistic-ascriptive pattern. Such a system tends to be focused around kinship and local community, and to de-emphasize the need for powerful and legitimate larger centers of authority such as the state. Given a weak achievement orientation, such systems see work as a necessary evil. Morality converges around the traditionalistic acceptance of received standards and arrangements. There is an emphasis on expressive rather than instrumental behavior. There is little concern with the behavior of external authority as long as it does not interfere with expressive freedom. Such systems also tend to emphasize diffuseness and elitism. The status conferred by one position tends to be accorded in all situations. Thus if a man plays one elite role, he is respected generally.[12]

[10] A comprehensive specification of the norms and behavior involved in concepts of political, social, economic, and intellectual modernization may be found in John Whitney Hall, "Changing Conceptions of the Modernization of Japan," in Marius B. Jansen (ed.), *Changing Japanese Attitudes toward Modernization* (Princeton: Princeton University Press, 1965), pp. 20–23 and footnote 19.

[11] The pattern variables have been applied in various discussions of social and economic development. For examples, see Fred W. Riggs, "Agraria and Industria—Toward a Typology of Comparative Administration," in William J. Siffin (ed.), *Toward the Comparative Study of Public Administration* (Bloomington: Indiana University Press, 1959), pp. 23–116; Joseph J. Spengler, "Social Structure, the State, and Economic Growth," in Simon Kuznets, Wilbert E. Moore, and Joseph J. Spengler (eds.), *Economic Growth: Brazil, India, Japan* (Durham: Duke University Press, 1955), esp. pp. 379–384; Bert F. Hoselitz, *Sociological Aspects of Economic Growth* (New York: The Free Press of Glencoe, 1960), pp. 29–42, 59–60; David C. McClelland, *The Achieving Society*, pp. 172–188; G. A. Theodorson, "Acceptance of Industrialization and Its Attendant Consequences for the Social Patterns of Non-Western Societies," *American Sociological Review*, 18 (1958), 437–484.

[12] Parsons, *The Social System*, pp. 198–200. For a comparative social-psychological study of the orientations of comparable samples of adolescents in Buenos Aires and Chicago where the findings are congruent with Parsons' assumptions about differences between North American and Latin American values, see R. J. Havighurst, Maria Eugenia Dubois, M. Csikszentmihalyi, and R. Doll, *A Cross-National Study of*

Although the various Latin American countries obviously differ considerably—a point which will be elaborated later—it is interesting to note that a recent analysis of the social structure of the most developed nation, Uruguay, describes the contemporary situation there in much the same terms as Parsons does for the area as a whole. Aldo Solari has summed up some of his findings about his own country:

> It is clear that particularism is a very important phenomenon in Uruguayan society and it prevails over universalism. A great number of facts support this. It is well known that the prevailing system of selection for government employees is based on kinship, on membership in a certain club or political faction, or friendship, etc. These are all particularistic criteria. A similar phenomenon is present in private enterprise where selection of personnel on the basis of particularistic relations is very common. The use of universalistic criteria, such as the use of standardized examinations, is exceptional. Quite frequently when such universalistic criteria seem operative, they are applied to candidates who have been previously selected on the basis of personal relationships.[13]

Ascriptive ties are also quite strong in Uruguay, linked in large part to the importance of the family in the system. Concern with fulfilling family obligations and maintaining family prestige leads propertied Uruguayans to avoid risking the economic base of the family position. The concerns of the middle class which tend to affect the expectations and norms of the whole society are for "security, moderation, lack of risk, and prestige."[14]

The sources of Latin American values have been generally credited to the institutions and norms of the Iberian nations, as practiced by an Iberian-born elite during the three centuries of colonial rule. Those sent over from Spain or Portugal held the predominant positions, and in the colonies "ostenta-

---

Buenos Aires and Chicago Adolescents (Basel: S. Karger, 1965). The authors report that the Chicago group differs from the Buenos Aires one in being "more self-assertive and autonomous . . . more resistive to authority . . . more instrumental . . . the Buenos Aires group are more expressive in their orientation to the world" (p. 79).

[13] Aldo E. Solari, *Estudios sobre la Sociedad Uruguaya* (Montevideo: Arca, 1964), p. 162.

[14] *Ibid.*, p. 171.

tiously proclaimed their lack of association with manual, productive labor or any kind of vile employment."[15] And Spain and Portugal, prior to colonizing the Americas, had been engaged for eight centuries in conflict with the Moors, resulting in the glorification of the roles of soldier and priest, and in the denigration of commercial and banking activities, often in the hands of Jews and Moslems. Iberian values and institutions were transferred to the American continent. To establish them securely, there were constant efforts by the "Church militant" to Christianize heathen populations, the need to justify morally Spanish and Portuguese rule over "inferior" peoples, Indians, and imported Africans, and the fostering of a "get-rich-quick mentality" introduced by the *conquistadores,* but reinforced by efforts to locate valuable minerals or mine the land, and most significantly by the establishment of the *latifundia* (large-scale plantations) as the predominant form of economic, social, and political organization.[16] Almost everywhere in Latin America, the original upper class was composed of the owners of *latifundia,* and these set the model for elite behavior to which lesser classes, including the businessmen of the towns, sought to adapt.

And as Ronald Dore points out, in *arielismo,* the Latin American scorn for the pragmatism and materialism now usually identified with the United States, "there is an element that can only be explained by the existence of a traditional, landed upper class."[17] The period of the predominance of

[15] Frederick B. Pike, *Chile and the United States, 1880–1962* (Notre Dame: University of Notre Dame Press, 1962), p. 78. The strength of these values may be seen in the fact that for much of the colonial period, at the University of San Gregorio in Quito, "Applicants for entrance had to establish by a detailed legal process 'the purity of their blood' and *prove that none of their ancestors had engaged in trade."* Harold Benjamin, *Higher Education in the American Republics* (New York: McGraw-Hill, 1965), p. 16 (my italics).

[16] For a collection of papers dealing with the social structure of *latifundia* in different parts of the Americas, see Division of Science Development (Social Sciences), Pan American Union, *Plantation Systems of the New World* (Washington: Pan American Union, 1959), and Charles Wagley and Marvin Harris, "A Typology of Latin American Subcultures," *American Anthropologist,* 57 (1955), 433–437.

[17] R. P. Dore, "Latin America and Japan Compared" in John J. Johnson (ed.), *Continuity and Change in Latin America* (Stanford: Stanford University Press, 1964), p. 245. He indicates also that the absence of such attitudes in Japan is related to "the attenuation of the ties

latifundia social structure is far from over. In most Latin American nations (Mexico, Bolivia, and Cuba are perhaps the major exceptions), agriculture is still dominated by *latifundia*. Thus, farms of 1,000 hectares or more, which constitute 1.5 per cent of all farms in Latin America, possess 65 per cent of the total farm acreage. *Minifundias* (small farms of under 20 hectares) constitute 73 per cent of all farms, but less than 4 per cent of the acreage.[18] The high-status social clubs of most major cities are still controlled or highly influenced by men whose families derived their original wealth and status from *latifundia*. In spite of repeated demands for land reform, little has been done to reduce the economic source of the influence of *latifundia* families.[19] Hence the continuation of pre-industrial values in much of Latin America can be linked in large part to the persistence of the rural social structure which originally fostered these values.[20] Even in Uruguay, which has long been dominated by the metropolis of Montevideo, one finds that much of the upper social class of the city is composed of members of powerful old landowning families. Many of those involved in commercial and banking activities have close kinship ties with the large cattle raisers

that had bound the feudal aristocracy and gentry [which] began at the end of the sixteenth century and was completed in 1870." For a discussion of the concept of *arielismo*, see Kalman H. Silvert, *The Conflict Society: Reaction and Revolution in Latin America* (New Orleans: Hauser Press, 1961), pp. 144–161.

[18] United Nations Economic and Social Council. Economic Commission for Latin America, *Provisional Report on the Conference on Education and Economic and Social Development in Latin America* (Mar del Plata, Argentina: 1963. E/CN.12/639), p. 250.

[19] Thomas F. Carroll, "Land Reform as an Explosive Force in Latin America," in John J. TePaske and Sydney N. Fisher (eds.), *Explosive Forces in Latin America* (Columbus: Ohio State University Press, 1964), pp. 81–125.

[20] Wagley and Harris, *op. cit.*, pp. 439–441; Frank Tannenbaum, "Toward an Appreciation of Latin America," in Herbert L. Matthews (ed.), *The United States and Latin America* (Englewood Cliffs: Prentice-Hall, 1963), pp. 32–41; José Medina Echavarría, "A Sociologist's View," in José Medina Echavarría and B. Higgins (eds.), *Social Aspects of Economic Development in Latin America*, Vol. II (Paris: UNESCO, 1963), pp. 33–39; Gino Germani, "The Strategy of Fostering Social Mobility," in Egbert De Vries and José Medina Echavarría (eds.), *op. cit.*, I, pp. 222–229; Charles Wagley, *Race and Class in Rural Brazil* (Paris: UNESCO, 1952), pp. 114–145; Bernard J. Siegel, "Social Structure and Economic Change in Brazil," in Kuznets, Moore, and Spengler (eds.), *op. cit.*, pp. 405–408.

and *estancieros*. And the upper rural class maintains considerable influence on the society as a whole through its control over the main agricultural organizations, and the continued strength of a widespread ideology which states that the wealth of the country depends on land, and on the activities of those who farm it.[21]

In many countries the prestige attaching to landownership still leads any businessmen to invest the monies they have made in industry in farms.[22] A study of the Argentinian elite indicates that similar emphases are important there also, in spite of the influence of its cosmopolitan, 6 million-strong capital city Buenos Aires:

> Insofar as the entrepreneurial bourgeoisie moved up in the social scale, they were absorbed by the old upper classes. They lost their dynamic power and without the ability to create a new ideology of their own, they accepted the existing scale of social prestige, the values and system of stratification of the traditional rural sectors. When they could they bought *estancias* [ranches] not only for economic reasons, but for prestige, and became cattle raisers, themselves.[23]

In Chile, too, many analysts have suggested that much of the behavior and values of the urban bourgeoisie reflect their effort to imitate and gain acceptance from an extremely conservative land-based upper class. Less than 10 per cent of the landowners own close to 90 per cent of the arable land; this group shows little interest in efficient productivity and sustains semi-feudal relations with its workers.[24] One possible "superficial advantage" of the close identification of the urban middle class with that of the old aristocracy has been suggested by a North American commentator. "Because this group has in its political, social, and economic thinking so closely reflected the attitudes of the aristocracy, there has been almost no disruption as middle sectors have won increasing power

[21] Solari, *op. cit.*, pp. 127–129, 113–122.
[22] J. Richard Powell, "Notes on Latin American Industrialization," *Inter-American Economic Affairs*, 6 (Winter 1952), p. 83.
[23] José Luis de Imaz, *Los que mandan* (Buenos Aires: Editorial Universitaria de Buenos Aires, 1964), p. 160.
[24] Pike, *op. cit.*, pp. 280–283.

in Chilean politics." But he notes that, while producing political stability, this role "may also have contributed to economic and social stagnation."[25]

Similar patterns have been described by many students of Brazilian society to account for the strong emphasis on family particularism within industrial life there. Brazil, of course, as the last major country to retain slavery, as a former empire which ennobled its leading citizens, and as the most rural of South America's major countries, can be expected to retain many of the value emphases of an elitist traditional culture, even among the successful "new classes" of its relatively highly developed southern regions.

> Rather than considering themselves a new "middle class," these newly successful groups have come to share, with the descendants of the old landed gentry, an aristocratic set of ideals and patterns of behavior which they have inherited from the nobility of the Brazilian empire. . . .
> One of these aristocratic values relevant to economic change is what Gilberto Freyre has called a "Gentleman complex"—a disposal of manual labor in every form. . . . Just as in the past when manual labor was the lot of slaves in Brazil, it is considered today to be the work of the lower class. . . .
> [S]emi feudal relationships continue to dominate the social and economic relations of the simple rural worker. . . . The traditional relationships between the small upper [landed] class and the rural peasant and the growing class of urban workers are important factors in economic growth. The institutions and the value system of this upper class affect the ideology of change, the entry of foreign capital into the country, the encouragement and development of appropriate skills, and other acts facilitating economic growth. To a large extent it is their "aristocratic" values and ideals which provide many of the life expectations and incentives . . .[26]

[25] *Ibid.*, p. 287. This book was published in 1962, before the victory of the left-wing Christian Democrats.

[26] Siegel, *op. cit.*, pp. 406–411. See also Charles Wagley, *An Introduction to Brazil* (New York: Columbia University Press, 1963), pp. 126–131. A summary of a detailed study of Brazilian industrialists reports that other than European immigrants and their offspring, "Most of the new industrialists were simply large landowners diversifying into manufacturing. Those who did not actually retain their plantations, retained strong links with the land. Their style of life hardly changed; their social attitudes changed not at all." See Emanuel de Kadt, "The Brazilian Impasse," *Encounter*, 25 (September 1965), 57. He is report-

The stress on values as a key source of differences in the rate of development of economic and political institutions has been countered by some students of Latin America; they point to the Southern states of the American union as an example of a subculture which has been relatively underdeveloped economically, which has lacked a stable democratic political system, and which has placed a greater emphasis on violence and law violation to attain political ends, than the rest of the country. And as these scholars point out, the white South is the most purely Anglo-Saxon and Protestant part of the United States.

The American South resembles much of Latin America, including Brazil, in having an institutional structure and value system erected around a plantation (or *latifundia*) economy, which employed large numbers of slaves, and which, after the abolition of slavery, developed a stratification hierarchy correlated with variations in racial background. From this point of view, the clue to understanding the economic backwardness and political instability of Brazil and much of Spanish America lies in their structural similarities with the American South, rather than in those values which stem from Iberian or Catholic origins.[27] This argument is strengthened by analyses of the differences between southern and northern Brazil. The southern part of the country, which was much less involved in large-scale slave labor agriculture, can be compared with the north, in much the same way as the United States' North varies from its South. Southern Brazil and northern United States are much more developed economically, and they place more emphasis on the "modern" value system—achievement, universalism, and the like—than do the warmer regions of their countries.

There are certain similarities in another American country, Canada, in its internal cultural and economic differentiation.

---

ing on the findings in Fernando Henrique Cardoso, *Empresário Industrial e Desenvolvimento Econômico* (*no Brasil*) (São Paulo: Difusão Européia do Livro, 1964).

[27] See Sanford Mosk, "Latin America versus the United States," American Economic Association, *Papers and Proceedings*, 40 (1950), pp. 367–383. See also Gilberto Freyre, *New World in the Tropics. The Culture of Modern Brazil* (New York: Vintage Books, 1963), pp. 71–72, 82–87, 193–195.

French Canada, historically, has been slower to develop than English Canada. Much of its economic development has been dominated by entrepreneurs from English-speaking backgrounds.[28] An analysis of French-Canadian businessmen, based on interviews, reports their economic value orientations in terms very reminiscent of the studies of Latin American entrepreneurs.[29] Although not so unstable politically as the Southern United States or most of Latin America, Quebec has long exhibited symptoms of political instability (an opposition party system is perhaps less institutionalized there than in any other populous province); charges of political corruption, illegal tactics in campaigns, violations of civil liberties, and the like seem much more common in Quebec than in the English-speaking provinces.[30] Quebec is certainly Latin and Catholic (if these terms have any general analytic or descriptive meaning), but it obviously has not had a plantation culture, nor a significant racial minority, although it could be argued that the English-French relationships resemble those of

[28] See Bernard Blishen, "The Construction and Use of an Occupational Class Scale," *Canadian Journal of Economics and Political Science*, 24 (1958), 519–531; Yves de Jocas and Guy Rocher, "Inter-Generational Occupational Mobility in the Province of Quebec," *Canadian Journal of Economics and Political Science*, 23 (1957), 377–394; John Porter, *The Vertical Mosaic: An Analysis of Social Class and Power in Canada* (Toronto: University of Toronto Press, 1965), pp. 91–98, *passim.*

[29] Norman W. Taylor, "The French-Canadian Industrial Entrepreneur and His Social Environment," in Marcel Rioux and Yves Martin (eds.), *French-Canadian Society*, Vol. I (Toronto: McClelland & Stewart, 1964), pp. 271–295.

[30] One French-Canadian analyst has argued that "historically French-Canadians have not really believed in democracy for themselves." He suggests "that they have never achieved any sense of obligation towards the general welfare, including the welfare of the French-Canadians on non-racial issues." Pierre Elliot Trudeau, "Some Obstacles to Democracy in Quebec," in Mason Wade (ed.), *Canadian Dualism* (Toronto: University of Toronto Press, 1960), pp. 241–259. On the general problems of, and weakness of, democracy in Quebec see Herbert Quinn, *The Union Nationale* (Toronto: University of Toronto Press, 1963), esp. pp. 3–19, 23, 65–67, 126–129, 131–151; Gerard Dion and Louis O'Neill, *Political Immorality in the Province of Quebec* (Montreal: Civic Action League, 1956); Arthur Maheux, "French Canadians and Democracy," in Douglas Grant (ed.), *Quebec Today* (Toronto: University of Toronto Press, 1960), pp. 341–351; Frank R. Scott, "Canada et Canada Français," *Esprit*, 20 (1952), 178–189; and Michael Oliver, "Quebec and Canadian Democracy," *Canadian Journal of Economics and Political Science*, 23 (1957), 504–515.

white-Negro, or white-Indian, in other countries of the
Americas.

Various analyses of the weakness of democracy in Quebec
argue that religious-linked factors are relevant. Years before
becoming Prime Minister, Pierre Trudeau stated:

> French Canadians are Catholics; and Catholic nations have
> not always been ardent supporters of democracy. They are
> authoritarian in spiritual matters; and since the dividing line
> between the spiritual and the temporal may be very fine or
> even confused, they are often disinclined to seek solutions in
> temporal affairs through the mere counting of heads.[31]

And many have pointed to the differences in the economic
development of the two Canadas as evidence that Catholic
values and social organization are much less favorable to economic development than Protestant ones have been. As S. D.
Clark has reasoned, "in nineteenth century Quebec religion
was organized in terms of a hierarchy of social classes which
had little relation to the much more fluid class system of
capitalism, and sharp separation from the outside capitalist
world was maintained through an emphasis upon ethnic and
religious differences and through geographic isolation."[32]

These comparisons between the United States' North and
South and English and French Canada show that structure
and values are clearly interrelated. Structure such as a plantation system combined with a racially based hierarchy is functionally tied to a given set of "aristocratic" values, antipathetic
to an emphasis on achievement, universalism, and hard work.
But any value system derived from given sets of historical
experience institutionalized in religious systems, family structures, class relations, and education will affect the pace and
even direction and content of social and economic change.

If we turn now to studies focusing directly on the relationship between values and entrepreneurial behavior, the available materials from many Latin American countries seem
to agree that the predominant values which continue to inform the behavior of the elite stem from the continued and

[31] Trudeau, *op. cit.*, p. 245; see also Quinn, *op. cit.*, pp. 17–18.
[32] S. D. Clark, *The Canadian Community* (Toronto: University of
Toronto Press, 1962), p. 161.

combined strength of ascription, particularism, and diffuseness. Thomas Cochran has examined the literature from various American cultures, as well as from his own empirical research, and has conjectured that Latin American businessmen differ from North American ones in being:

> 1) more interested in inner worth and justification by standards of personal feeling than they are in the opinion of peer groups; 2) disinclined to sacrifice personal authority to group decisions; 3) disliking impersonal as opposed to personal arrangements, and generally preferring family relations to those with outsiders; 4) inclined to prefer social prestige to money; and 5) somewhat aloof from and disinterested in science and technology.[33]

Somewhat similar conclusions are reported in various surveys of managerial attitudes in various Latin American countries. These indicate that role specificity, i.e., separation of managerial from other activities, is relatively less common there than in more developed areas. A Latin American manager "is quite likely to devote part of his office hours to politics or family affairs."[34] Bureaucratic and competitive norms are comparatively weak. Personal characteristics are valued more than technical or organizational ability.[35]

Family particularism is much more common among Latin American business executives than among their counterparts in more developed nations. "Managers are frequently selected on the basis of family links, rather than specialized training." The entire managerial group often came from one family, and the "great majority of managers interviewed either considered this to be an appropriate arrangement under the conditions of their country, or had not thought of alternatives."[36]

[33] Thomas C. Cochran, *The Puerto Rican Businessman* (Philadelphia: University of Pennsylvania Press, 1959), p. 131; see also pp. 151–154 and Cochran, "Cultural Factors in Economic Growth," *op. cit.*

[34] Albert Lauterbach, "Managerial Attitudes and Economic Growth," *Kyklos*, 15 (1962), 384. This study is based on interviews with managers in eight countries.

[35] Eduardo A. Zalduendo, *El empresário industrial en América Latina: Argentina* (Mar del Plata, Argentina: Naciones Unidas Comisión Económica para América Latina, 1963. E/CN12/642/Add 1), p. 46.

[36] Albert Lauterbach, "Government and Development: Managerial Attitudes in Latin America," *Journal of Inter-American Studies*, 7

In Brazil, even the growth of large industries and corporate forms of ownership have not drastically changed the pattern. In many companies the modal pattern seems to involve an adjustment between family control and the rational demands of running a big business. Either the children or the in-laws of the old patriarch are technically trained, or the company involves a mixed system of family members working closely with technically educated nonfamily executives. However, the type of managers employed by family groups is known as *hombres de confianza* (men who can be trusted), and have been selected more for this quality than for their expertise.[37]

Most analysts of Latin American business behavior agree that a principal concern of the typical entrepreneur is to maintain family prestige; thus he is reluctant to give up the family-owned and -managed type of corporation. Outsiders are distrusted, for the entrepreneur "is acutely aware that any advantage that may be given to somebody outside his family is necessarily at the expense of himself and his own family."[38] From this evolves an unwillingness to cooperate with others outside of one's firm, and a defensiveness toward subordinates, as well as toward creditors, distributors, and others. Such assumptions about the behavior of others are, of course, self-maintaining, since people tend to behave as significant others define them, thus reinforcing a mutual state of distrust. In the family-dominated firms which constitute such a large proportion of Latin American business, non-family, middle-management personnel will often be untrustworthy and inefficient, since they will lack identification

---

(1965), 202–203; see also L. C. Bresser Pereira, "The Rise of Middle Class and Middle Management in Brazil," *Journal of Inter-American Studies*, 4 (1962), 322–323.

[37] Fernando H. Cardoso, *El empresário industrial en América Latina: Brasil* (Mar del Plata, Argentina: Naciones Unidas Comisión Económica para América Latina, 1963, E/CN/12/642/Add. 2), pp. 25–26; for a description of the way in which *hombres de confianza* were incorporated into a major Argentinian industrial complex see Thomas C. Cochran and Ruben E. Reina, *Entrepreneurship in Argentine Culture. Torcuato Di Tella and S.I.A.M.* (Philadelphia: University of Pennsylvania Press, 1962), pp. 266–268; see also de Kadt, *op. cit.*, p. 57, for a summary of Brazilian evidence on this point.

[38] Tomas Roberto Fillol, *Social Factors in Economic Development. The Argentine Case* (Cambridge: M.I.T. Press, 1961), pp. 13–14.

with firms in which "the 'road upward' is blocked by family barriers," and they are given limited responsibility.[39] This fear of dealing with outsiders even extends to reluctance to permit investment in the firm. For many Brazilian "industrialists, the sale of stocks to the public seems to involve . . . a loss of property. . . ." A Brazilian market research survey reported that 93 per cent of entrepreneurs interviewed stated "that they had never thought of selling stock in their enterprise."[40] As Emilio Willems points out, "such a typically modern institution as the stock-market in large metropolitan centers failed to develop because the most important joint-stock companies are owned by kin-groups which handle transfer of stock as a purely domestic matter."[41]

Although not statistically typical of Brazilian entrepreneurial behavior, some of the practices of the largest Brazilian firm, the United Industries, which in 1952 employed 30,000 workers in 367 plants, indicate the way in which family particularism and other traditional practices can continue within a massive industrial complex. In spite of its size, it is owned largely by the son of the founder, Francisco Matarazzo, Jr., and various family members. "The bleak and impeccably dressed Francisco, Jr., controls his empire from a pigskin-paneled office that is fitted with a buzzer system to summon top executives, who, on leaving, *must bow their way backward from his presence.*"[42]

The managers of foreign-owned companies, whether Brazilian or foreign are different in their behavior. They tend to emphasize a high degree of rationalization and bureaucratic practice in running their firms. Although they are interested in securing personal loyalty from subordinates, it is not the basic requirement for employment. The executive personnel are ambitious and competent employees, concerned with their

[39] *Ibid.*, p. 61.
[40] Cardoso, *El empresário industrial en América Latina*, p. 31; Siegel, *op. cit.*, pp. 405–408. Robert J. Alexander, *Labor Relations in Argentina, Brazil, Chile* (New York: McGraw-Hill, 1962), pp. 48–49.
[41] Emilio Willems, "The Structure of the Brazilian Family," *Social Forces*, 31 (1953), 343.
[42] Richard M. Morse, *From Community to Metropolis. A Biography of São Paulo, Brasil* (Gainesville: University of Florida Press, 1958), p. 229 (my italics).

personal success, and valuing ambition in themselves and others.[43]

The lack of a concern with national interests or institutional development among Latin American entrepreneurs has been related by Albert Hirschman to what he calls an "ego-focussed image of change," characteristic of badly integrated, underdeveloped societies. Individuals in nations dominated by such an image, "not identifying with society," will view new developments or experiences simply as opportunities for self-aggrandizement. Although seemingly reflecting a desire to get ahead, this orientation, which inhibits efforts to advance by cooperation with others "is inimical to economic development, [since] . . . success is conceived not as a result of systematic application of effort and creative energy, combined perhaps with a 'little bit of luck,' but as due either to sheer luck or to the outwitting of others through careful scheming." And Hirschman, like other analysts of Latin America, sees the inability to trust and work with others as antithetical to effective entrepreneurship.[44]

A 1960–1961 analysis of the "technological decisions" of Mexican and Puerto Rican entrepreneurs, compared with foreign-born managers of subsidiaries of international companies, supports these interpretations.

> Differences among foreign and national enterprises in ways of attracting capital, handling labor relations, arranging technical flexibility, channeling information internally and externally (and even willingness to respond to impertinent interview questions) are all consistent with an interpretation that the native entrepreneurs view society as probably malevolent and that the foreigners would have stayed home if they agreed [with this view of society].[45]

Attitudes to money similar to those frequently reported as characteristic of a nonindustrial, traditional population have been reported in studies of Latin American business leaders. A short-range rather than a long-range orientation is com-

[43] Cardoso, *El empresário industrial en América Latina*, pp. 35–39.

[44] Albert O. Hirschman, *The Strategy of Economic Development* (New Haven: Yale University Press, 1958), pp. 14–19.

[45] W. Paul Strassmann, "The Industrialist," in Johnson, *op. cit.*, pp. 173–174.

mon: make money now "and then live happily—that is, idly—
ever after."[46] This means that entrepreneurs frequently prefer
to make a high profit quickly, often by charging a high price
to a small market, rather than to maximize long-range profits
by seeking to cut costs and prices, which would take more
effort.[47] Although the concept of immediate profit "in industrial enterprises usually meant within one year or else after
paying back initial loans," this does not reflect a Schumpe-
terian assumption about the reward or encouragement necessary to entrepreneurial risk-taking. Rather, the overwhelming
majority of the Latin American businessmen interviewed argued that risk is to be avoided, and that "when there is risk
there will not be new investment," that investment risk is a
luxury which only those in wealthy countries can afford.[48]
Reluctance to take risks may be related to the strong concern
with family integrity, with viewing business property much
like a family estate. "Where bankruptcy might disgrace one's
family, managers will be more cautious than where it is regarded impersonally as expedient corporate strategy."[49]

It is important to note that these generalizations about the
attitudes and behavior of Latin American entrepreneurs are
all made in a comparative context. Those who stress their
commitment to particularistic and diffuse values are generally
comparing them to North Americans, or to a model of rational, bureaucratic, competitive enterprise. However, as contrasted with other groups within their societies, Latin American entrepreneurs, particularly those involved in large-scale
enterprise, tend to be the carriers of "modern" values. Thus
one analysis of Colombian businessmen points out: "They are
urban people in a rural country. In a relatively traditionally
oriented society, their values are rational and modern."[50]

[46] Lauterbach, "Managerial Attitudes and Economic Growth," p.
379; Fillol, *op. cit.,* pp. 13–14.

[47] One report on Panama comments that "their business philosophy
. . . is that of the gambler or plunger. . . . They prefer low volume
and high markup; they want quick, large profits on small investment.
They cannot think in pennies." John Biesanz, "The Economy of Panama," *Inter-American Economic Affairs,* 6 (Summer, 1962), 10.

[48] Lauterbach, "Government and Development," pp. 209–210. Powell,
op. cit., pp. 82–83.

[49] Strassmann, *op. cit.,* p. 173.

[50] Aaron Lipman, *El empresário industrial en América Latina: Colombia* (Mar del Plata, Argentina: Naciones Unidas Comisión para

The impact of Latin American orientations to entrepreneurial behavior has been summed up in the following terms:

> Comparatively the Latin American complex: 1) sacrifices rigorous economically directed effort, or profit maximization, to family interests; 2) places social and personal emotional interests ahead of business obligations; 3) impedes mergers and other changes in ownership desirable for higher levels of technological efficiency and better adjustments to markets; 4) fosters nepotism to a degree harmful to continuously able top-management; 5) hinders the building up of a supply of competent and cooperative middle managers; 6) makes managers and workers less amenable to constructive criticism; 7) creates barriers of disinterest in the flow of technological communication; and 8) lessens the urge for expansion and risk-taking.[51]

The emphases on the value orientations of entrepreneurs as a major factor in limiting economic development in Latin America may be criticized for de-emphasizing the extent to which the values themselves are a product of, or sustained by, so-called structural or economic factors. Thus, it has been suggested that the unwillingness to delegate responsibility to nonfamily members reflects the objective dangers of operating in unstable political and economic environments. Such conditions dictate extreme caution and the need to be certain that one can quickly change company policy so as to avoid major losses or bankruptcy as a result of government policy changes, change in foreign exchange rates, and the like. An "outsider" presumably will not have as much interest in the finances of the firm, or the authority to react quickly. Rapid inflation, high interest rates, and other instability factors would all seem

---

América Latina, 1963. E/CN/12/642/Add. 4), p. 30; Guillermo Briones, *El empresário industrial en América Latina: Chile* (Mar del Plata, Argentina: Naciones Unidas Comisión para América Latina, 1963. E/CN/12/642/Add. 3), p. 35. It should be noted that most of the above generalizations about Latin American entrepreneurs are based on interview data. And as Fernando Cardoso points out, such data may tend to be at variance with actual behavior. Many of those interviewed are well educated and aware of the nature of a modern entrepreneurial outlook. Cardoso suggests that the actual behavior of those interviewed is much less modern and rational than would be suggested by the interviews. Cardoso, *op. cit.*, pp. 47–48, 59.

[51] Cochran, "Cultural Factors in Economic Growth," pp. 529–530.

to inhibit long-range planning and encourage a quick and high profit. There can be little doubt that such structural factors help to preserve many of the traditionalistic practices. And such a conclusion would imply the need for deliberate government policies to create a stable environment, such as planned investment policies, regulation of inflation, and restrictions on the export of capital.

But if the existence of interacting supportive mechanisms, which will inhibit economic growth, is admitted, the fact remains that similar generalizations have been made about the effect of values on attitudes and behavior of other groups and institutions. For example, an analysis of Argentine politics before the military coup points to the effect of these values in preventing stable political life. "Argentina's class-bound politics assume that no public measure can be good for almost everybody, that the benefit of one group is the automatic loss of all others."[52] Although Argentina is, after Uruguay, socially the most developed nation in Latin America, highly literate and urbanized, its citizens still do not accept the notion of, nor do they show loyalty to, a national state which acts universalistically. Argentina is instead characterized by the "survival of localistic, sub-national views and loyalties archetypical of the traditional society. . . ."[53] Similarly in the largest country in Latin America, it "is a well known fact that local government, party politics, and bureaucracy in Brazil still largely reflect family interests which are of course a variance with the principles of objective management as dictated by democratic rule."[54]

Efforts to "modernize" values and behavior are not solely, or even primarily, located in the economic or political spheres. Rather, those professionally concerned with ideas and values, the intellectuals, may play a decisive role in resisting or facilitating social change. As John Friedmann has pointed out, the intellectual in developing countries has three essential tasks to fulfill, "each of which is essential to the process of

[52] Kalman H. Silvert, "The Costs of Anti-Nationalism: Argentina," in Silvert (ed.), *Expectant Peoples: Nationalism and Development* (New York: Random House, 1963), p. 350.
[53] *Ibid.*, p. 353.
[54] Willems, *op. cit.*, p. 343.

cultural transformation: he mediates new values, he formulates an effective ideology, and he creates an adequate, collective [national] self-image."[55] In Latin America, however, the large body of literature concerning the values of the extremely prestigious *pensadores* or intellectuals, whether creative artists or academics, agrees that they continue to reject the values of industrial society, which they often identify with the United States. A survey of the writings of Latin American intellectuals points up this conclusion: "There is no school of literature in Latin America, which argues that technology and technological change represent values which should be adopted, cherished, and used as a means to a more meaningful life."[56] Even when modern technology is accepted as a necessary precondition for social betterment, it is often described as a threat to the traditional values of the society.[57]

Some of the factors which sustain these attitudes, even in the face of the recognized need of the nations of Latin America to change to get out of the "humiliating" status of being considered "underdeveloped" or even backward, have been suggested in an interesting comparison of the different ways in which Japan and Latin America reacted to similar concerns.

When seeking to define a national self-image in a nationalistic frame of mind, one is most likely to seize on those features which supposedly differentiate one from one's major international antagonist. For Japan this point of counter-reference, the thou than which one has to feel more holy, has been the West generally and in the twentieth century America more particularly. For Latin America, since the beginning of this century at least, it has been almost exclusively America. But in differentiating themselves from Americans, the Japanese could point to the beauties of their tight family system; their patriotic loyalty to the Emperor contrasting with

[55] John Friedmann, "Intellectuals in Developing Countries," *Kyklos,* 13 (1964), 524.
[56] William S. Stokes, "The Drag of the *pensadores,"* in James W. Wiggins and Helmut Schoeck (eds.), *Foreign Aid Reexamined* (Washington: Public Affairs Press, 1958), p. 63; see also Fred P. Ellison, "The Writer," in Johnson (ed.), *op. cit.,* p. 97.
[57] Stokes, *op. cit.,* see the footnotes to these articles for references to the large literature by Latin Americans and others emphasizing these points.

American selfish individualism; the pacific subtleties of Buddhism contrasting with the turbulent stridency of Christianity; and so on. But it was not as easy for a Latin American to establish the Latin American differentiae in terms of family, political, or legal institutions. He had to fall back on "spirit" and attitudes; and since the most visible American was the businessman, he tended—*vide arielismo* as Ellison describes it—to make his dimension of difference the materialist-spiritual one. Thus by scorning American devotion to technology and profit, he made something of a virtue out of the stark fact of economic backwardness. For their part the Japanese had enough superior arguments with which to fortify their uncertain sense of their superior Japaneseness without resorting to this one, with its inhibiting effect on indigenous economic growth.[58]

While much of the anti-United States sentiment is presented in the context of left-wing critiques, *pensadores* of the right—those who uphold the virtues of tradition, Catholicism, and social hierarchy—also are aggressively opposed to North American culture, which they see as "lacking culture, grace, beauty, as well as widespread appreciation of aesthetic and spiritual values."[59] And a report on the writings of Chilean conservative intellectuals states that more than one hundred works have been published which "are as hostile to basic United States social, economic and political patterns as to Russian communism."[60]

The values fostered by the *pensadores* continue to be found in much of Latin American education as well. Most analysts of Latin American education agree that, at both university and secondary school level, the content of education still reflects the values of a landed upper class. Even in the second most developed Latin American country, Argentina, a study of national values points out that the traditional landed aristocratic disdain for manual work, industry, and trading continues to affect the educational orientations of many students. When an Argentine seeks to move up, "he will usually try to do so, not by developing his manual skills or by accomplishing business or industrial feats, but by developing his *intellectual* skills. He will follow an academic career typically

[58] Dore, *op. cit.*, p. 245.
[59] Pike, *op. cit.*, p. 251.
[60] *Ibid.*, p. 254.

in a field which is not 'directly productive' from an economic point of view—medicine, law, social sciences, etc."[61]

As Jacques Lambert has put it:

> A ruling class deriving its resources from landed property looks to education for a means not of increasing its income but rather of cultivating the mind. The whole public education system has been organized as a preparation for higher education, and more particularly for the type of education provided in the faculties of law, which gave instruction not only in law but also in political and social science, for a class of political leaders.[62]

There is considerable resistance at both secondary and university levels to changing the curriculum to adapt to the needs of mass education in an urban industrial society. President Lleras of Colombia, for example, complained that students in the secondary schools "are studying the same courses as in the 19th century."[63] The Brazilian sociologist Florestán Fernandes suggests that the "democratization" of education in his country has meant "spreading throughout Brazilian society the aristocratic school of the past."[64] The school here reinforces the disdain for "practical work," and diffuses these values among the upwardly mobile.

> Education has remained impermeable to economic, social and political revivalist influences. Misunderstanding and contempt of popular education has subsisted, and the excessive prestige enjoyed by the humanistic culture of the old upper class, as patrons of a corresponding type of anti-experimental book-learning, has been perpetuated. The school continues to be an isolated institution divorced from man's conditions of existence and specializing in the transmission of bookish techniques, potted knowledge and routine intellectual

[61] Fillol, *op. cit.*, pp. 17–18.

[62] Jacques Lambert, "Requirements for Rapid Economic and Social Development: The View of the Historian and Sociologist," in De Vries and Echavarría, *op. cit.*, p. 64.

[63] Robert W. Burns, "Social Class and Education in Latin America," *Comparative Education Review*, 6 (1963), p. 232.

[64] Florestán Fernandes, "Pattern and Rate of Development in Latin America," in De Vries and Echavarría, *op. cit.*, pp. 196–197; see also Oscar Vera, "The Educational Situation and Requirements in Latin America," in De Vries and Echavarría, *op. cit.*, pp. 294–295; and Wagley, *An Introduction to Brazil*, pp. 103–104.

concepts. Formal education, in a word, is guarded from any impact that would adjust it to the constructive social functions which it should properly carry out in a society aiming at homogeneity and expansion.[65]

In Chile, one prominent educator, Julio Vega, wrote in 1950 "that education must begin to emancipate itself from the social prejudices which lead 99 per cent of those entering the *liceo*—somewhat the equivalent of the United States high school, but organized around an entirely different curriculum and dedicated to a different social purpose—to want to be professionals, so as to gain access to the world of the aristocracy." And many have argued that the educational system has taught middle-class Chileans "to think like an aristocrat of the past century and to hold in disdain manual labor and those who perform it."[66]

These generalizations about the strength of the traditional humanist bias in Latin America may be bolstered by reference to comparative educational statistics. Latin America as an area lags behind every other part of the world in the proportion of its students taking courses in engineering or the sciences. As of 1958–1959, 34 per cent of all West European undergraduates were studying science or engineering, in contrast to 23 per cent in Asia (excluding Communist China and India), 19 per cent in Africa, and 16 per cent in Latin America.[67] The comparable figure for the major Communist countries including the Soviet Union and China is 46 per cent.[68] China now trains more engineers per year than any other country except the Soviet Union and the United States. And 90 per cent of all China's scientists and engineers have

---

[65] Fernandes, *op. cit.*, p. 196.

[66] Pike, *op. cit.*, pp. 288–289. "There is a lengthy list of works suggesting that the educational structure in Chile foments class prejudice, leading the middle class to shun labor and the laboring classes, while striving to emulate the aristocracy" (p. 442, footnote). This work contains a detailed bibliography.

[67] J. Tinbergen and H. C. Bos, "The Global Demand for Higher and Secondary Education in the Underdeveloped Countries in the Next Decade," O.E.C.D., *Policy Conference on Economic Growth and Investment in Education, III, The Challenge of Aid to Newly Developing Countries* (Paris: O.E.C.D., 1962), p. 73.

[68] Frederick Harbison and Charles A. Myers, *Education, Manpower and Economic Growth* (New York: McGraw-Hill, 1964), p. 179.

been trained since 1949.[69] In Uruguay, on the other hand, slightly over half the students in higher education have been enrolled in faculties of humanities, fine arts, and law, about ten times as many as in the scientific and technical faculties. In Chile, in 1957, less than one-sixth of the students were studying science or engineering, and the increase in the numbers in these faculties between 1940 and 1959 was less than the growth in total university enrollment. "In Communist countries, of course, the proportions are almost exactly reversed; Czechoslovakia had 46 per cent in scientific and technical faculties and only 6.4 per cent in humanities, arts, and law."[70] Among Third World nations, only Israel with 42 per cent of its students in science and engineering, and Nigeria with 40 per cent, approached the Communist nations in degree of dedication of higher education to development training objectives.[71]

The situation is now changing in some Latin American countries; but it is significant that a comparative analysis of trends in higher education completed for UNESCO noted particularly that, as compared to other regions, in Latin America there "has been no concerted efforts . . . to strengthen interest and achievement in science and the related fields."[72] In the largest Latin American country, Brazil, enrollment in universities has increased ten times, from 10,000 to 101,600, between 1912 and 1961. However, the percentage of the total studying engineering was 12.8 in 1912 and 12 in 1961.[73] A study of students in seventeen middle schools (*ginásios*) in São Paulo indicates that the large majority hoped to enter one of the traditional prestige occupations. And Brandão Lopes comments that his findings indicate "the

[69] *Ibid.,* p. 88.
[70] *Ibid.,* pp. 115–119.
[71] James S. Coleman, "Introduction to Part IV," in J. S. Coleman (ed.), *Education and Political Development* (Princeton: Princeton University Press, 1965), p. 530.
[72] Frank Bowles, *Access to Higher Education,* Vol. I (Paris: UNESCO, 1963), p. 148.
[73] Robert J. Havighurst and J. Roberto Moreira, *Society and Education in Brazil* (Pittsburgh: University of Pittsburgh Press, 1965), p. 200. And engineering in Brazil and other parts of Latin America often means the traditionally socially prestigious field of civil engineering, not mechanical, chemical, or industrial.

permanence of traditional Brazilian values relating to work in an environment in which economic development demands new specialties."[74] The absence of French Canadians in leading roles in industry has been explained as a consequence of Canada's educational system, which resembles that of Latin America. Until the 1960's secondary education in Quebec was largely "based on private fee-paying schools," whose curriculum reflected "the refined traditions of the classical college. In the main, French-Canadian education was never geared to the provision of industrial skills at the managerial or technical level. The educational system was inappropriate for the kind of society that by 1950 Quebec was becoming. It was an outstanding example of institutional failure."[75]

Another reflection of the strength of "aristocratic" values in the Latin American educational system is the phenomenon of the part-time professor. It has been estimated that less than 10 per cent of the professors at Latin American universities receive salaries intended to pay for full-time work. As one Uruguayan professor once said to me, "To be a professor in this country is a hobby, a hobby one engages in for prestige." Obviously when men spend most of their time earning their living away from the university, often in an occupation such as the law which is unrelated to their academic work, they cannot be expected to make major contributions to scholarship, or to devote much time to guiding students.[76]

To describe this system as "aristocratic" may seem ironic, but comparative research on other subjects indicates that the "conception that public social service is performed best when [one] . . . is not paid, or is paid an honorarium, is basically an aristocratic value linked to the concept of *noblesse oblige*." Conversely, inherent in egalitarian ideology "has been the principle that a man should be paid for his work."[77] In a comparative analysis of the position of leaders of voluntary

---

[74] Brandão Lopes, "Escôlha ocupacional e origem social de ginasianos em São Paulo," *Educação e Ciencias Sociais*, 1 (1956), 61, 43–62. This study is reported in Wagley, *An Introduction to Brazil*, pp. 125–126.

[75] Porter, *op. cit.*, pp. 92–93.

[76] Benjamin, *op. cit.*, pp. 60–66, 94–97, 120–123.

[77] Lipset, *The First New Nation*, p. 195; see also Chapter 11 of this book, p. 403.

organizations in the United States and various European nations, I presented data which indicated that there are many more full-time paid leaders of such groups in the United States than in much of Europe. And I concluded:

> The inhibitions against employing a large number of officials permeate most voluntary associations in the European nations and reflect the historic assumption that such activities should be the "charities" of the privileged classes. The absence of a model of *noblesse oblige* in an egalitarian society fostered the American belief that such voluntary associations, whether they be the "March of Dimes," social work agencies, or trade unions, should be staffed by men who are paid to do the job. In a sense, therefore, it may be argued that the very emphasis on egalitarianism in America has given rise to the large salaried bureaucracies which permeate voluntary organizations.[78]

In the early days of the Latin American and European universities, they were staffed either by members of well-to-do families or the clergy. Such academics required no financial support from the university.[79] The high prestige of the university in Latin America is to some extent linked to its identification with the elite, with the assumption that professors and graduates, "doctors," are gentlemen.[80] However, such an identity is not dependent on the universities' contribution to society, and is clearly dysfunctional in any society which seeks to develop economically, or to make contributions to the world of science and scholarship. And it may be suggested that the resistance to "modernizing" the curriculum and to "professionalizing" the professoriate stems from the desire to maintain the diffuse elitist character of the role of the intellectual.[81] In contemporary times, when relatively few

[78] *Ibid.*
[79] Stokes, *op. cit.*, p. 70.
[80] Lambert, *op. cit.*, p. 64.
[81] Ironically, the powerful leftist student groups in the various Latin American countries constitute a major force resisting university modernization. See John P. Harrison, "The Role of the Intellectual in Fomenting Change: The University," in Tepaske and Fisher, *op. cit.*, pp. 27–42. In Venezuela, they have opposed tightening up examination standards. See Orlando Albórnoz, "Academic Freedom and Higher Education in Latin America," in S. M. Lipset (ed.), *Student Politics* (New York: Basic Books, 1967), pp. 283–292.

professors in fact can support themselves from family income, the diffuse elite status of the professor encourages him to use the status to secure wealth or power outside the university. Thus the professoriate as a status, as the equivalent of an aristocratic title, may be converted into high position on other dimensions of stratification. As one recent study of the Latin American university concludes about the behavior of the *catedrático*, the chairholder:

> With his name, title, connections, civil service status and lifelong position ensured, he is often tempted to use his chair as a mere rung on the long social climb to power. Once made "catedrático," he no longer has to worry much about teaching and even less about research. Aided and sustained by his university post, he is at last free to launch up on a successful professional or even political career.
>
> It is expected that a full professor will amass a modest personal fortune in the exercise of his profession as a lawyer, doctor or engineer . . . [Sometimes] these professional activities are also used as further stepping stones on the road to administrative, political or diplomatic positions . . .[82]

ECONOMIC GROWTH AND THE ROLE OF THE
"DEVIANT" IN ANTI-ENTREPRENEURIAL CULTURES

The argument that Latin American values are antithetical to economic development can, of course, be pitted against the fact that a considerable amount of economic growth has occurred in many of these countries. Clearly, in the presence of opportunity, an entrepreneurial elite has emerged. The logic of value analysis would imply that the creation or expansion of roles which are not socially approved in terms of the traditional values should be introduced by social "deviants." This hypothesis is basic to much of the literature dealing with the rise of the businessman in different traditional societies.

In his classic analysis of economic development, Joseph Schumpeter pointed out that the key aspect of entrepreneurship, as distinct from being a manager, is the capacity for leadership in innovation, for breaking through the routine and

[82] Rudolph P. Atcon, "The Latin American University," *Die Deutsche Universitätszeitung,* 17 (February, 1962), 27.

the traditional.[83] From this perspective the analysis of the factors which resulted in the rise of an entrepreneurial group leading to economic growth under capitalism is comparable to the study of the conditions which brought about anti-capitalist revolutionary modernizing elites of various countries in recent decades. The approach which emphasizes the theory of deviance assumes that those who introduce change must be deviants, since they reject the traditional elite's ways of doing things.[84] As Hoselitz puts it, "a deviant always engages in behavior which constitutes in a certain sense a breach of the existing order and is contrary to, or at least not positively weighted in the hierarchy of existing social values."[85] In societies in which the values of the dominant culture are

> not supportive of entrepreneurial activity, someone who is relatively outside of the social system may have a particular advantage in entering an entrepreneurial activity. The restraints upon entrepreneurial activity imposed by the network [of social relations] would be less effective against such a person. Thus, an immigrant may be outside of many of the networks of the nation and freer to engage in entrepreneurial activity,[86]

in other words, freer socially to deviate.

If we assume, in following up such generalizations, that within the Americas the value system of Latin America has discouraged entrepreneurial activity, while that of the English-speaking Protestant world of the United States and Canada has fostered it, then a comparative study of the backgrounds of entrepreneurs in these countries should reveal that those of Latin America are recruited disproportionately from sociologi-

[83] Joseph Schumpeter, *The Theory of Economic Development* (New York: Oxford University Press, 1961), pp. 74–94.

[84] Bert Hoselitz, "Main Concepts in the Analysis of the Social Implications of Technical Change," in Hoselitz and Moore, *op. cit.*, pp. 22–28.

[85] Hoselitz, *Sociological Aspects*, p. 62; Peter T. Bauer and Basil S. Yamey, *The Economics of Underdeveloped Countries* (Chicago: University of Chicago Press, 1957), pp. 106–112.

[86] Louis Kriesberg, "Entrepreneurs in Latin America and the Role of Cultural and Situational Processes," *International Social Science Journal*, 15 (1963), *op. cit.*, 591.

cal "deviants," while those of North America should come largely from groups which possess traits placing them inside the central structures of the society. An examination of the research data bearing on this hypothesis indicates that it is valid.

In many countries of Latin America, members of minority groups, often recent immigrants, have formed a considerable section of the emerging business elite. "In general it appears that immigrants took the lead in establishing modern manufacturing before World War I [in Latin America]."[87] Recent studies in various countries reveal comparable patterns. Frequently, these new entrepreneurs come from groups not known for their entrepreneurial prowess at home, such as the Arabs and the Italians, although Germans and Jews are also among those who are to be found in disproportionate numbers in business leadership. A study of Mexican business leaders found that of 109 major executives, 26 had foreign paternal grandfathers; among the "32 outstanding business leaders in Mexico, 14 reported a foreign paternal grandfather."[88] Analysis of the backgrounds of 286 "prestigious" entrepreneurs, taken from the Argentine *Who's Who*, indicates that 45.5 per cent were foreign born.[89] However, many of those born in Argentina are "among the first generation born in the country."[90] Classifying the sample by origins, Imaz reports that only 10 per cent came from the traditional upper class, and they, as in many other Latin American countries, are concentrated in industries which processed agricultural products, so that their role in industry is an extension of their position as a landed class. Among the rest, almost all are of relatively recent foreign origin.[91] Data from a survey of the heads of 46 out of the 113 industrial establishments in Santiago, Chile, which employ more than 100 workers in-

---

[87] Strassmann, p. 164.
[88] Raymond Vernon, *The Dilemma of Mexico's Development* (Camridge: Harvard University Press, 1963), p. 156.
[89] Imaz, p. 136.
[90] *Ibid.*, see also Germani, *op. cit.*, pp. 223–226; and Zalduendo, *op. cit.*, p. 10. The census of 1895 reported that 84 per cent of the 18,000 business establishments were owned by foreign-born individuals. Cochran and Reina, *op. cit.*, p. 8.
[91] Imaz, *op. cit.*, pp. 138–139.

dicate that 76 per cent of them are immigrants or the children of immigrants.[92] An earlier study of the Chilean middle class reports that as of 1940 the overwhelming majority of the 107,273 foreign born in the country were in middle-class, largely self-employed occupations.[93] In Brazil also "the majority of industrial entrepreneurs are immigrants or descendants of relatively recent immigrants."[94] Thus in São Paulo, 521 enterprises out of 714 were owned by men in these categories.[95] In the other economically developed states, Rio Grande do Sul and Santa Catarina, "almost 80 per cent of the industrial activities . . . were developed by people of European immigrant extraction."[96]

Similar patterns may be found in the less developed and more traditional countries. Thus, in a recent study of Peru, François Bourricaud traces in detail the continued control of members of the ancient oligarchy over much of the economic life of the country, their maintenance in much of agriculture and traditional business and banking of the *patron* system, and family and clan control. However, in the new and risky enterprises, those which have produced the new rich of the country, one finds many recent immigrants.[97] In Colombia, like Peru, a country with relatively little immigration, a study of the members of the National Association of Industrialists reports "that in 1962, 41 per cent of a sample of business

[92] Briones, *op. cit.*, p. 10.

[93] Julio Vega, "La clase media en Chile," in *Materiales para el estudio de la clase media en la américa latina* (Washington, D. C.: Pan American Union, 1950), pp. 81–82, as cited in Pike, *op. cit.*, p. 279.

[94] Benjamin Higgins, "Requirements for Rapid Economic Development in Latin America: The View of an Economist," in De Vries and Echavarría, *op. cit.*, p. 169.

[95] Emilio Willems, "Immigrants and Their Assimilation in Brazil," in T. Lynn Smith and Alexander Marchant (eds.), *Brazil. Portrait of Half a Continent* (New York: Dryden Press, 1951), p. 217. These apparently are largely from Italian, German, Jewish, and Lebanese backgrounds. See also Pereira, *op. cit.*, p. 316; Richard Morse, "São Paulo in the Twentieth Century: Social and Economic Aspects," *Inter-American Economic Affairs*, 8 (Summer, 1954), 21–23, 44; George White, "Brazil: Trends in Industrial Development," in Kuznets, Moore, and Spengler, *op. cit.*, pp. 57, 60–62.

[96] Wagley, *An Introduction to Brazil*, p. 87.

[97] François Bourricaud, *Pouvoir et societé dans le Pérou Contemporain* (Paris: Armand Colin, 1967), Chapter I.

Values and Entrepreneurship in the Americas 109

leaders in Bogotá were immigrants from other countries."[98]
In Panama, in 1940 before the decree "nationalizing" commerce, "nearly 45% of the men actively engaged in commerce or manufacturing were foreigners."[99] The various studies of the backgrounds of the Latin American entrepreneurial elite indicate that on the whole they are a well-educated group, the majority of them in most countries are university graduates. And a study of the origins of students at the University of São Paulo suggests that much of the separation in career orientations between those of native background and others takes place while in school. Thus, the proportion of students of non-Brazilian background is higher among the students than in the population of the city; only 22 per cent are of purely Brazilian descent. Even more significant is the fact that students with a higher proportion of foreign-born ancestors tend to enroll in the "modern" faculties, such as economics, engineering, pharmacy, and the like. Those with preponderantly Brazilian family backgrounds are more likely to be found in the more traditional high-prestige schools such as law and medicine. And the author of this study comments:

> The children of foreign-born parents . . . are more inclined to take advantage of the new opportunities in occupations which have emerged from the economic development of the city of São Paulo. One should consider the fact that in Brazil, the schools of Law and Medicine convey special social prestige to their students. It is easier for a not completely assimilated adolescent of foreign descent to ignore that prestige than for a "pure" Brazilian.[100]

Similarly, at the University of Chile, the School of Physics suffers from low prestige, "which diminishes the attractiveness of the field. . . ." A recent study of Chilean university students reports:

[98] Aaron Lipman, "Social Backgrounds of the Bogotá Entrepreneur," *Journal of Inter-American Studies,* 7 (1965), 231.
[99] Biesanz, *op. cit.,* p. 9.
[100] Bertram Hutchinson, "A origem sócio-econômica dos estudantes universitários," in Hutchinson (ed.), *Mobilidada e Trabalho* (Rio de Janeiro: Centro Brasileiro de Pesquisas Educacionais Ministério de Educação e Cultura, 1960), p. 145.

Who, then, are the students in this school? Why have they rejected the natural and well-formed paths of career choice? The most obvious are those who are immigrants or sons of immigrants—primarily German refugees and Italian emigrés . . . A second and frequently overlapping group is composed of students who are critical of the traditional alternatives.[101]

Immigrant and minority groups have shown comparable abilities to take advantage of, or to create, opportunities in other parts of the underdeveloped world. Thus in sub-Saharan Africa, Arabs, Indians, and to a lesser extent Chinese, form a large part of the commercial world. In Southeast Asian countries, Chinese constitute almost the entire business community; Indians were important in Burmese economic life before they were expelled. It should be noted that it is not only "immigrants" who have been disproportionately successful. Minority religious groups such as Christians have entered the universities in relatively large numbers in various Asian states, even where they are a tiny minority in the entire population. In Indonesia, for example, more than 15 per cent of the new students entering Gadjah Mada University in 1959–1960 were Christians, although few people adhere to Christianity. In general in Southeast Asia, there is

a relatively high proportion of youth from minorities enrolled in universities and [they have a] . . . reputation as better academic achievers than youth from majority elites. Such minorities . . . include the Karens and the Indians in Burma, the Chinese in Thailand, the "burghers" in Ceylon, the Bataks and Chinese in Indonesia, and other Christians in all these countries.[102]

The creative role of the deviant, or the outsider, has in part been conceptualized by the term "marginal man," who for various reasons is partially outside the culture in which he is living, is less socially integrated in the structures which maintain conformity, and is therefore not so committed to the established values of the larger order. Hence men of this

---

[101] Myron Glazer, *The Professional and Political Attitudes of Chilean University Students* (Ph.D. thesis: Department of Sociology, Princeton University, 1965), 78–79.

[102] Joseph Fischer, "The Student Population of a Southeast Asian University: an Indonesian Example," *International Journal of Comparative Sociology*, 2 (1961), 225, 230.

sort are more likely to be receptive to possibilities for change.[103] An analysis of those who successfully took advantage of the opportunity to shift the use of land in the vicinity of São Paulo from subsistence agriculture to lucrative commercial crops (mainly the growth of eucalyptus for firewood) illustrates this process. More than 90 per cent of those who became small-scale, relatively well-to-do entrepreneurs were recent settlers in the area, "immigrants or children of immigrants . . . or members of a small but flourishing Protestant sect (the *Evangelistas*) . . ."

> Almost all of the recent settlers were as poor as the *caboclos* [the native, lowest status rural dwellers] when they arrived. They managed to see new alternatives when they arose, to buy up small plots of land and gradually increase their holdings, mostly at the expense of the *caboclos* . . . It is worth testing . . . the proposition that *participation in newly valued activities among members of low economic and prestige classes varies inversely with length of residence in a locality*. Old settlers at depressed levels have inherited habits of belief, a morality and expectation of role rights and obligations associated with their statuses . . . that they are only slowly adaptable in the presences of altered opportunities. One of the most striking occurrences in the changing situation within the *municipio* under consideration is the fact that several *caboclos* sold or were seeking to sell their properties to prospective entrepreneurs, and then turned around and hired their labor out for wages.[104]

The traits which are often associated with economic innovation lead their bearers to be frowned upon or even hated by those who adhere to the conventional traditions of the society, or who resent the success of others. Thus in Brazil, Gilberto Freyre reports that many of non-Portugese descent have

> shown a lack of finer moral scruples which has given many of them the reputation of being morally or ethically inferior . . . [Their actions which lead to success in politics and business] are given as an example of the fact that the sons of "immigrants" are morally inferior to the sons of old

[103] See Robert Park, *Race and Culture* (Glencoe: The Free Press, 1950), pp. 345–392; Everett Stonequist, *The Marginal Man* (New York: Russell & Russell, 1961).
[104] Siegel, *op. cit.*, pp. 399–400 (emphases in the original).

Brazilian families as political leaders, businessmen, and industrial pioneers. Of course, sons of immigrants who follow such careers are freer than the members of old and well-known families from certain moral controls that act upon men deeply rooted in their towns or countries or regions.[105]

It is indicative of the extent to which Latin Americans identify entrepreneurial or commercial abilities as "alien" to their tradition and values that ethnic myths are invented to explain the success of those of native background who do succeed. Thus both in Colombia, where the citizens of Antioquia have evidenced entrepreneurial abilities far exceeding those of other sections of the country, and in Mexico, where residents of Monterrey have shown comparable skills, the story is widely believed that both groups are descended from *maranos,* secretly practicing Jews who publically changed their religion after 1492.[106] These stories have been disproven by historical research, but the fact that many accept them as gospel tells much about attitudes toward entrepreneurship. The same factors may be involved in Gilberto Freyre's report, citing various writers, that the major center of business enterprise in Brazil, São Paulo, is "probably the nucleus of the Brazilian population with the largest strain of Semitic blood."[107]

The logic of the analysis suggested here, however, does not agree with the thesis that innovating entrepreneurs in developing societies must be recruited disproportionately from the ranks of social "deviants," as some have interpreted data such as these. Rather, it points with Weber to the fact that many minority groups have not shown such propensities. Clearly the Catholic minorities in England, or other Protestant countries, were much less likely than the general population

[105] Freyre, *op. cit.,* p. 161.

[106] Strassmann, *op. cit.,* p. 166.

[107] Gilberto Freyre, *The Masters and the Slaves: A Study in the Development of Brazilian Civilization* (New York: Alfred A. Knopf, 1963), p. 36. Freyre does not evaluate this thesis; rather, as with many other tales concerning Jewish traits and abilities, he seems to be gullibly accepting. "The farmers with a deep love for the land and a thorough knowledge of agriculture were sometimes abused or exploited in Brazil by those of their fellow countrymen whose passion was for commercial adventure and urban life—most of them probably Jews" (Freyre, *New World in the Tropics,* p. 50).

to engage in entrepreneurial activity. In his analysis of the divergent consequences for economic behavior of Protestantism and Catholicism, Max Weber pointed to the greater business accomplishments of the Protestant *majority* as compared to the Catholic minority in Germany.[108] The key issue, as Weber has indicated, is the value system of the various groups involved. Latin America and some other less developed traditional societies are so vulnerable to economic cultural "deviants" because the predominant values of the host culture are in large measure antithetical to rational entrepreneurial orientations. Where national values support economic development, the Weberian emphasis on value would suggest that the innovating business elite would be drawn not from deviants but rather from the "in-group," from persons with socially privileged backgrounds.

An examination of the social characteristics of North American business leaders in both Canada and the United States bears out these assumptions. Compared with most other nations in the world, the United States and English-speaking Canada have been among the most hospitable cultures to economic development. The Protestant ethic as fostered by denominations spawned of Calvinist and Arminian origins strongly influenced all classes in these societies, the United States somewhat more than Canada. And a study of the business leaders of the United States in 1870, the period of its take off into industrial development, indicates that 86 per cent of them came from "colonial families" settled in the country before 1777. Only 10 per cent were foreign-born or the children of foreign-born.[109] More than 98 per cent of the post-Civil War business elite were Protestants. Although the proportions of those of non-Anglo-Saxon, non-Protestant, and foreign-born parentage have increased over the years, they have always remained considerably lower than their proportion in the population as a whole.[110] Canadian data are avail-

[108] Weber, *op. cit.,* pp. 38–46.
[109] Suzanne Keller, *The Social Origins and Career Lines of Three Generations of American Business Leaders* (Ph.D. dissertation: Department of Sociology, Columbia University, 1953), pp. 37–41.
[110] See S. M. Lipset and Reinhard Bendix, *Social Mobility in Industrial Society* (Berkeley: University of California Press, 1959), pp. 137–138.

able only for the post-World War II period, but it should be
noted that Canada's emergence as a major industrial society
largely dates from the war. Previously its economy somewhat resembled that of Argentina, being largely dependent
on agricultural exports. The Canadian case is extremely interesting since the country is composed of two separate
cultures—English Protestant and Latin Catholic. And a comprehensive report on the Canadian elite shows a clear-cut
picture: where cultural values congruent with entrepreneurship are ascendant, the business elite will be recruited largely
from the dominant culture group, not from minorities. Thus
those of Anglo-Saxon Protestant background are overrep-
resented, while those of Latin, Catholic, and minority origins
are underrepresented.

> An examination of the social origins of the economic elite
> shows that economic power belongs almost exclusively to
> those of British origin, even though this ethnic group made
> up less than half of the population in 1951. The fact that
> economic development in Canada has been in the hands of
> British Canadians has long been recognized by historians. Of
> the 760 people in the economic elite, only 51 (6.7 per cent)
> could be classified as French Canadians although the French
> made up about one-third of the population in 1951. . . .
> There were no more than a handful who . . . could be clas-
> sified as top-ranking industrialists in their own province.
>
> Ethnic groups of neither British nor French origin, which
> made up about one-fifth of the general population, were
> hardly represented at all. There were six Jews (.78 per cent
> of the sample as opposed to 1.4 per cent of the general popu-
> lation) . . . [O]nly 78 (about 10 per cent) were Catholic
> . . . 43 per cent of the population in 1951 was Catholic.[111]

In seeking to account for the low representation of French
Canadians in the economic elite, even within Quebec, John
Porter points out that the evidence does not fit the assumption that it is largely a result of the greater power of the British
Canadians. For French Canadians do quite well in other
power structures, e.g., politics, the intellectual world, and religion. French weakness in industry seems related to elements
in their culture comparable with those in much of Latin
America.

[111] Porter, *op. cit.,* pp. 286–289.

The varying origins of the business elites of the American nations clearly indicate that "out" groups, such as ethnic-religious minorities, are given the opportunity to innovate economically when the values of the dominant culture are antithetical to such activities. Thus, the comparative evidence from the various nations of the Americas sustains the generalization that cultural values are among the major forces which affect the potentiality for economic development.

Although I have focused on the direct effects of value orientations on the entrepreneurial behavior of certain groups, it should be clear that any given individual or group supports the values of his or its effective social environment. Although national values may discourage entrepreneurial activities, ethnic or religious subgroups, or links to foreign cultures may encourage them for those involved. One explanation of the comparative success of members of some minority groups in Latin America, such as the Anglo-Argentines, is that they continue to respect their ancestral national culture more than that of their host society. The fact that many ethnic minorities in some Latin American nations continue to send their children to schools conducted in their ancestral language and to speak it at home attests to their lack of acceptance of national culture and values.

The key question basically is whether one is involved in a network of social relations which sustain or negate a particular activity. Viscount Mauá, Brazil's great nineteenth-century economic innovator, although a native Brazilian, was adopted while in his early teens by an English merchant in Rio de Janeiro; his biography clearly indicates that he became an "alien" within his native culture, that English became his "native" language, the one in which he thought and wrote his private thoughts."[112] Conversely, as we have seen, many successful entrepreneurs are drawn away from total commitment to their business life by an involvement in social networks and reference groups which supply more prestige than their vocation. One of Argentina's most successful entre-

[112] Anyda Marchant, *Viscount Mauá and the Empire of Brazil* (Berkeley: University of California Press, 1965), pp. 81, 83, 208–209, 241.

preneurs, who was an immigrant, built up a complex network
of industrial companies, took the time to study at the university, accepted an appointment as an associate professor of
Economics and Industrial Organization at the University of
Buenos Aires, when he was fifty years of age, sought to secure
a regular chair three years later, and bought a 6,600-acre
estancia, on which he spent much time.[113] To facilitate the
emergence of a given new role in a society, it is necessary to
help create social recognition for it within meaningful subgroups. The leaders of Meiji Japan have provided an example of the way in which one nation did this. To raise the
prestige of the business class,

> . . . social distinctions [were] granted to the presidents
> and main shareholders of the new companies. The presidents
> were given the privilege of the sword and family name. They
> were appointed by the government, as officials were. A presi-
> dent could walk directly into the room of a government offi-
> cial while common people had to wait and squat outside the
> building. Many other minor privileges were granted.[114]

It is important to recognize that the introduction of new
activities by those linked to "foreign" cultures or minority
religions is not simply one of the various ways to modernize
a society. Innovations which are associated with socially marginal groups are extremely vulnerable to political attack from
those who would maintain traditional values. Consequently
efforts at economic modernization, changes in the educational
system, or social customs which are introduced by "outsiders," may have much less effect in modifying the central
value system than when they are fostered by individuals who
are members of the core group, as occurred in Meiji Japan.

Although much of the discussion thus far has involved the
presentation of evidence concerning *the* Latin American
value system, it is obvious that there is considerable variation
among Latin American nations, as there is among the

[113] Cochran and Reina, *op. cit.,* pp. 147–151. It is worth noting that
his two sons studied for their Ph.D.'s abroad, and that both are professors, one in economics and the other in sociology.

[114] Johannes Hirschmeier, *The Origins of Entrepreneurship in Meiji
Japan* (Cambridge: Harvard University Press, 1964), p. 35.

English-speaking countries. Thus, many of the distinctions which have been drawn between Argentina and Uruguay on the one hand and Brazil on the other refer to the greater egalitarianism and universalism in the former two. Or the earlier and greater degree of working-class consciousness in Chile (indicated by the strength of Marxist parties) as contrasted with Uruguay and Argentina may be a consequence of the greater elitism, ascription, and particularism of Chile, which was a major center of population concentration under colonial rule, while the values of the latter two were modified by their later formation as immigrant cultures.

Uruguay (and to a somewhat lesser extent Argentina) differs from the rest of Latin America in being relatively committed to a historically rooted egalitarian ideology. This value orientation stems from the effects of widespread immigration, which helped provide a mass urban base for reformist political movements. As Gino Germani indicates, immigration "played a great part in the destruction of the traditional pattern of social stratification."[115]

The emphasis on egalitarianism in both Argentina and Uruguay is perhaps best reflected in the extension of their educational systems, which have long led all other Latin American nations in the proportions attending school, from primary to university. This commitment to education may have played a major role in facilitating economic growth during the late nineteenth century and the first three decades of the twentieth. However, when egalitarianism is associated with particularistic and ascriptive orientations, it seemingly serves to strengthen the concern with security mentioned earlier, and early successful pressures (more in Uruguay than Argentina) for welfare state measures. Both countries, today, face difficulties, brought about in large measure because earlier governments responsive to popular pressures have dedicated a large share of national revenues to welfare.

Efforts to do more than present loose illustrations of this type must await systematic comparative work on all the Latin American republics, as sociologists at the Di Tella Institute

[115] Germani, *op. cit.*, p. 226. Argentina cultural traits are discussed in Fillol.

in Buenos Aires are now doing.[116] They are attempting to codify systematically a large variety of qualitative and quantitative materials, covering more than a century, to test out various hypotheses concerning the sources of differentiation within Latin America.

CHANGES IN VALUE ORIENTATIONS

The evidence presented thus far would seem to indicate that, regardless of the causal pattern one prefers to credit for Latin American values, they are, as described, antithetic to the basic logic of a large-scale industrial system.[117] However, as noted earlier, it should be recognized that these descriptions are all made in a relative or comparative context, that Latin American economic behavior is evaluated either in comparison with that in the United States, or other developed nations, or against some ideal model of entrepreneurship. The value system of much of Latin America, like Quebec, has, in fact, been changing in the direction of a more achievement-oriented, universalistic, and egalitarian value system, and its industrial development both reflects and determines such changes. Many Latin American entrepreneurs are hiring nonfamily members as executives, and in various ways have acted contrary to the supposed norms. To some extent this

[116] See Torcuato S. Di Tella, Oscar Cornblit, and M. Ezequiel Gallo, "Outline of the Project: A Model of Social Change in Latin America," *Documentos de Trabajo* (Buenos Aires: Instituto Torcuato Di Tella Centro de Sociologia Comparada, n.d.).

[117] Alexander Gershenkron has shown how entrepreneurial activities in nineteenth-century Russia "were at variance with the dominant system of values, which remained determined by the traditional agrarian pattern. . . . The nobility and the gentry had nothing but contempt for any entrepreneurial activity except its own. . . . Divorced from the peasantry, the entrepreneurs remained despised by the intelligentsia." He argues, however, that while such cultural values may "indeed delay the beginning of rapid industrialization," they cannot stop it. Their effect, rather, is to hold back the pressures for industrialization so that they finally burst out in periods of rapid growth. However, he also concludes that in Russia "the delayed industrial revolution was responsible for a political revolution," i.e., the Bolshevik seizure of power. *Economic Backwardness in Historical Perspective* (Cambridge: Harvard University Press, 1962), pp. 59–62, 28.

may reflect the fact that a large segment of the creative and successful entrepreneurs are members of minority ethnic groups. More important, perhaps, is the fact that bureaucratic corporate enterprise has an inherent logic of its own; those who build such organizations, or rise within them in once-traditional societies, are either "deviants" who have the necessary new orientations, or men who develop them. Paternalistic feudal attitudes toward workers are characteristically more common in the less developed Latin American countries than in the more industrialized ones, a finding which parallels the situation within Spain.[118] There, the more developed an area, the more "modern" the attitudes of its entrepreneurs.

Such developments have been analyzed by Fernando Cardoso in his study of the industrial entrepreneur in Brazil. The shift from the values of the *patron* to those of the modern professional entrepreneur occurred with the emergence of large-scale industries, such as automobile manufacturing or shipbuilding. He points out that the rapidity of the adjustment to modern orientations depends on the attitudes of the entrepreneurs involved. And the same individuals and companies often react in what appear to be contradictory ways. These dual orientations, modern and traditional, reflect in part the mixed character of the Brazilian economy, which may still be characterized as incipient industrial capitalism.[119] The heterogeneity of entrepreneurial environments and orientations has, as yet, prevented the emergence of a consistent ideology to which most adhere.[120] Hence, Cardoso points to changes in values with growing industrialization, although he does not challenge the general description of Latin American economic behavior, as still applying to much of the Brazilian present.

Values clearly change as societies become economically

[118] Amando do Miguel and Juan J. Linz, "Movilidad Social del Empresario Español," *Revista de Fomento Social*, 75–76 (July–December, 1964).

[119] Cardoso, *Empresário Industrial*, p. 157 and *passim*.

[120] A very similar point is made about the heterogeneity of outlook among the Argentinean entrepreneurs by Imaz, *op. cit.*

more developed.[121] Many of the generalizations made about Latin American or other relatively underdeveloped societies, in contrast to the United States or northern Europe, were made, and are still being made, about such countries as Spain, France, or Italy, when they are compared with more economically developed countries.

Only a short time ago, economic "stagnation" in these European Latin countries was interpreted as the consequence of values incongruent with enterprising behavior. That breakthroughs in development occur for a variety of reasons in different countries is obvious. Values dysfunctional to economic growth may inhibit but not prevent growth, if other factors are favorable. As the history of various nations has suggested, processes or conflicts about values may foster the emergence of groups motivated to achieve economically. But conclusions such as these do not offer any prospect for change, other than to suggest the need for detailed careful study of the relevant factors suggested by social science theory in each country, or simply to add to the amount of investment capital available in a given country. I would like, therefore, to turn to a discussion of the various ways which seem open to those who deliberately seek to change values so as to foster the emergence of entrepreneurial elites.

The experience of Japan, the one non-Western nation which has successfully industrialized, suggests that the key question may not be the creation of new values so much as the way in which cultural ideals supporting tradition can give rise to those supporting modernity, that the shift from tradition to modernity need not involve a total rejection of a nation's basic values.[122]

In discussing this problem, Reinhard Bendix notes that in Weber's *The Protestant Ethic and the Spirit of Capitalism*, a study of the resolution of the contradiction between the co-

[121] For a statement of the ways in which economic development may change values, see Albert O. Hirschman, "Obstacles to Development: A Classification and a Quasi-Vanishing Act," *Economic Development and Cultural Change*, 13 (1965), 385–393.

[122] For example, see Robert Bellah, *Tokugawa Religion* (Glencoe: The Free Press, 1957); James C. Abegglen, *The Japanese Factory* (Glencoe: The Free Press, 1958); Marion J. Levy, Jr., "Contrasting Factors in the Modernization of China and Japan," in Kuznets, Moore, and Spengler, *op. cit.*, pp. 496–536; and Hirschmeier, *op. cit.*

existing traditional and modern within a developing society, Western Europe, Weber observed that Reformers continued to be concerned with their salvation and accepted the traditional, Christian devaluation of worldly pursuits. The emergence of the "spirit of Capitalism" represented a direct outgrowth of this early anti-materialistic tradition of Christianity, a growth which occurred without replacing this tradition. Linking Weber's approach to the various analyses of the preconditions for Japanese development, Bendix points out that the Samurai under the Tokugawa regime became a demilitarized aristocracy loyal to the traditional Samurai ethic of militancy, even though the Tokugawa regime pursued a public policy of disciplined pacification, of the avoidance of conflict or competitive struggles to change a status or power relationship among the feudal lords. After the Meiji Restoration of 1868, the virtues of achievement were socially accepted. The traditional Samurai ethic applied to a competitive world now meant that any self-respecting Samurai was obliged to show his ability and desire to win. Thus in nineteenth-century Japan, as in Reformation Europe, "modern" economic orientations emerged through the application of traditional values and sources of individual motivation to new structural conditions, rather than the supplanting of one set of values by another. Since Japan and Western Europe are the only two non-Communist cultural areas which have developed successfully on their own, the finding that achievement values seemingly emerged out of a redefinition of traditional values, rather than the adoption of new ones, has obvious implications for those contemporary underdeveloped cultures which seek to industrialize.[123]

In seeking for culturally accepted orientations which will lead a section of the elite to "split off" and endorse "modern" values, Talcott Parsons suggests that nationalism, concern for the international status of one's society, can motivate those who are most oriented to foreign opinion to press for

[123] See Reinhard Bendix, "Cross-Cultural Mobility and Development," in Neil Smelser and S. M. Lipset (eds.), *Social Structure and Social Mobility in Economic Development* (Chicago: Aldine Publishing Company, 1966), pp. 262–279. See also Hoselitz, *op. cit.*, pp. 8–82; and Hirschmeier, *op. cit.*, pp. 44–68.

new attitudes toward industrialization. And within the existing elites such people are most likely to be found among intellectuals, especially "those who have had direct contacts with the West, particularly through education abroad or under Western auspices at home."[124] In the name of fostering the national welfare, major changes may be introduced, which would be more strongly resisted if they were perceived as serving the interests of a subgroup within the society, such as the businessmen. In Uruguay, governmental actions which are justified by a nonrevolutionary national development ideology are seen by the workers as another rationalization of the ruling class to consolidate its power.[125]

If the source of new development concerns is to be nationalism rather than self-interest, then the means are more likely to be perceived in the political rather than in an autonomous economic arena.[126] And within the political arena, it is necessary to disassociate the policies advocated from any identification with possible foreign control. In Latin America today, support of "socialism" as opposed to "capitalism" becomes a way in which intellectuals may advocate industrialization without being accused of seeking to foster foreign "materialistic" values which are destructive of the spiritual values of the society.[127]

A "socialist" ideology of economic development may be conceived of as a functional alternative to the Meiji elite's use of loyalty to the Emperor, Shinto, and the nation, when seeking to industrialize Japan. The problem which can best be met by a revolutionary nationalist ideology justifying the rejection of the past has been well put by Gerschenkron:

> In a backward country the great and sudden industrialization effort calls for a New Deal in emotions. Those carrying out the great transformation as well as those on whom it imposes burdens must feel, in the words of Matthew Arnold, that

---

[124] Talcott Parsons, *Structure and Process in Modern Society* (New York: The Free Press of Glencoe, 1960), pp. 116–129.

[125] Solari, *op. cit.*, p. 172.

[126] See also Gustavo Lagos, *International Stratification and Underdeveloped Countries* (Chapel Hill: University of North Carolina Press, 1963), pp. 3–30, 138–160.

[127] Ellison, *op. cit.*, pp. 96–100.

> . . . Clearing a stage
> Scattering the past about
> Comes the new age.

Capitalist industrialization under the auspices of socialist ideologies may be, after all, less surprising a phenomenon than would appear at first sight.[128]

In formulating such ideologies, Latin America is at a disadvantage compared with the "new nations" of Asia and Africa. Most of the latter have recently attained independence under the leadership of mass parties whose revolutionary ideology subsumes the values of egalitarianism, achievement, universalism, and collectivity orientation. Traditional practices may be attacked as antithetical to the national interest and self-image. In much of Latin America, however, many traditional values and practices are regarded as proper parts of the national identity. Supporters of these traditional practices cannot be challenged as being anti-nationalist. Conversely, the initial steps toward attaining a national economic system in the United States were facilitated by its being "in many senses an underdeveloped country when it was transformed into a new nation-state by a revolution led by a new elite."[129] The new United States faced the need to break down the particularistic loyalties and values of the "indigenous aristocracy" of each little colony. And under the aegis of the ideology proclaimed in the Declaration of Independence, the revolutionary elite modified "the social institutions inherited from the British to the needs of a continental political economy."[130] Latin America, however, did not use its revolutionary struggle for independence to legitimate major social and economic changes; rather, independence often confirmed the control of the traditional landed class in power. Hence, as segments of the elite have awakened in recent decades to the need for such changes, they find it difficult to create the political institutions and national consensus needed to foster new values.

[128] Gerschenkron, *op. cit.,* p. 25.
[129] Robert Lamb, "Political Elites and the Process of Economic Development," in Bert Hoselitz (ed.), *The Progress of Underdeveloped Areas* (Chicago: University of Chicago Press, 1952), p. 30.
[130] *Ibid.,* p. 138.

Perhaps Mexico is the best example of a systematic effort at value change in Latin America. The Mexican Revolution transformed the image and legitimate political emphases of the nation. It sought to destroy the sense of superiority felt by those of pure Spanish descent by stressing the concept of *Mexicanidad,* and by a glorification of its Indian past.[131] There are almost no monuments to Spaniards from Cortés to independence in 1814. Emphases on white racial descent are socially illegitimate. The values of the Mexican Revolution are similar to those of the other Western revolutions—the American, French, and Russian. Although Mexico clearly retains major elements of the traditional Latin American system, it is the one country, other than Cuba, which has identified its national ethos with that of equality and an open society. And with the sense of a collective revolutionary commitment to growth and egalitarianism, one finds that business activities, which are sanctioned by government approval, are presented as ways of fulfilling national objectives. A detailed account of the way in which the Revolution affected value change concludes:

> [The] Revolution fostered a shift from ascription to achievement as the basis for distributing income, and from particularistic to universalistic standards as the basis for distributing political and economically-relevant tasks among performers . . .
>
> Finally, it is evident that the nationalist character of the Revolutionary movement together with the broad area of congruence between politically significant new class interests

[131] As one student of Mexican politics comments: "[T]he distinctive feature of a revolution is that it establishes new goals for the society; it reorganizes society, but it must first reorganize the values which that society accepts; a successful revolution means the acceptance as 'good' of things which were not regarded as good before, the rejection as 'bad' of things previously acceptable or commendable. . . . Prior to the [Mexican] revolution, the Indian was semiofficially regarded as an inferior being, to be kept out of sight as much as possible, being prohibited by Porfirio Díaz's police from entering the Alameda, the public park in the center of Mexico City, for example. After the revolution, Mexico's Indian heritage became a matter of national pride, to be stressed in her art and her history, to be studied at length in her universities." From Martin Needler, "Putting Latin American Politics in Perspective," in John D. Martz (ed.), *The Dynamics of Change in Latin American Politics* (Englewood Cliffs: Prentice-Hall, 1965), p. 25.

and social goals has assisted the shift from self-orientation to collectivity orientation in the performance by the new elite of its social role.[132]

Many of the conclusions about the impact of the Revolution on Mexican society which have been drawn from institutional and anthropological research have recently been reiterated in an opinion survey focusing on the effect of the Revolution on political attitudes and behavior. The authors compared Mexican responses on a number of items to those of Italians, choosing the latter nation as another Latin, Catholic, semi-developed state which does not have a commitment to revolutionary ideals. Among their findings are:

> In Mexico, 30 per cent of the respondents express pride in some political aspect of their nation—ten times the proportion of respondents in Italy, where only 3 per cent expressed such pride. A large proportion in Mexico also express pride in its economic system—in particular, they talk of economic potential and growth. In contrast, few Italians express pride either in the political aspects of their nation or in the economic system. . . .
>
> There is some evidence . . . that the continuing impact of the Revolution explains part of the attachment to their political system that Mexican respondents manifest. Respondents in Mexico were asked if they could name some of the ideals and goals of the Mexican Revolution. Thirty-five per cent could name none, while the remaining 65 per cent listed democracy, political liberty and equality, economic welfare, agrarian reform, social equality and national freedom. . . . Those respondents who mentioned goals of the Revolution were then asked if they thought those goals had been realized, had been forgotten, or were still actively being sought. Twenty-five per cent of the 614 respondents in this category think the goals have been realized, 61 per cent think that they are still being sought, and only 14 per cent think they have been forgotten.[133]

---

[132] William P. Glade, Jr., "Revolution and Economic Development: A Mexican Reprise," in Glade and Charles W. Anderson, *The Political Economy of Mexico. Two Studies* (Madison: University of Wisconsin Press, 1963), pp. 50–52; for a detailed account of the way in which the revolution affected changes in values see pp. 33–36, 39–43, 44–45, and *passim*.

[133] Sidney Verba and Gabriel A. Almond, "National Revolutions and Political Commitment," in Harry Eckstein (ed.), *Internal War* (New York: The Free Press of Glencoe, 1964), pp. 221–222, 229.

The Mexican Revolution, of course, did not involve simply a symbolic transfer of power, as has occurred in a number of other Latin American countries. Rather, it is the one major Latin American nation in which genuine land reform occurred. The old dominant class of large landowners has been eliminated. "The large landholders disappeared at the pinnacle of the social order, together with their luxury consumption, no-work value system and the belief in the innate inequality of social segments."[134] The rapid economic growth rate of Mexico in recent decades has been credited by many to the consequences of this revolution in changing the value system, in making possible the rise of a middle class that is self-assured about its own role. It "is fairly abstemious and frugal; it is devoted to modernization and education and recognizes economic achievement as a worthwhile end." Conversely, its neighbor, Guatemala, provides a "good comparative-control" case of a nation of similar social structure and history, but which has not changed its basic agricultural system and consequent class structure and value system, and shows little economic progress; the term retrogression would be more apt.[135]

The positive example of Mexico and the negative one of Guatemala, and many other countries as well, suggest that those concerned with Latin American economic development and social modernization might best devote themselves to an analysis of the conditions for revolutionary transformation of class relationships, particularly at the current stage of development in the rural areas. Presumably the quickest way to initiate major changes in values is through (social) revolutions which remove those dominant strata which seek to maintain their position and traditional values. A recent study

---

[134] Manning Nash, "Social Prerequisites to Economic Growth in Latin America and Southeast Asia," *Economic Development and Cultural Change*, 12 (1964), 230; Pablo Gonzáles Casanova, *La Democracia en México* (México, D. F.: Ediciones ERA, 1965), p. 41. Clarence Senior, *Land Reform and Democracy* (Gainesville: University of Florida Press, 1958).

[135] Nash, *op. cit.*, pp. 231, 232–233. See also Frank Brandenburg, "A Contribution to the Theory of Entrepreneurship and Economic Development: The Case of Mexico," *Inter-American Economic Affairs*, 16 (Winter 1962), 3–23.

of sociological changes in Mexico concludes that in the new middle class

> there is evidence that the Revolution, by reducing the level of affluence and power of *cacique* families and by redistributing hacienda lands, has had a considerable psychological impact on the population in the direction of strengthening attitudes of independence and initiative and, conversely, reducing those of submissiveness.[136]

Analyses of the ways in which revolutions have fostered value change have pointed to how new regimes have sought to encourage economic development by changing the content of their education systems, not only in terms of more vocational education, but also through introducing achievement themes. In Mexico, through "the ideological values in Mexican socialism, achievement motivation was accorded a key position. . . ."

> The process of inculcating achievement values in 1939 through textbooks took at least two forms. First, the texts gave universalistic and achievement values to the workers' movement. All workers were equal; their individual progress and status within the movement depended on their own aggressiveness and accomplishment on the job. This value orientation served to break down the traditional emphasis placed on social immobility and status achievement by birth and blood, both ascriptive-based values. Secondly, a high value was placed on the very activity of hard effective work, where men got their trousers dirty and their hands callused. Work was a noble and honorable endeavor in life. These achievement values were to be absorbed by the children who read how the son idolized his hard-working father. Later, in 1959 . . . in the field of education, the central idea presented to the child was the need to study, to excel, and to improve one's intellectual self. Related to the progress of education and to achievement was the stress placed upon developing personal discipline and a sense of responsibility.[137]

The educational system of Communist China has similarly exerted strong pressure on very young children for individual

---

[136] Glade, *op. cit.*, p. 43.

[137] Walter Raymond Duncan, *Education and Ideology: An Approach to Mexican Political Development with Special Emphasis on Urban Primary Education* (unpublished Ph.D. thesis, Fletcher School of Law and Diplomacy, 1964), 167, 204–205.

competitive achievement.[138] The teaching materials used in Chinese kindergartens in stories, songs, and games "reveal a highly sophisticated program of training conducive to individual achievement motivation."[139] These are apparently designed consciously to break down the "noncompetitive, group-oriented environment based on compatible relationships" fostered by the traditional pre-Communist family.

David McClelland has analyzed the emphases on achievement in Chinese education as reflected in the content of children's readers for "three Chinas," the Republican era of 1920–1929, Taiwan during 1950–1959, and Communist China for the same period. The stories of the 1920's showed a very low concern for achievement. The achievement emphases are markedly higher in Taiwan and Communist China, with the latter showing China "for the first time . . . above the world average."

> The predominantly U. S. influence on Taiwan has increased the amount of achievement concern in stories used there, but not as decisively as among the Communists on the Mainland. The quantitative data are supported even more strongly by qualitative analysis of the stories themselves. For instance the achievement concern in the Taiwanese stories is largely concentrated in tales of Western heroes—e.g., Magellan, Alexander Graham Bell, George Washington—whereas on the Mainland it saturates stories dealing with local and indigenous Chinese heroes.[140]

Data from various other nations undergoing ideological revolutions suggest similar conclusions. Thus the analysis of the content of children's readers in 1950 as compared with 1925 indicates that a "wave of high n Achievement . . . is common in newly independent countries."[141] This finding supports the earlier generalization that the "old" underdeveloped states of Latin America are at a disadvantage compared

---

[138] John Wilson Lewis, "Party Cadres in Communist China," in James S. Coleman, *op. cit.*, p. 425; see also Richard H. Solomon, "Educational Themes in China's Changing Culture," *The China Quarterly*, No. 22 (April–June 1965), 154–170.

[139] Lewis, *op. cit.*, p. 425.

[140] David McClelland, "Motivational Patterns in Southeast Asia with Special Reference to the Chinese Case," *Journal of Social Issues*, 19 (1963), 12–13.

[141] *Ibid.*, p. 10.

to the "new" ones of Asia and Africa in seeking political consensus for anti-traditional values. Analysis of Russian children's stories in 1925 and 1950 also reveals a considerable increase in achievement themes between the two periods. And case studies of post-World War II Russian defectors "strongly suggest that n Achievement may be higher in individuals brought up wholly under the Soviet system since the Revolution than in an earlier generation."[142] A comparison of the actual n Achievement test scores of a sample of factory managers and of professionals in the United States, Italy, Turkey, and Communist Poland also suggests the positive inpact of Communist ideology on such orientations. The achievement orientation scores of the Poles were close to those of the Americans, and both were much higher than the Italians or Turks.[143]

EDUCATION AND THE MOTIVATION FOR
INNOVATING ENTREPRENEURIAL ELITES

Although revolution may be the most dramatic and certainly the most drastic method of changing values and institutions which appear to be inhibiting modernization, the available evidence would suggest that reforms in the educational system which can be initiated with a minimum of political resistance may have some positive consequences. Changes in the educational system may affect values directly through the incorporation of modern values to which students are exposed; indirectly they may help to modify the occupational structure by both increasing the numbers trained for various "modern" professions and helping to increase the status of positions needed in a developing economy. Clearly the way in which nations conceive of elite status may affect the supply of talent available for leadership in economic development. Thus, a high evaluation of occupations associated with traditional sources of status—the land, the military, humanistic intellectual occupations, and the free professions—tends to direct talent into occupations which do not contribute much to

---

[142] McClelland, *The Achieving Society*, pp. 412–413.
[143] *Ibid.*, pp. 262, 288.

industrial development. And in cultures with such occupational values, the children of the successful entrepreneurs of lowly, often foreign, origin frequently go to university to find means of entering the learned professions, politics, the arts, or similar occupations. Such behavior is likely to reduce both the talent and capital available for entrepreneurial expansion.

To analyze the value system inherent in university structures in detail would take us considerably beyond the limits of this discussion. A detailed effort to do just this by Michio Nagai, Japan's leading educational sociologist, argues that the values of higher education are in fact achievement orientation, universalism, and functional specificity, among others. Nagai derives the need for these value orientations in the university from a consideration of the requirements for genuine scholarly creativity. Universities which do not stress these values cannot be oriented toward the attainment of scholarly goals, and cannot protect themselves from outside interference with academic freedom.[144] There have been, of course, many universities, particularly in Latin America, which have not adhered to these values. Links with politics or religion have involved diffuse role obligations in which faculty have not been free to teach or publish findings in violation of the ideologies of groups of which they are a part. Ascriptive appointive, admission, or grading policies have sometimes reduced the adequacy of educational institutions as trainers of innovative elites motivated to achieve within a competitive system. But one may suggest that the more the universities of Latin America or other parts of the underdeveloped world are absorbed into the international world of scholarship, the more likely they are to reflect the values of this reference group in their internal systems, and to teach these to their students.

There is, of course, no simple relationship between the values of modern science and the way universities or even industrial concerns and government agencies operate in different countries. The Japanese system illustrates a formula

[144] Michio Nagai, *The Problem of Indoctrination: As Viewed from Sociological and Philosophical Bases* (Ph.D. Thesis: Department of Sociology, Ohio State University, 1952, multilith), pp. 36–39 and *passim*.

whereby a "modern" nation may maintain particularistic and ascriptive traits while also developing rigidly universalistic and competitive patterns which guarantee the recruitment of talent into elite positions.

Members of various Japanese organizations—business, academic, or governmental—are given particularistic protection once they are admitted to membership. There is little competition for promotion or salary increases; men move up largely by seniority. Similarly, within the school and university system, little competitive grading occurs; almost everyone is promoted and graduated. And the graduates of various elite institutions are accorded almost "ascriptive" rights by others, e.g., leading business firms and government bureaus tend to hire most of their executive trainees from a few select universities, much as they have done for decades.

Universalism enters into the Japanese educational and business systems at two stages, first at admission to university, and second at entrance into the lower rungs of business or government executive ladders. The entrance examinations for Japanese universities are completely competitive; admission is solely a function of how well the students do on them, and many children of university professors, politicians, and the wealthy do not qualify for admission to the prestigious universities. Before admission, no one has any special claim to be accepted. Once admitted, however, grades do not serve as an important basis for future selection. While a prospective employer may not learn much about a student from his grades, he can be fairly certain that almost any graduate of Tokyo, Kyoto, Waseda, and other high-quality universities will be among the very top group in the country in general intelligence, and in ability to benefit from higher education. And as a further guarantee of quality there is another impersonal level of competition; job applicants must often take examinations as a precondition for civil service or business employment.

The Japanese system, therefore, permits particularism to operate in every personal relationship, while recruiting in a manner designed to ensure that the elite will be both highly motivated in achievement terms and well qualified. A teacher will not fail a student—i.e., someone with whom he has a personal relationship—nor will an employer or supervisor subject a subordinate to a humiliating lack of confidence. But the competitive entrance examinations, in which the examiners judge people with whom they have no personal relationship or obligation, meet the requirements of both particularistic and universalistic values.

It is significant that other industrialized societies which have emphasized ascription and particularism have also worked out means to handle the dilemma. In Britain, entrance to university has not been difficult until recently, but final grading has been handled on a completely universalistic basis. Examiners from other universities are always involved in awarding final examination grades to assure that local faculty do not give special preference to their own students. And the grade which a graduate receives—first- or second-class honors, or lower—or, often more importantly, the status of his school (Oxbridge or not), remains with him as one of the major attributes which defines his place in government, business, and other institutions for the rest of his life. In France there is universalistic competition in receiving grades and in being admitted to elite schools at various levels.

Conversely, it may be pointed out that a society which strongly emphasizes universalism and achievement in its values may permit a great deal of particularism and ascription. Political patronage has continued in America to a greater degree than in many more particularistic European nations; nepotism may be found in industry; influence and family background may affect admission policies to universities, e.g., the children of alumni and faculty are often given preference over those with better records even in some of the best universities. It may be suggested that where a society has strong norms which fulfill certain basic requirements of the system, it does not need explicit rules. North Americans will yield to particularistic obligations, but within self-imposed limits, to avoid harming the institution by helping incompetents. Hence the very emphasis on achievement and universalism in the North American value system would seem to reduce the need for the kind of rigidly universalistic examination system which exists in Japan, where all the normative pressure is in the direction of particularism. And North American institutions are much less inhibited about dismissing students or employees for lack of ability.

Thus it would appear that modernizing societies require either strong values or rules sustaining achievement and universalism. *They need not reject their traditional value system if they can work out mechanisms to guarantee that a large section of the elite will be composed of men who are highly motivated and able to achieve.* However, much of Latin America and some other nations in the less developed parts of the world have not succeeded in doing either. Men from privileged backgrounds may be admitted to university, take courses in which it is easy to pass and get a degree, and then secure a high position on the basis of whom they know, or through family ties. These countries have not yet found mechanisms to associate talent with elite status. And those reformist student movements which resist making admission and examination standards more rigorous are, in effect, helping to maintain the traditional order.

There is, of course, considerable pressure on many Latin American state universities to change because of the increasing numbers of applicants. Today, in some countries, large numbers fail to qualify for university entrance.[145] However, the entrance examinations have been subject to severe criticism in many countries for being biased in favor of those educated traditionally in private schools.[146]

An admissions system which is biased against the children of the less well to do also discourages enrollment in courses leading to "modern" vocations as distinct from the traditional elite ones. Studies of occupational choices of university students indicate that the career aspirations of the less well to do resemble those of youth from minority ethnic backgrounds. They are both more likely to seek to achieve through studying subjects such as business, engineering, or practical sciences. The source of the class bias in recruitment to Latin American universities is not solely, or even primarily, in the preference given to those whose pre-university training is in traditional subjects. Rather, it lies in the fact that the road to university graduation requires a relatively high family income.

---

[145] Benjamin, *op. cit.*, pp. 67–71, 97–99, 123–127, 148–153.
[146] Bowles, *op. cit.*, pp. 147–152.

And in poor countries, where most families have no possible economic reserve, they will not be able to sustain their children through the higher levels of schooling. In Latin America, about two-thirds of all secondary school students attend private schools which charge fees, a factor which undoubtedly operates to increase class discrimination. As compared even to other underdeveloped regions, Latin America has done little to "identify and encourage able students . . . to provide programmes for part-time students, although it is known that a sizeable proportion of the students in higher education support themselves through employment, and there is no programme for external or correspondence students. Perhaps most important of all, the number of students who receive financial assistance must be discounted as negligible."[147] This situation, of course, means that the overwhelming majority of students at Latin American universities are from quite privileged backgrounds.[148] The distribution of class backgrounds may become more rather than less discriminatory in the future, if higher education does not expand rapidly. For greater selectivity brought about by a more rapid increase in demand than in places available will increase the relative advantage of those from well-to-do, culturally privileged homes, who can prepare for admission examinations after having attended good private schools, or having private examination tutors.[149]

Evidence that a deliberate policy to encourage students to take modern rather than traditional subjects can work in Latin America has been presented by Risieri Frondizi, former rector of the University of Buenos Aires, who reports that the initiation of "a program of fellowships, offered only in fields like science and technology," cut the number studying law in half within three years, while the modern subjects gained greatly.[150]

The rulers of Meiji Japan have provided an excellent ex-

---

[147] *Ibid.*, p. 148.

[148] Burns, *op. cit.*, pp. 230–238; Kalman H. Silvert, "The University Student," in Johnson, *op. cit.*, pp. 207–210.

[149] Havighurst and Moreira, *op. cit.*, pp. 104–105.

[150] Risieri Frondizi, "Presentation," in Council on Higher Education in the Americas, *National Development and the University* (New York: Institute of International Education, 1965), p. 30.

ample of the way in which a development-oriented elite consciously used the educational system both to provide the needed cadre of trained and highly motivated people and to enhance the status of those occupations needed for modernization. Shortly after the restoration, technical "education was introduced at the university and middle-school levels, and it covered a broad range of theoretical science and practical instruction in agriculture, trade, banking, and, above all, industrial technology."[151] In addition to the various government schools in these fields, Japanese businessmen helped start private universities such as Keio and Hitotsubashi, designed to train for executive business positions students who could absorb the norms of modern business rationality as part of their education.[152]

Another major problem of Latin American universities is the curricula and status orientations of students which encourage vast numbers to work for degrees in subjects which are not needed in large quantity. Educational policy often encourages such maladjustments by making it much easier to secure a degree in subjects such as law or the humanities rather than the sciences or engineering. Clearly it is an implicit policy decision to pass students in the former fields for less and easier work than in the latter, a decision which says, in effect, "We will overtrain and overencourage a section of our youth to aspire to occupational roles which are overcrowded and which do not contribute to social and economic modernization." Malcolm Kerr's comment about such policies in Egypt applies to many underdeveloped countries:

> The passively accepted assumption is that in these fields, where tuition fees are very low and nothing tangible is sacrificed by increasing the attendance at lectures, freedom of opportunity should be the rule. In reality, of course, a great deal is sacrificed, for not only does the quality of education drop, but a serious social problem is made worse, and thousands of students beginning their secondary schooling continue to be encouraged to aim for the universities rather than for the secondary technical education which would be more useful to themselves and to the economic progress of the country.[153]

[151] Hirschmeier, *op. cit.,* pp. 127, 128–131.
[152] *Ibid.,* pp. 164–171.
[153] Malcolm H. Kerr, "Egypt," in Coleman, *op. cit.,* pp. 190–191.

These comments are clearly relevant in judging how education, particularly higher education, supports the elite in contributing to political stability and economic growth. First, as Arthur Lewis has suggested, there is some reason to suspect that the status concomitants linked to education per se should vary with the proportion and absolute size of the population that is educated. A relatively small higher educational establishment will encourage the retention, or even development, of diffuse elitist values among university graduates, while if a large proportion of the university-age population attends school, the pressures should be in the opposite direction.[154] In much of Latin America, university students almost automatically "become part of the elite. It matters little whether a student is the son of a minister or the son of a workman. His mere enrollment at the university makes him one of the two per thousand most privileged in the land."[155] Conversely, in the United States, with its mass educational system, few university graduates may expect to attain high status; many of them will hold relatively low positions in nonmanual work; and a certain number will even be employed in manual occupations. Where comparatively few attend university, as in Britain, graduates who fail to achieve a status comparable to most of their fellow graduates will feel discontented; their reference group will be a higher successful group. The same analysis may be made with regard to the different implications of education for status concerns in the Philippines as contrasted with Senegal. A Filipino who attends the massive University of the Far East must know that few of his fellow students can expect an elite position; Senegalese students, like many in Latin America, however, know that among their classmates are the future economic and political leaders of the country.

A related consequence of increase in the numbers who attain higher levels of education should be an increase in the amount of high-achievement orientation in a nation. Studies of the occupational goals of college students in nations with

---

[154] For a discussion of the consequences of moving from a small elite system to mass higher education in Japan, see Herbert Passin, "Modernization and the Japanese Intellectual: Some Comparative Observations," in Jansen, *op. cit.*, pp. 478–481.

[155] Atcon, *op. cit.*, p. 16.

tiny systems of higher education suggest that the large majority of them expect positions in government work.[156] Since some form of white-collar employment must be the goal of college and secondary students, a sharp increase in their numbers should make talent available for a variety of technical and entrepreneurial roles. As Tumin and Feldman have indicated:

> From the point of view of a theory of stratification, education is the main dissolver of barriers to social mobility. Education opens up the class structure and keeps it fluid, permitting considerably more circulation through class positions than would otherwise be possible. Education, further, yields attitudes and skills relevant to economic development and such development, in turn, allows further opportunity for persons at lower ranks.[157]

The thesis that sees positive effects from the expansion of universities has been countered by these arguments: a transfer of educational techniques from developed to underdeveloped societies sometimes results in dysfunctional efforts at innovation; an "overexpansion" of educational resources may create a frustrated, and hence politically dangerous, stratum whose political activities undermine the conditions for growth; the "educated" often develop diffuse elitist status and cultural sustenance demands so they refuse to work in the rural or otherwise "backward" parts of their country; the educated often resist doing anything which resembles manual employment; and rapid educational expansion results in many being poorly educated, while reducing the opportunities available to the small minority of really bright students.[158]

There is no doubt, of course, that the rapid expansion of an educational system may result in an oversupply of persons with relatively high expectations of employment, salary, and

[156] See K. A. Busia, "Education and Social Mobility in Economically Underdeveloped Countries," *Transactions of the Third World of Congress of Sociology,* Vol. V (London: International Sociological Association, 1956), pp. 81–89.

[157] Melvin Tumin with Arnold S. Feldman, *Social Class and Social Change in Puerto Rico* (Princeton: Princeton University Press, 1961), p. 7.

[158] H. Myint, "Education and Economic Development," *Social and Economic Studies,* 14 (1965), 8–20.

status. The increase in the numbers of educated people in a developing economy necessarily means that as education becomes less scarce it should command less status and income. The process of adjusting expanded levels of higher education to reduced rewards is obviously a difficult one, and often results in political unrest. And as Arthur Lewis has pointed out, "upper classes based on land or capital have always favoured restricting the supply of education to absorptive capacity, because they know the political dangers of having a surplus of educated persons."[159] One must, however, separate the problem of the possible political consequences of educational expansion from the economic ones. As Lewis indicates,

> as the premium for education falls, the market for the educated may widen enormously. . . . The educated lower their sights, and employers raise their requirements. . . . As a result of this process an economy can ultimately absorb any number of educated persons. . . . One ought to produce more educated people than can be absorbed at current prices, because the alteration in current prices which this forces is a necessary part of the process of economic development.[160]

The argument against expansion is largely political rather than economic, and calls for a detailed examination of the sociological consequences. Mexico affords an example of the way in which economic growth and emphases on new values may reduce the tensions inherent in rapid educational expansion. William Glade contends that although the educated were often frustrated in pre-revolutionary Mexico, "the more or less steady expansion of the private sector activity since the mid-1920's" has meant a continuing demand for trained persons. "Secondly . . . with the over-all expansion of the social, economic, and political structure there came a widening range of socially approved channels for the realization of achievement."[161]

[159] W. Arthur Lewis, "Priorities for Educational Expansion," O.E.C.D., p. 37.
[160] *Ibid.*, pp. 37–38.
[161] Glade, *op. cit.*, pp. 44–46; for my discussions of the conditions which affect student participation in various forms of politics see S. M. Lipset, "University Students and Politics in Underdeveloped

To sum up the discussion of universities, the expansion of the educational system is of unquestioned benefit in providing the requisite skills, aspirations, and values essential to modern occupational roles. Not only expansion is required but the content of education should also be broadened. Specifically, education should be directed toward inculcating innovative orientations and teaching problem-solving techniques in all fields of knowledge. This would mean emphasizing and rewarding creative and independent effort on the part of students. The problem suggested earlier of the potentially disruptive political consequences of overproduction of university graduates would presumably be reduced if expansion is accompanied by a modernizing of the educational system. Underemployed graduates with modern, innovative orientations are perhaps less likely to seek traditional political solutions to their plight, and more prone to look for other possible avenues toward achievement.

Proposals such as expansion and curricula change are easy to make but difficult to put into practice. Proposals to transform radically and to expand the educational system would meet, first of all, the opposition of present elites who are identified to some extent with the present system, and see such changes as a threat. Considerable innovative skill may have to be applied to overcome such opposition.

The conclusion to this discussion of education also brings us full circle to a recognition of the need to change class relationships in order to foster a change in values. Governments and parties which are deliberately concerned with the need to change values must also seek for ways to foster the rise of new occupational strata to status and power, and the reduction of the privileged position of old power groups, such as the land-linked traditional oligarchies who have little interest in economic growth, social modernization, expanded opportunities for talent, or democracy and equality.

Countries," in S. M. Lipset (ed.), *Student Politics* (New York: Basic Books, Inc., 1967), pp. 3–53, and S. M. Lipset, "Student Politics in Comparative Perspective," in S. M. Lipset and Philip Altbach (eds.), *Students in Revolt* (Boston: Beacon Press, paperback, 1970), pp. xv–xxxiv; and my chapters, 1–4, in S. M. Lipset and Gerald Schaflander, *Passion and Politics* (Boston: Little-Brown, in press, 1971).

The following chapter continues the effort to show how variations in values affect behavior through an examination of the differences in the structure and activities of Jewish communities.

CHAPTER 4

The American Jewish Community in a Comparative Context

Most research on Jewish communities around the world tends to investigate the "Jewishness" of such communities, and to ask to what extent given communities are assimilating or retaining their "Jewishness." Such a point of view may be justified from a religious orientation; that is, one may ask to what extent certain basic tenets and practices of a given form of Judaism are being followed in any community. But from an intellectual perspective it is difficult to defend the position that the study of the Jews should be organized around the maintenance or decline of "Jewishness." Rather, any effort to develop a systematic study of Jewish communities must be developed in a comparative context. It is impossible to study the sources of variation in the beliefs and practices of comparable subgroups in different countries without a conceptual framework and methodology which dictates a systematic comparison of the larger societies to which these groups belong.

Some years ago in a comparative discussion of Jewish communities published in *Commentary*, Milton Himmelfarb attempted to revive Heine's Law as a methodological guide to such investigations. Heinrich Heine suggested over a century ago that the only way one could understand the variations

in the behavior of Jews in different countries was by seeing
these differences as adaptations to the dominant behavior patterns within the Gentile community. There is much evidence
for this view. Thus British Jewry has a structure somewhat
like that of the dominant, high-status Church of England;
the Chief Rabbi roughly corresponds to the Archbishop of
Canterbury. Upper-class Gentile Englishmen are formally, at
least, orthodox; they adhere to the traditional Anglican Creed
and practice; nonconformist Protestantism has been lower-
status in England. In the United States the dominant form of
Christianity is congregationalist in organization and "liberal"
in theology. And American Jewry, including orthodoxy, is also
congregationalist in its religious structure. It is true that American Jews attend synagogue less than the entirety of American
Protestants attends church. However, well-educated Protestants do not go to church as frequently as less-educated ones.
I would guess that a comparison of American Jews with
socially and intellectually comparable Protestants would reveal
that the Jews are, in fact, similar in their religious involvement. Similar logic may be applied to the situation in France.
There, the Jewish religious organization resembles that of the
Catholic Church; it is "Episcopal." However, the French
Gentile community has been divided historically between a
clerical segment, traditionally anti-Semitic, and an anti-clerical
part, favorable toward Jewish rights. The Jews have been
placed by French history in the anti-clerical, or, if you will,
non-Catholic community, a community which regards all
religious adherence as outmoded. Hence, French Jewry also
has been extremely irreligious; in effect, most native-born
French Jews have behaved religiously like the rest of the non-
Catholic half of France. (The large Argentinian Jewish community closely resembles the French in these respects.)
Rather than give further general impressionistic comparisons
of this type, I would like to illustrate my general methodological thesis with a discussion of the Americanism of the
American Jewish community, for which there is ample
evidence.

Many have pointed to the lack of centralized organization
within the American Jewish community as a source of weakness. Rabbi Mordecai Kaplan has presented the Reconstruc-

tionist proposal for the creation of a *kehilla,* a formal community structure such as once existed in eastern Europe, which would be built around the community centers. The eminent sociologist Robert MacIver, in his famous Report on Jewish organizations made at their behest, also called for more community integration, for greater co-operation, for the merger of organizations performing similar functions, and other integrative measures. Both Kaplan and MacIver, however, were thereby asking American Jews to do something which other Americans refuse to do. The emphasis on achievement, on competition, on individualism, stressed by foreign observers from Tocqueville and Martineau in the first half of the nineteenth century down to recent visitors, affects organizations as it does individuals. Competitive pluralism has characterized associational life within many "communities" in America. Competition and lack of systematic co-operation is also typical of the American Negro community. More than two decades ago the sociologists Edward Shils and Morris Janowitz concluded their analysis of American fascist groups with the comment that these groups did not constitute an effective threat because of the inability to get together. The factionalism and lack of party discipline of American political parties which so astonishes Europeans is but another example of the same general phenomenon. In a sense, these behavior patterns may be considered as examples of one of the dominant value emphases in American culture, that of self-orientation as distinct from and stronger than collectivity orientation, to use one of Talcott Parsons' pattern-variables discussed in the previous chapters. And the American emphases on self-orientation and achievement are in turn related to the stress on equality. As Tocqueville well noted, when one thoroughly destroys aristocratic privileges and values, one opens "the door to universal competition." To urge the American Jewish community to return to, or to adopt, a community structure derivative from the much more elitist society of Europe is to ignore the interrelationships between subgroup systems and the social system of the larger society.

The various religions in America also reflect the values and pattern of organization of the larger society. Even the Catholic Church with its centralization of theological authority in Rome has been unable to avoid conforming. In the late nineteenth century Pope Leo XIII publicly complained about heretical tendencies within the American Church. He was concerned about the preoccupation with materialistic and Puritanical values. Most recently, the French Dominican R. L. Bruckberger has contended that American Catholics resemble American Baptists or Presbyterians more than they do Mexican or Italian Catholics.[1] In *The First New Nation* I report in some detail on the similarities in descriptions and analyses of American religion made from the early nineteenth century down to the present by foreign visitors, both lay and clerical.[2] Almost without exception, such commentators have noted that every American with whom they talked had a religious affiliation, belonged to or supported some denomination. But almost as common is the observation that Americans were reluctant to discuss the content of their own religion or to recommend its advantages to others. The standard American attitude for over a century and a half seems to have been that all religious affiliations and beliefs are good.

Fundamentalist or orthodox true believers have argued that such an attitude reflects a basic secularization of religion, that American religion has no effect on behavior, that it is merely a weekly conventional ritual. I question this conclusion. In a multi-religious nation, in which no denomination comes close to having a majority of the population among its members, and in which many social situations—school, work, politics—bring together men of differing religions, a general consensus that religious affiliations are irrelevant to other relationships is essential. Even when men believe strongly in their own faith—and there is much evidence that most Americans do so believe—they must be willing to accept the convention that the secular and religious spheres of life are separate, for the sake of an integrated society. This does not, however, conflict with the generally accepted and broadly asserted value, for man and society, of religion in general. One may even urge Americans to fulfill those moral obliga-

[1] See R. L. Bruckberger, trans. C. G. Paulding and V. Peterson, *Image of America* (London: Longman's, Green, 1960).

[2] S. M. Lipset, *The First New Nation* (Garden City: Doubleday-Anchor, 1968), chapter 4.

tions based on religious tenets. But such obligations must necessarily be restricted to the limited area of "Golden Rule" morality in which all agree. The alternatives to such a public and common religious creed are limited to those of a national religion with almost universal adherence, intense religious controversy, or a large, often majority, segment of nonbelievers, the situation most common in present-day Europe. Compared to Jews in most of present-day Europe, American Jews are much more likely to belong to and attend a synagogue, much as American Protestants and Catholics have a higher rate of church attendance than their European coreligionists. It should also be noted that despite greater freedom and opportunity to join the majority culture, American Jewry has had a lower rate of inter-marriage than western European Jews. Thus, American religious communities are properly described as irreligious only in contrast to the orthodoxy inherited by Christians and Jews alike from medieval Europe.

The pattern of shearing away ancient rituals characteristic of various religions in the process of their adaptation to modern America is not a recent phenomenon. In *American Judaism* Nathan Glazer recalls[3] that at the founding of Hebrew Union College in 1883 (perceived at that time not as the theological seminary of a distinct Reform movement but simply as an academy to train rabbis), shrimp (a non-Kosher food) was served at an opening ceremonial dinner. Almost all the rabbis present remained and only two or three objected and walked out. The tendency to ignore ritual, already dominant in the large community (over a quarter of a million Jews) of the 1880's, was reversed as a result of the mass migration of orthodox Jews from eastern Europe between 1890 and the First World War. The renewed power of orthodox religion simply reflected the export of the religious culture of the Pale to America. It is thus not surprising that with the emergence of an American Jewry, composed increasingly of the native-born, the forces which modified religious ritual before the mass immigration have reasserted themselves.

[3] Nathan Glazer, *American Judaism* (Chicago: University of Chicago Press, 1957), p. 57.

If we turn to the widely observed tendency of American Jews, as individuals, to obtain higher education and to shift from self-employed business occupations to the more intellectually prestigious though financially less rewarding salaried professions, especially academic and nonacademic scientific and culturally creative positions, we see here also a reflection of the predominant national value pattern. An increasing proportion of Americans, currently close to 40 per cent of the college-age population, enter institutions of higher learning. Almost 90 per cent of those from higher-status professional and business managerial families do so. Studies of the backgrounds of college students majoring in different subjects reveal that the liberal arts, the more intellectually oriented areas of university education, tend to recruit students from higher-status background, while the more vocational subjects, such as engineering, business, and education (for elementary and secondary school teaching), draw heavily from the upwardly mobile, those of working-class or lower-status ethnic background. The propensity of American Jews to send their children to universities, and the increasing trend of the offspring of well-to-do businessmen and independent professionals to study subjects leading to a creative intellectual or scientific career, rather than to enter the family business, reflects a pattern common among non-Jew as well. A study by *Fortune* magazine of the way of life of the leading executives in the automobile industry in the early 1960's reported that this group of highly paid leaders of a major American industry, many of whom were of relatively lowly origin, typically boasted to one another about the intellectual accomplishments of their children as nuclear physicists, writers, and academics. The group, almost totally non-Jewish, included many who reported to the *Fortune* interviewer that they were proud of their earning enough to help their $8,000-a-year academic or research scientist son make his way in the world. Thus the children of the well-to-do New York Jewish clothing manufacturer and the Protestant midwestern vice-president of General Motors appear to have similiar aspirations and attainments. By the end of the decade the college student scions of the upper-middle class liberal Protestants and Jews were working together as leftist student activists, a phenomenon discussed in Chapter 10.

The intellectual achievements of American Jews in the university and elsewhere have sometimes been contrasted with the lesser achievements of English Jewry. Here again, the reduced academic orientation of Jews in Britain reflects the values of the larger society. In the late 1950's only 4 per cent of university-age English youth entered a university. By 1970, even if one includes, as one should, the various other non-university institutions and types of training in Britain which are contained within universities and colleges in the U.S., the total proportion entering higher education would still be under 15 per cent in contrast to close to 45 per cent in America. In 1957, only 13 per cent of the children of men in professional and managerial positions entered British universities, a great contrast with the nearly unanimous pursuit of higher education among those from the same strata in America. And while the large majority of leading English business executives still have not attended a university, a 1957 study indicates that 87 per cent of top executives in 287 major American companies held a Bachelor's degree, and 32 per cent had attained one or more advanced graduate degrees.[4] A study of the most important leaders in American business and governmental life reports that as a group they have much more formal education than the average college graduate.[5] The differences in British and American values and attitude toward education affect not only the Jews of both countries, the bulk of whom are but two generations away from Jewish communities in eastern Europe; they also have sharply affected educational orientations in the liberated colonies of Britain and America. Few have noticed that the two major former American colonies, the Philippines and Puerto Rico, have as large a college population proportionate to the relevant age group as any country in western Europe. Former British colonies, including Jamaica, a Caribbean island somewhat comparable in population to Puerto Rico, and Malaya, whose indigenous

[4] See F. C. Pierson *et al.*, *Education of American Businessmen: A Study of University—College Programs in Business Administration* (New York: McGraw-Hill, 1959).

[5] W. Bell, *et al.*, *Public Leadership* (San Francisco: Chandler, 1961).

population is of similar ethnic stock to the Philippines, have fewer than one per cent of the college age group in institutions of higher learning. America's Jews, like the residents of America's former colonies, reflect in their behavior the national belief that everyone should attend college. And, conversely, groups in Britain or those outside who have absorbed British educational values behave correspondingly. (Of course, in rough comparisons of this kind, one must ignore differences of standard: a British-type undergraduate education differs markedly from one on the American model. But here I am concerned less with quality than with aspirations and social consequences.) It should be noted, of course, that Britain is gradually changing in its educational structure in the process of becoming more equalitarian, and that English Jews like English Gentiles are showing increasing interest in higher education and in thus widening the base of support of creative intellectual and scientific endeavors.

While I have stressed the extent to which the American Jew reflects American society, some sociologists, such as Robert Park and Nathan Glazer, have even argued that the Jews are the *most* American of all groups in the nation, that they exhibit the predominant American traits in a more integrated fashion than any other group. Park, who is one of the major founding figures in American sociology, urged more than forty years ago that courses on the history, culture, and behavior of the American Jews should be included as a *required* part of the curriculum of all American high schools, that by studying the American Jews in detail, Americans of all backgrounds could learn to understand their nation and themselves.[6] Glazer has argued that Jews everywhere are more sensitive to trends in the larger society than are others, and, being completely free in America to choose their modes of behavior, they often anticipate the general patterns of the future. Robert Park, who I think would have agreed with Glazer, urged, too, that American social scientists should take as a major topic for research the study of the Jews.

Park's two recommendations, courses on Jewish culture and history and intensive social science analysis of Jewish

[6] Robert Park, *Race and Culture* (Glencoe, Illinois: The Free Press, 1950).

behavior, were not adopted. The first, of course, was never seriously discussed, while the failure of the second is worthy of detailed investigation as part of the sociology of knowledge. Gentile social scientists, while revealing a considerable fascination with Jewish life, have, I think, avoided studying the Jews precisely because of the large number of Jews in their fields. Sustained contact with Jews suggests to them, I suspect, that Jewish social scientists would do a better job of understanding the Jewish community than an outsider. But, in fact, with relatively few exceptions, Jewish social scientists with a general reputation in their discipline have also abstained from writing about American Jews. Ely Ginsberg of Columbia and Daniel Bell and Nathan Glazer of Harvard are the major exceptions which come to mind, and only the latter has actually engaged in a major scholarly work on the subject.[7] (Parenthetically, it may be noted that as far as I know, David Mandelbaum of Berkeley is the only Jewish American anthropologist who has ever written professionally about Jewish communities abroad—other than those in Israel.) The failure of Jewish social scientists to engage in research on the Jews reflects their desire to be perceived as American rather than Jewish intellectuals. To write in depth about the Jewish community would seemingly expose them to being identified as "Jewish Jews," as individuals who are too preoccupied with an ethnic identity, and who lack the universalistic orientation prized by social scientists and American intellectuals generally. The strength of this attitude among Jewish intellectuals as a group is demonstrated by the comments in a *Commentary* symposium published in 1961.[8] The editors of *Commentary* asked about fifty young Jewish intellectuals (almost all under thirty-five), many of whom were already prominent, to comment on their attitudes toward being a Jew and to things Jewish. The standard reply of almost all who answered was that they did not see what there was to comment about. They were American Jews, but they felt that the fact of their

---

[7] I am ignoring the excellent work done by men employed by Jewish institutions, and by those with specific appointments to posts on Jewish topics, e.g. Jewish History, Near Eastern Languages, Yiddish Literature, etc.

[8] "Jewishness and the Younger Intellectuals: A Symposium," *Commentary*, 31 (April 1961).

ethnic or religious background had little to do with their roles
as creative intellectuals. It is fairly obvious that these men and
women must have had little insight if they really believed this.
The fact that they espouse such a conception is, however,
what is significant for the purposes of this discussion. American Jewish intellectuals want to receive recognition as individuals, and thus far the larger society has encouraged them
in this aspiration. How much this behavior reflects a capitula-
tion to assimilationist pressures, to a desire to escape from
Jewishness in any form, and how much it is an adaptation
to the general American convention that each person can
and should remain identified with his religious background,
with the stricture that such differences should not affect relations in secular roles, remain a topic for future investigation
(if anyone is interested in such a study).

To understand the American Jew, it is necessary to be sen-
sitized to factors in American life which used to be discussed
in Marxist circles as the problem of "American exceptionalism." Given the absence of a Socialist movement in America,
the limited character of working-class consciousness, the
equalitarian social relationships, and the gap in living standards between the American lower strata and those elsewhere,
a frequent topic of discussion was whether the analyses and
political tactics fostered by Marxists in other capitalist nations
were appropriate to the United States. And, of course, most
American Jews, including a majority of those belonging to
Zionist organizations, seem to believe that the conditions
which bred major anti-Semitic movements in other nations do
not exist in the United States, that "American exceptionalism"
applies to anti-Semitism as well as to socialism. I have dealt
with the sources of various special American characteristics
in *The First New Nation,* and in the previous chapters. I
should like, however, to iterate two key factors which are
particularly relevant to any understanding of the way in
which America responds to Jews. Most visible as a special
variable is the role of immigration in forming the United
States. No other nation has as many religions and ethnic
groups whose presence is accepted as a permanent part of the
society. In contrast, the Latin American countries have been
predominantly Catholic; the English speaking parts of the

Commonwealth are composed largely of descendants of immigrants from the British Isles. For well over a century the United States has sustained a national ideology which defined efforts to emphasize ethnic-religious differences as un-American. The frequent "nativist" and anti-Catholic movements, which derived much of their strength from the Protestant rural and urban poor, had to be put down by the authority structure.[9] Thus, unlike the situation of Jews elsewhere, those in America were never defined as the largest visible out-group, as one which differed in basic traits from the overwhelming majority. In the United States Jews have been but one of a very large number of religious-ethnic groups, many of whom were subject to some antagonism and discrimination from those who arrived earlier. In Poland, in France, in Germany, and in other parts of Europe, anti-Semitism has traditionally been the one most important, often almost the only, historic source of internal group prejudice. It has existed in the United States, but as one of many competing prejudices, much less salient on the whole than prejudice against Negroes, Orientals, Catholics, and whichever is the most recent group of impoverished slum-dwelling immigrants, such as Puerto Ricans in New York. Studies of the major post-war right-wing extremist leaders and movements indicate no propensity among their supporters to be anti-Semitic. Those who believe in conspiratorial theories of politics, such as the belief that Communists control key segments of the American government, do not appear to translate their paranoid beliefs into generalizations about the Jews.[10]

From a long-run perspective on the situation of the Jew, perhaps a more important factor than the impact of diverse immigrant groups is the predominant value system. As, noted in Chapter 2, many commentators on American values (Louis Hartz, Clinton Rossiter, and others) have urged the predominant political tradition with which America, as a nation, is identified is a liberal or left-wing one. An American Socialist writer, Leon Samson, seeking during the depths of the Great

[9] S. M. Lipset and Earl Raab, *The Politics of Unreason: Right-Wing Extremism in the United States, 1790–1970* (New York: Harper and Row, 1970).
[10] See Daniel Bell, ed., *The Radical Right* (New York: Doubleday, 1963) and Lipset and Raab, *op. cit.*, chapters 6–10.

Depression of the 1930's to explain why efforts to build Socialist movements made such little headway, argued convincingly that socialism as an ideology faced the problem of
competing with Americanism, a political ideology whose *values* concerning the good society were similar to those of socialism. Samson compared the writings of prominent American
conservatives and businessmen on the nature of preferred
social relations with those of leading Marxists, from Marx on
down. And he reported that, property relations excepted (the
economic content of Socialism), the Marxists and the American conservatives agreed in describing the good society as one
which stresses equality of interpersonal relations and of
opportunity which urges the necessity for hard, efficient work,
and which judges each man by his work, not his origins.[11]

The orientations toward men and groups stemming from
equalitarian values and the structure of a society composed
of many ethnic-religious groups, have given American Jews
opportunities for acceptance as individuals such as have never
existed in any predominantly Gentile society in history. The
Jew can be part of American society in a way that has never
been true elsewhere. And this real access, combined with
the sensitivity to others resulting from a long history as an
out-group minority in other societies, enables the Jew to become, as Park and Glazer suggested, the most American of
Americans. I do not want to imply, of course, that there are
no basic differences between Jews and other groups, since
these persist even when one compares Jews and non-Jews
with similar sociological characteristics. A variety of evidence
suggests that the intellectual orientation of Jews is greater than
that of non-Jews. No other American ethnic-religious group
has been as successfully upward-mobile as the Jews. Sociological studies have indicated that Jews differ from various Christian groups on a variety of morality issues, from a relatively
low rate of divorce to attitudes toward different types of law
violations.[12] All studies of Jewish political attitudes and behavior agree that they are far more liberal and even radical

[11] See L. Samson, *Toward a United Front: A Philosophy for American Workers* (New York: Farrar and Rinehart, 1933).
[12] See G. Lenski, *The Religious Factor* (Garden City: Doubleday,
1961), pp. 148 ff.

on most issues than are others with comparable socio-economic status.[13]

The one group of social scientists who have studied Jews systematically are those working on the problem of alcoholism. They are fascinated by the fact that Jews have a much lower rate of alcoholism than any other major ethnic-religious group.[14] Jews show different patterns of spending than others at the same level of income. They contribute more to charitable causes; they spend more on the "good life" for themselves and their families than do Protestants at the same income level.[15] The combination of a positive attitude toward intellectual activities, relatively greater wealth, and propensity to contribute to worthy causes mean that in many cities Jews play a disproportionately important role in supporting major cultural institutions, both as contributors and consumers.[16]

If these comments have any theme, it is that the comparative study of the Jew must be linked inseparably with the comparative study of the Gentile. To focus on the study of the Jews or any other people or religious group alone is wrong methodologically and will result in erroneous conclusions.

The next section, Part III, shifts to a more theoretical level in an effort to suggest the basic determinants of political conflicts in both underdeveloped and industrial societies.

[13] See Lawrence Fuchs, *The Political Behavior of American Jews* (Glencoe, Illinois: The Free Press, 1954), and references and discussion in Chapter 10 of this book.

[14] See C. R. Snyder, *Alcohol and the Jews, a Cultural Study of Drinking and Sobriety* (Glencoe, Illinois: The Free Press, 1958).

[15] See Marshall Sklare, ed., *The Jews: Social Patterns of an American Group* (Glencoe: Illinois, The Free Press, 1958).

[16] John Gunther, *Inside U.S.A.* (New York: Harper & Brothers, 1951).

PART III

SOCIAL STRATIFICATION AND POLITICS

.

CHAPTER 5

Issues in Social Class Analysis

Concern with social class and social stratification is as old as social thought. The ancient Greek philosophers were extremely conscious of the effects of stratification, and propositions about stratification may be found throughout many of the writings of Aristotle and Plato. Thus Aristotle, in discussing the conditions for different types of political organization, suggested in essence that constitutional government—limitation on the powers of the political elite—is most likely to be found in societies with large middle classes, while city-states characterized by large lower classes and small middle and upper classes would be more likely to be governed as dictatorships based on mass support, or as oligarchies. This general approach has been elaborated in contemporary studies of the social requisites of democracy. Plato, in the *Republic*, discussed the conditions for a genuine equalitarian communist society and suggested that the family is the key support of inequality—that is, of social stratification. His argument,

Reprinted with the permission of the Publisher from "Social Class" in David Sills (ed.), *International Encyclopedia of the Social Sciences* (New York: The Macmillan Company & The Free Press, 1968), XV, 296–316. Copyright © 1968 by Crowell Collier and Macmillan, Inc.

which is still followed by many contemporary sociologists, was that individuals are motivated to secure for other family members, for whom they feel affection, any privileges that they themselves enjoy. Hence, in every society there is a built-in pressure to institutionalize inequality by making it hereditary. Plato argued that the only way to create a communist society would be to take children away from their parents and to have the state raise them, so as to eliminate the tendency toward inherited social privilege.

Most of contemporary sociological theory and research on social class, however, does not stem from the Greeks. The emphasis of the Enlightenment on the possibility of social laws and of their discovery through observation and comparative study must be taken as one of the principal methodological breakthroughs. Institutional regularities, such as those governing class, status, and political relationships, became objects of disinterested inquiry as things in themselves, thus reversing the notion, dominant in the Middle Ages, that the temporal sphere was nothing more than an auxiliary part of a supernatural plan, subject to the principles of natural law.

The Enlightenment served to erase the assumptions about hierarchy, class, and intergroup relationships that stemmed from the medieval model of an organic Christian civilization. Thus, the basis was being laid for a science of society.

But it was Karl Marx, more than anyone else, who carried this scientific perspective into the study of social class, even going so far as to derive his idea of class from what he called the scientific laws of history. He then not only accepted the premise that social phenomena possess their own laws, but also set out to discover the underlying variables and how they are expressed under differing historical conditions. Thus, if one were to award the title of father of the study of social class to any individual, it would have to be to Marx. He made class the central aspect of his analysis of society and of his theory of social change. Though most latter-day sociologists have disagreed with many, if not most, of Marx's assumptions about stratification, many of the non-Marxist or anti-Marxist ideas on the subject have come about in reaction to Marx's original formulations.

This does not mean, of course, that there were not other

important eighteenth-century and nineteenth-century figures who used stratification concepts in a sophisticated manner. Marx obviously was a child of his times; many of his ideas, sometimes in almost identical form, can be found in the writings of others. The Marxist formulation, laid down in the chapter "Social Classes" in *Capital*,[1] that there are three major economic classes in modern society—landlords receiving rent, capitalists profit, and workers wages—is derived directly from Ricardo's *Principles*, published in 1817, a work that also presented the labor theory of value.[2] Adam Smith's great book, *The Wealth of Nations*, is an important work for the study of stratification, as are other writings of the school of Scottish philosophers of his day.[3] The American founding fathers contended that all complex societies are stratified and that there is an inherent basis of conflict among groups with diverse economic and class interests. Various American Marxist groups have, in fact, sought to legitimate Marxist doctrine as compatible with classic American thought by pointing to the similarities between the ideas presented in No. 10 of *The Federalist* and various writings of Marx.[4] However, these precursors of Marxism influenced sociology primarily through their influence on Marx himself. It was he who formulated the theory of class so powerfully that he defined the terms of the argument for later sociological thinkers.

TYPES OF THEORETICAL APPROACH

Approaches to the fact of social inequality have differed in the extent to which they emphasize change or stability in social systems. These differences in theoretical orientation have to a considerable extent reflected political differences. Reformists or radicals have seen reactions against social inequality and social class differences as sources of social

[1] Karl Marx, *Capital*, III (Moscow: Foreign Languages Publishing House, 1962), 862–863.
[2] David Ricardo, *Principles* (New York: E. P. Dutton & Co., Inc., 1937).
[3] Adam Smith, *The Wealth of Nations* (London: Methuen & Co., 1930).
[4] Daniel de Leon, *James Madison and Karl Marx* (New York: New York Labor News Co., 1932).

change, which they are inclined to favor. Theorists with more conservative political tastes have justified aspects of the existing order by trying to show the functions performed by hierarchy in all social systems. Concern with social change has generally been associated with interest in social classes, that is, groups within stratified collectivities that are said to act politically as agents of change. Those stressing the functional basis of inequality have been interested in social stratification and in the purposes served by differential rewards, particularly in prestige, for various positions in social systems.

Those using the concept of social class to interpret the dynamics of social change have assumed that the creation of new occupational or economic roles has often resulted in the emergence of groups that initially were outside the traditional hierarchical system. As these new groups attempt to stabilize their position within society, they come into conflict with older, privileged strata whose status, economic resources, or power they challenge. The new groups also often develop sets of values, both secular and religious, that enhance their position by undermining the stability of the prior value system and the structure of privilege it justified. Thus historical change is viewed basically as a consequence of the rise of new classes and the downfall of old ones; it is assumed that complex social systems are inherently unstable and that conflicts stemming from inequality cause pressure for changes in the system.

In contrast, functional theorists have assumed that social systems must be treated as if they were in equilibrium. From this point of view, it is necessary to relate the various attributes of the social hierarchy to the conditions for social stability. Class, therefore, has been seen by these theorists not as an intervening variable in the process of social change but, rather, as a set of institutions that provide some of the conditions necessary for the operation of a complex society. These conditions, basically, amount to the need for a system of differentiated rewards as a means of institutionalizing the division of labor: differentiation by status and income is posited as a necessary part of the system of motivation required to place individuals in the various positions that must be filled if society is to operate.

The interest of students of social change in why men rebel, why they want change, has led to an emphasis within the tradition of class analysis on the way in which inequality frustrates men and leads them to reject the *status quo*. Functional analysts, on the other hand, are much more concerned with how the social system gets men to conform, to seek and remain in various positions in society, including ones that are poorly rewarded or require onerous work. The former, in other words, often ask how systems of stratification are undermined; the latter seek to know how and why they hold together.

It is important to note that while any analysis of social class must necessarily deal with social stratification as well, these two terms are not synonymous. Theories of social class refer to the conditions affecting the existence of strata that have developed or should develop some "consciousness of kind," that is, some sense of existence as a group attribute of society. Stratification refers to the entire complex of hierarchical differentiation, whether group-related or not. Although this discussion is about social class, much of the analysis in it will involve stratification, since it is impossible to account for the way in which social classes are formed, change, and affect other aspects of society without referring to stratification systems as such.

I have distinguished two polar traditions of social thought that do not, of course, occur in pure form in real life. Marx, the foremost student of class and social change and the advocate, par excellence, of instability and revolution, was also aware of the functional aspects of social stratification. Many of his writings attempt to show how ideologies, values, and patterns of behavior—all at different class levels—serve to maintain the stability of the social order. In fact, Marxian analysis is replete with functional propositions.

The functionalists, on the other hand, are of course aware that change and conflict occur and that men not only accept but also reject the given stratification system. Thus (as is noted in more detail below) the most influential stimulator of functional thought in sociology, Émile Durkheim, sought to show the way in which strains in value emphases within the same system lead individuals and groups to reject the dominant value system and to deviate from expected forms of behavior. Where Marx saw alienation as inherent in social inequality, Durkheim suggested that anomie, or rulelessness, is endemic in all complex social systems.

To see the way these concerns with stability and change, with alienation, and with the formation of class sentiments have evolved in modern social thought, it is necessary to turn to an examination of the work of some of the key theorists, particularly Marx, Weber, and Durkheim.

THE MARXIST THEORY OF CLASS

Marxist sociology starts from the premise that the primary function of social organization is the satisfaction of basic human needs—food, clothing, and shelter. Hence, the productive system is the nucleus around which other elements of society are organized. Contemporary sociology has reversed this emphasis by stressing the distribution system, the stratification components of which are status and prestige. To Marx, however, distribution is a dependent function of production.

Stemming from the assumption of the primacy of production is the Marxist definition of class: any aggregate of persons who play the same part in the production mechanism. Marx, in *Capital,* outlined three main classes, differentiated according to relations to the means of production: (1) *capitalists,* or owners of the means of production; (2) *workers,* or all those who are employed by others; (3) *landowners,* who in Marx's theory seemingly differ from capitalists and are regarded as survivors of feudalism.[5] From Marx's various historical writings, it is clear that he had a more complex view than this of the hierarchical reality and that he realized, for instance, that there is differentiation within each of these basic categories. Thus, the small businessmen, or petty bourgeoisie, were perceived as a transitional class, a group that will be pressed by economic tendencies inherent in capitalism to bifurcate into those who descend to the working class and those who so improve their circumstances that they become significant capitalists.

[5] Marx, *op. cit.*

Although Marx differentiated classes in objective terms, his primary interest was in understanding and facilitating the emergence of class consciousness among the depressed strata. He wished to see created among them a sense of identical class interests, as a basis for conflict with the dominant class. The fact that a group held a number of objective characteristics in common but did not have the means of reaching organized class consciousness meant for Marx that it could not play the role of a historically significant class. Thus, he noted in "The Eighteenth Brumaire of Louis Bonaparte" that the French peasants of that period possessed many attributes that implied a common class situation:

> The small-holding peasants form a vast mass, the members of which live in similar conditions, but without entering into manifold relations with one another. Their mode of production isolates them from one another, instead of bringing them into mutual intercourse. The isolation is increased by France's bad means of communication and by the poverty of the peasants. . . . In so far as millions of families live under economic conditions of existence that separate their mode of life, their interests and their culture from those of other classes, and put them in hostile opposition to the latter, they form a class. In so far as there is merely a local interconnection among these small-holding peasants, and the identity of their interests begets no community, no national bond and no political organization among them, they do not form a class.[6]

Nikolai Bukharin, one of the leading theoreticians of the Russian Communist party, who was more concerned with sociological theory and research than any other major Marxist figure, attempted to formalize the differences among the workers, the peasants, and the lumpenproletariat (unattached laborers), making the workers a class and the other two not classes. His analysis, based on the events of the early decades of the twentieth century, was elaborated beyond that of Marx.

The working class is exploited by a visible common oppressor, is brought together by conditions of work that encourage the spread of ideas and organization among them,

[6] Karl Marx, "The Eighteenth Brumaire of Louis Napoleon," in Marx, *Selected Works*, I (Moscow: Foreign Languages Publishing House, 1962), 334.

and remains in a structured conflict situation with its employers over wages and working conditions. Consequently, over time it can become a conscious class.

Table 4–1.

BUKHARIN'S ANALYSIS OF CLASS CONDITIONS

Class properties	Peasantry	Lumpen-proletariat	Proletariat
1. Economic exploitation	+	−	+
2. Political oppression	+	+	+
3. Poverty	+	+	+
4. Productivity	+	−	+
5. Freedom from private property	−	+	+
6. Condition of union in production, and common labor	−	−	+

Source: N. Bukharin, *Historical Materialism* (New York: Russell, 1965), p. 289.

Marx, however, did not expect there to be a high correlation between objective class position and subjective revolutionary class consciousness until the point at which the social system in question broke down: if there was to be total class consciousness in any given society, then by definition it would be in the midst of revolution. In normal times, structural factors press deprived strata to become conscious, but the inherent strength of the ruling class prevents class consciousness. The dominant class possesses social legitimacy, controls the media of communication, is supported by the various mechanisms of socialization and social control, such as the school and the church, and, during its period of stability is able to "buy off" those inclined to lead or participate in opposition movements. The Marxist term that characterizes the ideology of the lower class in the period of the predominance of the other classes is "false consciousness."

Marx was not very concerned with analyzing the behavior of the capitalist upper class. Basically, he assumed that the powerful parts of such a class must be self-conscious and that the state as a vehicle of power necessarily serves the interests of the dominant class in the long run. But more important to Marx than the sociology of the privileged class was that of the workers; the important question for research and action concerned the factors that would bring about working-class consciousness.

The dilemma of the Marxist theory of class is also the dilemma of every other single-variable theory. We can locate a class member objectively, but this may tell us little about the subjective correlates (social outlook, attitudes, etc.) of class position. Marx never actually said that at any given point in history or for any individual there would necessarily have to be a relationship between class position and the attitudes of class members. He did believe, however, that common conditions of existence create the necessary base for the development of common class attitudes, but that at any point in time, sharp discrepancies may exist between class position and class attitudes or behavior. Marx attempted to deal with this problem by his theory of transitional stages in the development of class. The first stage, in which a class is a class "in itself" (the German *an sich*), occurs when the class members do not understand their class position, the controls over them, or their "true class interests." The proletariat, as long as they are simply fighting for higher wages without recognizing that this is part of a necessary class struggle between themselves and the bourgeoisie that will end in the victory of one or the other, are a class *an sich*. In ideal-type terms the opposite of the class in itself is the class "for itself" (*für sich*). The class *für sich* is a self-conscious class, a large proportion of whose members consciously identify with it and think in terms of the class's struggle with another class. As long as most persons in a lower class think in *an sich* terms, the behavior of class members will be characterized by intraclass competition in which individual members of the class strive to get ahead of other members. In such a period, class conflict will be weak. Only when *für sich* attitudes develop does the class struggle really emerge. Members of a lower class who do not yet identify with their class are, according to Marx, thinking in terms of values or concepts that are functional for the stability of the position of the dominant class. Any individual, therefore, though objectively a member of the lower class, may subjectively be identified with or may be acting in ways which correspond to the position of another class. At different periods varying portions of an underprivileged population may be either *an sich* or *für sich*. One of the purposes of Marxist analysis is in the investigation of this discrepancy. In discussing the rise of the bourgeoisie, Marx suggested that the period during which the bourgeoisie was a class *an sich* was longer and required greater effort than the period during which it became self-conscious and took political class action to overthrow feudalism and monarchy.[7] Implicit in this discussion of the development of the bourgeois class is the idea that the emergence of self-consciousness among the workers will also take a long time. Marx in fact suggested "making a precise study of strikes, combinations and other forms of class activity" in order to find out how the proletariat organizes itself as a class.[8]

■ *Alienation.* A key element in the Marxist sociology of the exploited is the Hegelian concept of alienation. Men are distinguished from animals—are less animal and more human—insofar as they become increasingly self-conscious about and freely selective of their work and conditions of life. Insofar as men do not freely choose their work but, rather, do whatever tasks are set before them, simply in order to exist, they remain in a less than human state. If work (or leisure) is imposed on man, so far from being free, he is objectively exploited and alienated from the truly human, that is, autonomous, condition.[9]

Alienation, for Marx, is an objective, not a subjective, condition. It signifies lack of autonomy, of self-control. The fact that workers may say that they like their work or social conditions does not mean that they are free actors, even if they think they are. Thus, in a slave society the fact that some slaves may have believed that they preferred to be slaves, and even that they were better off as slaves than as freed men, did not change the fact that objectively they were slaves. Similarly, the fact that a wage worker likes his conditions of work does not affect his position of being alienated and economically exploited or his potential as a free human being. In this

[7] Karl Marx, *The Poverty of Philosophy* (New York: International Publishers, 1963), pp. 146–147.
[8] *Ibid.,* p. 147.
[9] Karl Marx, *Early Writings* (New York: McGraw-Hill, 1964), pp. 120–134.

sense, class society is akin to slavery. Class society must produce alienated individuals who are distorted, partial people. Marx therefore sought to document the facts about alienation and to understand the conditions under which estrangement, resentment, and, ultimately, political class consciousness would arise. Both class and alienation, he thought, would be eliminated by ending the private ownership of the means of production, for as long as people are working for others, they do not have conscious control over their life space and therefore are not truly human. Fully human society would come about when the production system could produce abundance in an absolute sense, when the machines produced enough food, clothing, and shelter for all men, to have as much as they needed, so that they could then devote themselves not to fighting over the scarce fruits of production but to fostering the activities of the mind. In essence, he was arguing that all class societies were pre-human and that class must disappear.

THE WEBERIAN APPROACH TO STRATIFICATION

While Marx placed almost exclusive emphasis on economic factors as determinants of social class, Weber suggested that economic interests should be seen as a special case of the larger category of "values," which included many things that are neither economic nor interests in the ordinary sense of the term. For Weber, the Marxist model, although a source of fruitful hypotheses, was too simple to handle the complexity of stratification. He therefore sought to differentiate among the various sources of hierarchical differentiation and potential cleavage. The two most important sets of hierarchies for Weber were class and status.[10]

■ *Class.* Weber reserved the concept of class for economically determined stratification. He defined a class as being composed of people who have life chances in common, as determined by their power to dispose of goods and skills for the sake of income. Property is a class asset, but it is not

[10] Max Weber, *Essays in Sociology* (New York: Oxford University Press, 1946), pp. 180–195. Edited by H. H. Gerth and C. W. Mills.

the only criterion of class. For Weber, the crucial aspect of a class situation is, ultimately, the market situation.

The existence of large groups of people who can be located in a common class situation need not produce communal or societal action—that is, conscious, interest-determined activity —although it should produce *similar* reactions in the sense that those in the same class situation should exhibit similar behavior and attitudes without having a sense of class consciousness. These similarities, such as patterns of voting behavior or of drinking habits, reflect the effect of variations in life chances among the classes.

Weber, like Marx, was concerned with the conditions under which class consciousness arises. For him, however, there was no single form of class consciousness. Rather, which groups develop a consciousness of common interest opposed to those of another group is a specific empirical question; different groups acquire historical significance at different times and in different places. The extent of consciousness of kind depends to a considerable degree on the general culture of a society, particularly the sets of intellectual ideas current within it. Concepts or values that might foster or inhibit the emergence of class-conscious groups cannot be derived solely from knowledge about the objective economic structure of a society. The existence of different strata subjected to variations in life chances does not necessarily lead to class action. The causal relationship posited by Marx between the fact of group inferiority and other aspects of the structure that might be changed by action had to be demonstrated to people; consciousness of it need not develop spontaneously. The presence or absence of such consciousness is not, of course, a fortuitous matter. The extent to which ideas emerge pointing to a causal relationship between class position and other social conditions is linked to the transparency of the relationship—that is, to how obvious it is that one class will benefit by action directed against another.

An examination of the history of class struggles suggested to Weber that conflicts between creditors and debtors are perhaps the most visible form of conflict flowing from economic differentiation. The conflict between employers and workers is also highly visible under capitalism, but it is essentially a special case of the economic struggle between buyers and sellers, a form of interest tension normal within a capitalist market economy. It involves an act of creative imagination and perception to develop an ideology that the tension between employer and worker requires an attack on the entire system of private ownership through the common action of all workers against the capitalist class. Such an act is much more likely to come from the intellectuals, who thereby present the workers with an ideological formula, than from the workers themselves. In this respect, Weber came to conclusions similar to those drawn by Lenin, who also argued that workers by themselves could only reach the stage of economism, of trade union consciousness—that is, of conflict with their employers over wages and working conditions. For Lenin, as for Weber, the emergence of revolutionary class consciousness requires leadership, much of which would be drawn from other strata—in Lenin's case, the elite or vanguard party.[11] Weber explicitly formalized the conditions that facilitate the emergence of class consciousness in terms that incorporated the principal elements of the Marxist scheme almost intact, although he made the significant and important addition of common status:

> Organized activity of class groups is favored by the following circumstances: (a) the possibility of concentrating on opponents where the immediate conflict of interests is vital. Thus workers organize against management and not against security holders who are the ones who really draw income without working. . . . (b) The existence of a class status which is typically similar for large masses of people. (c) The technical possibility of being easily brought together. This is particularly true where large numbers work together in a small area, as in the modern factory. (d) Leadership directed to readily understandable goals. Such goals are very generally imposed or at least are interpreted by persons, such as intelligentsia, who do not belong to the class in question.[12]

[11] V. I. Lenin, *What Is To Be Done?* (New York: International Publishers, 1929).

[12] Max Weber, *The Theory of Social and Economic Organization* (London: Routledge and Kegan Paul, 1947), pp. 427–428.

Weber's condition (a) is essentially a rephrasing of Marx's antagonism factor, though Weber made a distinction, not made by Marx, concerning the direction of the antagonism—in this case, toward the visible overseer. Condition (b) was never explicitly discussed by Marx. Condition (c) is borrowed directly from Marx. As for condition (d), in Marx's works it appears as the role of the party, although Marx never faced up to the problems that arise when a workers' party has a middle-class leadership.

▪ *Status.* The second major dimension of stratification, status, refers to the quality of perceived interaction. Status was defined by Weber as the positive or negative estimation of honor, or prestige, received by individuals or positions. Thus it involves the felt perceptions of people. Those in a similar status position tend to see themselves as located in a comparable position on the social hierarchy. Since status involves perception of how much one is valued by others, men value it more than economic gain.

Weber argued that since status is manifest, consciousness of kind is more likely to be linked to status differentiation than to class. In other words, those who are in a higher or lower status group are prone to support status-enhancing activities, whether or not these activities can be classed as political. Those groups with high status will be motivated to support values and institutions that seemingly serve to perpetuate their status. Weber regarded economic class as important primarily because it is perceived as a cause of status. Since it is usually easier to make or lose money than it is to gain or lose status, those in privileged status positions seek to dissociate status from class, that is, to urge that status reflects factors such as family origin, manners, education, and the like—attributes that are more difficult to attain or lose than economic wealth.

There is, of course, as Weber pointed out, a strong correlation between status and class positions. However, once a group has attained high status through given achievements, its members try to limit the chances that others will replace them. And this is often done by seeking to deny the original source of individual or family status. The economic and class orders are essentially universalistic and achievement-oriented.

Those who get, are. He who secures more money is more important than he who has less. The status order, on the other hand, tends to be particularistic and ascriptive. It involves the assumption that high status reflects aspects of the system that are unachievable. Thus it operates to inhibit social mobility, up or down. Weber, in his writings on status, echoed the functional analysis of the role of style presented by Veblen.[13] For Weber, as for Veblen, the function of conspicuous consumption—that is, of emphasis on pragmatically useless styles of consumption that take many years to learn—was to prevent mobility and to institutionalize the privileges of those who had risen to the top in previous years or epochs. Status groups are therefore identifiable by specific styles of life. Even though the original source of status was economic achievement, a status system, once in existence, operates independently of the class system and even seeks to negate its values. This, as Weber and Veblen both suggested, explains the seemingly surprising phenomenon that even to an industrial capitalist society, money-making is considered vulgar by many in privileged positions, and the children of those who have made money are frequently to be found in noncommercial activities.

■ *Class relations and status relations.* The distinction between class and status is also reflected in the different nature of the key set of interactions that characterizes each. Class relations are defined by interaction among unequals in a market situation; status is determined primarily by relations with equals, even though there are many status contacts among unequals. The sanctions, in the case of status, are greater when violating the norms for relations with equals than those for relations with unequals.

One value of differentiating between class and status is that while these two dimensions of stratification are correlated, there are many cases in which they are discrepant. Thus individuals or groups may be higher in status than in class, or vice versa. Weber argued that such discrepancies are important aids to understanding the dynamics of social change and of conflict; he detected an inherent strain between

[13] Thorstein Veblen, *The Theory of the Leisure Class* (New York: Modern Library, 1934).

the norms of the market and those of status systems. Markets are the dynamic source of tension for modern industrial society. Success or failure in the market constantly upsets the relative position of groups and individuals: groups high in status and wealth often lose their relative economic position because of market innovations, failure to adjust to change, and the like, while others rise suddenly on the scale of wealth. Those who had status and its frequent concomitant, legitimate access to political authority, exert their influence and power against the *nouveaux riches*. For example, a common interpretation of the behavior of the French bourgeoisie during the Revolution of 1789 is that they had not pressed for economic rights and power because they already possessed all they needed. Rather, they had wanted to force the monarchy and aristocracy to accord them high status. Similarly, Weber's disciple Robert Michels suggested that the political radicalism of many quite wealthy European Jews before World War I was a consequence of their having been denied a status position commensurate with their class level in society.[14]

■ *Social structure and political conflict.*   An industrial society characterized by an elaborate, highly institutionalized status structure *combined* with the class tensions usually found in industrial societies is more likely to exhibit class-conscious politics than is one in which status lines are imprecise and not formally recognized. It has therefore been argued that Marxist, class-conscious parties have been stronger in societies, like the Wilhelmine Germany in which Weber lived most of his life, that maintain a very visible and fairly rigid status system derived from preindustrial society than in class societies, such as the United States, that lack a feudal tradition of estates. Moreover, insofar as the dynamics of a successful industrial society undermine the ascriptive status mechanisms inherited from the feudal precapitalist order, the amount of political conflict arising from class consciousness is reduced. Hence it would seem to follow from Weber's analysis that the growth of industrial capitalism, and the con-

[14]Robert Michels, *Political Parties* (New York: Free Press Paperback, 1966), pp. 247–248. (This book was first published in 1911.)

sequent imposition on the stratification system of capitalism's emphases on achievement and universalism, weaken rather than increase class-linked consciousness of kind. This thesis of Weber's that stresses the consequences of structural changes on class relationships has been paralleled by T. H. Marshall's analysis of the relationship between citizenship and social class.[15] Citizenship, for Marshall, is a status that involves access to various rights and powers. In premodern times citizenship was limited to a small elite; social development in European states has consisted to a considerable extent in admitting new social strata—first the bourgeoisie and later the workers—to the status of citizen. The concept of the citizen that arose with the emergence of the bourgeoisie in the eighteenth century involved a claim to universalistic rights in the status order, as well as the political one. Marshall has suggested that class-conscious ideologies of the extreme sort are characteristic of new strata, such as the bourgeoisie or the working class, as they fight for the right to full social and political participation—that is, for citizenship. As long as they are denied citizenship, sizable segments of these classes endorse revolutionary ideologies. In turn, older strata and institutions seeking to preserve their ancient monopolies of power and status foster extreme conservative doctrines.

From this point of view, the history of political ideologies in democratic countries can be written in terms of the emergence of new social strata and their eventual integration into society and polity. In Europe, the struggle for such integration took the form of defining a place in the polity for the business strata and the working class alongside the preindustrial upper classes and the church. Unless class conflicts overlapped with continuing controversies concerning the place of religion, as they did in Latin Europe, or concerning the status of the traditional upper strata, as they did in Germany, intense ideological controversy declined soon after the new strata gained full citizenship rights.

■ *Power, status, and bureaucracy.*   Power, which in the Marxist analysis derives from class position, is a much more

[15] T. H. Marshall, *Class, Citizenship and Social Development* (Garden City: Doubleday-Anchor, 1965), pp. 71–134.

complex phenomenon in the Weberian model. Weber defined power as the chance of a man or group to realize their will even against the opposition of others. Power may be a function of resources possessed in the economic, status, and political systems; both status and class are power resources. Since men want higher status, they tend to try to orient their behavior to that approved by those with the higher status which they value. Power resources can also be found in institutions that command the allegiance of people—religions, parties, trade unions, and the like. Anyone with followers or, like the military, with control of force, may have access to power. In large measure, the relative weight of different power resources is determined by the rules of the political game, whatever these may be in different societies. The structure of legal authority and its degree of legitimacy influence the way in which power is secured.

For Weber, the key source of power in modern society is *not* to be found in the ownership of the means of production. Rather, the increased complexity of modern industrial society leads to the development of vast bureaucracies that become increasingly interconnected and interdependent. The modern state, with its monopoly of arms and administration, becomes the dominant institution in bureaucratized society. Because of the increasing complexity of operating modern social institutions, even economic institutions are brought into a close, dependent relationship with the administrative and military bureaucracies of the state. Increasingly, therefore, as all social institutions become more bureaucratized and the centralized state gains control of other social institutions, the key power resources become rigidly hierarchical large-scale bureaucracies.

■ *Bureaucratization and alienation.* This concern with bureaucracy as the key hierarchical power-related structure of the stratification system of industrial society (whether the society is formally capitalist or socialist is irrelevant) led Weber to formulate a source of alienation very different from that of Marx. For Weber, it was not only the wage worker who becomes alienated through his lack of control over his human needs; the bureaucrat is even more subject to obsessive demands. Bureaucracy, in fact, has an inherent tendency to destroy men's autonomy. It is characterized by formalism and it involves, in Weber's terms: (1) subordination; (2) expertise (and hence a rigid division of labor); (3) obeying fixed rules.[16] Even members of small, nonbureaucratic structures have their freedom reduced if these structures are involved with bureaucracies. In this conclusion, Weber agreed with Marx. However, for Weber the key depersonalizing element is the expectation that the bureaucrat will give absolute loyalty to the organization. Loyalty within a bureaucracy is impersonal; no personal attachments are supposed to interfere with the functioning of the system. Thus the depersonalization of loyalty became the equivalent of what Marx called the alienation of man from his labor. Weber argued that, as a social mechanism, bureaucracy assumes absolute discipline and a high level of predictability. People in bureaucracies fulfill role requirements rather than their personal desires. Rational action in bureaucracies is not an end in itself but, rather, an aspect of the structure of social interaction. Individuals both judge others and interact on the basis of universalistic norms; personal motives are not considered. The bureaucratic structure functions for its own ends, not those of the people within it. In theory, all individuals in bureaucracies are expendable and only positions are important.

Preparation for a bureaucratic career involves increasing conformity. Bureaucracy requires that individuals become highly specialized. Success depends on the individual's ability to conform. As one enters a bureaucracy, he loses much of his freedom to change his life alternatives. He becomes highly specialized and therefore cannot move from one firm or type of job to another. Such specialization, such conformity to narrow role requirements—to the needs of the "machine"—means dehumanization, or alienation from true human choice.

The alienation inherent in bureaucracy is, for Weber, independent of the system of property relations. Socialism means more rather than less alienation, because it involves greater bureaucratization. There is little difference between capitalist and socialist societies in their class relations and

---

[16] Weber, *Essays in Sociology*, pp. 196–198.

their propensity to alienation. The source of alienation lies in bureaucracy, which is inherent in industrial society.

The growth of bureaucratization also has the effect of separating work roles from other activities, with socially destructive consequences. An individual within a bureaucracy has to conform to efficiency rules, production standards, and other impersonal goals that have no meaning in his life outside work, since they are the bureaucracy's goals, not his; he conforms to them while at work, but gets no guidance as to how to behave in other activities. Weber can be interpreted as having believed that the nonbureaucratic part of life was becoming increasingly normless while bureaucratic structures were becoming increasingly normative. As social institutions become more bureaucratized, individuals learn how to behave within bureaucracies but not outside of them.

In a sense, Weber raised Marx's ideas about the nature and consequences of stratification to a higher order of generalization. Marx's conclusions were based mainly on his analysis of social relations under capitalism; this analysis presupposed a social system in which the fruits of production were scarce and control over the means of production was inequitably distributed. Weber, by using more general analytical categories, sought to deal with issues that cut through all complex social systems. Thus he characterized every complex system according to the distribution of economic and honorific life chances in it. While Marx stressed that social stratification is a result of economic scarcity, Weber emphasized that honor and prestige are themselves scarce: economic goods could increase, and everyone could gain in an absolute sense, but, since prestige is determined by relative ranking, if one went up, another went down. The latter form of stratification involves a zero-sum game, and consequently occasions continual tensions in any society with unrestricted social mobility.

Alienation also is presented as a broader category in Weber's work than in that of Marx. Basically, alienation from self involves compulsive conformity to norms: the alienated individual is role-bound. Since such compulsive conformity is inherent in bureaucracy, which Weber saw as the dynamic element in modern society, he was much more pessimistic about the future of society than was Marx.

Much of contemporary writing by intellectuals and social scientists about alienation is derived more from Weber than from Marx. For instance, the ideas advanced by Erich Fromm, David Riesman, William F. Whyte, Robert K. Merton, Arnold Green, and C. Wright Mills concerning the "bureaucratic," "marketeer," or "other-directed" personality, the "organization man," and, in general, the individual who seeks to get ahead by selling his personality, are all related to the effects of bureaucracy on individuals. Weber is the intellectual father of these and all similar discussions. His ideas, therefore, constitute not only a contribution to sociological analysis but also a basic source for the moral criticism of society. They usually have not been perceived as such because Weber's empirical conclusion, that all complex societies will be both stratified and alienative, leads to no positive moral solution. This is because for Weber (as for C. Wright Mills), the only society that really makes individual autonomy possible is the nonbureaucratized society of small producers, and societies of this type are rapidly vanishing.

FUNCTIONALIST APPROACHES

Although the ideas generated by Marx and Weber remain the most fruitful sources of theory on social stratification, much of contemporary sociology accepts the so-called functionalist approach to the subject. This approach is associated with the names of Émile Durkheim, Kingsley Davis, Talcott Parsons, and Robert K. Merton.

Durkheim and subsequent functionalists have assumed that since modern society has a complex and highly differentiated system of roles which must be performed, different men must be motivated to perform different roles.[17] They see man as a social animal whose needs are not primarily physical and satiable but, rather, culturally determined and potentially unlimited. However, if all individuals had the same set of unlimited desires, no complex social structure would be possible. Consequently, some social or moral force must shape

[17] Émile Durkheim, *The Division of Labor* (Glencoe, Ill.: The Free Press, 1947).

and limit these potentially unlimited desires. Society prescribes varying goals for different individuals and groups,
sets limits on these goals, and prescribes the means that may
legitimately be used to attain them.

In analyzing the function of stratification, functionalists
see it as the mechanism through which society encourages
men to seek to achieve the diverse positions necessary in a
complex social system. The vast variety of positions that must
be filled differ in their requirements for skill, education, intelligence, commitment to work, willingness to exercise power
resources against others, and the like. Functionalist theory
posits that in an unstratified society—that is, one in which
rewards are relatively equal for all tasks—those positions
which require more work, postponement of gratification,
greater anxiety, and the like will not be filled by the most able
people. The stratification system is perceived, therefore, as
a motivation system; it is society's mechanism for encouraging
the most able people to perform the most demanding roles
in order to have the society operate efficiently.

The theory also suggests that status—honorific prestige—is
the most general and persistent form of stratification because
what human beings as social animals most require to satisfy
their ego needs is recognition from others. Beyond a certain
point, economic rewards and power are valued, not for themselves, but because economic or power positions are symbolic
indicators of high status. Hence, the functionalist school of
stratification agrees with Weber that stratification, or differential hierarchical reward, is an inherent aspect of complex
society and that status as a source of motivation is inherently a scarce resource.

The emphasis in functional analysis on the need for hierarchical differentiation does not, of course, explain how men
evaluate different individuals in the stratification system. Parsons has pointed to three sets of characteristics which are
used as a basis of ranking. These are *possessions,* or those
attributes which people own; *qualities,* belonging to individuals and including traits that are ascribed, such as race, lineage, or sex, or that are attributed as permanent characteristics, such as a specific ability; and *performances,* or evaluations
of the ways in which individuals have fulfilled their roles—in

short, judgments about achievements. Societies, according to Parsons, vary considerably in the degree to which their central value systems emphasize possessions, qualities, or performances in locating people on the social hierarchy. Thus, ideally, a feudal social system stresses ascribed qualities, a capitalist society emphasizes possessions, and a pure communist system would assign prestige according to performance. Parsons has stated that no actual society has ever come close to any of these three "ideal-type" models; each society has included elements of all three. However, the variation in the core ideal values does inform the nature of the stratification system, patterns of mobility, and the like.[18]

If we assume, as most functionalists do, that the function of stratification is to act as a system of role allocation, then it follows that a key requisite for an operating social system is a relatively stable system of social rankings. That is, there must be consensus in a society about what sorts of activities and symbols are valued; without such consensus, the society could not operate. Given this assumption, an ongoing system of stratification requires a general set of ideological justifications. There must be various mechanisms which explain, justify, and propagate the system of inequality, and which cause men to accept as legitimate the fact of their own inequality. From an ideal-typical point of view, a system of stratification that is stable would set for various groups within societies goals that could be achieved by all within each group. Feudal societies, which theoretically separate the population from birth into distinct hierarchical strata which cannot be crossed, but within which men may succeed and gain social recognition for doing a good job, represent perhaps the extreme form of stratification as something that adjusts men to the needs of society. Theoretically, in a society in which individuals were socialized to accept attainable positions as the proper and necessary fulfillment of their role in life, men would feel "free" and satisfied. The sense of freedom, of being one's own master and of achieving what one thinks one wants to achieve, exists only where the means–ends relationship defined

[18] Talcott Parsons, "A Revised Analytical Approach to the Theory of Social Stratification," in R. Bendix and S. M. Lipset (eds.), *Class, Status and Power* (Glencoe, Ill.: The Free Press, 1953), pp. 92–128.

by society is stable—that is, where men do in fact get what they have been taught to want.

But it is extremely doubtful whether any such system of balanced means–ends relationships within a stratification system ever existed or could exist. The assumption that individuals seek to maximize the esteem in which they are held implies that those who are in low-valued positions are subject to punishment. To be valued negatively means to be told that one is no good, that one is bad. Consequently, it may be argued that there is an inherent tension between the need to maximize esteem and the requirements of a stratification system.

In actual stratification systems, this tension appears to be alleviated by various transvaluational mechanisms. That is, there seems in all societies to be a reverse stratification system, the most enduring form of which is usually found in religion. Inherent in many religions is the belief that wealth and power are associated with sin and evil, while virtue is associated with poverty. Christianity and Hinduism, for example, both posit that righteousness will somehow be rewarded in the hereafter, so that the virtuous poor will ultimately be able to look down upon the wicked rich. This mechanism, which holds out the hope of subsequent reward for adhering to the morality of the present, does not, of course, challenge the existing secular distribution of privilege. It does, however, reflect the inherent tension within stratified society: that there is both acceptance and rejection of the value system by the underprivileged.

■ *Durkheim and functionalist theory.*   Durkheim assumed that preindustrial society had been reasonably stable in that it had prescribed different sets of goals for different strata. He assumed that the lowly in feudal society had not resented not being high and that feudalism had been so organized that a man could and did obtain a sense of self-respect within his own group. Industrial society, he thought, is quite different. Society no longer provides the individual with definitions of means and ends that allow him to attain the goals his society defines as worthwhile. A highly integrated normative order such as feudalism had provided everyone with the possibility of feeling that his life was meaningful and successful within a given castelike stratum. In modern society, however, wealth and power become ends in themselves, and most people, unable to attain high prestige, find their own lives in conflict with social norms. Such conflict of norms leads to anomie, the breakdown of normative order, which becomes a chronic condition in industrial society.[19]

Industrial society prescribes universalistic goals in monetary or bureaucratic terms. Since the norms of the market place and the bureaucracy prescribe common orientations and similar goals for all, it is inevitable that many men will experience life as failure. For Durkheim, the weakness of the stratification system of industrial society is that, basically, it encourages only one set of values, those involving individual success. This pressure on the individual to achieve results produces anomie—Durkheim's equivalent of alienation. The higher rate of suicide in industrial as compared with traditional society was, in part, explained by Durkheim in these terms. The individual no longer has the sense of being socially integrated that was possible in a *Gemeinschaft* society, that is, one with a strong set of closely related means and ends linked to the religious system. The individual does not have the means to achieve the universalistic goals set by modern society, and the society's normative order does not support him in his daily life, guide his activities, or give him a sense that his life is worthwhile. When the normative structure collapses, when individuals lose their sense of being involved in meaningful means–ends relationships, many break down, engage in obsessive behavior, and lose their ability to relate to achievable goals, and some commit suicide.

The key to understanding Durkheim's contribution to the discussion of alienation and stratification is his emphasis on a stable society as a prerequisite for an integrated personality. The absence of an established harmony of means and ends, far from producing freedom, produces, according to Durkheim, resentment and apathy—the war of each against all. Durkheim's theory therefore leads to the ironic conclusion that people should feel freest in a closed, integrated system in

[19] Émile Durkheim, *Suicide* (Glencoe, Ill.: The Free Press, 1951), pp. 246–257.

which they have little choice of occupation or opportunity for social mobility, while in an open, universalistic system they should feel coerced, dehumanized, estranged. In the latter case it follows that they will also experience a need to, in Erich Fromm's words, "escape from freedom." Society's emphasis on success thus becomes the principal source of alienation.

Durkheim's analysis of anomie ties into Weber's discussion of the alienative properties of bureaucracy for, as Fromm, Merton, Riesman, and others have pointed out, to succeed in a bureaucratic society, one must not simply conform to a work role—one must sell one's personality to one's superiors. This implies that the rules for success are often very imprecise and hence create confusion about means and ends.

■ *Anomie, social change, and rebellion.* Durkheim's account of what Merton has called the "seeming contradictions between cultural goals and socially restricted access to these goals" is a key aspect of the theory of social change that is inherent in Durkheimian functionalism.[20] Since no complex society can achieve a complete balance between its emphases on ends and means, stratification systems always generate pressure on individuals and strata to deviate systematically from the cultural prescriptions of the society, and hence they foster social change. As Merton puts it:

> The distribution of statuses through competition must be so organized that positive incentives for adherence to status obligations are provided for *every position* within the distributive order. Otherwise, as will soon become plain, aberrant behavior ensues. It is, indeed, my central hypothesis that aberrant behavior may be regarded sociologically as a symptom of dissociation between culturally prescribed aspirations and socially structured avenues for realizing these aspirations.[21]

The outcome of the possible relations between approved goals and prescribed means has been analyzed in detail by Merton and by numerous other writers. These relations create

[20] Robert K. Merton, *Social Theory and Social Structure* (Glencoe, Ill.: The Free Press, 1957), p. 123.
[21] *Ibid.,* p. 134.

a variety of strains fostering change. Thus innovation in the means of getting ahead occurs among those who feel strongly the culturally prescribed mandate to succeed but lack such culturally approved means to do so as access to capital, skills, education, and proper ascribed background characteristics. Innovation may have positive and negative consequences from the point of view of society. On the positive side is the effort to get ahead by "building a better mousetrap," that is, by providing services that did not exist before, such as credit buying, which was first diffused by Jewish businessmen. On the negative side are the forms of innovation that are regarded as illegitimate. As Bell has pointed out, organized crime has constituted a major avenue of mobility in American life.[22] Minority ethnic groups and those of recent immigrant stock have contributed disproportionately to the ranks of professional criminals.

While Merton has elaborated on the sources of social and individual tensions in this area, more pertinent here is his emphasis that such tensions may also produce rebellion. Rebellion by the lower strata, he has argued, may be viewed as an adaptive response called for when the existing social system is seen as an obstacle to the satisfaction of legitimate needs and wants. In means—ends terms, rebellion involves the establishment of a new set of goals which are attractive to those who feel themselves "outcasts" in the existing system. When rebellion is not a generalized response but is limited to relatively powerless groups, it can lead to the formation of subgroups alienated from the rest of the community but united among themselves. Of course, rebellion may also take a political form in an effort to overthrow the existing society and replace it with one that stresses other values.

Emphasis on these and allied sources of rebellion advances the study of alienation and prospective lower-class rebellion beyond the concern with objective social inferiority and economic exploitation. The study of values in this context helps to explain the phenomenon that many quite poverty-stricken strata in different countries do not rebel and are often even

[22] Daniel Bell, *The End of Ideology* (Glencoe, Ill.: The Free Press, 1960), pp. 115–136.

conservative conformists, while other, relatively affluent strata, whose position is improving objectively, may provide the mass base for widespread rebellion.[23] It is clearly possible, under the means–ends formula, for a very lowly group to accept its place and income because it has achieved as much as it has been socialized to aspire to. Conversely, a much more well-to-do group whose aspiration levels have been raised sharply as a result of rapid urbanization, greater education, access to international media, recent involvement in industry, and exposure to the blandishments of unions and leftist political parties may experience the phenomenon of unlimited "rising expectations" and hence feel dissatisfied and prove receptive to a new myth which locates "the source of large-scale frustrations in the social structure and . . . portray[s] an alternative structure" that would be more satisfying.[24]

Functionalist sociology stresses the way in which stratification fulfills certain basic needs of complex social systems and so becomes one of the principal stabilizing mechanisms of complex societies. Like the Marxist and Weberian forms of analysis, it points to ways in which the demands of a stratification system press men to act against their own interests, and alienate them from autonomous choice. However, the focus in functionalism on means–ends relationships reveals the conflict-generating potential of stratification systems, in which goals are inherently scarce resources. Hence, functional analysis, like the other two, locates sources of consensus and cleavage in the hierarchical structures of society.

■ *Empirical studies.*   A considerable amount of the research on stratification by American sociologists has stemmed directly from functional analysis. Perhaps the most extensive single set of studies is contained in the many volumes by W. Lloyd Warner and his associates reporting on the "social class" (i.e., status) system of a number of American communities.[25] Warner, an anthropologist by training and originally a follower of Durkheim, argued that any effort to deal in

[23] Durkheim, *op. cit.*, p. 254.
[24] Merton, *op. cit.*, p. 156.
[25] W. L. Warner, J. O. Low, Paul S. Lunt, and Leo Srole, *Yankee City* (New Haven: Yale University Press, 1963).

functional terms with the social system of a modern community must relate many of the institutional and behavioral patterns of the community to the needs of the classes within them rather than to the larger system as such. Using the method of reputational analysis (asking people in the community to rank others and seeing who associated with whom as status equals), Warner located five or six social classes ranging from "upper-upper" to "lower-lower." Each of them was found to possess a number of distinct class characteristics, such as intrafamily behavior, associational memberships, and attitudes on a variety of issues. On the whole, Warner saw class divisions as contributing to social stability rather than to conflict, because the strata are separated into relatively distinct elements that have a more or less balanced and integrated culture. He interpreted his data as indicating that those in lower positions tend to respect those above them in the status hierarchy and to follow their lead on many issues. While most sociologists would agree with Warner concerning the existence of the sort of status groupings that he described (Weber presented a picture of American status relations in much the same terms), many would disagree with him concerning the degree of consensus within the system as to where individuals are located and would tend to agree more with Merton that tensions and conflicts are inherent in any hierarchical order. It is interesting to note, however, that while the various community studies of the accorded status system do suggest considerable ambivalence about where various individuals or families rank, particularly if they are not close to the very top or bottom of the system, investigations concerning the prestige rankings of occupations indicate considerable consensus both within and among a variety of nations.[26] The prestige studies would seem to be in line with the assumption of functionalist theory that consensus in the desirability of different occupational roles is necessary in order to motivate the most competent individuals to seek those positions which are valued most.

[26] Robert S. Hodge, Donald J. Treiman, and Peter H. Rossi, "A Comparative Study of Occupational Prestige," in R. Bendix and S. M. Lipset (eds.), *Class, Status, and Power: Social Stratification in Comparative Perspective* (New York: The Free Press, 1966), pp. 309–321.

■ *Criticism of the functionalist approach.* Functionalist theory has been sharply criticized by a number of sociologists who argue that while systems of widespread inequality characterize all existing complex societies, this fact does
not demonstrate that inequality is a social requisite for a
stable society, as many functionalists argue. Rather, these
critics urge that systems of stratification persist and take the
varying forms they do because the privileged strata have
power and are able to impose their group interests on the society. The greater rewards in income and status received by
various positions reflect greater power more than the need
to motivate individuals to secure them. The value systems
related to stratification therefore reflect the functional needs
of the dominant strata, not those of the social system as
such.[27] A Polish sociologist, Wlodzimierz Wesolowski, has
suggested that functionalist sociologists, particularly Davis
and Moore, who have written the most comprehensive contemporary statement of the functionalist position, are wrong
when they emphasize the need for stratification as a system
of motivation in the form of material advantage or prestige.[28] He has contended that there are alternative systems
of social organization that can sharply reduce inequality in
prestige and income while motivating people to seek higher
education and fill responsible positions. Hence, class differences that derive from such forms of inequality may decline
greatly. Wesolowski, however, agrees with the functionalists
that complex social systems will continue to be organized on
hierarchical lines, because systems of authority and command
are necessary. Men will continue to be divided between those
who occupy "positions of authority . . . who have the right
(and duty) to give orders while the others have the duty to
obey them." And he has noted that Friedrich Engels, Marx's

[27] Melvin Tumin, "Some Principles of Stratification: A Critical Analysis," in Bendix and Lipset, *op. cit.,* pp. 53–58; Walter Buckley, "Social
Stratification and the Functional Theory of Social Differentiation," in
S. M. Lipset and Neil Smelser (eds.), *Sociology: The Progress of a
Decade* (Englewood Cliffs, N. J.: Prentice-Hall, 1961), pp. 478–484.
[28] Wlodzimierz Wesolowski, "Some Notes on the Functional Theory
of Stratification," in Bendix and Lipset, *op. cit.,* pp. 64–69. Kingsley
Davis and Wilbert Moore, "Some Principles of Stratification," in Bendix
and Lipset, *op. cit.,* pp. 47–53.

closest intellectual collaborator, who "said that in a communist system the State as a weapon of class domination would wither away, nevertheless, declared that it would be impossible to think of any great modern industrial enterprise or of the organization of the future communist society without authority—or superiority—subordination relationships."[29]

Wesolowski agrees with the functionalists that stratification is inevitable because differentials in authority relationships, not variations in income or prestige, are necessary. As he puts it, "if there is any functional necessity for stratification, it is the necessity of stratification according to the criterion of authority and not according to the criterium of material advantage or prestige. Nor does the necessity of stratification derive from the need to induce people for the acquirement of qualifications, but from the very fact that humans live collectively."[30]

Wesolowski has presented in general terms a formulation very similar to that of the German sociologist Ralf Dahrendorf, who has tried to reformulate Marx's theoretical assumptions so as to deal more adequately with certain structural changes in Western society—especially those which have resulted in the divorce of ownership from management that is characteristic of the modern corporation.[31] Many have argued that this separation negates Marx, since it means the disappearance of the class of private capitalists as a powerful stratum. Dahrendorf, however, has suggested that the only significant difference this change makes is that it is now more meaningful to speak of the differential distribution of *authority* as the basis of class formation than it is to speak of the ownership of the means of production. It is differential access to authority positions and, therefore, to power and prestige that gives rise to contemporary class conflict, for those who are excluded from authority in "imperatively co-ordinated associations" (a term Dahrendorf borrowed from Weber) will be in conflict with those who have command over them.

[29] Wesolowski, *op. cit.*, p. 68.
[30] *Ibid.*, p. 69.
[31] Ralf Dahrendorf, *Class and Class Conflict in Industrial Society* (Stanford: Stanford University Press, 1959). See also Gerhard Lenski, *Power and Privilege* (New York: McGraw-Hill, 1966).

Articulation of manifest interest and organization of interest groups then become the dynamite for social-structural change.

■ *Functionalism and Marxism.*   In urging that the universality of stratification, or hierarchical differentiation— though not, it should be noted, of social class—is linked to the functional requirements for a power hierarchy, Wesolowski has built an interesting theoretical bridge between Marxist and functionalist sociology. For his and Dahrendorf's lines of reasoning ultimately are not greatly different from the functionalist approach to power presented by Parsons. The latter, of course, does not emphasize the theme of power as self-interested, which is found in the Marxian tradition, or that of coercion, which was stressed by Weber. Rather, Parsons has suggested that power—in his terms, the ability to mobilize resources necessary for the operation of the system—should be viewed in value-neutral terms, as follows. Inherent in the structure of complex society, especially in the division of labor, is the existence of authority roles, holders of which are obligated to initiate acts that are socially necessary. Most of the things done by those at the summits of organizations or societies are necessary. If individuals and groups are to achieve their goals within the division of labor, it must include a complex system of interactions. The more complex the system, Parsons has argued, the more dependent individuals are on others for the attainment of their goals, that is, the less free or powerful they are. And power is basically control over the allocation of resources and roles so as to make a given system operative. Power, under any system of values, resides in having what people desire, because they will obey for the sake of getting what they want. Finally, unless the capacity to organize the behavior of those in a system existed, sharply differentiated societies could not operate.[32]

It should be noted that there is a coincidence of the Marxist and functionalist approaches to political power. Both approaches view it as a social utility—as the means, par excellence, through which societies attain their objectives, including the expansion of available resources. Elite theories of power,

_____

[32] Talcott Parsons, "On the Concept of Political Power," in Bendix and Lipset, *op. cit.*, pp. 240–265.

on the other hand, see it in "zero-sum" terms, that is, they assume a fixed amount of power, so that the gain of one group or individual necessarily involves the loss of others. Two reviews of C. Wright Mills's analysis of the American power elite—one by a functionalist, Parsons, and the other by the student of stratification who, among leading American sociologists, stands closest to Marxism, Robert S. Lynd—criticized Mills for having a zero-sum game approach to power and for identifying it with domination.[33] That is, both Lynd and Parsons agreed that power should be viewed, both sociologically and politically, in the light of its positive functions as an agency of the general community and that it is erroneous to view power, as Mills did, solely or even primarily in terms of powerholders seeking to enhance their own interests.

There is, of course, a link with stratification theory in Parsons' analysis of power, since he has assumed that what people value most are economic advantage and esteem. It follows from this that those who possess the qualities which place them at the upper levels of the economic and status hierarchies also have the most power. Money and influence, Parsons has noted, are exchangeable for power, since power is the ability to mobilize resources through controlling the action of others.

THE DIMENSIONS OF STRATIFICATION

The foregoing discussion of the Marxist, Weberian, and functionalist approaches to social class analysis has distinguished a number of issues that continue to concern sociologists. Instead of moving toward one concept of social class, students of stratification have generally reacted to an awareness of the complexity of the subject by differentiating a large number of apparently relevant concepts, most of

[33] C. Wright Mills, *The Power Elite* (New York: Oxford University Press, 1956). Talcott Parsons, "The Distribution of Power in American Society," *World Politics*, 10 (1957), 123–143. Robert S. Lynd, "Power in the United States," *The Nation*, 182 (May 12, 1956), 408–411, and "Power in American Society as Resource and Problem," in Arthur Kornhauser (ed.), *Problems of Power in American Democracy* (Detroit: Wayne State University Press, 1957), pp. 1–45.

which are directly derivable from the three traditions discussed above. The differences in approach have, in large measure, reflected variations in the intellectual concerns of the scholars involved.

Contemporary students of stratification continue to be divided into two groups, those who urge that there is a single dimension underlying all stratification and those who believe that stratification may best be conceptualized as multidimensional. That is, they disagree as to whether economic class position, social status, power, income, and the like are related to one underlying factor in most societies, or whether they should be considered as distinct although related dimensions of the stratification system. To some degree this controversy may be perceived as a continuation on a more formal level of the differences between the approaches of Marx and Weber. However, some of those who uphold the single attribute position are far from being Marxists. They do not believe that position in the economic structure determines all other aspects of status; rather, they would argue that statistical analysis suggests the presence of a basic common factor. For analytic purposes, however, the controversy cannot be resolved by statistical manipulation, since some of those who favor a multidimensional approach would argue that even if it turns out that these various aspects of stratification do form part of a single latent attribute, there is enough variation among them to justify the need to analyze the cases in which individuals or groups are ranked higher on certain dimensions than on others.

If we assume, as most contemporary sociologists do, that stratification may most usefully be conceptualized in multidimensional terms, we are confronted with the variations in dimensions which various theorists emphasize. The dimensions they have suggested may be grouped into three categories: (1) *objective* status, or aspects of stratification that structure environments differently enough to evoke variations in behavior; (2) *accorded* status, or the prestige accorded to individuals and groups by others; (3) *subjective* status, or the personal sense of location within the social hierarchy felt by various individuals. These approaches in turn may be further broken down in terms of important variables, as follows.

■ *Objective class concepts.* Perhaps the most familiar component of objective status is power position within the economic structure. This is essentially Marx's criterion for class: persons are located according to their degree of control over the means of production. In the first analysis this serves to distinguish owners from employees. Owners, however, may vary in their degree of economic security and power, as large businessmen differ from small ones, and workers also may vary according to the bargaining power inherent in the relative scarcity of the skills they possess.

Another important concept in this area is extent of economic life chances. Weber perceived economic status not only in terms of ownership but also in terms of the probability of receiving a given economic return, or income. Thus an employee role, such as engineer or lawyer, which gave someone a higher probability than a small businessman's of earning high income, would place him in a higher class position. Essentially, this dimension refers to power in the market. Indeed, the simple difference in income received has been suggested as the best way to measure economic class.

Variation in the relative status of different occupations has also been seen as an important criterion for differentiating positions in the economic hierarchy. This approach has increasingly come to be used in studies of social mobility. Occupational prestige is, of course, a form of accorded status, except that what is being ranked are occupations, not individuals or groups.

Another aspect of stratification that is sometimes perceived as an objective one is power, which may be defined as the ability to affect the life chances of others, or conversely as the amount of freedom from control by others. Power may also be conceptualized as the set of probabilities that given role relationships will allow individuals to define their own will—that is, to impose their version of order even against the resistance of others. This dimension is extremely difficult to describe in operational terms: how, for instance, does one compare the different amounts and types of power possessed by labor leaders, Supreme Court justices, factory owners, and professors? It is also argued that power should not be regarded as an aspect of stratification in itself, as if it were comparable with economic class, but, rather, as the dynamic resultant of the forces brought into play in different types of social situations. Authority—legitimate power within a formal structure—is clearly hierarchical, but the rank order of authority usually applies only to a given authority structure within a society, not to the society itself.

Finally, a number of sociological studies have treated education as a major determinant of objective status and as a dimension of stratification. The differences in behavior and attitudes of those who are higher or lower in educational attainments have been demonstrated by empirical research. On the theoretical level, it is argued that education, like the various economic dimensions, affects the life chances of individuals—their degree of security, their status, and their ability to interact with others. People are given differential degrees of respect and influence according to their level of education.

■ *Accorded status.* The dimension of accorded status is the one most sociologists tacitly or overtly refer to when they use the term "social class." This dimension involves the amount of status, honor, or deference that a given position commands in a society. Various methods are used to study accorded status, but in any case the location of individuals or groups in the status system depends on the opinion of the individuals who go to make up the system rather than the opinion of the sociologist who observes it. Accorded status, then, is a result of the felt perceptions of others, and a social class based on accorded status is composed of individuals who accept each other as equals and therefore as qualified for intimate association in friendship, marriage, and the like.

Since this concept depends on rankings by others, it is difficult to apply it to large-scale social systems, particularly nations, except at the level of the small uppermost social class. Individuals from different communities cannot rank each other unless they rely on criteria more objective than social acceptability. The social class consisting of individuals who have, roughly speaking, the same attributes will vary with size of community; for instance, the type of individual who may be in the highest social class of a small town will probably be in the middle class of a large city. It has, in fact, been argued that the larger the community, the more likely it is that accorded status will correspond to objective status. In other words, individuals who live in large communities are more prone to make status judgments about others on the basis of knowledge about their jobs, how much their homes are worth, how many years of education they have had, and the like.

Accorded status tends to become an ascribed characteristic, that is, one that can be inherited. "Background," which usually means family identification, is the way in which people define the source of accorded status. This implies that in addition to specific lineage, other visible ascribed characteristics, such as race, ethnicity, and religion, often constitute elements in status placement. In all societies that contain a variety of racial, ethnic, or religious groups, each such group is differentially ranked in honorific or status terms. Those groups which were present first and retain the highest economic and political positions tend to have the highest status. Thus in the United States, such traits as being white, Anglo-Saxon, and Protestant (preferably of the historically earliest American denominations, such as Episcopal, Congregational, or Quaker) convey high status on those possessing them. The status attributes of various socially visible groups are also determined by various typical characteristics of their members. Thus religious or ethnic groups which are poor on the average are of low status, and wealthy members of such groups tend to be discriminated against socially by comparably well-to-do members of more privileged groups (for instance, a well-to-do Baptist will have lower status in most American communities than a comparably affluent Episcopalian).

Status, it should be noted, is a power resource in much the same way as economic position or political authority. Since status involves being accepted by those in high positions, and since the desire for status is universal, men seek to accommodate their actions to those who can confer status on them.

■ *Subjective status.* Unlike objective and accorded class concepts, which locate individuals in the stratification hierarchy according to the judgments of analysts or of the community, subjective status categories involve efforts to discover the way in which the individual himself perceives the stratification hierarchy. In sociology there are essentially two main traditions of dealing with subjective positions, one based on the methodological device of self-identification and the other on reference group theory.

Self-identification. The technique of self-identification is used to determine the extent to which given individuals or portions of specific groups see themselves as members of a given class or other group that may be located in terms of stratification. Efforts to locate individuals have involved asking them to place themselves in one of a number of class categories furnished by the investigator in such questions as "Do you think of yourself as a member of the upper, middle, working, or lower class?"[34] The number of alternatives furnished respondents may, of course, be larger or smaller than this. Other investigators, instead of following this procedure, have sought to find out what categories people use to describe the social hierarchy.[35]

Reference group theory. The groups that individuals use as reference points by which to evaluate themselves or their activities are known in sociology as reference groups.[36] They can be, but need not be, groups to which an individual belongs. Thus a person may judge his degree of occupational achievement by comparing his attainments with those which preponderate among his fellow ethnic, racial, or religious group members, people he went to school with, neighbors, or those who are more privileged than he is and whose position he would like to attain.[37]

Reference group theory assumes that individuals rarely use the total social structure as a reference group but, rather,

[34] Richard Centers, *The Psychology of Social Class* (Princeton: Princeton University Press, 1949).

[35] Jerome Manis and B. N. Meltzer, "Some Correlates of Class Consciousness among Textile Workers," *American Journal of Sociology,* 69 (1963), 177–184.

[36] Herbert H. Hyman, *The Psychology of Status,* Archives of Psychology, No. 269 (1942).

[37] Merton, *op. cit.,* pp. 225–386.

that they judge their own status by comparison with smaller, more closely visible groups. The extent of satisfaction or dissatisfaction with status is held to depend on one's reference groups.

Reference groups are often derivable from structural factors; thus neighborhoods, factories, employers, schoolmates, and the like often constitute relevant reference groups. On the other hand, relevant reference groups may be manipulated, as when organized groups that are competing for support seek to affect the reference groups of those whose support they want so as to increase their sense of satisfaction or dissatisfaction.[88] The formation of class consciousness may be seen as a process in which members of the lower social strata change their reference groups: while class consciousness is dormant or incipient, the lower-class individual relates himself to various small groups; with the full emergence of class consciousness, he relates himself to aspects of the larger social structure.

OBJECTIVE AND SUBJECTIVE ORIENTATIONS

The fact that social class may be conceptualized both objectively and subjectively does not mean that these are in any sense mutually exclusive ways of looking at the social hierarchy. Almost all analysts, regardless of which approach they choose to stress, are interested in examining the interrelations between their conception of class and other factors, which they view either as determinants or as consequences of class variations. Thus, as has been noted, Marx was intensely interested in the subjective reactions of people to their location in the class structure.

It is significant that Richard Centers, who is most identified with the social-psychological approach to class as involving self-definition, initiated his study of the subject as a way of finding out to what extent American workers were class-conscious in the Marxist sense. In fact, Centers' work is more directly inspired by Marx than is that of many sociologists,

[88] S. M. Lipset and Martin Trow, "Reference Group Theory and Trade-Union Wage Policy," in Mirra Komarovsky (ed.), *Common Frontiers of the Social Sciences* (Glencoe, Ill.: The Free Press, 1957), pp. 391–411.

who are more wont to approach the subject in objective terms.
It should also be noted that there are close links between
elements in Marx's thought and contemporary reference
group theory. In seeking to suggest hypotheses that would
explain the relationship between objective position and anticipated subjective reactions, Marx advanced a theory of relative deprivation. He suggested that although objective improvement in the economic position of the workers could
take place under capitalism, this would not prevent the
emergence of "true" class consciousness, since the position of
the capitalists would improve more rapidly than that of the
workers. As he put it, the "material position of the worker
has improved, . . . but at the cost of his social position.
The social gulf that divides him from the capitalist has
widened."[39] In another work Marx illustrated this generalization with the story of a man who was very happy with a small
house in which he lived until a wealthy man came along and
built a mansion next door: then, wrote Marx, the house of
the worker suddenly became a hut in his eyes.[40]

Similarly, although Marx never dealt with the distinction
between class and status on a conceptual level, there are
frequent references in his historical writings to distinctions
among social strata in various countries. These distinctions
actually reflect what would now be called variations among
status groups. Perhaps the most interesting formulation
related to this question may be found in a major Marxist
classic by Engels. In discussing political life in nineteenth-
century England, Engels pointed out in very clear terms that
status may be an independent source of power, more important in a given situation than economic power:

> In England, the bourgeoisie never held undivided sway. Even
> the victory of 1832 left the landed aristocracy in almost
> exclusive possession of all the leading government offices. The
> meekness with which the wealthy middle class submitted to
> this remained inconceivable to me until the great Liberal
> manufacturer, Mr. W. E. Forster, in a public speech implored
> the young men of Bradford to learn French, as a means to
> get on in the world, and quoted from his own experience

[39] Karl Marx, "Wage, Labor and Capital," in Marx, *Selected
Works,* I, 273.
[40] Karl Marx, "Value, Price and Profit," in *ibid.,* pp. 268–269.

how sheepish he looked when, as a Cabinet Minister, he had
to move in society where French was, at least, as necessary
as English! The fact was, the English middle class of that
time were, as a rule, quite uneducated upstarts, and could
not help leaving to the aristocracy those superior government places where other qualifications were required than
mere insular narrowness and insular conceit, seasoned by
business sharpness. . . . The English bourgeoisie are, up to
the present day [1892], so deeply penetrated by a sense of
their social inferiority that they keep up, at their own expense and that of the nation, an ornamental caste of drones
to represent the nation worthily at all state functions; and
they consider themselves highly honored whenever one of
themselves is found worthy of admission into this select and
privileged body, manufactured, after all, by themselves.[41]

Clearly, what Engels was describing is a situation in which
an old upper class, which had declined in economic power,
continued to maintain its control over the governmental
machinery because it remained the highest status group in
the society. Those with less status but more economic resources conformed to the standards set up by the higher
status group.

■ *Stable and unstable status systems.*   The relationships among the different dimensions of stratification vary in
different types of societies and different periods; they are
probably at their weakest during periods of rapid social
change involving the rise of new occupational strata, shifts
from rural to urban predominance, and changes in the status
and authority of key institutions, such as religion and education. Of all the relatively stable types of society, the ones in
which the various dimensions of stratification are most closely
correlated are rural, caste, and feudal societies. The growth of
industrial and urban society in Europe and America has resulted in a system of stratification characterized by wide discrepancies between class and objective status, and between
both of these and the subjective attributes of status. Currently,
as Western society moves into a "postindustrial" phase characterized by a considerable growth in the white-collar, technological, and service sectors of the economy and a relative

[41] Friedrich Engels, *Socialism, Utopian and Scientific* (New York:
International Publishers, 1938), pp. 25–26.

decline in employment in manufacturing, the relationships among the dimensions have become more tenuous. Status, economic reward, and power are tied to educational achievement, position in some large-scale bureaucracy, access to political authority, and the like. In a predominantly bureaucratic society, property as such has become a less important source of status and social mobility. Complaints about alienation and dehumanization are found more commonly among students, intellectuals, and other sectors of the educated middle classes than among the working class. Most recently, sections of the communist movement have openly discussed the revolutionary role of university students and the petty bourgeoisie, and have seen the organized proletariat in Western society as a relatively conservative group, unavailable for radical politics.

These developments may reflect the fact that some of the most politically relevant discontent in the bureaucratic "affluent society" of the 1960s seems to be inherent in social tensions induced by *status inconsistencies*. However, the bulk of resentment against the stratification system is still rooted in objective deprivation and exploitation. The concept of status inconsistency introduced by Lenski, who derived it from Weber, refers, as I noted in Chapter 1, to the situation of individuals or groups that are differentially located on various dimensions of stratification.[42] Persons in such a situation are exposed to conflicting sets of expectations: for instance, those who are high in educational attainments but are employed in relatively low-paid occupations tend to be more dissatisfied than those whose stratification attributes are totally consistent. As evidence in support of this assumption it is possible to cite research findings that among the relatively well to do, those with discrepant status attributes are more likely to favor change in the power structure and to have more liberal or leftist attitudes than those with status attributes that are mutually consistent.[43] Consequently, the increase in status discrepancy inherent in situations of rapid social change

[42] Gerhard Lenski, "Status Crystallization: A Non-Vertical Dimension of Social Status," in Lipset and Smelser, *op. cit.*, pp. 485–494.

[43] I. W. Goffman, "Status Consistency and Preference for Change in Power," *American Sociological Review*, 22 (1957), 275–281.

should result in an increase in overall discontent and, among those in the more ambiguous status positions (which in the 1960s occurred largely in the well-educated middle strata), in greater receptivity to the myths justifying rebellion. In industrialized societies those who form the underprivileged strata but who have consistent status attributes remain politically on the left but show little interest in radical change. Because all social change generates status discrepancies, rebellious and extremist mass movements are more likely to be found during periods of rapid industrialization and economic growth, and in areas where immigration has caused sudden population growth, than in industrially mature urbanized areas.

▪ *The future of social class.*   To conclude on a note of irony, it may be observed that in a certain sense history has underwritten one of Marx's basic assumptions, which is that the cultural superstructure, including political behavior and status relationships, is a function of the underlying economic and technological structure. As Marx put it in the Preface to *Capital:* "The country that is more developed industrially only shows, to the less developed, the image of its own future."[44] Hence, the most economically developed society should also have the most advanced set of class and political relationships. Since the United States is the most advanced society economically, its class system, regarded as part of its cultural superstructure, should be more appropriate to a technologically advanced society than the class systems of the less developed economies of Europe. In addition, one might argue that the United States, since it lacks a feudal past, should evolve the institutions of a highly developed society in their purest form. Hence, an unpolitical Marxist sociology would expect the social class relationships of the United States to present an image of the future of other societies that are moving in the same general economic direction. Characteristic of such a social system is a decline in emphasis on social class, that is, a decline of distinct visible strata with a "felt consciousness of kind." The various dimensions of strati-

[44] Karl Marx, *Capital,* Vol. I (Moscow: Foreign Languages Publishing House, 1958), pp. 8–9.

fication are more likely to operate in a crisscrossing fashion, increasing the numbers who are relatively high on some components of status and low on others. Highly developed societies of this kind, whether variants of the communist or the capitalist model, are more likely to possess systems of social stratification—varied rankings—than social classes.

These comments suggest the need to view stratification in international as well as national terms.[45] The differences between the average per capita income of the poorest and wealthiest nations are on the order of 40 or 50 to 1, that is, much greater than the differences among social strata within the industrially advanced nations. These variations in national wealth constitute structural parameters that greatly affect the "class" relationships between nations. A Chinese communist has already advanced the thesis that the significant class struggle is between the predominantly rural nations, which are underdeveloped and very poor, and the urbanized, wealthy ones.[46] He has also argued that the wealth of the latter has to a considerable degree reduced the political expression of class tensions within them, but that this should be seen as a result of exploitation by the economically advanced countries of the underdeveloped ones. Whether this thesis is warranted by the facts of international trade relationships or not, it does seem true that any analysis of class structures and their political consequences must in the future consider the impact of variation in national incomes. Many in the elite of the poorer part of the world see themselves as the leaders of oppressed peoples; the radicalism of the intellectuals, university students, military officers, and the like in the less developed nations can be related to the social and economic inferiority of their countries, rather than to their position in the class structure. Such considerations take us far afield from the conventional Western sociological concerns with class relationships, but they clearly are relevant to any effort at

[45] Gustavo Lagos, *International Stratification and Underdeveloped Countries* (Chapel Hill: University of North Carolina Press, 1963); and Irving Louis Horowitz, *Three Worlds of Development: The Theory and Practice of International Stratification* (New York: Oxford University Press, 1966).

[46] Lin Piao, "Long Live the Victory of the Peoples' War," *The Peking Review,* 8 (September 3, 1965), 9–39.

specifying the sources of class behavior and ideologies. As sociology becomes more comparative in outlook and research, we may expect efforts to link class analysis of individual nations to the facts of international stratification.

The next chapter continues the discussion of stratification variables on a more empirical level by first enumerating the specific indicators of class used in political analysis, and then turning to a discussion of the way in which concern for moral factors, particularly religion, affects the impact of class on political choice.

CHAPTER 6

Class, Politics, and Religion in Modern Society: The Dilemma of the Conservatives

If class remains one of the main sources of party division, and if the lower strata back parties that advocate greater equality—parties that oppose the privileged elites—how can conservative parties compete in democratic elections? Concern with this problem led conservatives the world over to oppose universal suffrage in the nineteenth century. Many explicitly argued that the extension of the suffrage would result in the end of private property rights. As T. H. Marshall and others have pointed out, these conservatives were, to a certain extent, correct. There has been an inherent bias in favor of the extension of equality in all democratic societies. Parties dominated by the privileged classes have had to make constant concessions to equalize opportunity and reward. Measures that a previous generation of conservatives objected to as radical or socialist are accepted by the next one.[1]

However, even though democratic societies do move to the left, there still remains the question of how conservatives retain enough strength to compete successfully with leftists; the leftists should be able to draw on the majority of "poor"

[1] T. H. Marshall, *Class, Citizenship and Social Development* (Garden City, N. Y.: Doubleday, 1964), pp. 65–122.

workers or rural groups that exist in almost every nation. A number of answers have been suggested to account for the ability of conservative political groupings to win significant lower-class support. This support is a requirement for political stability. For the legitimacy of a democratic polity rests on the opportunity for all significant actors to have access to power. If the conservatives were deprived of such opportunities, they would eventually lose their commitment to the democratic "rules of the game." No one wants to keep playing in a game that he can never hope to win.

There are two important sources of deviation from a purely class model of party choice: first those which are inherent in the operation of a system of stratification, which either directly lead the lower strata to accept the orientations of the privileged ones, or sustain divergent bases of stratification which press men to react differently; and, second, politically relevant values which are not closely related to social class. On an international scale, the most common sources of such values are religious institutions, although ethnic or minority racial status is a close follow-up. In this chapter I seek to point out in general terms how elements inherent in stratification and in varying religious commitments serve to reduce the link between a given position in the class hierarchy and political behavior.

THE COMPLEXITIES OF STRATIFICATION AND PARTY CHOICE

Some of the ways in which the workings of the stratification system itself reduce the electoral appeal of lower-class based parties are:

1. The normative system inherent in all stratified societies reduces the political effectiveness of the lower strata. To a very high degree, lower classes throughout history have acceded to the societal values that define them as being, in various respects, inferior to those of higher status. This has been true even in modern industrial societies, despite the influence of Marxism and the wide diffusion of egalitarian values. Implicit in the very concept of a stratification order is the assumption that people in lower-status positions are oriented

upward; that is, that most of them would like to move up in the social structure, whereas people in higher positions are rarely motivated to move down. Insofar as individuals in lower-class positions use people in higher positions as a reference group toward which they aspire or whose approval they desire to win, we would expect them to take over the values of the higher-status group. People in high positions will be unlikely to adopt political attitudes that are associated with those of low status, but some lower-class people will be proud to take over reactions associated with the higher classes.

Conservative parties and policies, which reflect upper-class values, have by and large been surrounded by a halo of high prestige and status, while left parties have been "tainted" by association with the lower classes.

2. The lower classes, by virtue of their inferior position in the structure and the fact that the dominant legitimate norms of culture are middle- and upper-class ones, are necessarily exposed to conflicting normative pressures as they become politically class conscious or leftist in their orientations. Politically, they tend to develop or accept values that are functionally related to their needs as underprivileged groups, but as individuals they are faced with the problem of reconciling lower-class norms with a conflicting set of values that are functional for the political and social position of the upper class. In large measure, the values transmitted by a culture tend to reinforce conservative predispositions and to challenge left-wing ones. Consequently, again we might expect this factor to create more deviation from the modal-class pattern among lower-class people than among middle- and upper-class people.

3. Lower-class individuals are more exposed to conservative values transmitted through the schools, media of mass communication, and other powerful agencies of persuasion than are well-to-do, middle-class people faced with propaganda or media favoring liberal or leftist politics. For example, in the area of newspaper reading, the large majority of the population in every Western country reads newspapers that support the conservatives politically. This means that voters predisposed to back conservatives will have this predisposition reinforced by the press and the magazines that they

read, whereas voters disposed to support leftist parties will have this predisposition contradicted by the mass media.[2] This pattern of exposure is intrinsic to a stratified society and will normally result in greater deviations from the modal-class political pattern within the lower strata than among the middle and upper strata.

4. The political advocates of change in the existing society must mobilize support from individuals and groups who adhere to the old institutional order. Normally, it is much harder to get people to *change* their opinions or political allegiances than it is to get them to *retain* the ones they have. Since the factors that operate to induce individuals or groups to recognize the need for change will necessarily not affect all persons in the stratum that is changing equally, it may be expected that political tendencies advocating major changes will secure only a portion of the potential support from the social base to which the changes appeal; the party with links to the historic status quo, on the other hand, may expect to retain most of its support from the privileged strata.

Those lower-class groups, which are isolated from the pressures that are pressing their strata toward new reform politics, will continue to adhere to the conservative tradition. Thus, it has been pointed out frequently that workers who are socially isolated from other workers but who are in close contact with persons in the middle class (such as personal servants, and workers in very small companies or stores) will continue to be conservative, although their pay and status may be low. Lower-class housewives, more isolated from political information than men, tend to be more conservative and traditionalistic in their political outlook than men.

5. The lesser deviation of upper- than of lower-class individuals from modal-class behavior patterns may be a result of the more homogeneous political environment of the higher-status persons. In all countries, persons in the middle class are more likely to belong to many voluntary organizations than are lower-class individuals. Most of these associations tend to be homogeneous in class terms. The more privileged

[2] See Stein Rokkan and Per Torsvik, "The Voter, the Reader and the Party Press," *Koelner Zeitschrift für Soziologie und Sozial-Psychologie,* 12 (1960), 278–302.

strata tend to travel and move around among people like themselves, in jet planes, in leading hotels, and the like. Studies of political interest and participation indicate that the higher the position individuals occupy in the social structure, the greater their interest and activity in politics. Consequently, middle- and upper-class individuals are more likely than those in less-privileged positions to be continuously exposed to political information and propaganda that reinforce their inherent class-based political predispositions.

Conversely, lower-class individuals, who are less prone to belong to formal organizations or to interact with individuals who are informed and opinionated about politics, are consequently less likely to secure information that points up the need for class political action.

6. The structure of interclass communication will increase the deviance from the modal-class response more among lower-class than middle-class individuals. Interaction between individuals who belong to different social strata is much more likely to result in the lower-status individual being affected by the opinions of those in the higher class than vice versa. (This is based on the earlier assumption that most lower-class individuals concur in the general evaluation system of any given complex society.) Social interaction between social strata should increase the deviation among the lower-status groups, but should not greatly increase the frequency of deviation among members of the higher group.

7. Individuals with higher status in contemporary society are inherently more sophisticated about the relevance of political action to self-interest. This assumption flows from the facts that: (a) higher status is associated with higher education, and greater education is conducive to increased political sophistication; (b) the more transparent the relationship is between governmental policies and the welfare of a group to which a person belongs, the more likely he is to understand the need for political action. In an industrial society, as Max Weber pointed out, the relationship between government action and consequences is much clearer for the self-employed person and for people involved in directing businesses or associations of various kinds than it is for lowly-employed persons. Lowly-employed individuals are more likely to view, as

personally relevant, power within the *plant* rather than within the *polity;* and (c), as already noted, higher status is associated with greater personal exposure of an individual to politically knowledgeable and active persons of the same background as himself.

These mechanisms (inherent in social stratification), by strengthening conservative parties and weakening left parties, help balance the left and right in stable societies where the attributes associated with high status have not changed. In many of the former colonial and so-called emerging nations, however, this assumption of relative stability and general acceptance of the attributes of high status does not hold true. In these nations, certain varieties of high status are associated with hated foreign imperialisms and with social institutions that are felt to perpetuate national inferiority. Thus, conservative parties backed by businessmen and/or the rural elite in underdeveloped nations do not necessarily have the advantage of traditional legitimacy and identification with the summits of the status system. Leftism and nationalism are often identified with the nation and the national elite. The lower strata, insofar as they are politically conscious, have been won to the side of leftism around the symbols of national independence. As I noted previously:

> In colonial situations, the native elites derive their status, or are protected in it, by virtue of their connection with the status and power of the foreign ruler. And with independence, the values of hierarchy, aristocracy, privilege, primogeniture, and (more recently) capitalism, all associated with the foreign imperialist power, are easily rejected.[3]

In a context in which a large section of the elite supports leftist ideological goals, and in which the large majority live in poverty, the chances for conservative parties representing the traditional elite to remain viable electoral alternatives to the predominant leftists are quite rare. Quite commonly, one dominant mass-based "leftist" party controls, a phenomenon to be discussed in the next chapter.

[3] S. M. Lipset, *The First New Nation: The United States in Historical and Comparative Perspective* (New York: Basic Books, 1963), pp. 76–77.

But let us return to the democracies of Europe and the English-speaking world. In these nations, regardless of whether conservatism is strengthened by being linked to the national tradition (as it is in Britain) or is not strengthened (as in the United States), conservative politicians know that they must find ways of securing considerable lower-class support. They cannot win without it. Conservative parties must attempt to reduce the saliency of class as the principal basis of party division by sponsoring nonclass issues, while leftist parties will seek to emphasize their anti-elitist objectives. The first of these efforts of conservatives is illustrated by the responses of both the pre-Civil War American (conservative) Whig party and later the post-Civil War Republicans to the anti-elitist Democratic party. The Whig party emphasized national-interest issues and symbols—patriotism, defense of traditional religious morality, and the use of military leaders as political leaders. (See Chapter 9.) The only two Whig presidential candidates who were elected against the Jacksonian Democrats were military hero generals. After the Civil War the Republican party successfully emphasized its role as the savior of the Union, and nominated a number of Civil War generals. More recently, the first successful Republican presidential nominee since the Depression was the hero of World War II, Dwight Eisenhower.

Another conservative tactic in some countries has been to attempt to introduce some sort of pseudo-leftist (anti-elitist) issues. For example, in late nineteenth-century Germany, some conservative leaders attempted to counter the growing support for socialism among the workers by the formation of workers' associations, which tried to deflect the working-class antagonism to capitalism and the upper classes onto the Jews.[4] The support given to the anti-elitist Fascists and Nazis in post-World War I Europe by some businessmen and conservatives was probably motivated by similar reasons.

The behavior of conservative parties, of course, will vary greatly with the number of competing parties. Where multiparty systems exist, there are a number of nonleft-wing political forces such as religious, liberal, conservative, regional,

[4] See Paul Massing, *Rehearsal for Destruction* (New York: Harper, 1949).

and agrarian parties, which do not seek an electoral majority, but instead try to maximize the support of the social base predisposed to them (for example, all coreligionists for a religious party, all farmers for an agrarian party, and all businessmen and professionals for a liberal party). In multiparty systems, the most successful nonleft party is usually the religious party. Issues affecting the place of religion in education and other areas of life have kept many working-class Europeans voting Christian Democratic rather than Social Democratic or Communist. Like secular conservative parties, the religious political groups deny the saliency of class, insisting that transclass moral values and allegiances should be the most important differentiating factors in politics.

Conservative parties in a political democracy usually seek to reduce the saliency of class as a basis of party controversy in order to win more lower-class votes. These efforts may take the form of (1) introducing national patriotic issues and nominating military heroes as candidates; (2) stressing noneconomic bases of cleavage such as religious or ethnic differences, or issues of morality; (3) the fostering of Tory socialism, that is, legislation designed to benefit the socioeconomic position of the lower strata; and (4) using a variant of pseudo-socialism and anti-elitism, a surrogate-exploiting scapegoat which will absorb the antagonism to the societal elite.

Leftist parties around the world have continued to use anti-elitist symbolism and class interest to mobilize the support of the lower classes against the conservative parties.

CLASS AND POLITICS: A MULTIDIMENSIONAL PROBLEM

In accounting for deviations from the correlation between class position and party choice, I have pointed to the modification of such choices by strengthening both the influence of traditional dominant strata and the significance of bases of cleavage not directly linked to class. To a considerable extent, however, the weakness of the correlation is a consequence of the pluralistic character of modern stratification. Stratification is multidimensional, but some political analysis has treated it as if it were unidimensional. There are many diverse ways of obtaining rewards and power and these affect political relations differently.

The assumption of the unitary nature of stratification, or perhaps more accurately the tendency to use only one indicator to locate an individual's class position, has had unfortunate effects on political and sociological research. As the earlier discussion of Weber's approach indicated, men may have a variety of stratification positions: "Only persons who are completely unskilled, without property and dependent on employment without regular occupation, are in a strictly identical class status."[5] He pointed out that "class statuses . . . are different with each variation and combination" of items that locate individuals in the social structure.[6]

A number of concepts have been suggested in the preceding chapter to account for variation in political behavior as the consequence of varying combinations of social positions. Listing even a few of them, this time on an empirical descriptive level, will indicate the complexity of this analysis, and some of the reasons why an unidimensional treatment of class and party must report a considerable degree of variance from the general relationships. Many of these stratification concepts have, in fact, been used as explicit bases of political appeals by different parties.

1. Income—the poorer versus the wealthier.
2. Sources of income—employees versus employers.
3. Occupational position hierarchy—unskilled, skilled, white-collar, professional, and so on.
4. Property-owners versus nonowners; landlords versus tenants.
5. Creditor-debtor status.
6. Accorded social status-honorific deference or prestige hierarchy, as determined in part by economic attributes, ethnic or religious background, duration of residence in community, and duration of possession of status-ascribing attributes (old wealth versus new, parental background, and the like).[7]

[5] Max Weber, *The Theory of Social and Economic Organization* (New York: Oxford University Press, 1947), p. 425.
[6] *Ibid.,* p. 424.
[7] This is the factor described as "social class" by W. L. Warner in his *Yankee City* series of books.

7. Power rankings—those that involve subordination on one side and superordination on the other. Labor leaders (possibly relatively low in status and income but with considerable power), civil servants and elected officers, and heads of organizations whose members are lowly, all present examples of positions that convey much less income and status than they do power. Conversely, men may have considerable status or income or both but may feel that they have very little influence on decisions that concern them, and hence react as political outgroups.

8. Subjective stratification reactions: in all of the above dimensions the individual's position is determined by objective attributes, or the status that he or his possessions are accorded by others. Individuals, however, may perceive their position in the stratification system in ways that diverge from the normal pattern.[8] The self-placement of the actors is usually described as *subjective* class, as noted earlier. The concept *reference* class, as we have seen, refers to the status group toward whose modal behavior an individual is oriented.

Knowledge of an individual's subjective or reference class will increase the ability to predict his political behavior. Workers who report themselves as "middle class," or who adopt middle-class consumption styles, are more likely to support conservative politics than those who identify with the working class.

The most interesting political aspect of the diverse stratification dimensions is the way in which incompatible stratification attributes subject individuals to contradictory political pressures.[9] On the most general level, of course, status discrepancies may be regarded as a special example of cross pressures operating on individuals or groups. Those involved in politically relevant status discrepancies should exhibit a lower level of interest and activity. On the other hand, as the earlier discussion of the concept has pointed out, extremist forms of political behavior have often been caused by the

[8] Richard Centers, *The Psychology of Social Classes* (Princeton: Princeton University Press, 1949).

[9] Gerhard Lenski, "Status Crystallization: A Non-vertical Dimension of Social Status," *American Sociological Review,* 19 (1954), 405–413.

strains of status discrepancies. Seemingly contradictory propositions of this kind may be compatible, if we assume that people under cross pressures may attempt to reduce the strains either by retreating into apathy, saying that they do not care which position triumphs, or by adopting a position that will reduce the strains in a more extreme manner and in a more committed fashion than persons not faced with the need to resolve cross pressures. Which reaction occurs will depend on other factors specific to the situation.

The types of extreme political behavior explained by reactions to status discrepancies are also quite diverse. Thus it has been suggested that the *nouveaux riches* have responded frequently to the experience of having wealth without the corresponding high status by giving support to leftist or egalitarian movements that challenge the legitimacy of the traditional basis of social status. As I indicated in the preceding chapter, this thesis has been advanced to account for the behavior of the bourgeoisie in the French Revolution, and for the leftism of relatively well-to-do Jews in various countries. Similarly it has been argued that groups whose social class position is higher than their occupational-economic class—the "decayed aristocracy"—are frequently ultrareactionary, defensive of traditional values and institutions. But it should be noted that these two examples of discrepancies have also been used to explain quite opposite political reactions. Analysts of the "radical right" in the United States have suggested that some American *nouveaux riches* react to the strains inherent in their position by becoming even more conservative than the old rich, that they seek to adapt to the value and behavior patterns that seem common in the status group above them.[10] It has been suggested also that old but economically declining upper classes are sometimes relatively liberal. The emergence before World War I of Tory Socialism in England and Progressive Republicanism in America has been explained as a consequence of the felt hostility of declining old wealth to the rising *nouveaux riches*—industrialists and capitalists—who had outstripped them economically. These speculations and historical interpretations indicate the limits

[10] See the various essays in Daniel Bell (ed.), *The Radical Right* (Garden City: Doubleday, 1963), and Lipset and Raab, *op. cit.*

of comparative political analysis. Similar status discrepancies have been used to account for arch-conservative behavior and liberal action. To differentiate the conditions under which one or the other occurs calls for specific analysis on a case-study basis.

It is difficult also to be precise about the effect of variations in power position. For example, the pure logic of stratification analysis, which urges that high position results in greater conservatism, would suggest that those who hold greater power as a result of leading the lowly will be more "conservative" than their followers. Presumably becoming a union leader or a Labour Member of Parliament heightens interaction with those high in the social structure, and affects the reference class of those in such position. These assumptions have been advanced to explain the presumed shift to the right of leaders of unions and left-wing parties. On the other hand, such leaders, while high in power and often high in income as well, are in a relatively low position in terms of social-status position. Daniel Bell has suggested that American labor leaders are more liberal than their followers, partly because of the strains in their stratification position. Many labor leaders resent being outranked in prestige by business leaders, and may react to this self-discrepancy by supporting liberal or radical political movements through which they can gain more power and status recognition and by attacking those groups that deny respect to their power positions. This analysis, of course, suggests that trade-union and other leaders of low-status groups, far from being conservative influences on the policies of their organizations, are in fact often more radical than their rank-and-file members, since they feel more status deprived.

It should be also noted, however, that conflicting and overlapping stratification rankings in stable societies tend to contribute more to the support of the right than of the left. It seems natural that individuals should attempt to adjust their perception of the environment to maximize their claim to as high a status as possible. The man who achieves high occupational position, for example, is likely to drop his memberships in organizations that are lowly in status, to move to a higher-statused neighborhood, perhaps even to leave his low-ranking church for one whose members are higher in position, and in general to try to take over the behavior pattern of higher social classes. Politically, this implies a pressure to become more conservative. This is another example of the conservative bias inherent in stratification referred to earlier. It should be clear, however, that this "conservative bias" is only one factor among many even in stable polities and is countered by others. Thus the worker who has moved to the suburbs may still receive left-wing stimuli from his shopmates, his union leader, and his conflicts with authority in the plant, all of which may override any pressures to conform to the more conservative values of his neighborhood. Or, as has been indicated above, many persons with a claim to higher status in one dimension find that they experience social rebuffs when they attempt to translate that claim to social status in another dimension and, as a result, become even more leftist than they might have been if their statuses were congruent.

RELIGION AND PARTY

Religion, next to factors directly inherent in the stratification systems, has been, perhaps, the most influential source of political diversity in electoral democracies. As a value-generating institution, religion must affect the nature of political discourse seriously. Religion informs much of the variation in such nonpolitical aspects of behavior as work habits, achievement aspirations, and parent-child relations.[11] A religious denomination is an important reference group for a member, from which he takes his standards of judgment in many matters. Different religious groups exhibit varying political identities, and one of the tasks of political analysis is to account for these variations. The most explicit form of religious participation in politics is, of course, the religious political party such as the Christian Democrats of various European nations. However, many countries that do not have explicitly religious parties are still greatly affected politically by religion. In dis-

[11] Melville Dalton, "Worker Response and Social Background," *Journal of Political Economy*, 55 (1947), 323–332; Gerhard Lenski, *The Religious Factor* (Garden City: Doubleday, 1961), pp. 75–119.

cussing the subject, therefore, I want to suggest, first, some
hypotheses concerning the impact of religion on political
choice and then examine the factors related to the presence
of clerical political parties.

There are at least three kinds of variation among religious
groups that bear on their political differentiation. These are:

■ 1. *Different social characteristics.* Church groupings differ in socioeconomic and ethnic composition as well
as in geographical concentration, and the interests of predominant sections of a denomination may become identified
with given political tendencies. Churches composed of the
more well-to-do, or the high-status ethnic strata, are often
politically conservative. Thus Catholics and Jews in the various English-speaking nations are much less likely to be Conservatives or Republicans than are Protestants, and the association is not solely a result of stratification positions;
Catholics or Jews are much more likely to back the more
liberal party than are Episcopalians (Anglicans) at the same
socioeconomic levels.

■ 2. *Different historical experiences.* When past
events have structured a relationship between a denomination and a political tendency, the relationship may continue
indefinitely. For example, in Europe churches that are, or
have been, state churches (established) tend to be associated
with conservative parties, while churches that have faced discrimination from the state tend to have links to the "out-
group" parties—parties that oppose both the religious and
secular establishments. In Britain, which still has a state
church, the out-group "nonconformist" (Baptist and Methodist, for example) sects and Catholics supported the Liberals in
the past, and back the Labour party today. In France, well-to-
do Protestants and Jews, as well as anticlerical voters of Catholic ancestry, tend to vote for the more left-wing parties, as
compared to committed Catholics of comparable economic
position.

Consequently, the policies of different parties may be linked
to the secular interests of a religious group. Thus, in much
of Catholic Europe, parties differ with respect to the issue of

state support for religious education. In the United States, the Democrats have always been less willing than their opponents to impose immigration restrictions (an issue of greater relevance to Catholics and Jews than to Protestants), have been more supportive of the Catholic position on public education, and have been more receptive to giving public posts and nominations for elective office to persons who are not of Anglo-Saxon Protestant background.

■ 3. *Different religious values.* Religious groups differ theologically in spheres of public morality as well as social welfare. These differences may affect political behavior when theological formulations carry with them political directives, as in the case of papal encyclicals. The papal encyclicals, on the one hand, have endorsed many "welfare-state" policies and, on the other, have condemned atheistic and materialistic socialism and communism. Religious values may indirectly predispose individuals to accept certain congruent secular political ideologies. Thus many observers have called attention to Protestantism's contribution to an emphasis on individualism, on self-reliance, on feelings of personal responsibility for success and failure, and on the interpretation of social evils as a result of moral turpitude. Catholicism, on the other hand, tends to be more accepting of human and societal weakness; it gives the Church authority to relieve the individual of some sense of responsibility, and emphasizes communal responsibility.

Similar differences between churches and sects affect their reaction to public morality. Groups such as the Anglicans, Lutherans, Greek Orthodox, and Roman Catholics, are or have been established churches. Membership in a *church,* in the sociological sense of this word, comes with birth. In the pure case, national citizenship and church membership go together—for instance, almost all Scandinavians are Lutherans; most Englishmen are formally at least Anglicans; and Latin Europeans are baptized as Catholics. Given a socially diverse laity, a tolerant attitude toward the possibility of "sinning" must emerge if continued loyalty to the church is to be assured. Acceptance of human frailty and the assumption that the faithful will not all be saints are natural consequences of legal establishment—the coincidence of church membership and citizenship. On the other hand, many Protestant groups that were once nonconformist sects rather than birthright churches still retain their evangelical sectarian character. New converts to these organizations, and birthright adherents on reaching adulthood, are expected to have joined as a result of a conscious voluntary decision; in some organizations a violent conversion experience has been required as a sign of sincere faith. Good standing in these groups has been contingent on righteous living according to precepts that are sometimes very concrete.

Religious values, of course, have directly affected politics insofar as morality issues (such as prohibition, gambling, divorce, or birth control) become salient. In a number of countries the parties that have drawn support from the more ascetic wings of Protestantism have tended to support measures seeking to inhibit or limit alcoholic beverages. This has been true of the American Republicans and the British and Scandinavian Liberals.

■ 4. *Religious and political dissent.*   It has been suggested that sects serve as a functional alternative for, or pave the way for, political discontent. New sectarian splits from dominant religions often seem to express the resentment of depressed strata with their inferior position. This is most manifest in transvaluational beliefs (reversing present values), which emphasize the identification between poverty and virtue. Given the combination of transvaluational elements and hostility to worldly matters often found together in such sects, these groups may reduce the predispositions of poorer groups to back radical political protest. During the Great Depression in the United States, when left-wing protest was minor, such sects grew rapidly. In India, Islam's and later Christianity's greatest successes have been in regions largely inhabited by Hindu outcasts.

On the other hand, religious protest, by severing sectors of the population from loyalty to the religious establishment, may serve to weaken their traditional political allegiances in the process. Many of the leaders and early supporters of the

British Labour party came from the "nonconformist" or "dissenting" sects.[12] In Czarist Russia, Leon Trotsky consciously recognized the political implications of religious dissent. In 1897, he deliberately sought his first working-class recruits from among the members of "the religious sects opposed to the Orthodox Church."[13] And studies in a variety of countries have pointed to direct connections between the social roots of religious and political extremism.[14]

■ 5. *The religious political party.*   The most explicit form of religious participation in politics is, of course, the religious political party. These parties exist in a large number of Catholic, Calvinist, and Moslem countries, but less frequently in non-Calvinist Protestant nations, and in India, Israel, and the various Buddhist states. It is difficult to differentiate between the religions that participate explicitly in politics from the ones that do not, since so many factors vary with national systems and historic experiences. The following generalizations have, however, been suggested.

a. The more a church conceives of itself as God-ordained and has an ecclesiastical constitution that is completely separated from state power, the more likely is it to be interested in government action. In the West, the Catholic best fits these conditions. As a church in the sociological sense, it assumes that it is God-ordained, and it claims authority over all persons born within it, rather than (as with Protestant denominations, which have sectarian origins) over those who voluntarily give it allegiance. Unlike other Christian *churches* (the Lutheran, the Anglican, and the Greek Orthodox), it is genuinely supranational, accepting an authority outside of the nation: the Pope. The other state-supported churches have been closely linked to those who hold power in their state, and their tie to state power prevents them from playing

[12] See Robert F. Wearmouth, *Methodism and the Working-Class Movements of England, 1800–1850* (London: Epsworth Press, 1937); A. D. Belden, *George Whitefield the Awakener* (London: S. Low, Marston, 1930), pp. 247 ff.; and Franz Linden, *Sozialismus und Religion* (Leipzig: Tauchnitz, 1932).

[13] Isaac Deutscher, *The Prophet Armed, Trotsky, 1879–1921* (London: Oxford University Press, 1954), pp. 30–31.

[14] See S. M. Lipset, *Political Man* (Garden City: Doubleday, 1960), pp. 106–108, for a summary and discussion of a number of these studies.

an independent political role. The politics of the three Baltic states before their absorption by Russia in 1939 illustrate decisively that Catholicism and Lutheranism respond differently even when all other circumstances are comparable. Catholic Lithuania was dominated throughout its democratic history by the Christian Democrats, who secured between 35 and 45 per cent of the vote in a multiparty system. In Estonia—as Lutheran as Lithuania is Catholic (more than 80 per cent)— a Lutheran Christian Democratic party never secured more than 7 per cent. And in Latvia, with a Lutheran majority and a large Catholic minority, the Lutheran party secured less than 5 per cent while the Catholic party secured a majority of the votes from the predominantly Catholic section of the country. Similarly in Germany, today, a much larger proportion of Catholics vote for the nominally nonsectarian Christian Democrats than do Lutherans, although the leaders of both churches back the party. And among people who adhere to the predominantly Lutheran Evangelical Church, a larger ratio of those who stem from the small Calvinist wing of the church support the religious party, than do those of Lutheran background. Seemingly Calvinism, where it retains its ancient strong faith, retains more of the attributes of the God-ordained universalistic church than any other Protestant group. In The Netherlands, there are two strong Calvinist parties.

b. Where a cultural community is threatened by outside values, and there is a close identity between the community and a given religion, religious parties are more likely to emerge. This proposition applied particularly to the situation of various colonial peoples before independence.[15] In Indonesia, Pakistan, Morocco, Egypt, and other nations, the Mohammedan religion served as a major basis around which to organize a nationalist movement. As religion is a sphere in which rulers find it difficult to interfere, it is often the least suppressed base of local autonomy. As in the case of lower class-based movements, latent nationalist movements have first taken the form of religiously oriented organizations, which prepare the way for a political movement.

[15] George M. Kahin, *Nationalism and Revolution in Indonesia* (Ithaca: Cornell University Press, 1952), p. 38.

In many of the postcolonial new states, religion has appeared as a basis of party formation, which is fostered by conservative strata. National identity and left-wing values are often intertwined; the purpose of independence is seen as the creation of a new and radical social order; and the leftist parties are, therefore, identified with the accepted national goals. Consequently, religion is the one institution with popular support around which an opposition to socialism may be based (see the following chapter for further discussion). This effort to use religion to strengthen conservatism in radically oriented new strata is not new, the early American conservatives tried similar tactics in their efforts to defeat the Jeffersonian Democrats.[16]

Religious parties vary considerably from country to country, and from period to period, in their social base, program, and position on various issues. In the nineteenth century, European churches that had been established belonged on the "right." They described themselves as "antirevolutionary." In contemporary times, however, the strong conservative commitment of most religious parties which stem from historic established churches has declined, partly because of the growing weakness of total ideologies in European politics generally. Basically, however, the centrist character of most religious parties results from the fact that they must appeal to the lower strata, while retaining the support of deeply religious conservatives. A religious party that is far over to the right (or to the left) would risk the possibility of alienating important sectors of the population from the church. The ultrarightist activities of the Austrian Catholic party in the 1920's actually led many Catholics to leave the Church.[17]

The factors that determine the presence or absence of a major religious party have been of particular importance in affecting the possibilities for socialist electoral victories in industrially developed nations. The countries that do not have religious parties are essentially divided along class lines politically, and the socialist parties have held majority power in some of them—a condition that has not occurred in the oth-

[16] Lipset, *The First New Nation,* pp. 81–88.
[17] Charles Gulick, *Austria from Hapsburg to Hitler* (Berkeley: University of California Press, 1948).

ers. Essentially, as will be elaborated later, there are three kinds of parties in contemporary Europe: working-class (socialist and communist); middle-class (liberals or conservatives, and occasionally agrarians); and religious (Catholic and Calvinist). The religious parties are in a deciding balance-of-power position in a number of countries. Their heterogeneous social base produces considerable internal factionalism, which enables these parties to be all things to all men. The right wing can appeal to the traditional conservative forces, while the left wing and the religious trade unions can appeal to the workers. Thus, any strain between the secular affiliations and interests of supporters of religious parties and the policies of governments dominated by them may be eased by identifying with a given wing of the party, or a functional organization linked to it such as a trade union or peasant league.

The social factors that are associated with support of religious parties, not surprisingly, are those that correlate with faithful adherence to religion as such. This is particularly noteworthy with respect to sex differences. In all nations, women are much more religious than men; and, consequently, in countries with religious parties, voters for secular (particularly left, anticlerical, or liberal) parties are disproportionately male, while a large majority of the electorate of the religious parties are usually women. Rural groups are customarily among the more religious part of the population, and also disproportionately give their support to religious parties.

It is obviously important but difficult to distinguish between the impact of religious beliefs on politics and the relationships between religious and political institutions. For example, the hypothesis advanced by Erich Fromm and others that the *Autorität Glaube* (faith in authority) of Lutheranism was congruent with Nazi ideology and facilitated its hold on power is compatible with the evidence of opposition to Hitler by some Protestant leaders. In the first case, Fromm was talking about predisposition to accept certain political ideologies flowing from religious tenets, while the second case involved a power conflict between leaders of an organized church and the state's efforts to deny its traditional rights.

It is not easy for sociologists to formulate propositions

about religion and politics that appear valid outside of specific contexts. For, as Max Weber noted, one of the chief determinants of the precise political role of religion in any given polity largely depends on historical circumstances, and therefore it is difficult to generalize easily about relationships. While general statements may be made about the functions of religion for a society, the variation in denominational structure and values limits propositions to highly specific complex contexts. Factors such as the following ones will affect the reality in any given nation: the number of different groups existing in one society; the pattern of ecological distribution of a denomination; the relationship of different religious groups to other structural sources of difference; the relative majority or minority position of a group; the extent to which a given electoral system encourages or discourages special interest parties; and many more. But complexity does not mean inability to generalize, and with value-generating institutions as with varying systems and orders of stratification, the political analyst is obligated to look for functional relationships.

The next section turns to a series of case studies of political cleavage in different parts of the world which concretely illustrate the way in which class and religious factors affect the nature of such tensions. I first seek to compare the varying political conflicts in the underdeveloped and the developed worlds. I then turn to an analysis of the processes of political modernization within Europe. The section is concluded with two discussions of factors which have affected changes in American politics.

PART IV

POLITICAL CLEAVAGES IN
COMPARATIVE PERSPECTIVE

CHAPTER 7

Political Cleavages in "Developed" and "Emerging" Polities

Although many discussions of the possibilities for democratic politics in the emerging nations of the "third world" are posed in terms of whether or not these nations can successfully absorb political models established in the developed countries, it is not really possible to speak of a "Western" political system. A variety of factors have contributed to the vast array of party systems existing in the developed nations.[1] These include the different ways in which mass suffrage parties first emerged, the various conditions under which lower-class parties formed their basic ideologies, whether a polity derives its authority from historic legitimacy or from post-revolutionary populism, the extent to which different nations have

[1] An effort to relate these systematically to theoretical assumptions about basic structures of social systems derived from the concepts of Talcott Parsons may be found in S. M. Lipset and Stein Rokkan, "Cleavage Structures, Party Systems, and Voter Alignments," in Lipset and Rokkan (eds.), *Party Systems and Voter Alignments* (New York: The Free Press of Glencoe, 1967), pp. 1–64. I have also discussed the factors related to varying political systems in various contexts in other books and do not want to repeat them here. See S. M. Lipset, *Political Man: The Social Bases of Politics* (Garden City: Doubleday, 1960), pp. 45–96, and *The First New Nation* (New York: Basic Books, 1963), pp. 207–317.

resolved the tensions flowing from the key power cleavages common in the history of Western industrial societies, such as the place of religion, universal suffrage, the distribution of national income and resources, and the variations in electoral systems. Clearly many of the existing differences reflect the institutionalization of past bases of opinion cleavage; once formalized in political parties these cleavages have survived the decline or disappearance of the original social conflicts which gave rise to party divisions. Parties, like all other institutions, tend to foster self-maintaining mechanisms. They necessarily seek bases of support and new issues to perpetuate themselves. And as Ostrogorski noted, loyalty to parties is often comparable to identification with a religious denomination.[2] Each party retains a body of loyal adherents who see their party allegiance as an important part of their identity.

Variations in national party systems are linked to historical factors but this does not prevent the formation of broad generalizations about the development of party systems in democracies of the developed world, for the purpose of comparison with the polities of the "third world." This chapter will deal briefly with some of the varying historical conditions which have affected Western party systems, particularly in their formative periods, in order to point out some major differences in the bases of cleavage in the existing and emerging democracies.

THE DEVELOPMENT OF WESTERN PARTY DIVISIONS

The modern political party is in large measure the resultant of the democratic electoral system. Before the establishment of the suffrage there were, of course, controversies about the policies of government. In the absolutist state, such disagreements were resolved at the level of the monarchy. As the upper social strata, such as the landed nobility, sought to restrict the powers of the king, parliaments of various kinds

---

[2] M. Ostrogorski, *Democracy and the Organization of Political Parties* II: *The United States* (Chicago: Quadrangle Books, 1964), pp. 173, 223–224, 305–306. See my discussion of Ostrogorski's text in the Introduction to that edition.

emerged and shared some of the state's power. In these parliaments, men with common interests, values, or backgrounds joined together into loose factions which some historians have called parties. These groups, however, had no common program, little or no organization, and little discipline. They did not seek to gain power through elections, but did so by breaking off support from other factions, or by winning the backing of the king. Where an electorate existed, it was usually quite small and under the control of the local nobility, as in Great Britain.

As forms of electoral democracy advanced in nineteenth-century Europe, a contest developed in most countries between two elements, usually labeled liberals and conservatives. The liberals generally supported democratic reforms and some further extension of the initially quite limited suffrage, opposed an established church and religious control of education, and hence attracted to their ranks men who favored a variety of social and economic reforms. The conservatives tended initially to oppose extension of the suffrage (although they changed to support it in some countries, seeing the possibility of drawing support from "deferential" lower strata who responded to conservative efforts to improve their circumstances on the basis of *noblesse oblige*), to support the privileges of the traditional church, and to have the backing of the more traditionalist elements in society such as the old dominant landed class and the nobility. Given a very restricted electorate, these parties lacked cohesion. Local notables controlled their constituencies regardless of how they voted in Parliament and despite the consequences of government policies. The two parties were subdivided into various factions and new combinations kept re-forming within them.[3]

The introduction of the working class as a political force, however, soon changed this picture. As the workers organized into trade unions and legal or semi-legal political groupings, the upper classes gradually made concessions to the demand for adult suffrage. Sometimes these concessions were a result of the fear of revolution; at other times they were

[3] Maurice Duverger, *Political Parties* (London: Methuen, 1954), pp. xxiii–xxxvii; Max Weber, *Essays in Sociology* (New York: Oxford University Press, 1946), pp. 100–115.

owing to fulfillment of the democratic ideology of a victorious liberal group; and often they resulted from the efforts of one or another party to increase its base of electoral support. Conservatives felt they could rely on the votes of the religious and tradition-minded peasantry in many countries.[4] The inauguration of manhood suffrage, however, whatever the reason for its adoption, changed the nature of politics. The techniques necessary to win votes in a mass electorate required, as Ostrogorski indicated, the creation of the party organization. Thus the first formal party organizations emerged in American cities. Tammany Hall and its brethren were necessary for the mobilization of the voters. Considerable funds were required for campaigning and professional politics developed in response to a felt need.

In Europe, as Max Weber pointed out, the socialist parties were the first to adapt successfully to the new situation and create bureaucratic parties dominated by professional politicians.[5] These parties had an elaborate formal structure, dues-paying members, and branches which held regular meetings. They established party newspapers and created a network of groups tied to the party such as social clubs, women's associations, and youth organizations. They also formulated the concept of rigid party discipline, that the elected representatives were responsible to the party and must act according to party demands.

The emergence of the socialists as a political force within the context of manhood suffrage changed the structure of much of European politics. Mass-based religious and agrarian parties developed in a number of countries, and tended to adopt many of the organizational procedures of the socialists. The conservatives and liberals were also forced to react to the logic of dealing with a mass electorate by adopting organizational procedures in many ways similar to those of the Ameri-

---

[4] In 1861, Napoleon III advised the Prussian government to introduce universal suffrage "by means of which the conservative rural population could outvote the Liberals in the cities." F. Meinecke, *Weltbürgertum und Nationalstaat* (Munich: G. R. Oldenbourg, 1922), pp. 517–518; F. Naumann, *Die Politischen Parteien* (Berlin-Schönberg: Buchverlag der Hilfe, 1910), pp. 16–17.

[5] Weber, *op. cit.,* pp. 103–104; Guenther Roth, *The Social Democrats in Imperial Germany* (Totowa: The Bedminster Press, 1963), pp. 252–254.

can or socialist parties. On the whole, however, those parties which are lineal descendants of nineteenth-century liberal and conservative parties, led by notables, have never been so successful in creating large-scale membership parties as parties stemming from mass organizations such as the Marxist and religious ones.

CLASS TENSIONS AND POLITICS IN THE
FORMATIVE PERIOD OF WESTERN POLITICS

The modern ideological conflicts affecting industrial society originated in the problem of locating old pre-industrial upper classes, the church, the mass citizenry, and the working class within the polity. In the United States the place of the old upper class, religion, and suffrage was determined before the working class became a significant force. Thus, the workers did not have to fight their way into the electorate; the right of universal suffrage existed before the class existed. In much of Europe, on the other hand, these issues remained to be fought out together. In Germany, Austria-Hungary, Sweden, and Belgium, universal suffrage for males was not granted until shortly before or during World War I.[6] The aristocracy and even the monarchy retained important areas of power and privilege. And the established church continued to fight to retain or regain ancient privileges. In the Latin countries, particularly France and Italy, the Catholic Church rejected— almost until World War I—any cooperation between Catholics and the state which had denied the Church privileges it demanded on moral grounds. The working class left, therefore, was often at war with the old right, with organized religion, and with the bourgeoisie.

The prolonged intensity of class conflict in many continental nations was owing to the overlap of economic class conflict with "moral" issues of religion, aristocracy, and status. Because moral issues involve basic concepts of right and wrong, they are much more likely than economic matters to result in civil war or at least sharp class cleavage. To work out compromises over wages and hours or tax policy

[6] Duverger, *op. cit.*, p. 46.

is easy. To compromise with what is held to be heresy or a basic threat to the right way of life is much more difficult.

When accounting for the variations in class consciousness and class conflict among different industrial societies, we must examine the differences in the dynamics of their status systems. In general, the more rigid the status demarcation lines in a country, the more likely the emergence of explicit class-oriented parties. This variation in structure and its consequences may be illustrated by contrasting the political histories of the United States and Europe. Because the United States did not inherit a fixed pattern of distinct status groups from a feudal past, the development of working-class political consciousness required an act of intellectual imagination. American workers had to be "taught" that they were members of a common "class" and that they should cooperate against other classes. In Europe, however, workers were placed in a common class by the value system of the total society. In a real sense, workers absorbed a "consciousness of kind" from the social structure. Socialists did not have to teach them that they were in a different class; the society and the upper classes did it for them.

Nevertheless, there is considerable variation in the political behavior of different classes among European countries. The British have had a strong Labour party for over half a century, but it has always been less "radical" than most of the socialist parties on the continent. Never having had a Marxist phase and always friendly to religion, it adopted socialism as a goal only toward the end of World War I. Moreover, the Labour party does not oppose the monarchy, and its leaders accept aristocratic and other honorific titles from the Crown. The comparative moderation of British class conflict and politics has been related to several factors: its aristocracy assimilated the leaders of new classes, first the bourgeoisie and later labor; its period of rapid industrialization occurred before the emergence of socialist movements; and the rights of citizenship—universal male suffrage and the freedom to form unions—were granted prior to the formation of large-scale political and economic organizations by labor. Thus the emphasis on status classes in Britain facilitated the forming of class political groups which could operate from their beginning to obtain "more" for their members and supporters without having to fight for their place in the polity. Some analysts of German politics have contended that the great stress on *Stände,* estate or status groupings, explained the close ties of status group and party support in pre-Hitler Germany. "Probably in no other country would the analysis of the social composition of party organizations show it to be so homogeneous as do the results of sociological studies of the electorate."[7] The great emphasis on status differences in Germany accounted for the large number of middle- and upper-class parties, each representing a distinct status group and having a distinct ideology.

Similarly, the cleavage between the Socialists and Communists within the German working class reflected status concerns. Communist support came disproportionately from the less skilled *lumpen* elements among the workers. To this lower stratum the German socialist movement exhibited a hostility not found elsewhere.[8]

The greater propensity for political extremism of both left and right in German history is related to the strong desire to preserve *Ständ* rights. On the one hand, the Prussian aristocracy sought to retain their control over the major institutions of the polity, even to the extent of denying the middle classes access to most leading positions. Like the English aristocracy they sought to win the support of the masses against the bourgeoisie by passing many welfare measures. But unlike the English they did not allow workers' organizations and leaders to have full citizenship rights. From 1878 to 1891, the Socialists were outlawed as a party and Prussia, the main state of the Reich, did not have equal suffrage until Germany was defeated in World War I.[9] This

---

[7] Theodore Geiger, *Die Soziale Schichtung des Deutschen Volkes* (Stuttgart: Ferdinand Enke, 1932), p. 79.

[8] See Robert Michels, "Die Deutschen Sozialdemokratie I. Parteimitgliedschaft und soziale Zusammensetzung," *Archiv für Sozialwissenschaft und Sozialpolitik,* 26 (1906), 512–513; Robert Michels, *Sozialismus und Fascismus* I (Karlsruhe: G. Braun, 1925), pp. 78–79; Robert Lowie, *Toward Understanding Germany* (Chicago: University of Chicago Press, 1954), p. 138.

[9] There was, of course, adult male suffrage in the federal parliament, but the three-chamber voting system of Prussia, which discriminated heavily against the workers, served to prevent the large Socialist bloc in the federal parliament from having much influence, and this meant

refusal to allow the workers' leaders a share in political power forced the socialist movement to maintain a revolutionary posture in its ideology.

German middle-class support of the Nazis may also be linked to the strong status emphasis in the culture. Studies of this phenomenon have assumed they were motivated by a desire to maintain their privileges, threatened by the universalistic values incorporated in the Weimar Republic and fostered by the Social Democrats, and undermined by the economic catastrophe of the 1930's. The Nazis appealed strongly to this aspect of German middle-class values.

In southern and western Germany, where status lines were less rigid, the conservative classes had been willing—even before World War I—to admit the workers' political movement into the body politic by enacting universal suffrage. And conversely, the workers' movement demonstrated that it did not want to destroy the state, but to be admitted to it. As contrasted with Prussia, the socialist parties in these states developed a moderate and pragmatic ideology, gave considerable support to Bernstein revisionism, and even backed "bourgeois" cabinets. Conversely, the most reactionary elements in German society had their primary base in the most feudal region of the country, Prussia-beyond-the-Elbe. In the 1912 Reichstag, only four of the Conservative party members were elected from non-Prussian constituencies, and of the fifty-one Prussian conservatives forty-five were aristocrats who came from these eastern regions characterized by the predominance of large landowners.[10]

The same regions heavily supported enemies of the Weimar Republic. The Conservatives, remaining hostile to the republic, secured their strength basically in the same nonmodern areas as they did before the war. And while the aristocratic supporters of conservatism, on the whole, did not join the Nazis before 1933, the various analyses of electoral statistics

that the struggle for political democracy had still to be waged. "The federal constitution, as written by Bismarck, had made the federal government practically an appendix of the Prussian cabinet." See Carl Landauer, *European Socialism* (Berkeley: University of California Press, 1959), pp. 366–368.

[10] Theodore Schieder, *The State and Society in Our Times* (London: Thomas Nelson & Sons, 1962), p. 121.

during the early 1930's in Germany reveal that the support of Nazism came disproportionately from those strata least involved in modern industrial society. According to the census of 1933, a large majority of Germans lived in rural areas or communities with less than 25,000 population, and these sections gave the Nazis far greater support than did the more urbanized and industrialized larger cities. Similarly, the larger the proportion of the labor force employed in small business establishments, the higher the Nazi vote. "The ideal-typical Nazi voter in 1932 was a middle-class self-employed Protestant who lived either on a farm or in a small community, and who had previously voted for a centrist or regionalist political party strongly opposed to the power and influence of big business and big labor."[11]

The presence in the same country of large working-class extremist movements (e.g., anarchist and Communist) and ultrareactionary political tendencies among the middle and upper classes has been explained by many political analysts as a consequence of certain unique elements in social structure. Schumpeter, for instance, has argued that the persistence of the power and social influence of a nobility until quite late in the capitalist period in Britain and Germany, unlike the situation in the three Latin countries (France, Italy, and Spain), played an important role in reducing the working class's antagonism to the state. His thesis is that the aristocracy served as "protective strata" for the workers, helping to enact various social reforms, and thus giving them a sense that the state might be an effective instrument of social improvement. In countries where status differences remained strong, but which lacked a still powerful aristocracy that could foster a variant of anti-bourgeois "Tory socialism," as in the southern Latin nations, the workers became alienated from state and society as they developed conscious political and economic aims.[12]

A related hypothesis suggests that the peculiarly unstable politics of these nations has been a product of cultural factors which inhibited economic growth and led their business

---

[11] Lipset, *Political Man*, p. 149.

[12] Joseph Schumpeter, *Capitalism, Socialism and Democracy* (New York: Harper Torchbooks, 1962), pp. 134–139.

classes to follow the logic of pre-capitalist and mercantilist society. As Mario Einaudi once put it:

> [I]n those countries where the development of the middle classes has been stunted and limited so that their twentieth century bourgeoisie bears a striking resemblance to the bourgeoisie of the days of Louis Phillipe, there will be a continuing strong assertion of political views which have disappeared in those countries in which "everybody" belongs to the middle class.[13]

The Latin business classes preserved far longer than their counterparts in northern Europe a semi-feudal stratum with strong emphasis on family property and stability. To a greater extent than in the more mature industrial nations, family-owned concerns continued to play a dominant economic role and to follow pre-capitalist emphases on maintaining intact the family fortune and status; this limited their willingness to take economic risks or to enter into competition. The politics of the bourgeoisie were oriented toward maintaining the stability of existing business, i.e., protecting marginal producers.[14] As discussed in Chapter 3, this pattern is even more prevalent in Latin American countries.

Management in these countries retained conceptions of their proper authority over workers that emerged during early industrialization which were inappropriate to class relations in a mature industrial society. They continued to expect particularistic loyalties from their employees, to think it proper to deny them the right to collective bargaining. In the relatively small family-owned businesses, the processes of bureaucratization and rationalization—stable definition of rights and duties, systematic universalistic ordering of authority relationships, publicity of decisions, division of labor with the appearance of personnel experts or specialists in labor relations, and

[13] Mario Einaudi, " 'Social Realities' and the Study of Political Parties" (unpublished paper).

[14] See the various articles by David Landes: "French Entrepreneurship and Industrial Growth in the XIXth Century," *Journal of Economic History*, 9 (1949), 49–61; "French Business and the Business Man: A Social and Cultural Analysis," in Edward M. Earle (ed.), *Modern France* (Princeton: Princeton University Press, 1951), pp. 334–353; and "observations on France: Economy, Society and Polity," *World Politics*, 9 (1957), 329–350.

so on—did not emerge. Any threat to limit the rights of the business classes either by state or trade-union action was bitterly resented and opposed on moral grounds as an effort to undermine the very fabric of the social order, private family property.

The working class in these "halfway" industrialized countries found it difficult to develop legitimate, stable trade unions, and their political parties were unable to secure major structural improvements. As a result, the more politicized or class-conscious elements within the class continued to maintain the attitudes of alienation from the body politic characteristic of workers during the period of early rapid industrialization.[15] The emphasis within the society on status differentiation facilitated the emergence of strong class-conscious groupings. And to a much greater extent than elsewhere, these movements adhered to revolutionary anti-social doctrines, first those of anarcho-syndicalism and later of communism. This was the response of the Latin working class to being "in the society, but not of it."[16] And the revolutionary ideology of the working-class groups reinforced the fears and hostility of the middle and upper classes to any proposal that might give these groups increased access to power within industry or the state.

As in Germany, those sections of France and Italy resembling other industrialized capitalist nations (e.g., in having large-scale bureaucratized industries) were the ones in which the business classes demonstrated a greater willingness to accept trade-unionism as a legitimate and permanent part of the industrial system and in which anarcho-syndicalism was weakest. Before 1914 in France and Italy, the Socialists were most powerful in the areas of large industry; the anarcho-syndicalist unions were strongest in the areas where the particularistic values of small business were dominant. A

[15] "Sluggish economic growth may generate the deepest and longest lasting protest by reason of the society's inability to provide well-being and social justice to match social aspirations and by reason of the economic elite's failure to inspire confidence," Val Lorwin, "Working Class Politics and Economic Development in Western Europe," *American Historical Review*, 63 (1958), 350.

[16] See Bruce H. Millen, *The Political Role of Labor in Developing Countries* (Washington: The Brookings Institution, 1963), pp. 38–39; Lorwin, *op. cit.*, pp. 345–346.

similar pattern in Communist and Socialist support was found in France between World War I and World War II. The Communists in general inherited the centers of syndicalist strength. Since World War II, however, the Communists have replaced the Socialists as the dominant working-class party and are disproportionately strong within large industry, a point which will be elaborated in Chapter 7.

Variations in the working-class politics of the three major Scandinavian nations have been accounted for by the social consequences of the historic timing and pace of early industrialization, factors alluded to here in discussing other countries. The Danish labor movement has always been among the most moderate in Europe; the Swedish one underwent a period of considerable radicalization in the first decade of this century; while the Norwegian leftists exhibited their most revolutionary phase during and shortly after World War I. The Norwegian historian Edvard Bull has developed the most widely accepted explanation for the variations among these countries:

> He focused on one central "marco" variable: *the suddenness of the changes brought about by industrialization.* He developed a general proposition . . . : the *slower* the growth of industry and the more of its labor force that can be recruited from already established urban communities, the less leftist the reactions of the workers and the less radical their party; the *more sudden* the growth of industry and the more of its labor force has to be recruited from agriculture and fisheries, the more leftist the workers and the more revolutionary their party.[17]

[17] Summary of the main thesis of Edvard Bull, "Die Entwicklung der Arbeiterbewegung in den drei skandinavischen Ländern," *Archiv für die Geschichte der Sozialismus und der Arbeiterbewegung,* 10 (1922), in Stein Rokkan and Henry Valen, "Parties, Elections and Political Behaviour in the Northern Countries: A Review of Recent Research," in Otto Stammer (ed.), *Politische Forschung* (Köln: Westdeutscher Verlag, 1960), p. 110; see also pp. 107–108. The specific empirical results of Bull's analysis are presented in some detail in Walter Galenson, "Scandinavia," in Galenson (ed.), *Comparative Labor Movements* (New York: Prentice-Hall, 1952), esp. pp. 105–120. I have dealt with this material in *Political Man,* pp. 68–71. A detailed discussion of the relationship between the pace of industrialization and politics may be found in my article, "Socialism-Left and Right-East and West," *Confluence,* 7 (Summer 1958), 173–192.

The history of these nations would seem to validate Bull's proposition. Denmark experienced gradual economic and urban growth; Swedish industry developed very rapidly from 1900 to 1914; while Norway had the highest rate of growth of all three between 1905 and 1920, and experienced the greatest radicalization. Further evidence may be adduced from many other nations to show that periods of large-scale dislocations of population occasioned by rapid industrialization and urbanization have often led to the expression of deep class conflict.[18] However, such tensions usually decline, as Engels put it, wherever "the transition to large-scale industry is more or less completed. . . . [and] the conditions in which the proletariat is placed become stable."[19]

The factors underlying the emergence of a moderate labor and socialist movement in Belgium before World War I further illustrate the syndrome determining the variations in intensity of European politics.[20] Belgium and Britain were the first two nations to industrialize in Europe; hence the worst of the social strains occasioned by rapid industrialization and urbanization occurred before the rise of the modern labor movement. As Val Lorwin states in explaining the differences between the Belgian and the French and German movements: "Belgium's industrialization began earlier, and it became more urbanized than France."[21] Such factors, however, do not explain why the Belgian conservatives showed a propensity to compromise with labor militancy, thereby preventing the development of the vicious circle appearing elsewhere, in which the aggressiveness of one class occasioned similar reactions from the other. In his comprehensive comparative study of European socialism, Carl Landauer suggests that the conflict was moderate in Belgium because historically

[18] Lorwin, *op. cit.,* p. 350; Lipset, *Political Man,* pp. 70–71; Mancur Olson, Jr., "Rapid Growth as a Destabilizing Force," *The Journal of Economic History,* 23 (1963), 529–552.

[19] Friedrich Engels, "Letter to Karl Kautsky," November 8, 1884, in Karl Marx and Friedrich Engels, *Correspondence 1846–1895* (New York: International Publishers, 1946), p. 422.

[20] "Belgian socialism from the start has been one of the most moderate labor movements." Felix E. Oppenheim, "Belgium: Party Cleavage and Compromise," in S. Neumann (ed.), *Modern Political Parties* (Chicago: University of Chicago Press, 1956), p. 162.

[21] Lorwin, *op. cit.,* p. 348.

it had been less of a *Ständestaat* than any of its neighbors and that industrialization and capitalism flourished where feudal values had been weakest:

> Belgium is a business country, with a weak feudal tradition—much weaker than in Germany, France, or Britain. . . . In Belgium, fewer upper-class people than elsewhere think that they owe it to their pride to resist the aspiration of the underprivileged . . . [E]ven less than in Britain or France and certainly less than in Germany was exploitation motivated by the idea that the humble must be kept in their places; in Belgium, more than anywhere else, was the desire to force the worker to accept small pay, long hours, and otherwise unfavorable conditions of employment a pure dollar-and-cent proposition. The argument that a prolonged strike, even if it leads to defeat of the workers, would be extremely hard on business had more of an echo and met with weaker counteracting tendencies in bourgeoisie and government than in several other industrial countries.[22]

The situation in Finland illustrates yet another dimension in the variables which determined the political process in pre-World War I Europe. In some ways, the factors which affected the ideological tensions in the Finnish party system resemble those operative in some of the emerging nations of the contemporary "third" world which are discussed below. In the nineteenth century, Finland was a duchy under the Czar of Russia. A small Swedish-speaking minority was heavily represented among the privileged classes. Universal suffrage and trade-union rights did not exist. A Socialist party, formed at the end of the nineteenth century, appealed to the class discontents of the newly emerging working class and the much larger farm-tenant population. In effect, however, as was to occur later in many colonial countries of Asia and Africa, the Socialists addressed themselves to the interrelated issues of class, cultural and linguistic needs, democratic rights, and national independence. This meant that, although the movement necessarily had to be revolutionary in its ideology, it could successfully appeal for support to strata far removed from the relatively small working class. And the winning of universal suffrage in 1906 (following on the

General Strike throughout the Czarist empire in 1905) resulted in the Socialists securing 40 per cent of the seats in Parliament, more than such parties won in any other nation in Europe. Their parliamentary support grew to 43 per cent in 1910 and 45 per cent in 1913. In 1916, the Socialists, still fighting the class, cultural, and national battles, actually secured a parliamentary majority. The subsequent strength of Finnish communism in large measure stems from the commitment to radical Marxian concepts fostered by the Finnish Socialists during the period of Czarist rule.[23]

Although the political expression of class tensions was to change considerably between the pre-1914 and the post-1945 situations, structural hypotheses similar to those used to account for variations in the earlier period would seem to be relevant for the latter. The values and behavior patterns inherent in the status system, the pace of industrial development and urbanization, the pattern of management-labor relations linked to the bureaucratization of enterprises, and the degree to which diverse sources of political cleavage overlap, all remain as key sources of variation in class politics.

TYPOLOGIES OF WESTERN PARTY SYSTEMS

It is impossible to locate the determinants of the varying party systems in the democratic developed nations by a simple analytic framework. The number of parties that exist is a function of the complexity and intensity of the social cleavages which seek political representation, and of the nature of the electoral system. Nations such as France, where the

[23] See Harry Laidler, *Socialism in Thought and Action* (New York: Macmillan, 1927), pp. 447–450, 489–490; Franz Borkenau, *World Communism* (Ann Arbor: Ann Arbor Paperback, 1962), pp. 104–106; Heikki Waris, "Finland," in Arnold Rose (ed.), *The Institutions of Advanced Societies* (Minneapolis: University of Minnesota Press, 1958), pp. 211–214; for a summary of studies of Finnish political behavior in recent years see Pertti Pesonen, "Studies on Finnish Political Behavior," in Austin Ranney (ed.), *Essays on the Behavioral Study of Politics* (Urbana: University of Illinois Press, 1962), pp. 217–234; for a statistical analysis of the way in which the Swedish domination of class position and prestige was overcome see Karl Deutsch, *Nationalism and Social Communication* (New York: John Wiley, 1953), pp. 104–107.

strains derivative from conflicts over the place of the church, the relations among diverse status groups, economic interest struggles, and orientations toward political authority have persisted for more than a century, have a complex cleavage structure difficult to resolve within a two- or three-party system. This issue of the number of parties has been discussed in detail elsewhere and need not be repeated here.[24]

Similarly, the factors which affect the degree of ideological intensity, and the extent to which the democratic rules of the game are accepted by all important actors in the polity, are also too complex to be dealt with in detail in a discussion such as this. To a considerable extent, the intensity of cleavage and the character of attitudes toward the democratic system are associated with the severity of strains experienced by significant strata. Those strata which experience the tensions of rapid industrialization and urbanization tend to be much more radical than those inured to being part of an urban industrial society; nations in which democratic rights (full suffrage and trade unions) for all have been institutionalized prior to the emergence of a mass working class tend to have more moderate and legitimate opposition politics than those in which suffrage or trade-union rights were resisted deep into the present century; those nations which are relatively well to do and which have a high per-capita income reveal less significant strain between the classes and consequently less ideological politics; those countries which allocated citizenship rights to new classes, the bourgeoisie and later the workers, without requiring revolutionary overthrow of the symbolic source of traditional authority, the monarchy, also tend as a group to have more stable and less virulent politics than others.

If we turn now to an examination of the sources of party cleavage in contemporary democratic countries, it is clear that the role relationships which have proved most likely to generate stable lines of party support are largely aspects of stratification, as between higher and lower orders in status, income and power, or aspects of cultural differences, as

[24] See Lipset, *The First New Nation*, pp. 286–317, and Lipset and Rokkan, *op. cit.*

between specific groups which vary widely in their views of the nature and values of the good society.[25] The prototype of the first cleavage is class parties, of the second, religious parties. Differences rooted in stratification are likely to be most preponderant in economically developed stable polities in which much domestic political controversy may be described as the "politics of collective bargaining," a fight over the division of the total economic pie, over the extent of the welfare and planning state, and the like. Cultural or deeply rooted value conflicts are much more characteristic of the politics of developing countries with unstable polities. In such nations, in addition to conflicts rooted in class controversy, there is a division based on the differences in outlook related to institutions which originated in the pre-modern era, and to those which foster or are endemic in social and economic development. Examples of cultural conflicts include the confrontation of those who seek to maintain the traditional position of historic religion, the status and privileges of higher social strata such as the nobility, or social relationships within families and other institutions which represent a way of life characteristic of a relatively static rural society, against those who seek to change these patterns of behavior toward a more universalistic social system. Many of the variables associated with positions in a *Kulturkampf* are not linked to stratification, but to involvement in traditional or modern institutions and to generational experiences, for example, poor religious peasants may be conservatives, while well-to-do young professionals may be radical; the young and better educated may oppose the older and the less educated. Sex, too, may provide a basis for diversity where cultural issues are significant. The woman's role in most societies requires her to be more involved in religious institutions and less in modern economic ones, to be less educated on the average than men, and consequently to be more supportive of traditionalist parties than of modernizing ones.

If we consider the developed countries first, it is clear that in all of them there is a correlation between the generally

[25] For an effort at constructing a more formal typology, see Lipset and Rokkan, *op. cit.*

accepted degree of leftism or conservatism of political parties and their support in terms of stratification variables. The more liberal or left-wing parties are disproportionately supported by those with low income, by workers, by poorer farmers, by the less educated, by members of religious groups defined as low status, and by those invidiously identified in racial or ethnic terms.[26]

This pattern comes out most clearly in the five predominantly English-speaking democracies. In all of these countries the factors of lower-class status, Catholic religion, and recent immigrant background are associated with support for the Democrats or with Labour and Liberal politics. The size of the correlation varies among these nations and other factors enter as well, but it seems clear that stratification as rooted in occupation, income, religion and ethnicity, perceived as status-defining variables, accounts for part of the variation in party support.[27]

The picture is somewhat more complicated in the various multiparty systems of continental Europe. In some of them, cleavages rooted in the preindustrial society of the late eighteenth and much of the nineteenth centuries continue to influence the nature of party division. Perhaps the most striking example of this is the name of the party which represents the views of the Dutch orthodox Calvinists, the Anti-Revolutionary party. The revolution which this party is against is the French Revolution of 1789.

Although there are great variations among them, these countries do have a number of elements in common. First, the historic cleavage between liberal and conservative, or religious parties, which arose in the nineteenth century before the rise of socialism as a significant force, has been maintained in most of them. In Scandinavia, this cleavage is represented by the continuation of strong Liberal and Conservative parties, in Catholic Europe and Germany by the existence of Christian Democratic parties and liberal or other anti-clerical bourgeois parties. All of these countries have strong working-

---

[26] These statements are documented in detail in Lipset, *Political Man,* and I will not reiterate the references here.

[27] See Robert R. Alford, *Party and Society. The Anglo-American Democracies* (Chicago: Rand McNally, 1963).

class oriented parties. Here, however, they differ greatly according to whether there is one dominant Social-Democratic party opposed by a small Communist party, or whether there is a mass Communist party which is larger than the Socialists, as in France, Italy, and Finland. A number of these countries, particularly the Scandinavian, also have agrarian or peasant parties.

In spite of the great diversity in the continental multiparty systems, class and religion would seem to be the preponderant sources of difference among the parties. Lower income and status are associated with voting for the working-class oriented parties. On the whole, where there are large Communist and Socialist parties, the latter derive greater support from the more skilled and better educated workers, although there are important exceptions, particularly in the case of Finland. Communists also tend to draw support among the socially uprooted in rapidly changing areas, and among those who have been unemployed in the past. The religious parties draw their backing from the centers of religious strength, regardless of class, and thus gain support from both rich and poor, although they are disproportionately strong among farm people and among women. The urban religious manual workers seem to have many of the same economic interests and policy orientations as the Social Democratic workers, and they usually adhere to Christian trade unions which work closely with socialist unions. The Liberal parties on the whole, parts of Scandinavia excepted, tend to be relatively small, 7 to 15 per cent, and to be based on the anti-clerical bourgeois and professional groups. Scandinavian Liberalism is somewhat different. It resembles the old English Liberal party and though backed by irreligious bourgeois and professional groups, also draws support from the quite religious Scandinavian equivalents of the English nonconformists, who oppose the Conservatives as supporters of the traditional Lutheran Church Establishment. The Scandinavian Conservatives, in turn, seem to be the party of the more well to do, both rural and urban, and of those involved in the traditional church.

The maintenance of the pluralistic party structure of Scandinavia is facilitated by a system of proportional representation which helps preserve diverse nonsocialist parties. They are under no pressure to unite before elections, though the differences among them have declined. The picture is somewhat different in Catholic and southern Europe. There, a lower level of economic development, failure to develop completely legitimate political institutions, and the superimposition of the various conflicts of the nineteenth century over the status of the old privileged classes, the position of the church, and the economic class struggle, have resulted in a cleavage structure which cannot be readily fitted into a broad two-party coalition structure. Broadly speaking, the "normal" division in these nations is a three-party one consisting of a large multi-class Catholic party, based disproportionately on the rural population, opposed by a large Socialist party rooted in the urban working class, with a much smaller middle-class oriented anti-clerical Liberal party, which holds the balance of power. This pattern is found in Belgium, Luxembourg, Germany, and Austria. In Holland, the problem is complicated further by the presence of three conflicting religions, each of which has its own party, but if the religious parties are considered as one force, the Dutch pattern resembles the above four nations. In France and Italy, however, the strains are clearly more intense, and both the clerical and anti-clerical sectors of the nation have been greatly divided, so that each has a five- to six-party structure.

THE PARTIES OF THE THIRD WORLD

In the first flurry of democratic enthusiasm after World War II, many believed that the newly independent states of Africa and Asia, as well as the "old" nations of Latin America, would support democratic polities strongly resembling those of Western Europe and the overseas English-speaking democracies. Currently, with the emergence of military and one-party regimes in many of these nations, an almost total pessimism concerning the democratic potential of these countries has replaced the early hopes. Scholars, journalists, and politicians from the stable democracies now conclude that they erred in anticipating democratic institutions in nations whose economy and culture were not yet ready to sustain the tensions of party conflict. Although it is much too early to make definitive conclusions about the polities of the "third" world, it is clear that neither extreme of optimism or pessimism concerning the future of democracy is justified. In fact, outside of the Communist nations, the majority of the peoples of Asia live in democratic polities, in which the press is relatively free and opposition parties operate openly within and outside of parliament. Only in sub-Saharan Africa and the Arab world can one say that one-party and absolutist regimes predominate.[28] Most Latin American nations would hardly be considered models of democratic polities, particularly since the military has intervened in the recent past to limit the possible results of election in Peru, Argentina, Ecuador, Bolivia, and Brazil, but a greater semblance of opposition rights is permitted in some of the Latin dictatorships, e.g., Argentina and Mexico. In non-Communist Asia states containing the bulk of the population are relatively democratic—India, Ceylon, Israel, Lebanon, Turkey, Malaysia, Singapore, South Korea, the Philippines, and Japan. Unfortunately, the same cannot be said for Burma, and the remaining Moslem states of the Asian continent, but these, while possessing many votes in the United Nations, contain considerably fewer people than the democratic Asian polities.

The considerably greater cultural and historical diversity of the "third" world than that of the developed nations complicates the search for a single set of factors associated with the propensity to sustain competitive party systems among the less developed nations. Evidence for the association between level of economic development, literacy, and the existence of a stable democratic polity is one step in this search.[29] More

[28] The special failing of democracy in Africa clearly deserves some attention. To some considerable extent it would seem to have some relationship to the fact of tribalism. The African states are not societies or nations, they are for the most part heterogeneous collections of linguistically and culturally distinct tribes or smaller nations, without a common language. Before becoming democratic polities they must first *become* polities. See René Servoise, "Whither Black Africa?" *Futuribles,* 1963, esp. pp. 264–267.

[29] Lipset, *Political Man,* pp. 48–67; James S. Coleman, "The Political Systems of the Developing Areas," in Gabriel Almond and J. S. Cole-

fruitful, perhaps, in the long run, are the attempts to locate, and even measure, the consequences for political development of varying rates of social mobilization, of the process by which diverse strata are "integrated" into the larger modernizing sector of society.[30] Such changes, however, may result in a breakdown in national solidarity and early efforts at a democratic polity, since rapid social change, with its consequent high rates of mobility, initially results in considerable social displacement, incongruencies of status, and makes for considerable discontent with existing institutions. Many have pointed out that such processes produce people who are "disposable," available for new, often authoritarian or irresponsible political movements. As European history well demonstrates, modernization involves "a succession of what might be called crises of access . . . [periods involving] a social and political adjustment to new claimants to power, prestige, status."[31] Thus the very tendencies which enhance the conditions necessary to sustain an integrated and democratic polity may destroy embryonic efforts at such developments. Gino Germani has, in fact, suggested that a condition for increasing the probability that the processes of mobilization and modernization will support rather than undermine the chances for democracy "consists in the possibility of these social processes occurring in successive stages. In other words, a nation requires sufficient time and opportunity between stages of mobilization [incorporation of additional segments of the population] to integrate each given stratum. This is what occurred in the West both with respect to political integration

---

man, (eds.), *The Politics of the Developing Areas* (Princeton: Princeton University Press, 1960), pp. 538–544; Everett Hagen, "A Framework for Analyzing Economic and Political Change," in Robert Asher (ed.), *Development of Emerging Countries* (Washington: Brookings Institution, 1962), pp. 1–8; Charles Wolf, Jr., *The Political Effects of Economic Programs* (Santa Monica, The Rand Corporation, February 1964), RM–3901–ISA, pp. 19–33; P. Cutright, "National Political Development," *American Sociological Review*, 28 (1963), 253–264; and Irma Adelman and Cynthia T. Morris, *Society, Politics, and Economic Development* (Baltimore: Johns Hopkins, 1967).

[30] See Karl Deutsch, "Social Mobilization and Political Development," *American Political Science Review*, 55 (1961), 493–514.

[31] Kalman H. Silvert, "Some Propositions on Chile," *American Universities Field Staff Reports Service*, West Coast South America Series, 11 (1) 1964, 10.

and other forms of participation."[32] The hypotheses which
have been proposed concerning variations in extent or rate of
economic development, modernization, and mobilization, or
integration of populations, and the special characteristics of
the polities of the "third" world are yet to be tested by rigorous comparative research.[33] There are few efforts to differentiate among the types of party systems which exist within
these countries, as has been attempted for the Western democracies. To do so at this early stage of the comparative studies
of these nations would be rash, considering the scarcity of
intensive studies of their political parties.[34] The following
part of this discussion will seek to bring out some additional
patterns of political cleavage and of political development in

[32] Gino Germani, "Social Change and Intergroup Conflicts," Dittoed,
1963 (translated by I. L. Horowitz), p. 15. See also Gino Germani,
Política y Sociedad en una Epoca de Transición (Buenos Aires: Editorial Paidos, 1962).

[33] There is an extensive theoretical literature attempting to differentiate the conditions of politics in underdeveloped nations from those in
the developed countries. As yet, however, such writings have led to
few research studies designed to test out the propositions in them. See,
for example, Claude E. Welch, Jr. (ed.), *Political Modernization* (Bel-
mont, Calif.: Wadsworth, 1967); Gabriel Almond and G. B. Powell, Jr.,
Comparative Politics (Boston: Little, Brown, 1966); J. P. Nettl, *Political Mobilization* (New York: Basic Books, 1968); Lucien W. Pye, *Aspects of Political Development* (Boston: Little, Brown, 1966); David
Apter, *The Politics of Modernization* (Chicago: University of Chicago
Press, 1965); Gabriel Almond, "Introduction: A Functional Approach
to Comparative Politics," in Almond and Coleman (eds.), *op. cit.*,
pp. 3–64; James S. Coleman, "Conclusion: The Political Systems of the
Developing Areas," *ibid.*, pp. 532–576; John H. Kautsky, "An Essay on
the Politics of Development," in Kautsky (ed.), *Political Change in Un-
derdeveloped Countries* (New York: John Wiley, 1962), pp. 3–119; Ed-
ward Shils, "Political Development in the New States," *Comparative
Studies in Society and History*, 2 (1960), 265–292, 379–411; Zbigniew
Brzezinski, "The Politics of Underdevelopment," *World Politics*, 9
(1956), 55–75; Edward Shils, "On the Comparative Study of New
States," in Clifford Geertz (ed.), *Old Societies and New States* (New
York: The Free Press of Glencoe, 1963), pp. 1–26; Kalman Silvert and
Frank Bonilla, "Definitions, Propositions, and Hypotheses Concerning
Modernism, Class and National Integration," in Kalman Silvert (ed.),
Expectant Peoples (New York: Random House, 1963), pp. 439–450;
and S. N. Eisenstadt, *Essays on Sociological Aspects of Political and
Economic Development* (The Hague: Mouton, 1961), pp. 9–53.

[34] Although much has been written on these nations, there is little
knowledge in depth about them. For example, George Blanksten reported as recently as 1960 that "only one Latin American political party
has been the subject of a full-scale monographic study." See "The Politics of Latin America," in Almond and Coleman, *op. cit.*, p. 479.

the emerging nations, without attempting to arrive at any definitive statement on the factors involved and their inter-relationships.

The emerging political pattern of Latin America, military intervention apart, is closer to those of Europe than are those in the other areas of the developing world. Nineteenth- and early twentieth-century party conflicts resemble those of Latin Europe, from which Latin America derived much of its culture, religion, and earlier political ideologies.[35] The first cleavages were largely between pro-clerical, rural upper-class dominated Conservative parties and anti-clerical, bourgeois controlled Liberal parties. Socialist and anarcho-syndicalist movements arose in the working class left before World War I in a number of countries, but secured relatively little strength.[36] During the interwar period, and since World War II, however, political movements have emerged which are comparable to many in Africa and Asia. These movements express various forms of nationalist, anti-imperialist doctrine, oppose foreign domination of the economy, and seek through state control or ownership of the economy to foster rapid economic development. The ideological content of such parties has varied greatly. Between the late 1930's and the end of World War II, some, such as the movements of Perón in Argentina, Vargas in Brazil, and the M.N.R. in Bolivia, took over many of the trappings of Fascism or Nazism. They differed, however, from European fascist movements in being genuinely based on the working class or poor rural population. Since the war each adopted conventional left-wing ideologies, and has cooperated with various Communist movements (Trotskyist in Bolivia, orthodox in the other two). Others have been aligned continually with the Communists, explicitly or in the manner of fellow travelers. Communist parties have been particularly strong in Chile

[35] Donald M. Dozer, *Latin America: An Interpretive History* (New York: McGraw-Hill, 1962), pp. 369–414, and *passim;* George N. Blanksten, *op. cit.,* pp. 481–487; H. Davis (ed.), *Government and Politics in Latin America* (New York: Ronald Press, 1958); John J. Johnson, *Political Change in Latin America* (Stanford: Stanford University Press, 1958).

[36] Moisés Poblete Troncoso and Ben G. Burnett, *The Rise of the Latin American Labor Movement* (New York: Bookman Associates, 1960).

and Brazil. Still other movements such as the Acción Popular of Fernando Belaúnde Terry in Peru, the Acción Democrática of Rómulo Betancourt in Venezuela, and the National Liberation Movement of José Figueres in Costa Rica, may best be described as nationalist Social Democrats, comparable to the Indian Congress party. Most recently, Christian Democratic parties have arisen in many of the Latin American nations, as in Chile and Venezuela, tending on the whole to be relatively leftist supporters of land reform, economic planning, and of state intervention to foster economic development. And the various leftist movements have drawn considerable support from university students and intellectuals, a social category which includes a considerable segment of the university graduates in underdeveloped states.[37] The Castro movement is an example of a successful effort based initially on youthful members of the modernizing elites.[38]

A special pattern of "elitist" leftism which has appeared in many parts of the "third" world is military support for radical social reforms, i.e., for economic development and modernization. The military in a number of countries such

[37] As Shils has pointed out, in the socially less differentiated underdeveloped states the concept of intellectual is broader than in the more advanced countries. It includes "all persons with an *advanced modern education* and the intellectual concerns and skills ordinarily associated with it. . . . [T]he intellectuals are those persons who have become modern not by immersing themselves in the ways of modern commerce or administration, but by being exposed to the set course of modern intellectual culture in a college or university," *op. cit.,* pp. 198–199; for a discussion of students as intellectuals and their politics see also pp. 203–205, and see the articles on Latin American students and universities in S. M. Lipset and Aldo Solari (eds.), *Elites in Latin America* (New York: Oxford University Press, 1967), pp. 343–453; in S. M. Lipset (ed.), *Student Politics* (New York: Basic Books, 1967), pp. 283–354; and in the issue on "Students and Politics" of *Daedalus,* 97 (Winter 1968).

[38] That Castro's initial following was largely based on young, well-educated middle-class Cubans has been documented by Theodore Draper. He points out that of Castro's 18 cabinet members in 1960, everyone was a university graduate, that they were of middle- or upper-class background, and professionals or intellectuals occupationally. Theodore Draper, *Castro's Revolution, Myths and Realities* (New York: Praeger, 1962), pp. 42–43. Draper also points out that the list of Cuban defenders of Castroism who were interviewed by C. Wright Mills in his effort to present the authentic voice of the Cuban Revolution for his book *Listen Yankee* did not include a single worker or peasant. "Without exception, his informants were middle-class intellectuals and professionals" (p. 21).

as Turkey, parts of the Arab world, some in South and Southeast Asia and in Peru, have helped place leftist politicians or officers in power. The basis for military "leftism" would seem to be the concern of many officers to enhance national strength and prestige in a world in which these positions are seemingly a function of the degree of national economic development. While there is no necessary common interest shared by the nationalist leftist elites and the military in underdeveloped areas, governments based on such alliances have operated in many countries such as Burma, Pakistan, Egypt, Mexico, and Indonesia. In countries dominated by traditional-minded oligarchies, the military has often represented the only well-educated, Western-oriented, nationalist group favorable to modernization and capable of taking and holding power.[39] On the other hand, in other parts of Latin America mass-based reformist politicians have been overthrown by military juntas with links to traditional oligarchies. It should be noted, moreover, that the pessimistic conclusions of Morris Janowitz concerning the inability of the military leaders to engender successfully the processes necessary for economic and social development *when they take power in their own right* would seem to be warranted.[40]

The predominant pattern of political cleavage characteristic of those emerging nations which retain some version of demo-

[39] Harry Benda includes military officers in the category of the "westernized intellectuals" in the emerging nations, pointing out that they "were often the first group to receive Western training," and consequently became a force for modernization, which often brought them "fairly close to the socialism so prevalent among non-western intelligentsias in general." "Non-Western Intelligentsias as Political Elites," in John H. Kautsky, *op. cit.*, pp. 239–244; John J. Johnson (ed.), *The Role of the Military in Underdeveloped Countries* (Princeton: Princeton University Press, 1962); Morroe Berger, *Military Elites and Social Change* (Princeton: Princeton University Center of International Studies, 1960); Sydney N. Fisher (ed.), *The Military in the Middle East* (Columbus: Ohio State University Press, 1963); Edwin Lieuwen, *Arms and Politics in Latin America* (New York: Praeger, 1960); Lucien Pye, "Armies in the Process of Political Modernization," *European Journal of Sociology*, 2 (1961), 82–92.

[40] Morris Janowitz, *The Military in the Political Development of New States* (Chicago: University of Chicago Press, 1964). For a specification of the sharply different political roles, which may be played by the military in unstable polities, see Gino Germani and Kalman Silvert, "Politics, Social Structure and Military Intervention in Latin America," *European Journal of Sociology*, 2 (1961), 62–81.

cratic politics is a division between modernizing and traditionalist elements, which overlaps with, and to a considerable extent supersedes, the traditional left-right stratification-based conflict of the older and more stable polities. To an important degree, socialism and communism are strong because they are symbolically associated with the ideology of independence, rapid economic development, social modernization, and ultimate equality. Capitalism is perceived as being linked to foreign influences, traditionalism, and slow growth. Hence leftist movements secure considerable backing from the better educated who favor modernization. In many nations in Asia, Latin America, and Africa the better educated who are also more well to do are often the most significant backers of the more aggressively leftist tendencies.[41] There is ample evidence for this in the support of conservative parties by both impoverished religious peasants and the landholding elite, while backing for the left is drawn heavily from the better-educated members of the urban white-collar and professional classes, with the urban proletariat and peasants only entering as a force on the left after the modernizing elite groups have turned to them for support.[42] This pattern is brought out clearly in Japan. That nation, although more developed than any other country outside Europe or the English-speaking countries, has resembled the other emerging nations in its politics. In the 1920's, leftist groups were most successful among the students and other sections of the elite.[43] Public-

[41] The appeal of left-wing ideologies to the intellectuals and other sections of the university-trained intelligentsia in the underdeveloped nations has been analyzed in some detail. See Morris Watnick, "The Appeal of Communism to the Peoples of Underdeveloped Areas," in R. Bendix and S. M. Lipset (eds.), *Class, Status and Power* (Glencoe: The Free Press, 1966), pp. 428–436; Hugh Seton-Watson, "Twentieth Century Revolutions," *The Political Quarterly*, 22 (1951), 251–265; John H. Kautsky, *op. cit.*, pp. 44–49, 106–113; Edward Shils, "The Intellectual between Tradition and Modernity: The Indian Situation," *Comparative Studies in Society and History*, Supplement I (1961), 94–108. Perhaps the most comprehensive treatment of the subject is Edward Shils, "The Intellectuals in the Political Development of the New States," in John H. Kautsky, *op. cit.*, pp. 195–234.

[42] See Glaucio Ary Dillon Soares, "The Politics of Uneven Development: Brazil," in S. M. Lipset and Stein Rokkan, *op. cit.*, pp. 467–496.

[43] "A . . . factor that contributed to the fears of the ruling class was that 'bolshevization' was believed to be penetrating the sons of promi-

opinion surveys completed in recent years reveal that since World War II, education has been more highly correlated than class position with modernism and leftism. University students and graduates disproportionately back variants of socialism. On the other hand, less educated poor peasants and workers who are still tied to traditional social structures (e.g., workers in the highly paternalistic, numerous small factories and shops) support the conservative party.[44]

Tendencies similar to those in pre- and post-war Japan are evident in many other less developed emerging nations among university students and occupations requiring higher levels

---

nent men, the intelligentsia and the university students who formed the true *elite* of Imperial Japan or who would do so in the future. . . . [A Home Ministry Police Report stated:] 'After the Great Earthquake [1923] graduates from colleges and high schools, the so-called educated class, were most susceptible to the baptism of bolshevist thought. . . .' A situation in which the organization of the workers and farmers was so slight as to present no problem, but in which the *elite* and educated class had become 'bolshevized,' is completely abnormal according to the laws of Marxism. . . . [W]hat gave the rulers of Imperial Japan nightmares until the last was the 'bolshevization' of the State from within rather than revolution from below." Masao Maruyama, *Thought and Behaviour in Modern Japanese Politics* (London: Oxford University Press, 1963), p. 77.

[44] A study based on interviews with a sample of 3,000 Japanese men reports that the most radical segment are "the employed professional specialists. They are more in favor of denuclearized neutrality than laborers or blue-collar workers. They lend as much support to political strikes called by labor unions as do the laborers themselves. Most of the white-collar stratum favors and gives support to the socialist parties." Research Society on Japanese Social Structure, "Special Traits of White-Collar Workers in Large Urban Areas," *Journal of Social and Political Ideas in Japan,* 1 (August 1963), 78. A 1958 national sample reported heavy Socialist support among professionals and managerial groups. See Z. Sueutna, H. Aoyama, C. Hyashi, and K. Matusita, "A Study of Japanese National Character, Part II," *Annals of the Institute of Statistical Mathematics* (Tokyo), Supplement II (1961), 54; see also Joji Watanuki, "Patterns of Politics in Present-Day Japan," in S. M. Lipset and Stein Rokkan, *op. cit.,* pp. 448–449, 451–456; Robert A. Scalapino and Junnosuke Masumi, *Parties and Politics in Contemporary Japan* (Berkeley: University of California Press, 1962), p. 177; Douglas Mendel, *The Japanese People and Foreign Policy* (Berkeley: University of California Press, 1961), pp. 44–45, 47. A comprehensive report on many Japanese opinion surveys is Allan Cole and Naomichi Nakanishi, *Japanese Opinion Polls with Socio-Political Significance 1947–1957,* Vol. 1, *Political Support and Preference* (Medford: Fletcher School of Law and Diplomacy, Tufts University, 1960), *passim.*

of education.[45] Data from surveys of student attitudes in various countries reveal a tendency for those taking the more modern fields to be more leftist, while fields which train for the older professions, such as law, tend to be more traditionalistic. The findings from the student surveys are not so clear cut as one might anticipate, in part, perhaps, because of the differential utilization of graduates from different fields. Those studying "modern" subjects are more likely to find lucrative employment after graduation than are those who major in the more classic humanistic disciplines. The discrepancy between the needs of developing societies for technicians and scientists and the preference of students in some of them for the more traditional fields of law and the humanities often means that the latter are found disproportionately in the ranks of the "educated unemployed," or underpaid.[46] The inappropriateness of their university study for a subsequent career may thus contribute to the enhanced leftism of the university educated. In the larger sense, however, it may be argued, as John Kautsky has done, that the university trained,

[45] See S. M. Lipset, "University Students and Politics in Underdeveloped Countries," in Lipset (ed.), *Student Politics*, pp. 3–53; "Student Politics in Comparative Perspective," *Daedalus*, 97 (Winter 1968), 1–20; Kalman Silvert, *The Conflict Society: Reaction and Revolution in Latin America* (New Orleans: The Hauser Press, 1961), p. 166; T. B. Bottomore, *Elites and Society* (New York: Basic Books, 1965), pp. 86–104. An analysis of data collected from a sample of Indian students in 1951 by the Bureau of Social Science Research indicates that more than 40 per cent backed the Communist or Praha Socialist parties, both of which were quite weak among the general electorate. In some Latin American countries, such as Panama, El Salvador, Peru, Venezuela, and Brazil, Communists and pro-Castro groups are dominant in elections to the student councils. John Scott reports that "a number of important university campuses including those in Caracas, Michoacán, Lima, Santiago are virtually run by Communists." *How Much Progress?* (New York: Time Inc., 1963), pp. 123–125. In North Africa, also, university students are disproportionately to the left of the dominant politics. See Clement Moore and Arlie R. Hochschild, "Student Unions in North African Politics," *Daedalus*, 97 (Winter 1968), 21–50.

[46] The pattern of inappropriate career choice and educated unemployment is discussed in Justus M. van der Kroef, "Asian Education and Unemployment: The Continuing Crisis," *Comparative Education Review*, 7 (1963), 173–180; see also Joseph Fischer, "The University Student in South and Southeast Asia," *Minerva*, 2 (1963), 39–53; on the low economic rewards for Indian university graduates see Edward Shils, "The Intellectual between Tradition and Modernity," pp. 29–41.

as a class, constitute a socially dislocated group in underdeveloped states:

> The key role of the intellectuals in the politics of under-
> developed countries is largely due to their paradoxical position
> of being a product of modernization before modernization has
> reached or become widespread in their own country. In the
> universities, the intellectuals absorb the professional knowledge
> and skills needed by an industrial civilization; they become
> students of the humanities and social sciences qualified to
> teach in universities, and they become lawyers and doctors,
> administrators and journalists, and increasingly also scientists
> and engineers. When they return from the universities, whether
> abroad or not, the intellectuals find, all too often for their
> taste, that in their societies their newly acquired skills and
> knowledge are out of place. . . .
> During their studies, the intellectuals are likely to acquire
> more than new knowledge. They also absorb the values of
> an industrial civilization. . . . On their return, they find that
> these values, too, are inappropriate to the old society. . . .
> To the extent, then, that a native intellectual has substi-
> tuted for the values of his traditional society those of an
> industrial one—a process which need by no means be com-
> plete in each case—he becomes an alien, a displaced person,
> in his own society. What could be more natural for him than
> to want to change that society to accord with his new needs
> and values, in short, to industrialize and modernize it?[47]

The politics of developing nations must be seen, then, in
the words of the Japanese sociologist Joji Watanuki, as reflecting the cleavages of "cultural politics." By this is meant "the
politics where the cleavage caused by differences in value
systems have more effect on the nature of political conflict
than the cleavages based on economic or status factors."
While Watanuki does not deny "the working of economic
interest or status interest," he does argue that in countries
oriented toward rapid development such as Japan, one finds
"the relative dominance of cultural or value factors and the
superimposition and effects of these factors on others. . . ."[48]
Similarly, two students of comparative Latin American
politics, Kalman Silvert and Frank Bonilla, have postulated
the hypothesis that in the early phases of modernization or

[47] Kautsky, *op. cit.*, pp. 46–47.
[48] Watanuki, *op. cit.*, p. 457.

development of the "third" world, one should expect to find "very broad ideological alliances—all those in the innovating camp opposed to all those aligned against it."[49] As Watanuki notes, "cultural politics" are usually presented in *Weltanschauungen*, total ideological terms, in which all issues are "easily universalized as aspects of general principles, and are reacted to in highly emotional terms . . . sometimes suggesting the existence of a more deep-rooted basis for interest conflicts than actually exists."

It should be stressed that none of those who have commented on the politics of developing nations as reflecting value cleavages suggests the absence of class-linked political conflict.[50] They all note that *mass-based* leftist parties necessarily draw support from the workers or impoverished sectors of the rural population. Even the Castro movement, which originated among university graduates and drew much of its support from relatively well-to-do middle- and upper-class advocates of modernization, was able to secure heavy backing from the poor and uneducated after seizing power.[51]

These differences within the emerging nations, of course, have a parallel in the past, and to some extent in the present, in the developed countries in the form of the *Kulturkampf* over the place of religion, discussed earlier. Many of the educated, well-to-do bourgeois groups backed leftist anti-clerical parties in nineteenth-century Europe. The liberal parties stem from this source. The modern scientific professions, such as medicine, tended to back the left, while the professions rooted in tradition, such as the law, were heavily conservative. Teachers and professors in secular schools tended to be on the anti-clerical left. And even today these differences influence political behavior in nations such as France and Italy. Leftist

[49] "Definitions, Propositions, and Hypotheses Concerning Modernism, Class, and National Integration," Silvert and Bonilla, *op. cit.*, p. 443.

[50] In Japan, it is clear that even if university students, and young professionals, business executives, and the large majority of the intellectuals back the Socialists, Japanese business, both small and large, supports the conservative Liberal-Democrats. Almost all of the vast sums contributed for campaign purposes by Japanese business go to the latter, while the trade unions are the financial backers of the socialist parties. See James R. Soukup, "Comparative Political Finance: Japan," *Journal of Politics*, 25 (1963), 737–756.

[51] Maurice Zeitlin, *Revolutionary Politics and the Cuban Working Class* (Princeton: Princeton University Press, 1967).

parties, while primarily based on the lower strata, do draw some support from the historically anti-clerical (modernized) sectors of the middle class.[52]

But if the modernizing-traditional division contributes strongly to the support which the radical left draws from privileged elite groups in the emerging nations, it is also true that the conditions under which democratic politics are attempted in these states produce heavy support for the left from the lower strata as well, thus making it very difficult for conservative parties to find significant bases of support. This is, in part, because the large mass of the population in such nations live in impoverished conditions. But poverty alone does not breed discontent. In much of nineteenth-century Europe, conservative parties, led by members of the privileged classes, secured heavy backing from the urban and rural poor. They had the weight of traditional legitimacy and identification with the summits of an established status system on their side. Poor persons, like all others, had been reared to accept the old institutional order. Generally speaking, as elaborated in the previous chapter, people are unlikely to change opinions or allegiances which they have held for a long time. Hence leftist groups, modernizing factions, and others favoring large-scale change in the nineteenth century found that significant segments of the lower strata refused to support them. And conservatives, such as Bismarck and Disraeli, consciously sought to keep such support for conservative politics by following a deliberate policy of *noblesse oblige,* of favoring various welfare measures which would enhance the circumstances under which the poorer classes lived. Under such conditions, leftist or innovating parties became serious contenders for political office only after a long and arduous struggle for support.

Those mechanisms inherent in all stratified societies which serve to secure lower-class acceptance of the values of the system thus help to balance the relative strength of conservative and leftist parties. The leftists appeal to the interests of the more numerous lower strata, but the "deference vote"

[52] These continuities are discussed in S. M. Lipset and Mildred Schwartz, "The Politics of Professionals," in H. M. Vollmer and D. L. Mills (eds.), *Professionalization: A Reader in Occupational Change* (Englewood Cliffs: Prentice-Hall, 1966), pp. 299–310.

provides the conservatives with a large segment of the votes of the underprivileged. (Japan, Thailand, Iran, and Ethiopia, monarchies which were never colonies, seemingly still retain a large deferential population.)

In many of the new and emerging nations, however, the assumption that the lower classes enter the polity still showing deference to traditional institutions, values, and privileged classes does not hold.[53] Many high-status positions are associated with hated foreign imperialisms, and with social institutions regarded by large sections of the modernizing elites as contributing to the perpetuation of national inferiority. Thus conservative parties backed by businessmen and/or the rural elite face the difficulty that they do not have the weight of traditional legitimacy or a significant "deference vote" on their side.[54] Leftism and nationalism are often identified with the nation and the modernizing elite. The lower strata, insofar as they are politically conscious, may be won to the side of a radical leftism identified with symbols of national independence.

In such a contest, in which one large section of the elite supports leftist ideological goals, and in which the large majority of the population lives in poverty, the chances are small for the existence of conservative parties representing the tradi-

[53] Uganda provided an interesting special case of the continuity of traditional mechanisms of authority. Uganda contained a large African monarchy, Buganda, which remained politically autonomous and united under its hereditary monarchy during British rule. Consequently, as Apter has pointed out, Buganda was one of the few large native African states whose population retained that "extraordinary devotion to the king whose hierarchical authority represents what Weber calls hereditary charisma." See David Apter, *The Political Kingdom in Uganda* (Princeton: Princeton University Press, 1961), p. 457.

[54] The weakness of political conservatism in new nations does not mean, of course, that traditional attitudes with respect to other aspects of behavior are also weak. An excellent Indian study points out in detail that the same peasants who vote for modernizing, and even radical, politicians are often strongly attached to the old ways of their village life and resist innovation in agricultural practices. See Kusum Nair, *Blossoms in the Dust* (New York: Praeger, 1962). The distinction between traditional and modern attitudes may be made analytically, but in practice individuals and groups will vary considerably in the extent to which they hold attitudes which are seemingly incongruous. See on this Kalman H. Silvert, "National Values, Development, and Leaders and Followers," *International Social Science Journal*, 15 (1963), 560–570.

tional elite, or stressing the need for gradual rather than rapid change, as viable electoral alternatives. But as I have noted elsewhere:

> Although conservative groups in most new nations are deprived of the link with historic national values which they have in old states, there is at least one traditional institution with which they may identify and whose popular strength they may seek to employ: religion. The leftist national revolutionaries, in their desire to remake their society, often perceive traditional religion as one of the great obstacles; attitudes and values which are dysfunctional to efforts to modernize various institutions are usually associated with ancient religious beliefs and habits. And the efforts by the leaders of new states to challenge these beliefs and habits serve to bring them into conflict with the religious authorities.
>
> A look at the politics of contemporary new nations indicates that in many of them religion has formed the basis for conservative parties. . . .[55]

In Latin America, for example, religious-linked traditionalism furnishes a large base of support for conservative parties, particularly in relatively unchanging rural areas.[56] In a number of Moslem countries such as Turkey, Morocco, Pakistan, Malaysia, and Indonesia, religious-linked parties have been able to win considerable support when contesting elections. Similarly, in India, the Hindu religion currently provides a base around which a conservative party, the Jana Sangh, may win support. With very few exceptions, however, religious-linked traditionalism does not appear strong enough to provide conservative opposition parties with a sufficient mass

---

[55] S. M. Lipset, *The First New Nation*, pp. 78–79; see also pp. 74–90 for a discussion of factors which weaken potential strength of conservative parties in new states.

[56] See Soares, *op. cit.*, pp. 484–486, 491, for an analysis of the way in which illiteracy, "apathy, religion and traditional values . . . immunize and sterilize the peasants [of impoverished, north-east Brazil] against class organization and the germ of ideological rebellion." Analyses of voting choices in Chile through use of survey data reveal that degree of adherence to Catholicism is the principal correlate of vote decision. See Ruth Ann Pitts, *Political Socialization and Political Change in Santiago de Chile* (M.A. thesis in sociology, University of California, 1963); Brunhilde Velez, *Women's Political Behavior in Chile* (M.A. thesis in sociology, University of California, 1964).

appeal to form a significant alternative to modernizing radical movements.

CONCLUSIONS

The differences in the bases of party and ideological cleavage between the developed and underdeveloped world are of more than academic interest to the student of comparative politics. Clearly, the fact that a considerable section of the embryonic (student) and actual elites of the "third world" adhere to seemingly extreme versions of leftist ideologies, while the bulk of the university-educated elites of the developed countries espouse conservative or moderate reform doctrines, makes mutual understanding and communication difficult. (The militant student movement which emerged in the United States and many European countries during the late 1960's has not upset this generalization. According to opinion surveys, the extreme left is still a small minority, under 10 per cent, among the student population.) In developed Western societies, parties are increasingly agencies of "collective bargaining," representing the conflicting demands of diverse groups and strata. In the emerging nations, parties, particularly left-wing or nationalist ones, and in many of these nations all parties fit this category, see themselves not as representatives of particular groups which seek "more" of the total national pie, but rather as the bearers of programs and ideologies most likely successfully to mobilize society for a massive effort at economic development. In the developed nations, Marxism and Socialism are primarily the ideologies of the less well to do, and are naturally opposed by the privileged sectors. In the underdeveloped nations these ideologies serve as slogans to legitimate the efforts of certain elite strata to become or remain the ruling class, and to exact sacrifice from and impose hardships upon the poor for the sake of achieving the attributes of an economically powerful state.[57]

---

[57] As David Apter has pointed out, the elites of rapidly developing societies require a political myth which will bind to them the masses suffering the dislocations of industrialization and modernization. What religious belief did for the Western countries, he argues, "political religion" must do for the currently emerging nations. See "Political Reli-

It should be clear that efforts to generalize about the relation of given statuses and roles to political behavior, seen in terms of the historic left and right categories set in nineteenth- and twentieth-century Europe, prove inadequate when applied to most of the "third" world of Asia, Africa, and Latin America. This chapter has attempted to introduce a discussion of comparative party systems by pointing out some of the historical and other factors which account for diversity in bases of political cleavages. A comprehensive theory of politics which accounts for the behavior of all organizations calling themselves "parties," whether operating in the stable democracies, new states, or totalitarian regimes, is yet to be developed.[58] Meanwhile, we may conclude that exporting models of party systems and ideologies which "work" in advanced industrialized areas to less advantaged ones is not only bad social science, but much worse, may result in disastrous politics, as when ideologies of the Western underprivileged serve to justify intensive exploitation by the new ruling classes of the capital-accumulating Communist and "third" worlds. Rather than serving to articulate and justify the demands of the working class, as in the Western industrialized nations, the ideologies of the left as often applied by elites in the developing countries serve to mask a basic cleavage of interest between rulers and ruled, and to legitimate the political myth of a monolithic identity of elites and masses. In nineteenth- and twentieth-century Europe, Marxism and socialism have called to the attention of the workers and the poor generally that

gion in the New Nations," in Geertz (ed.), *op. cit.,* pp. 57–104. The English sociologist T. B. Bottomore has also suggested that "Marxism . . . is the Calvinism of the twentieth century industrial revolutions," *op. cit.,* p. 94.

[58] This does not mean that I believe that it cannot be developed. I would agree here with the programmatic statement made by Edward Shils for the Committee for the Comparative Study of New Nations in which he asserts, concerning efforts to deal with the politics of all nations: "Our task in this regard is to find the categories within which the unique may be described, and in which its differences with respect to other situations may be presented in a way that raises scientifically significant problems. Orderly comparison is one necessary step in the process of systematic explanation. . . ." "On the Comparative Study of the New States," *op. cit.,* p. 15. This article is an excellent statement of the problems and ambitions of comparative political sociology as derivative from Max Weber.

there is a basic continuing conflict over economic returns between themselves and those who control the means of production; in the contemporary Communist and the authoritarian states of the underdeveloped world, Marxism and socialism are defined to mean that the interests of both the controllers of the economy and the impoverished workers and peasantry are the same.[59] In nineteenth-century Europe, Marxism justified a struggle for the creation of free trade unions which exercised the right to strike, and for the rights of free speech, press, assembly, and competitive representative parties; in the contemporary Communist and many "third" world countries, Marxism is used by the ruling strata to supply arguments denying all of these rights.

This use of Marxism as the ideology of the aspiring elites of preindustrial societies was, of course, never anticipated by Marx and Engels. Rather, they conceived of socialist doctrines as helping to fulfill the aspirations of the working class in highly developed capitalist industrial societies. Socialist movements would only come to power in nations which had reached as high a level of industrialization as was possible under capitalism.[60] Socialism was never seen as an approach to rapid industrialization, rather it involved an effort to create a society with a higher state of genuine freedom in which workers and others would be liberated from the authoritarian restrictions inherent in bureaucratic industrial organization. Hence, the very concept of socialism as used by Marx and Engels had no

[59] Guy Hunter points out that in West Africa, socialism as advocated by the governing elite "includes above all the devotion to central planning of the use of resources, both human and material, for the common good. The West African press, both English and French, and the speeches of leaders hammer home again and again this planning theme, often opposed to the selfishness of the profit motive. . . .

"There is, however, little or no emphasis on the moral aspects of socialism, the gap between rich and poor. In tropical Africa as a whole exactly the reverse process is at present in full swing; the salaries and perquisites of the ruling group and of the whole professional and educated class are at or near the old expatriate level. . . . Despite constant inquiry, we could find little evidence of 'socialist' thinking in this moral sense, save among a few of the younger intellectuals in Lagos and Accra. . . ." *The New Societies of Tropical Africa* (London: Oxford University Press, 1962), pp. 288–289.

[60] A related discussion on the same point may be found in Adam Ulum, *The Unfinished Revolution* (New York: Random House, 1960), *passim*.

meaning except in a post-capitalist, post-industrial society in which machines liberated humanity from tedious work. Many Marxists, such as Rosa Luxemburg and Julian Martov, consequently, were horrified by the Bolshevik seizure of power in Russia in 1917, because they believed that it was sociologically premature, that it could only result in a severe distortion of socialism and hold back efforts to create the type of society, that is, that of libertarian socialism, envisaged by Marx and Engels. And, in fact, Marxism and socialism in the Soviet Union have served to justify as intensive a form of exploitation of human labor to secure "surplus value" for capital accumulation as the ruling class of any industrializing nation has ever attempted since the beginning of the Industrial Revolution.

The possibilities for the establishment and institutionalization of democratic procedures in the nations which now lack them are in large part dependent on the emergence of political cleavages rooted in interest and value differences that do not give any one political force predominant strength. A doctrine which denies sociological validity and political legitimacy to such differences once the party of the "workers" or the "people" is in power is a major obstacle to the formation of democratic polities. In this respect, Marxist doctrines as postulated in the underdeveloped world are profoundly different from those which justified the eighteenth- and nineteenth-century bourgeois revolutions in the West. The latter, although also organized under universalistic ideologies of equality which served to justify the aspirations of the new bourgeois elite to replace the old aristocratic one, nevertheless assumed the validity of interest differences, that the poor and the rich, the landed and the commercial classes, had separate interests. Democracy requires a recognition of the legitimacy of conflict and interest representation among the diverse groups in society, regardless of the form of economic organization. The breakdown of communication between Western and non-Western socialists is a result of the tremendous gap which exists between them given the considerably divergent connotations and social functions which socialism has taken on in different parts of the world. The possibility that socialism may regain in the "third" and Communist worlds its historic role as the ideology sustaining the lower strata's aspirations for more power, status, and income, cannot be ruled out. Endemic in its definition is an anti-elitist, egalitarian view of society. And as recent events in some of the Communist countries suggest, some do use the ideology of socialism to justify efforts to bring the accepted social myth and reality into harmony, much as in the United States men have used the American Creed to press for social equality.[61] The very concepts around which the members of the "new class" defend their right to exclusive possession of power may yet serve to undermine the autocratic systems which they have erected.

In Europe, at the advent of the modern era, the main sources of political tension revolved around the workers' struggle for citizenship, the right to take part in all decisions of the body politic on an equal level with others, against the dominant conservative aristocratic and business strata who controlled politics. In Latin America, as in Asia, leftist ideologies, usually of a Marxist variety, have been dominant among the modernizing elite and those identifying with nationalism. The polity is committed to giving the lower strata full political and social rights before the development of a stable economy which could support a large, relatively conservative urban middle class.

The left in most of Europe grew gradually in a fight for more democracy, for more personal and social freedoms, as well as in the struggle to reduce the discontents inherent in

[61] Evidence that the economically underprivileged do not share the views of the "socialist elite" concerning income differences comes from Communist Poland. An opinion survey inquiring into the proper level of differences in income for various occupations reported "that there is a strong correlation between the incomes of people and their views concerning a maximum scale of income differences. . . . The poll shows that factory workers, technicians, and certain groups of the intelligentsia with low salaries (teachers, post office workers, social service officials, etc.) are in favor of egalitarianism. On the other hand, an unfavorable attitude prevails among people of whom many have possibilities of high incomes." At the extremes, 54 per cent of the workers favored "relatively equal incomes" as contrasted with 20 per cent of the executives. Fifty-five per cent of the latter were strongly against narrowing the income gap, as compared with 8 per cent of the manual workers. But it should be noted that both the egalitarian-oriented less-privileged respondents and the more well-to-do defenders of inequality justified their opinions by "traditional slogans of the left." See S. M. Lipset, *Political Man*, pp. 224, 228–229, for references.

early industrialization. The right retained the support of the traditionalist, aristocratic elements in the society, and the political system eventually developed with economic development into a symbiotic relationship between a modified left and right. The result inevitably, as the next chapter tries to point out, is that political parties in Europe, even those of the left, have ceased being revolutionary—as many still are in most of the "third" world—and have become reformist.

CHAPTER 8

The Modernization of Contemporary European Politics

During the 1950's commentators on both sides of the Atlantic began to depict Western society by terms such as "The End of Ideology," "the post-industrial society," and the "post-bourgeois society."[1] While emphasizing different themes, these

[1] It is difficult to establish credit for the origin of this concept. Raymond Aron certainly deserves recognition for having presented it in the form which was widely followed by other writers in the West. See Raymond Aron, "Fin de l'age ideologique?" in Theodore W. Adorno and Walter Dirks (eds.), *Sociologica* (Frankfurt: Europaische Verlaganstalt, 1955), pp. 219–233, and *L'Opium des intellectuels* (Paris: Calmann-Levy, 1955), pp. 315–334. However, it should be noted that two major European scholars, T. H. Marshall and Herbert Tingsten, enunciated the same basic thesis without using the term in the late 1940's and early 1950's. Tingsten's early writings on the subject were presented in various articles in the Stockholm newspaper, *Dagens Nyheter*, while Marshall elaborated on the theme in his now almost classic essay, "Citizenship and Social Class," first presented in 1949 and reprinted in his volume *Sociology at the Crossroads* (London: Heinemann, 1963), pp. 67–127. See also Edward Shils, "The End of Ideology?" *Encounter*, 5 (November, 1955), 52–58; Herbert Tingsten, "Stability and Vitality in Swedish Democracy," *The Political Quarterly*, 26 (1955), 140–151; S. M. Lipset, "The State of Democratic Politics," *Canadian Forum*, 35 (1955), 170–171; Otto Brunner, "Der Zeitalter der Ideologien," in *Neue Wege der Sozialgeschichte* (Gottingen: Van den Hoeck und Ruprecht, 1956), pp. 194–219; Lewis Feuer, *Psychoanalysis and Ethics* (Springfield: Charles C. Thomas, 1955), pp. 126–130; Otto

commentators agreed that the growth of bureaucracy and "affluence" in Western industrial democratic society has made possible a social system in which class conflict is minimized. True, an argument does remain as to the relative income at any given moment of the rural sector, of different groups of workers, of private corporations, and so forth. But each group accepts the others' right to legitimate representation within the structure of representation and discussion.

The linkage between level of industrial development and other political and social institutions is obviously not a simple one.[2] Greater economic productivity is associated with a more equitable distribution of consumption goods and education—factors contributing to a reduction of intra-societal tension.[3] As the wealth of a nation increases, the status gap inherent in poor countries, where the rich perceive the poor as vulgar outcasts, is reduced. As differences in style of life are reduced, so are the tensions of stratification. And increased education enhances the propensity of different groups to "tolerate" each other, to accept the complex idea that truth and error are not necessarily on one side. (All of these consequences occur even though the relative distribution of *wealth does not* become less equal.)

An explanation for the reduction in the appeal of total

Kirchheimer, "The Waning of Opposition in Parliamentary Regimes," *Social Research*, 24 (1957), 127–156; Stein Rokkan. *Sammenlignende Politisksosilogi* (Bergen: Chr. Michelsens Institutt, 1958); Daniel Bell, *The End of Ideology* (Glencoe: The Free Press, 1960), esp. pp. 369–375; and S. M. Lipset, *Political Man* (Garden City, N. Y.: Doubleday, 1960), esp. pp. 403–417. Daniel Bell has written of the "post-industrial society." See his "The Post Industrial Society" (mimeographed, 1962). Ralf Dahrendorf describes comparable phenomena as the "post-capitalist society." See his *Class and Class Conflict in Industrial Society* (Stanford: Stanford University Press, 1959), esp. pp. 241–318, and Gunnar Myrdal, *Beyond the Welfare State* (New Haven: Yale University Press, 1960). George Lichtheim has commented on many of these ideas under the heading of the "post-bourgeois" society. See his *The New Europe* (New York: Frederick A. Praeger, 1963), esp. pp. 175–215; see p. 194. For an effort to sum up the empirical findings on the subject see M. Rejai, *et al.*, "Political Ideology: Empirical Relevance of the Hypothesis of Decline," *Ethics*, 78 (July 1968), pp. 303–312.

[2] For an excellent article on this subject see Val Lorwin, "Working Class Politics and Economic Development in Western Europe," *American Historical Review*, 63 (1958), pp. 338–351.

[3] See Simon Kuznets, "Economic Growth and Income Inequality," *American Economic Review*, 45 (1955), p. 4.

ideologies (*Weltanschauungen*) as simply derivative from the social concomitants inherent in increasing economic productivity is clearly oversimplified. T. H. Marshall has suggested that such extreme ideologies initially emerged with the rise of new strata, such as the bourgeoisie or the working class, as they sought the rights of citizenship, that is, the right fully to participate socially and politically. As long as they were denied such rights sizable segments of these strata endorsed revolutionary ideologies. In turn, older strata and institutions seeking to preserve their ancient monopolies of power and status fostered conservative extremist doctrines.

The history of changes in political ideologies in democratic countries, from this point of view, can be written in terms of the emergence of new strata, and their eventual integration in society and polity. The struggle for such integration took the form of defining the place in the polity of the old preindustrial upper classes, the church, the business strata, and the working class. The variation in the intensity of "class conflict" in many European nations has been in large measure a function of the extent to which the enduring economic struggle among the classes overlapped with the issues concerning the place of religion and the traditional status structure. Such controversies usually were perceived in "moral" terms involving basic concepts of right versus wrong, and hence they were much more likely than economic issues to result in sharp ideological cleavage and even civil war. The continuance of extremist movements in nations such as Germany and the Latin countries of southern Europe may be traced to the force of moral sentiments inherent in concerns for traditional status or religious privileges. Where such issues were resolved without becoming identified with the economic class struggle, then, as Marshall suggests, intense ideological controversy declined almost as soon as the new strata gained full citizenship rights. (But it should be noted that ethnic, racial or religious groups, like American blacks or Ulster Catholics, who still are deprived in citizenship terms will continue to find uses for extreme tactics and occasionally ideologies.)

Still a third factor related to the general decline in ideological bitterness has been the acceptance of scientific thought and professionalism in matters which have been at the center of political controversy. Insofar as most organized participants in the political struggle accept the authority of experts in economics, military affairs, interpretations of the behavior of foreign nations and the like, it becomes increasingly difficult to challenge the views of opponents in moralistic "either/or" terms. Where there is some consensus among the scientific experts on specific issues, these tend to be removed as possible sources of intense controversy. As the ideology of "scientism" becomes accepted, the ideologies of the extreme left and right lose much of their impact. Ironically, however, opposition to "scientism" has become particularly intense among left-wing student activists and their adult intellectual supporters. These groups correctly perceive "scientism" as a support for political gradualism.

But whatever the long-run sources of the reduction of the appeal of total ideologies (and there are short-run factors as well, such as the impact of wars both hot and cold), the fact remains that there has been a reduction in the intensity of class-linked political party struggles in most of Europe. This chapter surveys developments in the economies, social structures, and political parties of European societies which are relevant to an analysis of such trends. Within the context of a broad comparative analysis it also deals with the sources of deviations from these trends. The analysis thus seeks to define the elements in the changing structures which make for a lessening or persistence of class ideologies in different parts of Europe.

CLASS AND POLITICAL CONSENSUS AFTER 1945

The "miracle" of the postwar economic growth of Europe has been well documented. A combination of circumstances—the depression crises, prolonged experience with state economic intervention and planning under fascism or wartime regimes, the sharp increase in approval of socialist or welfare state concepts during and immediately following the war and the need for some years after the conflict to plan for and even furnish the capital for capital investment—resulted in a far greater amount of planning and government involvement in spurring economic growth than had existed in any democratic state before 1939.[4] The nationalization of businesses in France under the first De Gaulle regime surpassed the most grandiose ambitions of Third Republic Socialists, and systematic planning emerged in the early 1950's.[5] The Austrian economy is characterized by large-scale government ownership. Italy retained and even expanded the considerable government economic sector developed under Fascism. In Germany, the numerous dependent war victims and the presence of refugees from the East, comprising more than one-quarter of the population of West Germany, involved the state in welfare and other expenditures that took a large share of the gross national product for many years.[6] And in Britain, the Labour governments undertook an elaborate program of nationalization and welfare expenditures which have basically not been challenged by their Conservative successors.

In almost all of these nations, therefore, two general events of considerable significance for class behavior have occurred. On the one hand, many of the political-economic issues that occasioned deep conflict between representatives of the left and of the right were resolved in ways compatible with social-democratic ideology. On the other hand, the dominant strata, business and other, discovered that they could prosper through economic reforms that they regarded a decade earlier as the rankest socialist measures. The socialists and trade unionists found that their formal structural objectives, in many cases, had been accomplished with the cooperation of their political rivals. The need for government planning for economic

[4] For systematic data on government ownership generally in Europe, see John O. Coppock, "Government Expenditures and Operations," in J. Frederick Dewhurst, John O. Coppock, P. Lamartine Yates, and associates, *Europe's Needs and Resources. Trends and Prospects in Eighteen Countries* (New York: Twentieth Century Fund, 1961), pp. 436–442. See also Massimo Salvadori, "Capitalism in Postwar Europe," in *ibid.,* pp. 746–758.

[5] On the nature and extent of planning in postwar France see Pierre Bauchet, *La planification française. Quinze ans d'expérience* (Paris: Editions du Seuil, 1962).

[6] In "Germany in 1952, something like 37 per cent of the stock of industry was State-owned." Roy Lewis and Rosemary Stewart, *The Managers: A New Examination of the English, German, and American Executives* (New York: Mentor Books, 1961), p. 233. The figure is probably lower now.

growth and full employment was generally accepted; the obligation of the state to provide welfare services for the ill, the aged, and other dependent groups was viewed as proper by all parties; and the right of the trade union and political representatives of the workers to participate in decisions affecting industry and politics also was increasingly coming to be accepted. Domestic politics in most of these societies became reduced to the "politics of collective bargaining," that is, to the issue of which groups should secure a little more or less of the pie.

The transformation in class attitudes as reflected in political and interest group behavior is most noticeable in northern non-Latin Europe and among the socialist and Roman Catholic political parties. Large-scale extremist or avowedly authoritarian parties have almost completely disappeared north of France and Italy, with the exception of Finland and Iceland. The Norwegian and Austrian socialists who subscribed to a relatively left-wing Marxist view before World War II are now clearly moderate social-democratic parties.[7] The latter took part for twenty years in a stable coalition regime with the bourgeois People's party. The German Social Democratic party ruled its country for some years in alliance with the Christian Democrats and now governs in coalition with the liberal Free Democrats. The parties of the three German-speaking nations, Switzerland, Austria, and Germany, have given up any adherence to Marxism or class-war doctrines and are little concerned with any further expansion of the area of state ownership of industry.[8] The 1959 Godesberg Program

[7] See Hubert Ferraton, *Syndicalisme ouvrier et social-democratie en Norvège* (Paris: Armand Colin, 1960) for a detailed analysis of the transformation of the Norwegian Labor party from a radical oppositionist to a moderate governmental party. For a detailed account of the general changes in Norway see Ulf Torgensen, "The Trend Towards Political Consensus: The Case of Norway," *Acta Sociologica*, 6, Nos. 1–2 (1962), 159–172. For analysis of the changes in the Austrian parties, see Alexander Vodopivec, *Wer regiert in Österreich?* (Vienna: Verlag für Geschichte und Politik, 1961).

[8] For a detailed account of the changes in the approach of the Swiss Socialist party, a movement rarely discussed in social-science political analysis, see François Masmata, "Le parti socialiste suisse" (thesis for the Doctor of Research degree, École Politique, mimeographed, Paris: Foundation Nationale des Sciences Politiques, Cycle Supericur d'Études Politiques, 1963).

of the German party explicitly revoked the traditional policy of public ownership of the means of production.[9] An indication of the mood of European socialism may be found in a description of an international socialist conference:

> In July, 1958, the socialist international held a congress in Hamburg. The name of Karl Marx was mentioned exactly once. The old slogans of the class struggle and exploitation had disappeared. But the words "liberty," "democracy," "human dignity" came up again and again. . . . The principal theoretical speech was made by Oscar Pollack [famed theoretician of prewar Austro-Marxism]. His theme was, "Why is it that we cannot get the working classes excited about socialism any longer?" The answer that Pollack gave is that their lot is so improved, in a way which would have been incredible to nineteenth-century Socialists of any variety, that they are no longer easily moved by the slogans of class struggle and socialism.[10]

On the right, one finds that those parties which still defend traditional European liberalism (*laissez-faire*) or conservatism (social hierarchy) are extremely weak. The Scandinavian Liberals and Agrarians now accept much of the welfare state. Many Scandinavian bourgeois politicians, in fact, propose that their countries adopt Swiss political practice, a permanent coalition of all parties in which collective-bargaining issues are fought out and compromised within the cabinet.[11] The Roman Catholic parties, on the whole, have accepted the welfare state and economic planning, and have even supported increases in government ownership. They willingly participate in coalitions with socialist parties in many countries. Roman Catholic trade unions, once the bitter rivals of the so-called free or socialist unions in most Roman Catholic countries, either participate in the same unions as the socialists, as in Germany and Austria, or cooperate closely with the socialist unions, as in the Benelux nations. Issues concerning the rela-

[9] See Jossleyn Hennessy, "Productive Unrest in Germany," *New Society*, 1, No. 15 (January 10, 1963), 21–23. For the text of the new program which favors competition, see *Die Zeit*, 22 (June 7, 1963), 14.

[10] Bertram D. Wolfe, "A Century of Marx and Marxism," in Henry L. Plaine (ed.), *Darwin, Marx, and Wagner* (Columbus: Ohio State University Press, 1962), pp. 106–107.

[11] See Dankwart A. Rustow, *The Politics of Compromise* (Princeton: Princeton University Press, 1955), pp. 219–223.

tionship of church and state, particularly as they affect education and family legislation, still separate the left wing of the Roman Catholic parties from the socialists, but these are not of grave moment as compared to their agreement on economic and class matters. In Germany the traditional base of the opposition to a democratic regime, the regions beyond the Elbe, the homeland of the Junkers and feudal social relationships, is no longer part of the nation.[12] West Germany today is physically and socially largely comprised of regions and classes which historically have shown a willingness to sustain modern socioeconomic and political systems. Although once playing a major role in politics, the civil service and the army, the old aristocracy today participate little in these institutions.

Reactionary parties in postwar Europe have tended on the whole to be peripheral movements based on the outlying regions and strata which have not shared in the rapid economic growth, which find themselves increasingly outside of the new cosmopolitanism and which have lost out in the relative struggle for influence and status. Thus in Norway the Christian party, which seeks to further traditional values, is clearly a provincial party based on the lower middle classes of the rural and provincial communities.[13] Poujadism was the classic case of a movement appealing to the *resentments* of declining strata; its base was the backward parts of France which had been losing population, and the petit bourgeoisie whose relative position in French economy and society had worsened with the growth of the metropolis and large business and government. In Italy, the Monarchists and Neo-Fascists have recruited strength from roughly comparable groups, a pattern that has also characterized the support of the Austrian Freedom and the German National Democratic parties.[14]

Not unexpectedly, studies of the attitudes and behavior of the entrepreneurial strata in various parts of Europe suggest

[12] Theodore Schieder, *The State and Society in Our Times* (London: Thomas Nelson and Sons, 1962), p. 121.

[13] On Norway, see Stein Rokkan and Henry Valen, "The Mobilization of the Periphery," *Acta Sociologica*, 6, Nos. 1–2 (1962), 111–141.

[14] On France and Italy, see Mattei Dogan, "Political Cleavage and Social Stratification in France and Italy," in S. M. Lipset and S. Rokkan (eds.), *Party Systems and Voter Alignments* (New York: The Free Press, 1967), pp. 129–195.

that the managerial groups in the traditionally less developed countries of Europe, such as France and Italy, have been the most resistant to yielding their historic autocratic and paternalistic view of the role of management, a point elaborated in the previous chapter. "In general, France and Italy have been characterized by a large number of small enterprises, looked on by the family as a source of personal security and conducted in an atmosphere of widespread absence of trust."[15] The resistance to accepting trade unions as a legitimate part of the industrial system has been greater in these nations than anywhere else in democratic western Europe. And consequently, the presence of extreme views of class and industrial relations among leaders of workers and management has contributed to resisting the pressures inherent in industrialization to stabilize such relationships. The available evidence would suggest that Italian industrialists may be more resistant to accepting a *modus vivendi* with trade unions and the planning-welfare state than are the French, although, as shall be noted, the relative situation is reversed among the worker-based Communist parties of these countries.[16] It is difficult to account for these variations other than to suggest that fascism as practiced in Italy for two decades conditioned many Italian businessmen to a pattern of labor-management relations that they still long for. Conversely, however, fascism spared the Italian Communists the experience of having repeatedly to purge the various levels of leadership of a mass party. The party could emerge after World War II with close intellectual links to its prefascist, and more significantly pre-Stalinist, past and with a secondary leadership and rank and file whose major formative political experience was the Resistance rather than the Comintern.

Class conflict ideologies have become less significant components of the political movements supported by the middle

[15] See the various studies reported in Frederick Harbison and Charles A. Myers, *Management in the Industrial World. An International Analysis* (New York: McGraw-Hill, 1959). On Italy see also Joseph La Palombara "La Confindustria e la politica in Italia," *Tempi Moderni*, 4 (October–December, 1961), 3–16; on France see François Bourricaud, "Le 'Jeune Patron' tel qu'il se voit et tel qu'il voudrait être," *Revue Économique*, 6 (1958), 896–911; Lewis and Stewart, *op. cit.*, esp. pp. 165–187; Harbison and Myers, *op. cit.*, p. 123.

[16] See La Palombara, *op. cit.*, and Bourricaud, *op. cit.*, pp. 901, 903.

classes in Germany, Italy, and France. In Germany and in Italy, the Christian Democratic type parties, with their efforts to retain the support of a large segment of the unionized working classes, have made a trans-class appeal in favor of moderate changes. As compared to prefascist days, they have gained considerably at the expense of older, more class-oriented, more conservative parties. The classically liberal Free Democratic and Liberal parties receive about 7 per cent of the vote in each country. In France, the Christian Democrats (MRP) were not able to retain the massive upper- and middle-class conservative vote which the party inherited in the first elections of the Fourth Republic, as a result of the traditional right's being discredited by its involvement with Vichy. Large-scale anti-labor and anti-welfare state parties arose in the late 1940's and 1950's. The Gaullism of the Fifth Republic, however, has replaced such parties in the affections of the conservative and business part of the electorate. Gaullism is oriented to a trans-class appeal designed to integrate the lower strata into the polity, and it supports economic and social reforms which foster economic growth and reduce class barriers.

Looking at the policies of business toward workers and their unions, it would appear that Germany first, and much more slowly and reluctantly, France and Italy, in that order, have been accepting the set of managerial ideologies characteristic of the more stable welfare democracies of northern and western Europe.[17] Curiously, the one country in which research data exist which bear on the relationship between degrees of modernization and bureaucratization of industry and the attitudes of industrial managers in contemporary Spain. A study of the Spanish businessman by Juan Linz indicates clearly that the larger and more modern a factory, the more likely is its manager to believe in, or accept, modern personnel policies with their denigration of the particularistic

[17] Stanley Hoffman, "Paradoxes of the French Political Community," in Hoffman, *et al., In Search of France* (Cambridge: Harvard University Press, 1963), pp. 61–62; see also Laurence Wylie, "Social Change at the Grass Roots," in *ibid.,* p. 184. For a detailed analysis of the problems of analyzing the complexity of French economic life see Raymond Aron, *France Steadfast and Changing* (Cambridge: Harvard University Press, 1960), "Myths and Realities of the French Economy," pp. 45–77.

rights of *patrons* and their assumptions concerning universalistic treatment of subordinates. It is interesting to note that whether a manager is an owner or not seems to have little bearing on his attitudes on such issues. If the Spanish pattern occurs in the other Latin countries as well, it would suggest that those who argue that significant changes are occurring among managers in France and Italy are correct. As yet, however, few systematic comparative data exist on the subject, and many of the available analyses rely heavily on published statements of, or interviews with, the officials, that is, ideologues, of business associations. The latter tend to mouth, and probably even believe, the traditional *laissez-faire* and anti-labor ideologies which many of their members no longer follow in practice.

THE INTEGRATION OF THE WORKING CLASS

But if the evidence drawn from developments in various parts of the continent suggests that the secular trends press for political moderation, for the politics of collective bargaining, it is also important to note that these trends do not imply a loss of electoral strength for working-class-based parties. In fact, in all European countries varying majorities of the manual workers vote for parties which represent different shades of socialism. As the workers have become integrated into the body politic, they have not shifted from voting socialist to backing bourgeois parties. If anything, the opposite seems to have occurred. In the Scandinavian nations, for example, "all evidence indicates that social class explains more of the variation in voting and particularly more of the working-class voting than some decades ago. This has occurred simultaneously with the disappearance of traditional class barriers. As equality has increased the working class voters have been more apt to vote for the worker's own parties than before."[18]

A comparative look at the pattern of working-class voting in contemporary Europe reveals that with the exception of

[18] Erik Allardt, "Traditional and Emerging Radicalism" (mimeographed paper), p. 5.

Holland and Germany, the leftist parties secure about two-thirds or more of the working-class vote, a much higher percentage than during the depression of the 1930's.[19] The two exceptions are largely a by-product of the Roman Catholic-Protestant cleavage in their countries. The traditionally minority German and Dutch Roman Catholics have considerable group solidarity, and the Christian Democratic and Roman Catholic parties in these countries secure a larger working-class vote than occurs anywhere else on the continent. Close to 70 per cent of German Protestant workers vote Socialist, as do "humanist" and moderate Calvinist Dutch workers, as opposed to the conservative Dutch Calvinists, who are more like the Roman Catholics. The leftist working-class-oriented parties have increased their strength in much of Europe during the 1960's. It is clear, therefore, that the easy assumption made by many, concerning American as well as European politics, that greater national affluence would mean a weakening of the electoral support for the left is simply wrong. Regardless of how wealthy a nation may be compared to its past, all democratic countries, from the lands of the Mediterranean basin to Sweden, Australia, or the United States, remain highly stratified societies in which access to education, economic opportunity, culture, and consumption goods is grossly unequal. The nature of such inequalities varies greatly; in general the poorer a country, the greater the gap in the standard of consumption between the classes. However, in all countries the more deprived strata, in income and status terms, continue to express their resentments against the stratification system or perhaps simply their desire to be represented by politicians who will seek further to redistribute the goods of the society, by voting for parties which stand for an increase in welfare state measures and for state intervention in the economy to prevent unemployment and increase their income *vis-à-vis* the more privileged strata.

Greater national wealth and consequent lower visible class differentials, therefore, do not weaken the voting strength of the left as compared with the right; rather, their effects become most evident in the decline of ideological differences,

[19] See Mattei Dogan, "Le Vote ouvrièr en Europe occidentale," *Revue française de sociologie,* 1 (1960), 25–44.

in changes in the policies advocated by different parties. The leftist parties have become more moderate, less radical, in the economic reforms which they espouse. A look at the political history of Europe indicates that no mass lower class-based political party, with the single exception of the German Communists, has ever disappeared or significantly declined through losing the bulk of its votes to a party on its right.[20]

The loyalties once created for a *mass* left-wing party are rarely lost. The most striking testimony to this has been the ability of the Finnish Communist party to retain mass support and even to grow since World War II, in spite of the Russian invasion of the country in 1940, the subsequent war of 1941–1945, and the Russian annexation of Karelia. The Communists are able to secure a quarter of the vote even though 10 per cent of the population are refugees from the Russian-annexed territory. The support for the Communist party goes back to the Finnish Civil War, which followed the Russian revolution, when the Social Democratic party, the largest party under Czarist rule, divided into two roughly equal groups in reacting to Bolshevism. And although the Communist party was illegal for much of the period between the wars, it seemingly lost little backing. In recent years, it has grown somewhat during a period of rapid economic development and a sharply rising standard of living.

But if workers have remained loyal to the parties of their class on election day, they show much less commitment to these parties the rest of the year. All over Europe, both socialist and Communist parties have complained about losses in membership, in attendance at party meetings, and in the reading of party newspapers. Such changes attest to the growth of what French intellectuals have described as the problem of *dépolitisation*.[21] Another phenomenon illustrating these trends is the growing tendency of all the working-class organizations to place less emphasis on traditional *political* doctrines and to put more stress on representation of

[20] Although the German Communists secured about 16 per cent of the vote in 1932, they were never so large as the Social Democrats. The latter always retained their status as the predominant party of the workers. Hence even the German case is not a real exception.

[21] See especially the various articles in Georges Vedel (ed.), *La Dépolitisation, mythe ou réalité?* (Paris: Armand Colin, 1962).

concrete interests. Roman Catholic trade unions are also increasingly reluctant to intervene directly in politics.

In discussing the implications of changes such as these, a number of French political analysts have argued that what occurred in France in the 1950's and early 1960's, and presumably in some other countries as well, was not so much a decline in political interest (*dépolitisation*), as of ideology (*déideologisation*). Thus René Rémond, in introducing a general symposium on these issues, pointed out that while political parties have suffered a considerable decline in membership, this was not true of other French associations; that in fact there has been a considerable increase in the number of voluntary associations in France. Such groups, while nonpartisan, play important roles in politics in representing the specific interests of their members. The late André Philip even suggested that contemporary France finally is developing the social infrastructure recommended by Tocqueville as a condition for stable democracy, widespread support for secondary associations. He suggested that this is another consequence of modernization, since the pattern of commitment to one group which represents the individual totally is a characteristic of the early phase of development. In a modernized society, any given group or party will report a relatively low level of direct participation by their members or supporters since the segmentalized individual involved in many roles must support diverse groups, and hence seemingly takes on the role of spectator in most of them.[22]

It would seem as if much of France, radical intellectuals and students apart, has taken the plunge of finally dropping its historic commitments to total *Weltanschauungen* and seeing the problem of progressive social change as a pragmatic and gradual one. And insofar as Frenchmen are able to see some of the changes and policies which they advocate being adopted, even by a government which many of them distrust, their motivation to continue to participate in such pragmatic parapolitical activity continues.

[22] Colloque "France Forum," *La Démocratie à refaire* (Paris: Editions Ouvrières, 1963), "La Dépolitisation de l'opinion publique," pp. 15–74. The relevant comments of Rémond are on pp. 26–27; Philip's statements are on pp. 38–39.

There are many ways in which the more pragmatic orientation of Europeans manifests itself, but the changes in trade-union behavior are most noticeable. As already noted, in a number of countries socialist and Roman Catholic unionists are cooperating as they never did before World War II. The fact of such cooperation reflects the extent to which both have moved away from ideological or political unionism toward pragmatic or even, in the American sense of the term, "business unionism." In Italy and France, the trend toward a *syndicalisme de controle* is furthered by the emerging patterns of plant unions and supplementary factory contracts.[23] Such organization and negotiation for the first time involve the unions in dealing with the concrete problems of the factory environment such as job evaluation, rates, productivity, and welfare.[24] The pressures in this direction have come primarily from the non-Communist unions, although the Communist unions have also increasingly come to accept such institutions, more in Italy than in France.[25] The increase in economic strikes as distinct from political ones, though often resulting in an over-all increase of the strike rate, has been interpreted by some observers as reflecting the integration of the workers into the industrial system; an economic strike is part of a normal bargaining relationship with one's employer. Some suggested that the Italian strike wave of 1961 and 1962 was perhaps the first of this type since the war in that country.[26]

Other major strikes in the 1960's were also notable for the extent to which they increasingly resembled a typical American strike flowing from a breakdown in collective bar-

[23] See Jean Maynaud, "Apatia e responsibilita dei cittadini," *Tempi Moderni*, New Series 5, No. 9 (April–June 1962), 30–38.

[24] See Arthur M. Ross, "Prosperity and Labor Relations in Western Europe: Italy and France," *Industrial and Labor Relations Review*, 16 (1962), 63–85; see also Vera Lutz, *Italy, A Study in Economic Development* (London: Oxford University Press, 1962), pp. 222–223; and Joseph A. Raffaele, *Labor Leadership in Italy and Denmark* (Madison: University of Wisconsin Press, 1962), pp. 291–293.

[25] See Serge Moscovici, *Reconversion industrielle et changements sociaux* (Paris: Armand Colin, 1961), pp. 127–128.

[26] E. A. Bayne, "Italy's Seeds of Peril, Part IV," *American Universities Field Staff Reports Service*, Southeast Europe Series, 10, No. 4 (July 1962).

gaining. Most strikes usually ended by a negotiated settlement in which the unions secure more than they had been
offered initially. Few turned into political strikes, although the governments are directly involved in the negotia-
tions. Essentially there was increasing recognition on both
sides that the strike is a normal part of the collective-
bargaining process, although De Gaulle showed some initial
reluctance to concur, while he was President. In France the
Communist-controlled CGT did occasionally call for protest
strikes, while the much less politicalized unions affiliated to
the Socialist Force Ouvrière and the Roman Catholic CFTC
generally called trade-union strikes. The Communists were
forced to change their tactics, to shift from political protest to
economic strikes. The great French strikes of May and June
1968 were ended by a typical wages and hours agreement.
The CGT strongly opposed the demands by students that the
strikers adopt political objectives. The German New Left SDS
students were so dismayed by the lack of political support
from workers and the unions that they dissolved their national organization in the spring of 1970. These strikes in
Italy, Germany, and France may signify the beginning of a
new era in labor relations—one in which strikes are recognized as part of the normal bargaining relationship rather
than an embryonic civil war the outbreak of which is threat-
ening to leadership on both sides.[27]

The relative weakness of traditional leftist ideology in western and southern Europe is suggested also by various attitude
surveys taken since the 1950's. These studies indicate that the
actual sentiment favoring a "socialist solution" to economic
or social problems is much lower than the Socialist or Communist vote. It again demonstrates that people will vote for
such parties without commitment to the once basic ideological
values of these parties.

In Britain public opinion polls taken shortly before Labour
regained office in 1965 indicated that only 18 per cent of the
electorate favored more nationalization. Among Labour

[27] See Club Jean Moulin, *L'État et le citoyen* (Paris: Editions du
Seuil, 1961), "Vers le syndicalisme d'enterprise," pp. 271–279, for an
analysis of the structural pressures changing the nature of French
unionism.

party voters 39 per cent supported increased nationalization, 46 per cent would have left things as they were, and 15 per cent actually favored some denationalization. Conversely, only 43 per cent of the Conservatives advocated denationalization.[28]

A comparative analysis of attitudes toward ownership of industry in seven European countries based on interviews in the spring of 1958 reported strong sentiment favoring public ownership of industry only in Italy, the nation which has the largest support for radical ideologies in the form of large Communist and left-Socialist parties.[29]

In France, where about half the workers have voted Communist in most postwar elections, with another 20 per cent going to the Socialists, and a large majority voting for the Communist-controlled CGT trade-union federation in Social Security Board elections, opinion data suggest that the workers are not so hostile to the existing institutions as this record might imply. As early as 1956 a detailed survey of French workers reported that 53 per cent thought there was "confidence" in the relations between employees and management, as contrasted to 27 per cent who said there was "distrust." More than four-fifths believed their employer was doing his job well; nine-tenths thought the quality of the work done at their plant was good; only 13 per cent thought there was a great deal of waste in their firm; 57 per cent stated that they had a chance for a promotion at their work; and 86 per cent reported they liked their jobs. Although the Communists had secured the vote of a majority of French workers shortly before this survey, only 12 per cent of those interviewed stated they were very much interested in politics, about the same percentage as that which reported strong interest in trade-union activities.[30] And when asked in which country "the workers are best off," 54 per cent said the United States

[28] *Gallup Political Index*, Report No. 38, March 1963, p. 34.

[29] See studies completed by Affiliates of International Research Associates and reported in DIVO Institut, *Umfragen: Ereignisse und Probleme der Zeit im Urteil der Bevölkerung* (Frankfurt: Europaische Verlagsanstalt, 1959), p. 77.

[30] "The French Worker: Who he is, how he lives, what he thinks, what he wants." *Réalités*, 65 (April 1956), 8–18.

as compared with 14 per cent who answered the Soviet Union.[31]

How many of the French Communist voters actually adhere to a class-war perspective and a generally Communist view of politics is a question that is impossible to answer. French experts who have examined the available evidence from studies of workers' attitudes differ in their interpretations. Thus Raymond Aron suggests that the polls indicate that about two-thirds of French Communist supporters are "convinced Communists," while Mattei Dogan believes that less than half of them think of political action and the class struggle in the Marxist sense of the term.[32] During the strikes in May and June 1968 the Communist party strongly opposed the revolutionary objectives of the student radicals. The only party supporting them, in part, the Unified Socialist party (PSU), secured 3 per cent of the vote in the June 1968 elections. In the 1969 presidential election, the PSU candidate received 3.5 per cent.

The weakness of a sharp class-conflict view of politics in Germany is borne out by an opinion study which asked a sample of the electorate their opinions concerning class solidarity and party voting. Less than one-fifth took a purely class view of voting behavior, that is, that workers should always vote for the Socialists, and middle-class people always for the non-socialist parties. The majority agreed with the statement that workers or middle-class people might vote for either tendency, depending on the political situation and the issues involved. More than three-fifths of those in middle-class occupations, although predominantly non-socialist in their voting habits, agree with the opinion that the division between the bourgeoisie and the workers was no longer strong and that a doctor or a professor might vote either Christian Democratic or Social Democratic, depending on the particu-

[31] The findings of a study conducted for *Réalités* by IFOP, the French Gallup Poll; see also Charles Micaud, *Communism and the French Left* (New York: Frederick A. Praeger, 1963), pp. 138–139.

[32] Aron, *France Steadfast and Changing*, pp. 39–40; Mattei Dogan, "Il compartamento politico degli operai francesi," *Tempi Moderni*, 9 (April 1962), 26–27. Dogan reports that in 1952 the majority of workers supporting the Communists told interviewers that "the doctrine of this party was not the main reason for their vote" (*op. cit.*, p. 25). See also Micaud, *op. cit.*, pp. 140–141.

lar issues of a campaign. Conversely, only 30 per cent of the workers thought that a worker must always vote for the Social Democrats, while half of the worker respondents agreed with the statement that a worker should choose between the parties according to the issues.[33] As in France, the New Left ideological groups secured little adult support. In the September 1969 elections, the radical left ADP (Action for Democratic Progress) received 0.6 per cent of the national vote.

The ideology of the "open society" in which competent individuals can succeed seems to have permeated much of Europe, a phenomenon which may also contribute to a reduction of class tension. Thus surveys in a number of countries which inquired as to the chances of capable individuals rising socially in their country found large majorities which reported their belief that the chances were good. The percentages of respondents saying that chances were good were 90 in Norway, 88 in England, 72 in West Germany, and 70 in Belgium. The one European country covered in this study in which the proportion of those who were optimistic about mobility was less than half was Austria, but even there the positive answers outweighed the pessimistic ones, 49 per cent to 34 per cent. Italy and France were not covered in this comparative study. However, another set of surveys which inquired as to careers one would recommend to a young man found that the Italians ranked second only to the English in suggesting high-status professional occupations (62 per cent). The strongest French preference seemed to be for careers in the civil service, an orientation which distinguished them from

[33] Viggo Graf Blucher, *Der Prozess der Meinungsbildung dargestellt am Beispiel der Bundestagswahl 1961* (Bielefeld: Emnid Institut, 1962), pp. 73–75. See also Heinrich Popitz, Hans Paul Bahrdt, Ernst August Jures, and Hanno Kesting, *Das Gesellschaftsbild des Arbeiters* (Tübingen: Mohr-Siebeck, 1957), p. 233. Similar findings are reported in Alfred Willener, *Images de la société et classes sociales* (Berne: Stämpfli, 1957), pp. 153, 206. See also Ralf Dahrendorf, "Burger und Proletarier: Die Klassen und ihr Schicksal," in his *Gesellschaft und Freiheit* (Munich: Pieper, 1961), pp. 133–162, esp. p. 175; Rainer M. Lepsius, "Zum Wandel der Gesellschaftsbilder in der Gegenwart," *Koelner Zeitschrift für Soziologie*, 14 (1962), 450; Hansjurgen Daheim, "Die Vorstellungen vom Mittelstand," *ibid.*, 12 (1960), 252; and Renate Mayntz, *Soziale Schichtung und Soziale Wandel in einer Industriegemeinde* (Stuttgart: Ferdinand Emke, 1958), p. 103. For a poll of workers, see Institut für Demoskopie, *Jahrbuch der Öffentlichen Meinung, 1947–1955* (Allensbach: Verlag für Demoskopie, 1956), pp. 265, 267.

all other European nations except the Belgian. It should be noted also that the Italians and the French were least likely among the citizens of eleven European countries to recommend a career as a skilled worker or artisan to a young man.[34] There is some direct evidence that modernization results in a positive attitude by workers toward their occupational situation. A French study of the consequences of modernization in textile factories in northern France brings this out clearly. The author notes that the workers view the effects of technological innovation as a "good thing," that they see it as resulting in an increase in employment, greater possibilities for social mobility, and increased earnings.[35] The findings of French factory surveys with respect to worker reaction to modernization are paralleled in an early report on the comparative strength of the Communist party in five large Italian factories which varied in their degree of modernization. The less modernized the plants the larger the proportion of workers who belonged to the Communist party, holding size of plant constant.[36]

But if workers react positively to working in modernized, more bureaucratic work environments, if they see these as offering greater opportunity for higher earnings and mobility, if job satisfaction is actually higher in many of these, the fact remains that when one looks at the sources of left-wing strength, either in voting or in union membership, and in the extent to which men agree with "anti-capitalist" attitudes, such strength is to be found disproportionately in the larger factories and the larger cities.[37] This seeming contradiction reveals an interesting relation between the variables linked to the over-all characteristics of a national political class culture and the same variables operating within a given society.

[34] DIVO Institut, *op. cit.,* pp. 120, 124.

[35] Claude Durand, "Positions syndicales et attitudes ouvrières à l'égard du progrès technique," *Sociologie du travail,* 4 (1960), 351.

[36] Mario Einaudi, J. Domenach, and A. Garoschi, *Communism in Western Europe* (Ithaca: Cornell University Press, 1951), pp. 43–44.

[37] Dogan, *op. cit.,* p. 26. For reports of opinion data on characteristics of working-class vote, data on traits of union members and their attitudes drawn from a secondary analysis of the IBM cards of a survey of French workers completed by the French Institute of Public Opinion (IFOP) in 1956, see Richard Hamilton, *Affluence and the French Worker in the Fourth Republic* (Princeton: Princeton University Press, 1967).

As noted above, nations with a high level of industrialization and urbanization tend to have a low level of ideological conflict. But within nations, whatever the level of intensity of political controversy, larger factories and cities tend to be the strongholds of the left politics dominant in the country, Communist, Socialist, or Democratic.[38] Trade unions also are generally stronger in large factories in large cities. It would seem that while greater industrialization and urbanization with consequent greater national wealth make for a more stable polity, *within* any system these social factors are conducive to fostering working-class political and trade-union strength.

How might we account for this? In part it may be related to the fact that the large factory environment sustains fewer informal relations between members of different classes, reducing the possibility that the members of the lower class will be influenced personally by the more conservative and more prestigeful members of middle and higher classes such as owners, managers, and supervisors. And the more concentrated the members of a lower class are in a social environment, the easier it is for common class attitudes to spread among them and for representatives of class-oriented parties or other organizations to reach them and activate their anti-elitist sympathies.[39]

But although the emergence of large social environments that are class homogeneous facilitates the spread of lower class-based movements, the same factors operating in the social structure as a whole become linked with other tendencies operating to reduce class friction. On the working-class level these involve a rise in standards of living, educational levels, and opportunity for upward social mobility within industry.

---

[38] See Lipset, *Political Man,* pp. 263–267.

[39] German data indicate that the larger the plant a man works in the more likely he is to discuss politics with his fellow workers in the factory. Wolfgang Hartenstein and Gunther Schubert, *Mitlaufen oder Mitbestimmen* (Frankfurt: Europaische Verlanganstalt, 1961), p. 25. Conversely, the larger the size of the work unit, the fewer the workers who report that they chat informally with a higher up. See Juan Linz, "Cleavage and Consensus in West German Politics: The Early Fifties," in Lipset and Rokkan (eds.), pp. 293–294; Lipset, *Political Man,* p. 251; Hamilton, *op. cit.,* pp. 206–208; which report correlations of size of plant and radicalism. However, Eric Nordlinger, *The Working-Class Tories* (Berkeley: University of California Press, 1967), reports contrary findings for England.

In all countries with large Communist movements (Italy, France, and Finland), within any given structural environment, the better-paid workers are more moderate in their political views than the poorer ones. Modernization reduces the sources of worker hostility to management by altering the sources of managerial behavior. These trends involve a decline in the family-owned corporation and in the domination of the economy by the *patron* type who sees himself as all powerful, and the rise within the management strata of a corporate leadership characterized by a division of labor and by the requisite of formal higher education. Accompanying the growth in large systems is a consequent increased emphasis on universalistic and achievement values, on judging individuals on the basis of their specific roles as worker or manager. As management's resistance to formalizing the labor-management relationship gradually declines, union labor's commitment to an ideological view of unionism, as distinct from a business or pragmatic view, is also reduced.

THE NEW MIDDLE CLASS—THE BASE FOR EMPLOYEE POLITICS

The emergence of the new middle class—the increasingly large layer of clerks, salesmen, technicians, middle management, civil servants—has served to introduce as a major factor in the European polity a group which itself is so exposed to conflicting pressures from the left and the right that it can contribute to stabilizing class tensions. A broad middle class has a mitigating position because it can give political rewards to moderate parties and penalize extreme parties on both sides —right and left. Its members wish to obtain more for themselves and their offspring; they advocate universalistic equality in the educational and other aspects of the status-allocating mechanisms; they often uphold the extension of the welfare state. Yet their position among the relatively privileged in status and possession terms makes them supporters of political and social stability, of the politics of collective bargaining. And the larger a proportion of the electorate and the labor force formed by the new middle class, the more both the left and the right must take this group into account in determining their own policies. The political and trade-union influence of the new middle class is largely thrown on the side of pressing for greater opportunity, not greater social equality. The unions of the middle class are interested in maintaining, or even extending, the income gap existing between themselves and the manual workers. They often abstain from affiliating to the same central federation as the manual unions, and many of them are led by men who back "liberal" rather than labor parties. In some countries of Europe, and in Israel in recent years, there have been strikes by unions of salaried professionals in order to widen the gap between themselves and manual workers.[40] However, interest in income differences apart, these rapidly growing new middle classes press the political system toward consensus because as employees they favor many of the same statist policies that were long pressed by the representatives of the manual workers. Otto Kirchheimer in fact has argued that it is the very growth of

[40] On the behavior of white-collar workers in various countries see R. M. Blackburn, *Union Character and Social Class* (London: Batsford, 1967); Adolf Sturmthal (ed.), *White Collar Unions: Contemporary Developments in Industrialized Societies* (Urbana: University of Illinois Press, 1966). See also S. M. Lipset, "White Collar Workers and Professionals—Their Attitudes and Behavior Towards Unions," in William A. Faunce (ed.), *Industrial Sociology* (New York: Appleton-Century-Crofts, 1967), pp. 525–548; Michel Crozier, "Les attitudes politiques des employés et des petits fonctionnaires," in M. Duverger (ed.), *Partis politiques et classes sociales en France* (Paris: Armand Colin, 1955), pp. 85–99; *Petits fonctionnaires au travail* (Paris: Centre National de la recherche scientifique, 1955); "L'ambiguité de la conscience de classe chez les employés et les petits fonctionnaires," *Cahiers Internationaux de sociologie*, 28 (1955), 78–97; "Les relations de pouvoir dans un système d'organisation bureaucratique," *Sociologie du Travail*, 1 (1960), 61–75; "Classes sans conscience ou préfiguration de la société sans classes," *European Journal of Sociology*, 1 (1960), 233–245; "Le rôle des employés et des petits fonctionnaires dans la structure française contemporaine," *Transactions of the Third World Congress of Sociology* (Amsterdam: International Sociological Association, 1956), III, 311–319; Roger Girod, *Études sociologiques sur les couches salariées* (Paris: Marcel Rivière, 1961); Fritz Croner, *Die Angestellten in der modernen Gesellschaft* (Frankfurt: Humbolt, 1954); John Bonham, *The Middle Class Vote* (London: Faber and Faber, 1954); David Lockwood, *The Blackcoated Worker* (London: Allen and Unwin, 1958); E. Dahlstrom, *Tjänstemännen, Naringlivet och sämhallet* (Stockholm: Studieförbundet näringsliv och Samhälle, 1954). See also S. M. Lipset and Mildred Schwartz, "The Politics of Professionals," in H. M. Vollmer and D. L. Mills (eds.), *Professionalization* (Englewood Cliffs, Prentice-Hall, 1966), pp. 299–310.

these strata, who form the mass base of the "bourgeois" parties, that is largely responsible for the decline of ideology.[41]

It is important to recognize that the bourgeois parties are no longer bourgeois in the classic sense of the term. That is, the proportion of those who are self-employed, or who have close ties to the self-employed on the land or in the town, is an increasingly small part of the electorate. Most large parties now represent employees, manual or nonmanual. And while these strata differ in their orientations to many issues, they are also united on many welfare concerns. Swedish political history is an apt illustration of this point. The dominant Social Democrats were experiencing a secular decline in support, largely, according to survey analyses, because the white-collar segment of the population was growing relative to the manual sector. The party introduced a major reform, an old-age pension of 65 per cent of salary, in large part because their electoral researches had suggested such a proposal would be popular not only with their traditional manual supporters but with many white-collar workers. The proposal was ultimately carried in a referendum, and the party increased its national vote substantially. Even more significant, perhaps, is the fact that the Liberal party, which accepted the general principle of the enlarged pension, gained enormously at the expense of the Conservatives, who took a traditional position against high taxes and against increases in the functions of the state. This suggests that the political struggles of the future will increasingly take place between parties representing the status concerns and economic interests of the two employee strata, and that the parties drawing heavily from the self-employed will continue to lose influence.[42]

COMMUNISM RESISTS THE TREND

The dominant structural trend in Europe involves the final triumph of the values of industrial society, the end of rigid

[41] Kirchheimer, *op. cit.*, p. 148.

[42] It is interesting to note that a similar pattern has emerged within the United States. See Herbert J. McClosky, Paul J. Hoffman, and Rosemary O'Hara, "Issue Conflict and Consensus among Party Leaders and Followers," *American Political Science Review*, 54 (June 1960), 406–427.

status classes derivative from a preindustrial world, and increasing emphasis on achievement rather than ascription, on universalism rather than particularism, and on interaction among individuals in terms of the specific roles played by each rather than in terms of their diffuse generalized statuses. The heightening standard of living of the masses gives them greater market power and enables them to affect much of culture and societal taste. All these changes imply the emergence of a somewhat similar social and political culture, one which increasingly resembles the first advanced industrial society to function without institutions and values derivative from a feudal past, the United States. And as has been indicated earlier, this should mean the end of class-linked severely ideological politics.

Yet there is one major force which in a number of countries has rejected this view of European social change and which has done its best to block these trends—the Communist party. It is clear that the very existence of powerful Communist movements in countries such as France and Italy has been a major force perpetuating the institutions and values of the old society. In countries in which the Communists are the largest working-class party, in which they secure around a quarter of all votes, it has been difficult to elect a progressive government to office. If governments must secure a majority from the non-Communist three-quarters of the population, they have to rely in large part on the conservative and traditionalist elements. The fact that one-quarter of the electorate, constituting one-half or more of the social base of the "left," have been outside of the political game inevitably gives a considerable advantage to the conservatives. In effect, by voting Communist, French and Italian workers have disfranchised themselves. Thus not only does a mass Communist party serve to fossilize the ideological orientations characteristic of a preindustrial society among the working class, it contributes to preserving premodern orientations on the right.

A series of political developments—the revival of French Communist support recouping most of the electoral losses it suffered between 1956 and 1958 as a result of the Hungarian revolution and the Gaullist coup, the continued massive strength of Finnish Communism and the fairly continuous slow growth in the vote of the Italian Communists—each of which has occurred during long periods of prosperity and economic growth—would seem to contradict the thesis that economic growth and an improvement in social conditions enhance the prospects for political stability.[43] In these countries economic modernization has seemingly not been followed by a reduction in ideological tensions.

The countries with large Communist parties, however, remain among the less modernized of the big nations; their industry tends to be less centralized in large plants. Thus the proportion of German employees in plants with more than 1,000 workers is twice as high (38.9 per cent) as it is in France (17.6 per cent), while only 12 per cent of the employed Germans are in plants with fewer than 50 workers, in contrast to 37 per cent of the French.[44] The European countries in which communism is strongest are among those with a relatively small proportion of their total population living in metropolitan areas.[45] The rank-order correlation between the proportion of Communist votes in a nation and urbanization is minus .61, while the comparable correlation between left extremist voting and an index of industrialization is minus .76.[46] Insofar as the general pattern of politics, class relations, and other social attitudes is affected by the degree of bureaucratization of industrial and community life, it is clear that the nations with large Communist movements are on the whole among the less developed in these respects of the nations of Europe.

[43] E. A. Bayne, "Italy's Seeds of Peril," I, *American Universities Field Staff Reports Service,* Southeast Europe Series, 10, No. 1 (June 1962), 7, and "Unions on the March Again," *The Economist,* April 13, 1963, 137.

[44] For Germany see the *Statistisches Jahrbuch,* 1959, p. 179, and for France in 1954 see Institut national de la statistique et des études economiques, *Mouvement Economique en France de 1944 à 1957* (Paris: Presses Universitaires, 1958), p. 42.

[45] See Jack P. Gibbs and Kingsley Davis, "Conventional Versus Metropolitan Data in the International Study of Urbanization," in Jack P. Gibbs (ed.), *Urban Research Methods* (Princeton: Van Nostrand, 1961), pp. 422–424.

[46] William Kornhauser, *The Politics of Mass Society* (Glencoe: The Free Press, 1959), pp. 143, 150. The degree of urbanization was measured by the proportion of the population living in cities with more than 20,000 population, while industrialization was measured by the proportion of the labor force in nonagricultural occupations.

The comparative analysis of the consequences of economic growth on class relationships in relatively industrialized societies is further complicated by the fact that processes endemic in such improvement affect those workers who are accustomed to the industrial system differently from those who are drawn into it. For the former, increased bureaucratization of industry should make for improvement in income and the conditions of work, and thus should serve to moderate their propensity toward extremist politics. For the latter, the experiences of dislocation inherent in social and geographic mobility, particularly the shift from rural or small-town background to crowded urban slums, and from the pace and discipline of rural work to that of the factory, may increase their potential for support of political radicalism.[47] The need to adjust quickly to new social conditions and cultural norms makes individuals receptive to new values and ideologies which explain the sources of their discontent in revolutionary terms.[48] It should also be noted that the decline in the number of the chronically unemployed—from 2.5 million in 1950–1951 to well under a million in the early 1960's—in Italy may have increased rather than decreased the vote available to the extreme left. There are two empirical generalizations about the political behavior of the jobless and the formerly unemployed that hold true in a number of countries. First, the unemployed are much more likely than those regularly employed to be uninformed and apathetic about politics. Their insecurity would seem to reduce their availability for any "outside" interest, including the act of voting. Second, employed individuals who report a past experience of unemployment, or areas which were once centers of high rates of unemployment, are much more likely to exhibit leftist voting

[47] The change in the Italian occupational structure has been dramatic. See Bayne, "Italy's Seeds of Peril," II, No. 2 (June 1960), p. 6.

[48] See Edvard Bull, Jr., *Arbeidermilje under det industrielle gjennombrudd. Tre norske industristrok* (Oslo: 1958), as cited in Stein Rokkan and Henry Valen, "Parties, Elections and Political Behaviour in the Northern Countries: A Review of Recent Research," in Otto Stammer (ed.), *Politische Forschung* (Köln: Westdeutscher Verlag, 1960), pp. 107–108, 110; Lipset, *Political Man*, pp. 68–71. See also John C. Leggett, "Uprootedness and Working-Class Consciousness," *American Journal of Sociology*, 68 (1963), 682–692. Leggett also cites various historical studies which point to the link between "uprootedness" and radicalism.

propensities than those with more fortunate economic histories.[49]

The most comprehensive analysis of the sources of, and changes in, the support of a mass European Communist party, that of Erik Allardt in Finland, strongly suggests that economic growth in the less industrialized regions of a rapidly developing nation heightens the possibilities for extremist class-conscious politics. He points out that the characteristics of Communist strength in regions in which communism has gained greatly since World War II, the north and east, are quite different from those in the areas in which it has always been strong, the south and west. The latter are the original industrialized sections of the country. His detailed statistical analyses point to the conclusion that *"increase in Communist strength in all areas is related to changes which in one way or another are likely to uproot individuals."*[50] Ecological analysis indicates that increases in the per-capita income of the poorer regions are correlated highly with gains in Communist support. Allardt's analysis also suggests some of the factors underlying the continuation of Communist strength once attained. Stable Communist strength, that is, little fluctuations up or down, is associated with the older industrial areas in which the party has been strong since the Russian Revolution and which also give strong support to the Social Democrats. In such regions the Communists have erected an elaborate network of party-linked voluntary associations and leisure activities, so that, as in parts of France and Italy, one almost has a functioning Communist subculture unaffected by political events.

As already noted, it is doubtful that structural changes alone will result in the decline of a mass Communist party.[51]

---

[49] Lipset, *Political Man*, pp. 187, 198, 236; see also S. M. Lipset, *Agrarian Socialism* (Berkeley: University of California Press, 1950), pp. 176–177.

[50] Allardt, "Traditional and Emerging Radicalism," p. 21. In an earlier study Allardt has demonstrated that areas with the highest proportions of unemployed during the depression gave the highest support to the Communists in 1951–1954. See Erik Allardt, *Social Struktur och Politisk Aktivitet* (Helsingfors: Söderstrom, 1956), p. 84.

[51] Greece may be an exception to this generalization. See Marcello Dell' Omodarme, "Greece Moves toward Dictatorship," *Atlas*, 3 (1962), 301–305 (translated from *Communitá*, December 1961).

Where the party is strong, it endeavors, as in Finland, to isolate its base from serious influence by non-Communist sources. There are plenty of social strains inherent in the situation of the worker or poor peasant to reinforce acceptance of leftist doctrine, and a mass movement can claim that any improvements are the result of its agitation. The Communist sector of the electorate will join the democratic political game in the foreseeable future only if their party, as a party, does it. There is little doubt that if the various European Communist parties had been genuine national parties—that is, if their behavior had been largely determined by experiences within their own countries—they would have evolved in much the same way as the European socialist parties. And consequently, it is necessary to recognize that any predictions about their future behavior must be part of an analysis of developments within the Communist-controlled nations. The break between the Soviet Union and China permits genuine autonomy for all national Communist parties, so that the pattern of independence from Russian control emerging in Italy has occurred elsewhere as well.

The doctrinal base for such a change in the role of Communist parties has been advanced by various Yugoslav and Italian Communists.[52] The former have argued that there is a worldwide pressure for socialist innovations which is inherent in the nature of large-scale capitalist economic institutions. They accept the proposition that Communist movements and ideologies as they emerged in eastern Europe and Russia are appropriate for underdeveloped countries which have not had the experience of large and legally instituted labor, political, and union movements nor the experience of political freedom.[53] The more developed nations not only can avoid the experiences of the less developed Communist societies, but they can and are moving toward socialism while preserving political freedom. It has even been suggested that in the United States, socialist adjustments and institutions exist even though Americans refuse to accept the term socialism to

[52] An analysis of the similarities in the approaches of the Yugoslav and Italian Communists may be found in François Fejto, "Le parti communiste français et le 'polycentrisme,' " *Arguments,* 6 (1962), 69–70.

[53] See Walter Z. Laqueur, "The End of the Monolith: World Communism in 1962," *Foreign Affairs,* 40 (1962), 362.

describe the changes occurring within their society. Coexistence is possible, say these Yugoslavs, not only because major war is impossible in an atomic age, but because there is no basic cleavage between the Communist and the capitalist world, since the latter is ceasing to be capitalist in any traditional meaning of the term. Hence Communists in the developed countries will not have to make a revolution or come to power in their own right. By collaborating with other "progressive forces," they can hasten the emergence of socialist institutions.

The Italian Communist party has gradually modified its ideology so that some sophisticated observers would now describe it as a left social-democratic rather than a Communist party. Like the Yugoslav party, it no longer sees a fundamental dichotomy between capitalism and socialism, but rather argues that "there exists in the capitalist world today an urge towards structural reforms and to reforms of a socialist nature, which is related to economic progress and the new expansion of the productive forces."[54] And its late leader, Palmiro Togliatti, went on to argue the need to "correct" Lenin's position that "bourgeois state apparatus cannot be used for building a socialist society," in the light of "the changes which have taken place and which are still in the process of being realized in the world."[55] It denies the need for one-party dictatorship in Italy, and it has accepted Italian membership in the Common Market. Communist municipal office-holders work closely with business groups in fostering the interests of their cities, and party-controlled labor unions play a somewhat more responsible role in collective bargaining and Italian life generally than has been true for Com-

[54] Quoted in the Editorial Department of Hongqi, *More on the Differences Between Comrade Togliatti and Us* (Peking: Foreign Languages Press, 1963), p. 13.

[55] Togliatti's report, *op. cit.*, p. 130 (emphasis mine). For a discussion of some of the issues underlying the question of Marx and Engels' original position, the influence of the Paris Commune on them, and Communist revisionism, see S. M. Lipset, "The Sociology of Marxism," *Dissent,* 10 (1963), 59–69. This is a review article on George Lichtheim, *Marxism: An Historical and Critical Study* (New York: Frederick A. Praeger, 1961). This book must also be read in this context. Lichtheim argues that Marxism as a revolutionary doctrine is appropriate only to countries in the period of early industrialization.

munist unions in the past.[56] The Chinese Communists correctly point to the Italian party as the foremost example of reformist heresies among the nongovernmental parties. If the Italian electorate has not turned away from the Communists, the Communists have moved to the right. Thus the effect of a reduction in social strains among sections of the Italian workers may be reflected in the changed behavior of their party and unions.[57]

But if the experiences and the behavior of the Italian party suggest an adaptation to the emergence of stable political institutions and economic modernization in Italy, the French Communist party simply has adjusted more slowly and its policies until very recently seemingly challenged the underlying interpretation here.[58] The French party also had to react to the end of Soviet domination of party life and to economic modernization in France. But where the Italian party and its union federation, the CGIL, modified their programs and explicitly decided to cooperate "with what they termed the representatives of neo-capitalism," during the late 1950's, the French party in large part refused and remains in 1970 the most "conservative" communist party in Western Europe. It continued to insist that capitalism could not reform itself, that the workers could not make long-term improvements in their social situation, and that the unions must remain primarily political instruments. The Italian party decided to join forces with modernization, the French party

[56] In Italy see Giorgio Galli, "Italy," in Walter Laqueur and Leopold Labedz (eds.), *Polycentrism: The New Factor in International Communism* (New York: Frederick A. Praeger, 1962), pp. 127–140; and Giorgio Galli, "Italy: The Choice for the Left," in Leopold Labedz (ed.), *Revisionism* (New York: Frederick A. Praeger, 1962), pp. 324–336.

[57] For an indication of the diversity of opinion and level of open debate which exists among the leadership of the Italian Communist party, see the translations of the report published in *L'Unità*, the organ of the party, of a two-day debate within the central committee. Perry Anderson, "Debate of the Central Committee of the Italian Communist Party on the 22nd Congress of the C.P.S.U.," *New Left Review*, Nos. 13–14 (January–April, 1962), 151–192. For the history of open debate within the Italian party, see Guglielmo Negri and Paolo Ungari, "La vita dei partito," in Alberto Spreafico and Joseph La Palombara (eds.), *Elezioni e comportamento politico in Italia* (Cremona: Edizioni di Communitá, 1963), pp. 175–180.

[58] But for a different interpretation, see Lichtheim, *op. cit.*, p. 180.

continues to resist it.[59] The reasons for the differences in tempo of the parties are complex and I cannot detail them here.[60] Briefly, they would seem to relate to the fact that the French party was Stalinized and proletarianized in its leadership and membership during the 1930's and 1940's, while Fascism enabled the Italian party to escape some of these consequences; after 1944 it recruited and retained many non-Stalinist intellectuals in its organizations. Palmiro Togliatti, the leader of the Italian party until his death in 1964, though an official of the Comintern during the 1930's, more closely resembled the pre-Stalin leaders of Communism than his French equivalent Maurice Thorez, who won and maintained leadership as a result of following Stalin's every turn.[61] The variations in the Italian and French political systems have meant that elected local Communists have had more real power and involvement in running municipalities and other institutions in Italy than in France.[62] The Italian Socialists, in part because of their long Fascist experience, have been much less hostile to the Communists than have been the French Socialists. Hence the Italian party has never been so isolated from non-Communists as the French. These differences between the French and Italian Communist parties may be related to the facts that the Italian party has lost fewer members than the French (both parties have lost a considerable portion of their membership as compared with their postwar high point), and that the Italian party has done better at the polls during the 1960's.[63]

Communist parties without a Moscow-centered world party would be like national Roman Catholic churches without a pope, without the need to follow a dogma decreed from a

[59] See Pierre Fougeyrollas, "France," in Laqueur and Labedz, *op. cit.*, pp. 141–151.

[60] An excellent analysis of the differences between the Italian and French parties may be found in Fejto, *op. cit.*, pp. 66–72. A similar point is made by Laqueur, *op. cit.*, p. 369.

[61] See Ignazio Silone's essay in R. Crossman (ed.), *The God That Failed* (New York: Harper, 1949), pp. 106–112, and Antonio Gambino, "Togliatti's Balancing Act," *Atlas*, 3 (1962), 126–127 (translated from *L'Espresso*, December 31, 1961).

[62] See Michel Crozier, "La France, terre de commandement," *Esprit*, 25 (1957), 790–792.

[63] See Hamilton, *op. cit.*, pp. 27–28. See also Crozier, "La France, terre de commandement."

single source. And many observers predict that the individual parties will follow the road of Protestantism, of deviation, of variation, of adjustment to particular national conditions, much as the Social Democrats did half a century or more earlier. Those parties which operate within democratic societies will be under constant pressure to modify their totalitarian structures, as in fact the Italian party seems to be beginning to do.[64]

Given the history of the Communist movement, the training which its leaders have received in totalitarian methods, and the use of conscious deception, the acceptance (even though now critical) of the experiences of one-party regimes as a positive model, no one who cares about freedom can accept a Communist party as an equal player in a parliamentary game. On the other hand, the possibility that changes in the Communist world are permitting sufficient independence and variations among Communist parties to allow some of them to react to the forces which press them to act as regular participants within political democracies should not be ignored. The more positively involved are Communists and their *followers* in a political system which in fact is paying off socially and economically, the more difficult it will be for a given Communist party to renew an alienated stance among its supporters should the leadership decide to do so. Hence the possibility may be held out that the vicious circle of Communist-reactionary resistance to modernization in Latin Europe may be breaking down, not only as a result of the decline of the reactionary groups, but because of changes within Communism. Even Communism may be yielding to the pressures making for a decline of ideology and of class war.

CONTINUING SOURCES OF STRAIN

There are many sources of political strain within stable democratic societies. The stratification systems of all inherently involve a grossly inegalitarian distribution of status, income,

[64] Richard Lowenthal, "The Rise and Decline of International Communism," *Problems of Communism,* 12 (March–April 1963); see also Laqueur, *op. cit.,* pp. 371–373.

and power. Even the very "affluent" United States contains a large minority living in poverty by its own standards.[65] A look at consumption standards for Europe finds that very large minorities or majorities in different European countries still lack many items which are available to all but a few in the United States.[66] Status inequality would seem to be experienced as punitive by the lower classes in all systems. But while all societies present some ideological justification for enduring consumption and status inequalities, the concept of mass citizenship that arose with the Industrial Revolution undermines the stability of class systems because it implies, as T. H. Marshall put it, that "all are equal with respect to the rights and duties with which the status is endowed."[67] Hence he argues that modern democratic industrial society is historically unique in seeking to sustain a system of contradictory stratification values. All previous societies had class systems that assumed inequality, but they also denied citizenship to all except a small elite. Once full and equal political (manhood suffrage) and economic (trade-union organization) citizenship was established, the egalitarian emphasis inherent in the concept sustains a successful and continuing attack on many aspects of inequality. Much of democratic politics involves the efforts of the lower strata to equalize the conditions of existence and opportunity.

The tension between equality and inequality is endemic in modern industrial democratic society. The dominant strata will continue the attempt to institutionalize their privileges, to find means to pass on to their kin and offspring the privileges they have gained. This conflict, however, does not mean that one or the other tendency must triumph, or that the strain

---

[65] See S. M. Lipset, *The First New Nation* (New York: Basic Books, 1963), pp. 321–335 for an earlier discussion.

[66] A quick glance at any statistical table reporting on income or consumption standards in Europe suggests the extent to which European affluence is considerably below that of the United States. See J. Frederick Dewhurst, "Consumption Levels and Patterns," in Dewhurst *et al., op. cit.,* pp. 146–147, 161–162; P. Lamartine Yates, "Household Operations," in Dewhurst, *et al., op. cit.,* pp. 266, 267, 1005; Report of DOXA, 15, No. 16 (August 1961), p. 2; and "Tableau général de la consommation des français de 1950 à 1960," *Consommation,* 8 (July–December 1961), 5–174.

[67] Marshall, *op. cit.,* p. 87.

will destroy or even necessarily weaken the social fabric. The predominant character of modern industrial democracy, as a free and evolving society, is in part a result of the chronic tensions between the inherent pressures toward inequality and the endemic emphasis in democracy on equality.

The wave of writings in the 1950's that somehow saw in the growth of affluence in the Western world the emergence of a peaceful social utopia—which would not require continued political struggle between representatives of the haves and of the have-nots—ignored the extent to which the content of these very concepts changes as society evolves. As Marshall has pointed out, ever since the beginning of the Industrial Revolution almost every generation proclaimed a social revolution to elevate the lower strata. "From the 1880's to the 1940's people were constantly expressing amazement at the social transformation witnessed in their lifetime, oblivious of the fact that, in this series of outbursts of self-congratulation, the glorious achievements of the past became the squalid heritage of the present." [68]

But in spite of the progress leading one generation to proclaim the significance of recent social improvements, only a few years later others are arguing that the present conditions of the poor, of the lowly, are intolerable, that they cannot possibly be tolerated by free men who believe in equality. [69] And as Marshall indicates, such phenomena do not "mean that the progress which men thought they made was illusory. It means that the standards by which that progress was assessed were constantly rising, and that ever deeper probing into the social situation kept revealing new horrors which had previously been concealed from view." [70] The large literature dealing with poverty in the 1960's provided a new demonstration of Marshall's thesis.

The problem of the lower strata is now seen not only as a consequence of limited resources, but of "cultural deprivation" as well. It is clear that in all countries,

[68] *Ibid.*, p. 268.
[69] See Howe, *op. cit.*, pp. 325–326. See also John Goldthorpe and David Lockwood, "Not So Bourgeois After All," *New Society*, 1, No. 3 (October 18, 1962), 19.
[70] Marshall, *op. cit.*, pp. 269–270.

variation in participation in the intellectual culture serves to negate the dream of equal opportunity for all to mount the educational ladder; consequently, access to the summits of the occupational structure is still grossly restricted. In Sweden, for example, in spite of thirty-five years of Social Democratic government providing free access to universities together with state bursaries, the proportion of working-class children taking advantage of such opportunities has hardly risen. Few commodities are distributed as unequally in Europe as high-school and university education. The simple improvement in economic standards of living, at least at its present pace, does little to reduce the considerable advantages held by the culturally privileged strata to perpetuate their families in an equally advantaged position.[71] And socialist parties in a number of countries are beginning to look for ways to enhance the educational and cultural aspirations of lower-class youth. Here, then, is the most recent example of the conflict between the principles of equality inherent in citizenship and the forces endemic to complex stratified society that serve to maintain or erect cultural barriers between the classes. The latter operate as a consequence of the differential distributions of rewards and access to culture, and must be combated continually if they are not to dominate.[72]

In conclusion, this survey of economic and social developments accompanying the modernization of European society has shown compelling evidence for the moderation of ideological differences in Europe as a consequence of the increasing affluence of European nations, the attainment of economic as well as political citizenship by the workers, the gradual absorption and assimilation of the remnants of European society still living in feudal or otherwise underdeveloped economic and social conditions. The changes in parties of the left,

[71] See H. Bouterline Young, "Detection and Encouragement of the Talented in Italian Schools," *The British Yearbook of Education, 1962* (London: Evans Brothers, 1962), pp. 275–280. See also Christiane, Peyre, "L'Origine sociale des élèves de l'enseignement secondaire en France," in Jean Floud *et al., Ecole et société* (Paris: Marcel Rivière, 1959), p. 10.

[72] See Mark Abrams, "Social Class and Political Values" (paper presented to the British Sociological Association, Scottish Branch, Conference in Edinburgh, May 3–4, 1963), pp. 13–14.

especially Communist parties, to a more moderate orientation toward capitalist society and class conflict have been shown to be also related to broad changes in the international Communist world, as exemplified by the thesis of polycentrism and the reinterpretation of Marxism concerning the possibility of a rapprochement with capitalism. But it has also been pointed out that industrialization does not remove sources of tension. These sources are endemic to an industrial society which permits a relatively open struggle for the fruits of individual effort and which does not automatically give access to opportunity for individual advancement to those on the lower rungs of the status ladder. Finally, it has been argued that much of the ideological politics of the "Poujadist" left and right is a response to anachronistic orientations and forms of industrial organization still present in some sectors of European society, as among some peasants and small businessmen in France, or as a result of the preservation of outmoded forms of production and extraction, as in Britain and Belgium.

It should be clear, however, that not only do class conflicts over issues related to division of the total economic pie, influence over various institutions, symbolic status and opportunity, continue in the absence of *Weltanschauungen,* but that the decline of such total ideologies does *not* mean the end of ideology. Clearly, commitment to the politics of pragmatism, to the rules of the game of collective bargaining, to gradual change whether in the direction favored by the left or the right, to opposition both to an all-powerful central state and to *laissez-faire* constitutes the component parts of an ideology. The "agreement on fundamentals," the political consensus of Western society, now increasingly has come to include a position on matters which once sharply separated the left from the right. And this ideological agreement, which might best be described as "conservative socialism," has become *the* ideology of the major parties in the developed states of Europe and America. As such it leaves its advocates in sharp disagreement with the radical rightists and leftists at home, particularly the students and intellectuals among the latter, and at a disadvantage in efforts to foster different variants of this doctrine in the less affluent parts of the world.[73]

Much of the analysis in Chapters 6 and 7 has dealt with the interplay of class and cultural factors, the latter principally religion, in affecting the political cleavage structure in different parts of the world. The following two chapters concentrate on the United States. Since the United States has never had an explicitly religious party, and has a tradition of the separation of church and state, there has been a tendency to ignore the impact of religion on politics. In my earlier work, *Political Man,* I concentrated on the role of class in analyzing American politics. To complete the "American story," I have attempted to lay out in some detail the way in which religious cleavages modify and supplement the impact of class on partisan divisions.

[73] I have discussed the sources of student activism, the main remaining mass base for total ideological politics in articles published elsewhere. See especially my articles in S. M. Lipset (ed.), *Student Politics* (New York: Basic Books, 1967); S. M. Lipset and Philip Altbach (eds.), *Students in Revolt* (Boston: Houghton Mifflin, 1969).

CHAPTER 9

Religion and Politics in the American Past and Present

INTRODUCTION: INTERACTION OF RELIGION AND POLITICS

The interrelationship between religion and politics in the United States has been of interest to most analysts of American culture. To a considerable extent there has been general agreement that the fact of a pluralistic religious culture—the existence of many competing denominations—has contributed to the development and stability of American democracy. All American religions have been numerical minorities for much of our history, and hence have an "interest" in democratic liberties. Tocqueville's comment on the source of American Catholic commitment to democratic rights applies to most groups: "They constitute a minority, and all rights must be respected in order to ensure them the free exercise of their own privileges."[1] The prevalence of voluntary associations, many of which have played major roles in shaping political issues, seems causally related to the pattern of voluntary benevolent and moral associations which developed around the various denominations.

But if there is abundant discussion of the impact of religion as an institution on the general character of the polity, there is an understandable reluctance to deal with the way in which religious interest or belief enters directly into the main stream of political controversy, determining and structuring

[1] Alexis de Tocqueville, *Democracy in America* (New York: Vintage Books, 1954), Vol. I, p. 312.

the nature of party conflict. No political party now wants to be in the position of explicitly alienating any religious group, and no religious denomination wants to acknowledge an identification with one political party.

Yet it should be obvious, as has been noted in Chapter 5, that simply as an important value-generating institution and source of status and power, religion cannot exist without seriously affecting the nature of political discourse. Tocqueville, Bryce, and many other sophisticated foreign commentators on nineteenth-century America discussed the interaction between party choice and religious affiliation. A host of moral issues which separated the parties were clearly associated with religious belief. The modern assumption that a relationship between religion and politics violates "separation of church and state" has only in recent decades served to suppress serious intellectual inquiry into the interaction of these two key institutions.

Nothing is so revealing of the strength of the taboo on this subject as the story of the way in which the pollsters and others who have been gathering statistics on voting behavior had to be forced by the analysis of their data to accept the fact that religious affiliation had an independent effect on vote choice.

For many years, George Gallup, the head of the first permanent polling agency in the United States, did not inquire regularly concerning the religious affiliation of respondents in his election and other opinion surveys. The first major academic study of voting preferences based on interviews, that of Lazarsfeld and his associates in 1940, found a large difference in the party choice of Protestants as compared to Catholics, no matter what other factors, such as education and economic status, were held constant. This came as a considerable surprise to them, since there was no issue related to religion, as such, in this election.[2] As recently as 1959, Elmo

[2] Paul F. Lazarsfeld, Bernard Berelson, and Hazel Gaudet, *The People's Choice* (New York: Columbia University Press, 1948), p. 21. See the discussion of this development in Peter Rossi, "Four Landmarks in Voting Research," in E. Burdick and A. J. Brodbeck (eds.), *American Voting Behavior* (Glencoe: The Free Press, 1959), p. 18. Rossi reports that "Dr. Lazarsfeld related that George Gallup expressed disbelief when he told him of his finding that this religious factor was independently related to voting behavior" (p. 438).

Roper, who directs a second national survey group, wrote that there was no relationship between religious affiliation and voting.[3] And of course in writing about determinants of partisan choice in past elections, historians, other than those writing directly on religion, tended to concentrate on variations among socioeconomic groups, regions, and to some extent ethnic groups. Systematic investigation of the interrelationships of these factors with religion has only occurred in the last two decades.

Tracing the religious-political pattern in the United States is the chief concern of this chapter. The political history of the country is so short that this pattern is almost a matter of variations on one basic design. The first part of the chapter deals with the establishment of that design: the formative years and the one major realignment which took place around the middle of the nineteenth century. This is a sweeping attempt to describe the development of the basic religious-political pattern, without detailing the variations or passing contradictions which must attend any such broad historical generalization.[4]

This examination finds that such factors as these served to affect the basic political differentiation among American religious bodies: (1) social status, (2) economic class, (3) anti-Catholicism in both its religious and ethnic form, (4) level of concern with "public morality." The interplay of these and other variables in the religious-political pattern of twentieth-century America is then substantively examined. It becomes abundantly clear that political variation among religious groups is not just a matter of statistical curiosity, but it is closely related to the broad shaping of American political life.

[3] Elmo Roper, "The Myth of the Catholic Vote," *Saturday Review of Literature* (October 31, 1959), 22.

[4] In this chapter, I ignore most factors other than religion which have affected the varying social bases of support of American parties. This may give the unwarranted impression that I am trying to suggest that religion is the predominant factor. Obviously, this is not so, although it and class position are the two most important continuing ones. For an analysis of the significance of class factors see S. M. Lipset, *Political Man* (Garden City: Doubleday, 1963), esp. pp. 303–331. In a sense, this chapter is designed to complement the one on class and voting in the earlier volume.

THE BASIC DESIGN

■ *The formative years.*   America's first experience
with political differentiation among religious groups began
with the founding of the nation. The Episcopalian and Congregationalist churches became identified with the conservative
Federalists and Whigs, while the Baptist, Methodist, and Presbyterian churches were linked with the Jeffersonians and Jacksonians. Initially, this divergence was in some part the result
of the different social characteristics of these religious groups,
and in some part related to the fact that the former had
been state-established churches. Both before and after the
formation of the United States as a nation, it was not only a
country whose population was largely Protestant, but specific
Protestant denominations were the official state church. Almost all of the colonies had an established church, the Church
of England in the South and the Congregationalists in the
North. Although we now think of the Constitution as having
outlawed religious establishments when it laid down the principle of separation of church and state, in fact it did not. The
Bill of Rights states that *Congress* shall make no laws with
respect to the establishment of religion. Until the passage of
the Fourteenth Amendment in 1866, this provision did not
affect the individual states.

In some states these established churches were not disestablished until the second decade of the nineteenth century—in
the final case of Massachusetts not until 1833, forty-four years
after the adoption of the Constitution.[5] The struggle for the
disestablishment of the churches on the state level was related
to the party politics of its day. The original party fight was
between the liberal Democratic Republicans, led by Jefferson
and Madison and the conservative Federalists, led by John
Adams, Alexander Hamilton, and others. One of the differences between the Democratic Republican leaders, who in a
sense were the left-wingers of their day, and present liberal
political leaders, is that many of the former were Deists in

[5] See Euarts B. Greene, *Religion and the State* (Ithaca: Great Seal
Books, 1959), pp. 78–93.

their religious belief. They tended to look upon much of organized religion and most of the theologies of their day as outmoded medieval beliefs which would dwindle away. They were intellectually children of the Enlightenment. As in the case of the scholars of the European Enlightenment, they saw the modern world of the late eighteenth or early nineteenth century as growing beyond the superstitions which were regarded as hangovers from feudalism, medievalism, and a monarchical society.

Conversely, the more traditionalistic Federalists were concerned with maintaining various values and behavior patterns that persisted from colonial times. Many of them favored the preservation of established religions. The Congregationalist church was the established church for many years in three Federalist strongholds—New Hampshire until 1817, Connecticut until 1818, and Massachusetts until 1833.[6]

The defeat of the Federalists, first in the South where the Jeffersonians were dominant, then later in New England, was related to the disestablishment of the churches. It should be noted that while there was in this period a decline of religious institutions generally, the elimination of established religion was not in itself a defeat of religion; the Protestant denominations which were *not* established predictably supported the disestablishment of the state church.

The resolution of the Establishment issue in the early nineteenth century did not, of course, end the relationship between various denominations and party politics. Evidence drawn from an analysis of voting records would suggest that the link between the traditional high-status churches, Anglican and Congregationalist, and the more conservative party continued after the demise of the Federalists. Conversely, those denominations which were associated with lower-status groups, either in terms of ethnic origins, more recent immigrant status, or class composition, tended to be identified with the Democrats. Catholics, largely Irish, though not yet the major force they were to become, nevertheless were a noticeable group in some of the larger cities such as Boston and New York, and then as later were largely Democratic.

[6] See W. W. Sweet, *The Story of Religion in America* (New York: Harper, 1950).

These relationships between religion and party were, like all such statistical associations, a product of a number of factors. In part, they reflected an "interest" struggle among denominations; the established churches, past or present, were linked to the party of the Establishment, the Federalists. To some degree they were determined by traditions or values associated with certain denominations; the Calvinist groups, in particular, viewed Catholicism as representing great evil, the "antichrist" in Rome. Further, they flowed from class or status elements; the more well to do, who were also disproportionately members of the established churches, tended to support the more conservative party, while the poorer strata, who adhered to the new sects or the Catholic church, were Jeffersonians. The linkage between Catholics, plus others of more recent immigrant stock, and the Democrats were cemented at this early period in American history by the fact that the Federalists openly and avowedly tried to make life difficult for them, while the Jeffersonians defended their interests and rights.[7]

All the studies of voting behavior during this period agree that religious affiliation played a major role in differentiating the supporters of the two parties. The most detailed of them, that by Manning Dauer covering elections around 1800, reports that the Federalist party benefited considerably from Congregationalist support.[8] The Episcopalians, who had been the established church in the Southern states, also gave heavy backing to the conservative party. "The other religions whose members originally supported the Federalists were the German Reformed, Dutch Reformed, and Lutheran denominations . . . the Quakers, strongest in Pennsylvania, were generally Federalist, except when war threatened."[9] In areas which backed the Jeffersonians "the chief denominations were the Baptists . . . the Methodists and Presbyterians . . . concentrated in the back country geographically; and these same denominations plus the Irish Catholics in the

---

[7] John C. Miller, *Crisis in Freedom* (Boston: Little, Brown, 1951), pp. 43–44, 46–48.

[8] Manning Dauer, *The Adams Federalists* (Baltimore: Johns Hopkins Press, 1953), p. 25. See also Anson Stokes, *Church and State in the United States* (New York: Harper, 1950), Vol. I, pp. 408–410.

[9] Dauer, *op. cit.*, pp. 28–29.

towns."[10] It is difficult to estimate the extent to which such apparent differences in denominational political allegiance were directly related to the interest or theological positions of the churches, or reflected variations in socioeconomic position. The denominations which backed the Democrats all had an "interest" in disestablishment; they were largely composed of the less well to do; the Baptists and the Methodists were new sects whose ministers and adherents ranked low in the social hierarchy; the Presbyterians were largely a low-status Scotch-Irish immigrant group who had been rejected by the Puritans of New England and "were natural recruits for a leveling party."[11]

One would expect, however, that these groups would be among the most moralistic, and dislike the secularistic attitudes and policies of many Democratic leaders. The binding link between the "out-group" sects and the Deist party leaders would seem to have been a common dislike of the power and influence of the once established or traditional denominations. Insofar as the state enforced Christian norms, it reflected the past strength of the Establishment, and a decisive break between church and state meant the triumph of religious egalitarianism.

The highly visible character of the link between politics and religion may be seen in the comments of two ministers, one Congregationalist and the other Methodist, concerning the politics of the early nineteenth century. The Congregationalist recorded that the Jeffersonians included "nearly all the minor sects, besides the Sabbath-breakers, rum-selling, tippling folk, infidels, and ruff-scruff generally." The Methodist minister wrote: "The great mass . . . of the Methodist church and her adherents were Republicans. Every convert to Methodism in those times became a Republican if he was not one before. . . . On the other hand, Calvinism and Federalism were yoked together."[12]

[10] *Op. cit.*, on the Irish, see Carl Wittke, *The Irish in America* (Baton Rouge: Louisiana State University Press, 1956), p. 106.

[11] See Lawrence H. Fuchs, "Some Political Aspects of Immigration," in Joseph Fiszman (ed.), *The American Political Arena* (Boston: Little, Brown, 1962), p. 523, for a discussion of the role of the Scotch-Irish as "the core ethnic group of the Democratic party."

[12] Stokes, *op. cit.*, Vol. I, p. 676.

There is an abundant literature of sermons and articles which testifies to the close tie between Congregationalism and Federalism. The Jeffersonians were denounced from many pulpits as advocates of atheism and immorality. Inequality was defended as part of the divine scheme of things. Alexander Hamilton saw in the formation of a Christian Constitutional Society the salvation of the Federalist party. Even irreligious conservatives "considered religion indispensable to restrain the brute appetites of lower orders."[13]

Differences over the relationship of the church and state played a major role in structuring the revived two-party system which formed around supporters and opponents of Andrew Jackson. One of the first major rivals of the Jacksonians, the Anti-Masonic party, which was to become one of the major constituent elements in the Whig party, sought to bring together those who favored an alliance between church and state. And the Whig party basically took over this task.

> Battlegrounds shifted over time, but the lines drawn in the 1830's between "the Church and State party" and the "Jackson party" held fast. Struggles over Sunday laws, the sustained effort to open public assemblies with prayer, Jackson's refusal to act against Georgia for imprisoning missionaries to the Cherokees—on these and like issues, party differences were distinct, passionate and enduring.[14]

The Northern Whig spokesmen, like the Federalists before them, gave voice to the values of the dethroned Puritan Establishment. They argued that the state was a proper instrument to eradicate moral evils such as gambling and "grog selling," while the Democrats sought to limit the role of the state to the prevention of evils which resulted from individuals or groups being interfered with by others. The religious feeling and action that underlay the Federalist and Whig moralistic concerns may be seen in the activities of Lyman Beecher, who, as a key figure in the Congregationalist church, was also involved successively in Federalist, Whig, and later Re-

---

[13] Arthur Schlesinger, Jr., *The Age of Jackson* (Boston: Little, Brown, 1946), p. 16. See also Henry Adams, *The United States in 1800* (Ithaca: Great Seal Books, 1955), pp. 56–59.

[14] Lee Benson, *The Concept of Jacksonian Democracy: New York as a Test Case* (Princeton: Princeton University Press, 1961), p. 196.

publican politics. He, like many others of the New England theocrats,

> sought to reestablish a clerically dominated social order by means of voluntary social and moral reform societies that would give the clergy an influential role in forming public opinion and molding public legislation. The many 'benevolent societies' of the [Jacksonian] Period, which sought to evangellize the unchurched, to save the heathen, to sober the drunkard, to rescue the wayward female, to purify the Sabbath, to end dueling, to inaugurate Sunday Schools, and to send freed slaves back to Africa . . . [were composed largely of] the ministers and leading laymen and women of the Congregational churches.[15]

The party struggle was clearly not between religion and irreligion, although apparently most freethinkers and their organizations supported the Democrats, while the very devout, particularly among the older once-established groups, backed the Whigs.[16]

It is important to recognize that there was considerable congruence between the Jacksonian concern for secular egalitarianism and the struggle against the domination of the theocracy in religion. As McLoughlin puts it, "Here was the essence of the quarrel between the Whigs and the Jacksonians: the fight against aristocracy and privilege in politics had a clear parallel in religion."[17]

■ *The great realignment.*   The early religious-political pattern in America, therefore, found the more evangelical Protestants, particularly the Baptists, the Methodists, and the Presbyterians, backing the Jeffersonians-come-Democrats, along with the emerging Catholic population. The more deeply established and less evangelical Protestants, notably the Congregationalists and the Episcopalians, supported the Federalists and Whigs-come-Republicans. But by the time the two-party system had been recast in its durable Republican-Democratic mould after the Civil War, the Northern Method-

---

[15] William G. McLoughlin, "Introduction," Charles G. Finney, *Lectures on Revivals of Religion* (Cambridge: Belknap Press of Harvard University Press, 1960), p. xviii.
[16] Benson, *op. cit.,* pp. 198–207.
[17] McLoughlin, *op. cit.,* p. xix.

ists, Presbyterians, and Baptists were predominantly Republican. Since most American Protestants had by then become Baptists and Methodists, this realignment meant that native-born Protestants in general had become predominantly Republican.

There were, of course, a number of reasons for the shift of these several Protestant bodies. To begin with, both their socioeconomic level in society and their symbolic status rose rapidly. The high-status churches, Episcopal, Congregational, Quaker, and Unitarian, had not participated in the evangelical revivalism and expansion which the other Protestant groups underwent during the first half of the nineteenth century. The once-established churches remained disproportionately concentrated in the cities of the East, and declined in relative numerical importance. At the same time the influx of Roman Catholic immigrants, especially the Irish, swelled the working class. Thus, in terms of relative standing in the social scale, Methodists and Baptists, particularly the former, were both pulled and pushed upward. Simultaneously, these groups underwent in varying degrees the familiar shift from sect to denomination, a shift which was consonant with the forces changing their social position from without. In fact, these groups attained something of the status of "established churches" themselves. By 1850, two-thirds of the Protestants were Baptists and Methodists. Both groups had a sizable middle-class membership, and the Methodists possessed considerable urban strength.

With the increase in numbers and influence of these ascendant Protestant groups went a corresponding increase in willingness to use state power to enforce "their morality." There was still a kind of parallel between the fight against the political establishment and the fight against the (now unofficial) religious establishment, but the Baptists and Methodists began to move to the "other side" of the fight. They joined the older-established Protestant churches and the prevailing conservative political party in raising moral concerns as public issues. A purely religious dimension entered as a differentiating factor here. The Episcopalian church (like the Lutheran and the Catholic Churches) had come out of a tradition of having been state and total society churches, and never did see its religious mission as prescribing behavior, in the same way that the sects or denominations with sectarian origins typically do. Thus, in the early part of the nineteenth century, the surge of organizational movements to raise public morality—e.g., for temperance, peace, abolition of slavery, and maintenance of the Sabbath—was predominantly fostered by members of the old Federalist upper class and Congregational ministers, aided by the Presbyterians.

For example, the early nineteenth-century concern with the drinking habits and general state of morality among the population had strong class and political links. "The Federalists reasoned that if they could wean men from profanity, vice, and inebriation, the former sinners would be amenable to changing their political allegiance."[18] Reports of the day indicate that temperance and Federalism were closely identified by friends and foes alike.[19]

This early temperance movement had been dominated by members of the old Calvinist denominations, but its social base began to change in the 1840's. The rising evangelical sects also turned against the sin of drink. It was "becoming a potent sign of middle-class status, distinguishing the abstainer from the lower levels of the ne'er-do-wells, the unambitious and the irreligious."[20] As a matter of fact, the Baptists and the Methodists called for more drastic measures than did the earlier temperance leaders. The former favored total abstinence and eventually the passage of prohibition legislation, whereas the latter had advocated education to secure moderate drinking.[21]

Similarly, the leadership of the abolitionist organizations, begun in the 1830's, was drawn from substantial upper-middle-class and distinguished Federalist families, predominantly Congregational, Presbyterian, and Quaker, even though they

[18] Clifford S. Griffin, *Their Brothers' Keepers* (New Brunswick: Rutgers University Press, 1960), p. 37; John A. Krout, *The Origins of Prohibition* (New York: Alfred A. Knopf, 1925), pp. 83–100.

[19] Alice Tyler, *Freedom's Ferment* (Minneapolis: The University of Minnesota Press, 1944), p. 317; Joseph Gusfield, "Status Conflicts and the Changing Ideologies of the American Temperance Movement," in David Pittman and Charles R. Snyder (eds.), *Society, Culture and Drinking Practices* (New York: John Wiley, 1962), pp. 105–106.

[20] Gusfield, *op. cit.,* p. 107.

[21] Griffin, *op. cit.,* pp. 131–134.

included many Methodists, and were supported, of course, by Transcendentalist-Unitarian intellectuals.[22] However, a number of studies have associated the subsequent mass growth of the antislavery movement in the North with the emergent evangelical denominations.[23] Abolition had particular strength in areas which had been subject to successful revivalist campaigns.[24]

While the more evangelical denominations fostered abolitionist sentiment in the North, it is significant to note that membership in the very same churches was related to support for slavery in the South. Thus the three churches which split into Northern and Southern wings were the Presbyterians, Baptists, and Methodists. The Presbyterians suffered their first division in 1837–1838. "Although the split of New School and Old School was ostensibly along theological lines, in fact the South remained with the Old School, and the alliance of abolitionism and revivalism shaped the New School General Assembly."[25]

The Baptists and Methodists also separated long before the Civil War as a result of "contrasting attitudes on the part of the two sections of the church (North and South) on a moral question, slavery."[26] The positions of each of these evangelical denominations on opposite sides of the abolition question partly reflect the "settling in" of these groups, North and South, and their consequent support of their respective political establishments. It is notable, however, that abolition was an issue that lent itself to deep "moral" feeling on both sides, and was one therefore in which these denominations were able to commit themselves more thoroughly and with more religious vehemence than the Episcopalian, the Catholic, or the Lutheran bodies.

[22] David Donald, *Lincoln Reconsidered* (New York: Vintage Books, 1961), pp. 27–29.

[23] Franklin Hamlin Littell, *From State Church to Pluralism* (New York: Doubleday, 1962), p. 57; Tyler, *op. cit.,* p. 505; Benson, *op. cit.,* p. 212.

[24] Gilbert Barnes, *The Anti-Slavery Impulse, 1830–1844* (Gloucester: Peter Smith, 1957), p. 107; Littell, *op. cit.,* p. 64.

[25] Littell, *op. cit.,* p. 64.

[26] H. Richard Niebuhr, *The Social Sources of Denominationalism* (New York: Meridian Books, 1957), p. 194.

The clue to understanding these reactions lies in the attitudes toward sin which had emerged among the deeply religious evangelical American Protestants:

> The most significant characteristic of the Protestant attitude was a consciousness of the evil nature of sin. Protestant expounders made a simple and clear-cut distinction between right and wrong. Man was either saved or damned. Righteousness would be rewarded, sin punished. Sin must be fought. . . .
> Urged on by conscience, the dissatisfied soon found that the [basic community] sin was the sin of slavery. This cancer of society should be cut out, and stern duty called upon foes of sin to remove it. . . . These intense foes of the South were going to do everything possible to destroy slavery. They found their duty all the more compelling as the sin was largely in the body politic of the South, and attack upon it must weaken those who held power.[27]

Just as evangelical Protestantism helped to make the conflict "irrepressible" by bolstering the moral fiber of abolitionism, it served the same role south of the Mason-Dixon line by defining the sectional conflict as one of God versus Satan as well:

> The South, men said and did not doubt, was peculiarly Christian; probably, indeed, it was the last great bulwark of Christianity. . . . From pulpit and hustings ran the dark suggestion that the God of the Yankee was not God at all but Antichrist loosed at last from the pit. The coming war would be no mere secular contest but Armageddon, with the South standing in the role of the defender of the ark, its people as the Chosen People. . . .
> Every man was in his place because He had set him there. Everything was as it was because He had ordained it so. Hence, slavery, and indeed, everything that was, was His responsibility, not the South's. So far from being evil, it was the very essence of Right. Wrong would consist only in rebellion against it.[28]

[27] Roy Franklin Nichols, *The Disruption of American Democracy* (New York: Collier Books, 1962), pp. 35, 43.

[28] W. J. Cash, *The Mind of the South* (New York: Doubleday, 1954), pp. 91–93. See also Kenneth Stampp, *The Peculiar Institution* (New York: Alfred A. Knopf, 1956), pp. 158–162.

Roy Nichols has pointed up the specific denominational sources of the support of slavery:

> The bitter resentment welling up in the South was intensified by the fact that its people shared the prevailing Protestantism. . . . The Methodists, Baptists, and Presbyterians particularly set much store by preaching, and they stressed the Protestant tenets earlier described, emphasizing morals, conscience, and the hatred of sin. Stung to anger by attacks upon their institutions and by slurs upon their moral integrity, their pulpits became rostrums of defense. Thus southern clergymen fought northern ministers in the same Protestant vocabulary, but their themes differed. Southern divines became increasingly satisfied that slavery was ordained of God and justified in the Bible. God would condemn those who bore false witness against the South—the northern hypocrites who attacked the South as morally delinquent.[29]

Whatever other effects issued from this deep commitment of the major Protestant groups to the abolitionist issue, it certainly served both to facilitate and dramatize their great realignment in the North and West with the Republican party.

The shift away from the Democrats was made easier by the emergence of a number of "third parties," of which the Liberty party in the early 1840's and the Free-Soil party in 1848 were the most prominent. The latter ran Martin Van Buren, Jackson's Secretary of State and successor as President, as its presidential candidate, and drew into its ranks many Democrats. In addition, the tremendous increase in immigrant population, particularly Irish Catholics, made the evangelical Protestants more receptive to nativist propaganda, and presumably less happy within a party in which the immigrant groups played a major role. All during this period, "third" nativist parties such as the American or Know-Nothing party also served as a halfway house for a movement by Protestant Democrats away from their traditional party home to the Republican successors of the Whigs. The northern Know-Nothings included many foes of slavery, and the party disintegrated in the North because it refused to take a strong stand against the extension of slavery. While the Democrats

---

[29] Nichols, *op. cit.*, p. 48; see also Stanley Elkins, *Slavery* (Chicago: University of Chicago Press, 1959), p. 36.

were losing support among the once less privileged sects, the Whigs and Republicans retained the support of the members of the higher-status denominations.

These conclusions concerning changes in the voting allegiances of the various Protestant groups should be regarded as an informed guess. As yet, no hard analysis exists of this period other than Lee Benson's study of the election in New York State in the early 1840's. Examining the areas which give disproportionate support to the Liberty party, a small abolitionist organization, in the 1844 election, he reports that "its strongest support came from areas most likely to respond to the doctrines preached by New York rural evangelical sects. During the early 1840's, Baptists apparently led the antislavery hosts; Presbyterians and Methodists followed closely."[30]

The temperance and prohibition issues also played a major and interrelated role in recruiting evangelical Protestants to the anti-Democratic ranks. To a considerable extent, those active in abolition groups also strongly backed prohibitionist organizations, and vice versa. Antislavery candidates were often also advocates of prohibition. "In the 1850's, various combinations of antislaveryism, antiforeignism, and prohibitionism were electing hundreds of . . . men to office."[31]

But if these interrelated moral issues associated with the parties of the well to do and better educated resulted in defections from the Democrats of native-born adherents of the evangelical sects, the Democrats were able to recoup their losses from the heavy waves of immigration.

The overwhelming support which the Democrats secured from non-Anglo-Saxon immigrants, largely Germans and Irish Catholics, may be related to three factors which differentiated parties in the decades before the Civil War. The Democrats, as opposed to the Whigs and the Republicans, were much more oriented to serving the needs of the poor and new immigrants; they tended to oppose restrictions on liquor, whereas as we have seen their opponents supported them, and perhaps most important of all as far as the immigrants and Catholics were concerned, the Whigs and Republi-

[30] Benson, *op. cit.*, p. 212.
[31] Griffin, *op. cit.*, p. 220.

cans were often explicitly allied with various nativist and anti-Catholic organizations, such as the Native Americans and the Know-Nothings.

When the anti-foreign, anti-Catholic Know-Nothings broke up over the slavery question, the vast majority of them joined the Republicans in the North. Election data indicate that they had "served as a bridge between the old Whig party and the Republican party."[32] In New York State, where the Know-Nothings had received 34 per cent of the vote in the state elections of 1855, there was a heavy drop off in their support the following year, since "the Know-Nothing voters were deserting nativism to join the new favorite," the Republican party.[33] In the northwestern states in which there was a heavily foreign, particularly German, settlement, "the Know-Nothings cast their lot with the Republicans rather than nominate candidates of their own. Under their influence the Republican party in many northwestern states took on a decided nativist tinge. . . ."[34] In Indiana, the early Republican party was "tinged with the anti-foreign Know-Nothingism."[35] In Pennsylvania, the Republican and American parties cooperated closely in the election of 1856 on the state level. The Republicans officially endorsed a plan for a joint ticket of presidential electors for the two parties.[36] In Massachusetts, where the Know-Nothings had been stronger than anywhere else in the North, they formed "a *de facto* coalition with the rising Republican party."[37]

Before the 1860 presidential election, Republican Midwestern leaders, including Lincoln, made valiant efforts to destroy

[32] Lawrence F. Schmeckebier, "History of the Know-nothing Party in Maryland," *Studies in Historical and Political Science*, Johns Hopkins University 17 (1899), 40; Wilfred Binkley, *American Political Parties, Their Natural History* (New York: Alfred A. Knopf, 1947), p. 163.

[33] Louis D. Scisco, *Political Nativism in New York State* (New York: Columbia University Press, 1901), pp. 29–31.

[34] Ray Allen Billington, *The Protestant Crusade, 1800–1860* (New York: Rinehart, 1952), p. 395.

[35] Kenneth M. Stampp, *Indiana Politics during the Civil War* (Indianapolis: Indiana Historical Bureau, 1949), p. 5.

[36] Henry R. Mueller, *The Whig Party in Pennsylvania* (New York: Columbia University Press, 1922), pp. 233–234.

[37] Oscar Handlin, *Boston's Immigrants* (Cambridge: The Belknap Press of Harvard University Press, 1959), p. 204.

the impression that the party was anti-Catholic or anti-foreign, since in addition to the principle of equality itself, many of them realized that the foreign-born vote, particularly the German, could lose them the election if it went decisively against them. A detailed analysis of voting returns in Wisconsin indicates that this Republican effort, which was led by Carl Schurz, was unsuccessful. The Wisconsin Domesday Book project, "a superior Gallup Poll," concludes that five-sixths of the Germans backed Douglas against Lincoln, "because of the Know-Nothing nativism which the Republicans had absorbed."[38]

Even four years of war did not affect the basic correlates of party support. An analysis of voting returns in a number of states in the 1864 presidential election indicates relationships between various social factors and party presidential choice similar to those which differentiated Democrats and Whigs in the 1840's and were to distinguish Republicans and Democrats following the war. Lincoln's support came disproportionately from Protestants of New England and Anglo-Saxon background living in rural areas and small towns and "the better residential districts of the greater cities." Catholics, those of non-Anglo-Saxon recent immigrant background, particularly the Germans, and those living in the poorer districts of the large cities, were disposed to vote for McClellan, the Democratic candidate.[39]

In the late nineteenth and early twentieth centuries, outside of the one-party South, anti-Catholic and anti-immigrant politics which continued to exist tended to find a home inside of the Republican party. And on the issue of Catholic efforts to secure state funds for parochial schools, "often the local and State Democratic parties became allied with the Catholic point of view or at least were not hostile," while the Republi-

---

[38] See Joseph Schafer, "Who Elected Lincoln?" *American Historical Review*, 47 (October 1941), 51. Lincoln's advocacy of abstinence and prohibition legislation in Illinois could not have endeared him to the German voters.

[39] William F. Zornow, *Lincoln and the Party Divided* (Norman: University of Oklahoma Press, 1954), pp. 208–215. "Lincoln lost most of the counties where at least one-third of the population was foreign-born, or he polled a percentage less than he received for each state as a whole" (p. 212).

cans took "the opposite stand."[40] Running for governor of
Ohio in 1875, Rutherford B. Hayes worked fiercely to smear
the Democrats as subservient to Catholic designs. President
Grant struck a similar campaign note at a veterans' reunion
that fall by

> hinting darkly that unless the public schools were kept free
> from sectarian influence the nation might face a new civil
> war between the forces of patriotism and intelligence on
> the one side and superstition and ignorance on the other.
> . . . During the election of 1876 occasional Republican[s]
> charge[d] that the 'Romanish Church' was using the Demo-
> cratic party to overthrow the American school system. . . .[41]

In that year, James G. Blaine, the Republican leader in
the House of Representatives, introduced a constitutional
amendment which specified that no governmental authority
could allow any public property, revenues, or loans, to be
used for the support of any school or other institution under
the control of any religious sect. Although seeking to outlaw
support for private religious schools, the amendment explicitly permitted the "reading of the Bible in any school or institution," a clause which "revealed the Protestant inspiration
of the resolution," since Catholics had opposed Bible reading
which almost invariably meant use of a Protestant version.[42]
The Blaine proposal "failed to secure the necessary two-thirds
majority in a strictly party vote, Republicans voting for and
Democrats against it."[43] Republicans were not loath to continue the religious issues in the campaign since their election
platforms in 1876 and 1880 called for the passage of the
constitutional amendment proposed by Blaine, and more significantly, perhaps, Rutherford Hayes, their presidential candidate in these elections, had openly identified himself with
anti-Catholicism in 1875. And Blaine, the author of the anti-

[40] R. Freeman Butts, *The American Tradition in Religion and Education* (Boston: The Beacon Press, 1950), p. 142.

[41] John Higham, *Strangers in the Land* (New Brunswick: Rutgers
University Press, 1955), pp. 28–29; Stokes, *op. cit.*, Vol. II, p. 68.

[42] Butts, *op. cit.*, p. 143.

[43] Stokes, *op. cit.*, Vol. II, p. 68. For a detailed discussion of the relationship between the Republican party and various forms of
nineteenth-century nativism, see Lipset and Raab, *op. cit.*, especially
chapters 2 and 3.

Catholic amendment, was the Republican candidate in 1884. The largest single anti-Catholic organization of the late nineteenth century, the American Protective Association (A.P.A.), was organized in 1887. Politically, the A.P.A. operated as a faction of the Republican party, although it also involved many active in the Populist party in some states. "During the presidential campaign of 1892, the A.P.A. showed itself very friendly to the candidacy of Benjamin Harrison, a friendship that was stimulated, so it seems, by liberal assistance from the Republican campaign."[44] As it grew, the effort to capture "Republican primaries and conventions was . . . the predominant activity of the A.P.A. during the years 1893–95. . . . The Democratic party helped, by its strong anti-Know-Nothing attitude, to drive the A.P.A. wholly into Republican ranks."[45]

While the A.P.A.'s effort to dominate the party ultimately failed in its objective of converting the national level of the Republican party to its cause, it succeeded, in local elections both in Western and Eastern states, in fostering the Catholic issue, particularly as it related to the question of parochial schools as a basis of division between the parties.

As to the constant relationship between the Republican party and various nativist efforts to restrict immigration, John Higham in his detailed study of post-Civil War nativism concluded:

> From the outset the Republican party provided the main vehicle for restrictionist sentiment. It never monopolized or committed itself wholly to the movement, but it supplied the principal leaders, most of the energy, and most of the votes. Throughout the North and West the party tended to attract those who thought of themselves as "the better sort." It seemed the guardian of respectabiilty, morality, and standing. . . .[46]

It should not be surprising that a study of immigrant groups concludes that the two major Catholic ethnic groups, the Irish and the German, remained loyal to the Democratic party for the half century after the Civil War. The former, of course,

---

[44] Humphrey J. Desmond, *The A.P.A. Movement* (Washington: The New Century Press, 1912), pp. 67–68.
[45] *Ibid.*, p. 33.
[46] Higham, *op. cit.*, pp. 98–99.

played an increasingly important role within the party organization in the large cities, while, like "their Irish co-religionists, German Catholics tended to regard the Republican party as a vehicle for intolerant Puritans bent on prohibition, Sunday closing, and immigration restriction."[47]

THE DESIGN AT WORK: THE TWENTIETH CENTURY

The basic religious-political pattern crystallized in the latter part of the nineteenth century was one of increasing Catholic identification with the Democratic party as the party least antipathetic to newcomers and increasing Protestant identification with the Republican party as the party most closely allied with the American middle-class status quo of the time.

Following the Civil War, the link between Protestant orthodoxy and Americanism as a political ideology became closer than ever. The victory of the North was taken by many in the Northern churches as clear evidence that they had been fighting God's crusade and "it was but another short step to the enshrinement of the political instrument which, in the hands of Providence, had guided the Union to victory over slavery and disunion."[48] Sidney Mead concludes that there is general agreement among historians "that at the time Protestantism in America achieved its greatest dominance of the culture [the second half of the nineteenth century], it had also achieved an almost complete ideological and emotional identification with the burgeoning bourgeois society and its free enterprise system, so that in 1876 Protestantism presented a massive, almost unbroken front in its defense of the social status quo. . . ."[49]

James Bryce probably represented the informed consensus on the subject in the post-Civil War period, when he reported as of the 1880's: "Roman Catholics are normally Democrats,

[47] Maldwyn Jones, *American Immigrants* (Chicago: University of Chicago Press, 1960), p. 166.

[48] Sidney E. Mead, "American Protestantism since the Civil War: From Denominationalism to Americanism," in Abraham Eisenstadt (ed.), *American History. Book II: Since 1865* (New York: Thomas Y. Crowell, 1962), p. 174.

[49] *Ibid.*, pp. 186, 187.

because, except in Maryland, which is Democratic anyhow, they are mainly Irish. Congregationalists and Unitarians, being presumably sprung from New England, are apt to be Republicans. Presbyterians, Methodists, Baptists, Episcopalians . . . are mostly Republicans in the Northern States, Democrats in the South."[50] It is, however, difficult to be precise concerning the relation between party support and religious and ethnic group memberships from the Civil War to the Smith campaign in 1928. Historians, political scientists, and sociologists have in the main failed to analyze the basic data. The existing research does indicate, however, that lines of division held fairly firm during these decades. A summary of electoral researches in post-Civil War and early twentieth-century Wisconsin points this up clearly:

> During these late nineteenth-century decades, and persisting many decades later, much of Wisconsin's two-party division of the vote derived from circumstances usually described as "traditional." As elsewhere among northern voters, the Civil War had equated Republicanism with patriotism and respectability. This was especially true in the Wisconsin counties settled by Yankees from New England and upstate New York. Here identification with the cause of the Union often confirmed a preference for Republicans as the heirs of the Whigs, or perhaps of the Know-Nothings or even the abolitionists. The liquor issue also served to solidify the support which the temperance-minded, native American Protestants accorded the Republican Party.
>
> Conversely, the traditional Democratic support was heavily derived from those outside the scheme of values represented by the Yankee conscience. Both German and Irish immigrants found the Democratic party relatively congenial. Numerically the German element was more important, and even into the early part of the twentieth century, particularly until World War I, the rural counties settled mainly by Germans (Protestant or Catholic) turned out Democratic votes more or less in the pattern established by 1860. The city of Milwaukee also provided a substantial Democratic following of a similar traditional sort. . . .[51]

[50] James Bryce, *The American Commonwealth* (Toronto: The Copp, Clark Company, 1891), Vol. II, p. 36. Bryce also mentions that the support of the Democrats by "the Roman Catholic Germans [is owing] to the tacit alliance which has subsisted in many districts between the Catholic Church and the Democrats" (p. 32).

[51] Leon D. Epstein, *Politics in Wisconsin* (Madison: University of Wisconsin Press, 1958), pp. 35–36. Epstein is here summarizing "the

In Indiana, between 1868 and 1900, "an astonishing parallelism appears in the county-by-county division of party strength," and Key and Munger account for these continuities in party voting strength by the phenomenon of geographic concentrations of groups with similar cultural and religious origins who adhered to historic voting ties."[52]

Although continuities such as these are prevalent in American political history, it is clear that occasionally religious and ethnic groups do shift party or ideological ties. The linkages between the German Americans and the Democratic party were broken when the United States entered a war against Germany under a Democratic president in 1917. Much earlier, one may point to a decisive permanent change in the allegiance of a religious group, the Mormons, who gave up their identification with the Democratic party. The historic commitment of the Mormons to the Democrats was based on the fact that Joseph Smith, the founder of the church, had been a Democrat, that much of the persecution of the church had occurred under Republican administrations, and that Utah was admitted to the Union under a Democratic president, Grover Cleveland. This tie was decisively broken in 1900. In that year, McKinley carried the state against Bryan, although four years earlier Bryan had secured 80 per cent of the vote from the largely Mormon electorate.[53] The

---

careful and detailed studies of Joseph Schafer," published in a number of articles cited by Epstein on page 164. These loyalties were not simply maintained by tradition. In the early 1870's the Republicans passed a law "regulating saloons in a manner hostile to the German-Americans," and in the 1890's religious tensions were exacerbated by "a Republican law assumed to be hostile to the maintenance of parochial schools" (p. 163, n. 5). Samuel Lubell describes the traditional mainstay of the Iowa Democratic party before World War I as "the German-Americans, particularly the Catholic Germans." *The Future of American Politics* (New York: Doubleday, 1956), p. 180.

[52] V. O. Key, Jr., and Frank Munger, "Social Determinism and Electoral Decisions: the Case of Indiana," in Eugene Burdick and Arthur Brodbeck (eds.), *op. cit.*, p. 283.

[53] This shift has been explained as resulting from the fact that Utah and the Mormon church (as the largest economic as well as religious group in the state) were particularly concerned with protective tariffs for one of the state's major crops, sugar beets. The McKinley administration passed tariff legislation protecting domestic suppliers, while the Democrats opposed such tariffs.

state remained Republican until 1932, with the exception of the election of 1916. Similarly, Negroes, who had retained their historic allegiance to the Republican party from the end of the Civil War until the election of 1932, shifted to support the Democrats in successive contests.

But although such major changes occur, the available evidence suggests that there were no major adjustments in the pattern established in the nineteenth century outside of the solid South of disproportionate Catholic backing for the Democrats and Protestant preference for the Republicans. The strength of the correlation between the Catholic-Protestant division and party support undoubtedly rose and fell, but the difference remained basic. It has been argued by V. O. Key, Jr., that the election of 1896 was one of the "critical elections" in American political history in the sense that significant groupings growing out of the first Bryan-McKinley contest made long-term changes in loyalties.[54] In general, the candidacy of Bryan, who came out of the Midwest Bible Belt Populist tradition, resulted in a sizable increase in the Democratic vote in the plains and mountain states, and in a heavy loss in the East, where his inflationary program is presumed to have had a negative rather than a positive appeal to the less debt-ridden farmers and the urban strata. The contest, however, may not have affected the long-term relationship between religious-ethnic factors and party support; in fact, it may have even increased the correlation in the Eastern states. An analysis of changes in the vote between 1892 and 1896 in Massachusetts, which differentiated according to size of community, indicates that the Democrats lost most heavily in smaller communities, and retained considerable support in the larger communities in which they had previously been strong.[55]

---

[54] V. O. Key, Jr., "A Theory of Critical Elections," *Journal of Politics,* 17 (1955), 1–18.

[55] In Illinois, on the other hand, Bryan appears to have done much better in rural areas than in urban ones, a pattern which was probably true for much of the West. For Illinois see Duncan MacRae, Jr., and James A. Meldrum, "Critical Elections in Illinois: 1888–1958," *The American Political Science Review,* 54 (1960), 679–681.

Table 8-1.

SHIFTS IN DEMOCRATIC STRENGTH, 1892–1896, IN RELATION TO POPU-
LATION SIZE OF TOWNS

Population Size Groups	Mean Democratic Percentages 1892	Mean Democratic Percentages 1896	Mean Change 1892–1896	Per Cent 1896 Loss of 1892 Vote
1–999	34.0	14.7	19.3	56.8
2,000–2,999	38.8	18.3	20.5	52.6
10,000–14,999	46.7	26.9	19.8	42.4
50,000 plus	47.7	30.1	17.6	34.8

Source: V. O. Key, Jr., "A Theory of Critical Elections," *Journal of Politics,* 17 (1955), 14. Key did not compute the last column.

Since, according to Key, size of community was a rough index of religious and national origin variation—the small communities were largely Anglo-Saxon and Protestant, the larger cities had sizable segments of foreign-born Catholics —the evidence (see Table 8-1) would suggest that the campaign of 1896 may have actually reinforced the ethnic-religious correlations with party voting, at least as far as Massachusetts is concerned. On the national level, a study of this election which compared the vote in communities with more or less than 45,000 population within each state found that "in states in which the foreign-born constituted larger proportions of the population in comparison with other states, the urban population (more than 45,000) gave Bryan a larger proportion of the vote than he received in rural areas (less than 45,000)."[56] And the assumption that findings such as these reflect consistency in the ethnic-religious correlation is reinforced by an analysis of the vote within one large city, Boston. In Boston, the correlation between percentage of Democratic vote and percentage of foreign-born (principally Catholic) in each ward was about as high in 1892 as one ever secures when relating such factors, 0.88; in 1896 the relationship was slightly lower, although from a statistical point of view the difference was so small as to suggest practical identity, 0.82.[57]

[56] William Diamond, "Urban and Rural Voting in 1896," *American Historical Review,* 46 (1941), 303.
[57] Key, *op. cit.,* p. 15.

The Democrats clearly lost heavily among the poorer, immigrant, and Catholic population, as they did among those with the opposite characteristics, but the fact of this decline, particularly in the Eastern states, did not change the previously existing relationships. Unfortunately, the one detailed historical study of the statistical association between proportion of foreign-born (largely Catholic) and party voting, that by Robert Dahl of New Haven, begins with the election of 1904. His data indicate a high correlation (about 0.80) for 1904, which then dropped slightly in 1908, remaining "moderately close and steady until 1928," when the Smith campaign raised it to new heights.[58] Dahl suggests, too, that the seemingly radical candidacy of Bryan resulted in permanent losses to the Democratic party from more conservative Yankee Democrats. In general, the increasing identification of the Democratic party with the tremendous mass of Catholic immigrants and Irish leadership in Eastern cities served to convert most Yankees to the Republican standard. Protestant British, Scandinavian, and German immigrants, becoming accepted as members of the old stock, also joined the Republicans.[59] And the rural Midwestern Protestant votes which Bryan brought to the Democrats from the Populists in 1896 and 1900 returned to the Republican fold with the candidacy of Theodore Roosevelt in 1904.[60]

It is important to note in evaluating elections such as those of 1860, 1896, 1932, 1952, or 1964, in which one party made decisive gains, that the sheer fact of a large switch in votes from one party to another need not mean that there has been any change in the *relative* relationship of any given social group to a party. The increase may come more or less proportionately from all segments, so that the correlations between factors such as class or religion and party choice will remain relatively constant. This seems to have occurred in

[58] Robert Dahl, *Who Governs?* (New Haven: Yale University Press, 1961), p. 45.

[59] J. Joseph Huthmacher, *Massachusetts People and Politics* (Cambridge: The Belknap Press of Harvard University Press, 1959), pp. 14–15.

[60] Although this was apparently true for the country as a whole to judge by national voting statistics, it was apparently not true of Illinois. See MacRae and Meldrum, *op. cit.*, p. 680.

Boston between 1892 and 1896, when the Republicans gained greatly in all wards of the city but the correlation between proportion of foreign-born and presidential vote remained almost identical. In addition, it is possible that a major increase in the support of a given party may result more from the party's intensifying its support among strata previously identified with it, than from gains from traditionally negative strata. Thus, the elections of 1928 and 1960 clearly increased the existing relationship between religious affiliation and voting.

World War I and its aftereffects appear, however, to have affected the relationship of ethnic, and therefore religious, groupings to the two parties. Wilson had been elected in 1912 on a minority vote, the normal Republican support being divided between Taft and Roosevelt. However, in 1916, Wilson ran on an antiwar platform, while Charles Evans Hughes and the Republican party were much more sympathetic to the cause of the Allies led by Great Britain. The available evidence would suggest that various groups of non-Anglo-Saxon origin—the Irish who disliked Britain, the Jews who viewed Czarist Russia as the major anti-Semitic power of its day, and German and Scandinavian Americans who favored Germany —shifted to or remained with Wilson, while conversely there may have been an intensification of Anglo-Saxon "Yankee" backing for the Republicans.[61] Since the move to the Democrats included many traditionally Republican Scandinavian Lutherans, it is hard to estimate whether the Democrats gained or lost among Protestant voters.

Entry into war under Wilson, however, resulted in a major alienation of traditional Irish and Catholic support. In 1920, the Republicans won their greatest victory in history, securing 61.2 per cent of the national vote. In Massachusetts, with its large Irish-Catholic population, the Democratic party was unable even to nominate candidates for many local and congressional posts.[62] In Iowa, the "mainstay of the Democratic party has always been the German Americans, particularly Catholic Germans. So violent was their reaction against Wilson in 1920 that in some parts of Iowa the Democratic party

[61] Lubell, *op. cit.*, pp. 143–144.
[62] Huthmacher, *op. cit.*, p. 33.

all but disappeared. Candidates were not available to run for Congress on the Democratic ticket."[63]

James M. Cox, the Democratic candidate in that year, has himself well described what happened to him and his party:

> Leaders of three racial groups, Germans, Irish and Italian, had gone over to the Republican side. The Germans were angry with Wilson because of the war. The Irish were inflamed because Wilson did not make the independence of Ireland part of the Versailles treaty. The Italians were enraged because Fiume had been taken away from Italy. The Italians were practically solid.[64]

In 1924, the Democrats remained weak among the groups which had defected in 1920. Many of them voted for Senator Robert La Follette, on a third-party ticket.[65] He had been a major leader in resisting entry into the war, had campaigned vigorously for the independence of Ireland, and perhaps, most important of all, was the presidential candidate most avowedly opposed to the Ku Klux Klan, and most denounced by the Klan.[66] In Massachusetts, as in Illinois, most of his votes seem to have come from traditional centers of Democratic strength.

The rise of the Ku Klux Klan to prominence during the 1920's undoubtedly played an important role in preventing the Republicans from making permanent inroads among disaffected Democrats of Catholic and recent immigrant background. In much of the Northeast and Midwest, the Klan, like the A.P.A. before it, largely worked through the Republican party and had considerable influence in some of the state organizations. "In the East, where the Democratic Party was controlled largely by Irish Catholics, the Klan inevitably

[63] Lubell, *op. cit.*, pp. 180–181.

[64] James M. Cox, *Journey Through My Years* (New York: Simon and Schuster, 1946), pp. 272–273.

[65] In Illinois La Follette's vote came "from elements of the population which might have voted for Al Smith had he been nominated. . . . La Follette . . . obtained heavier support . . . from urban counties with heavy foreign-born population." The vote correlated 0.68 per cent with pro-wet sentiment on a 1922 referendum, and 0.54 per cent Catholic. MacRae and Meldrum, *op. cit.*, p. 677.

[66] Lubell, *op. cit.*, pp. 138, 149, 180; Huthmacher, *op. cit.*, p. 101.

associated itself more closely with the Republicans."[67] In addition, the Republicans had fostered both Prohibition and quota restrictions on immigration which were biased in favor of entrants from the Nordic Protestant nations, while the Northern Democratic members of Congress had shown opposition to these measures which were clearly unpalatable to most Catholics and others of recent immigrant stock.

The decline of the Democrats in presidential voting, particularly among Catholics and recent immigrant groups, did not mean that the party had lost its following among them. Some political analysts who have focused only on the presidential races have erred in suggesting that strong Catholic Democratic loyalties stem from 1928, the year Al Smith ran for President. They overlook the fact that the Democratic vote for state offices in many areas with large Catholic populations remained extremely high in the years during which the party declined heavily on the presidential level. In Massachusetts, in 1922, the Democratic percentage of the two-party vote for governor was 17.6 higher than in the 1920 presidential race. And the party gained much more in cities which had a large majority of foreign-born population than it did in communities which were predominantly native-born.[68] Similarly in 1924, when the Democratic presidential candidate secured only a quarter of the state's vote, the party's senatorial candidate, an Irish-American, captured almost half the vote, losing by only 18,000 in a poll of more than a million. In New York State, Al Smith was defeated for re-election as governor in 1920 by less than 100,000 votes, while Harding's majority over Cox was more than one million; two years later Smith was returned as governor with the largest majority in the history of New York's gubernatorial races.[69]

The results of these state contests suggest that despite the scrambled results of the 1920 and 1924 presidential contests, the traditional links between religion, ethnic group membership, class, and party support actually continued. The Demo-

[67] *Ibid.*, p. 89; see also Emerson Hunsberger Loucks, *The Ku Klux Klan in Pennsylvania* (Harrisburg: The Telegraph Press, 1936), p. 99; John B. Martin, *Indiana* (New York: Alfred A. Knopf), pp. 193–194.
[68] Huthmacher, *op. cit.*, p. 74; for Illinois data see MacRae and Meldrum, *op. cit.*, pp. 676–677.
[69] *Ibid.*, p. 94.

cratic party remained as the party through which Catholics, those of recent immigrant stock, and the poorer strata secured recognition, social mobility, and local interest representation. Key and Munger in their analysis of Indiana voting behavior indicate that this pattern of persistent loyalty to the state party, even when there are strong religious or ethnic pulls away from the party on the presidential level, occurred in 1928 and 1940 as well. In the former election the differentials between the presidential and state-office vote "strongly suggest that Protestant Democrats and perhaps Catholic Republicans responded to the situation by splitting their tickets. After the religious issue subsided, national and local party appeals were more nearly congruent and ticket splitting declined."[70] In the 1940 election, a largely Germanic area showed a large drop in support for Roosevelt, while the vote for the Democratic candidate for governor was much higher. In an analysis of public-opinion survey data in the 1950's Angus Campbell reported similar findings based on interviews with individuals. That is, the vote for state office and congressional contests remained linked to the usual correlates of party choice, while the presidential vote varied considerably.[71]

The story of the 1928 election in which Al Smith ran as the first Catholic to hold a presidential nomination of a major party has been told and analyzed by many.[72] This election aroused strong emotions and prejudices around the related issues of attitudes to Catholicism and Prohibition. The Smith campaign activated the poor, Catholic, Jewish, urban, immigrant groups, and alienated the small-town and rural native Protestants.[73] Lubell has argued that a profound "social upheaval stirred beneath the Smith vote. What Smith really embodied was the revolt of the under-dog urban immigrant against the top dog of 'old American' stock. His Catholicism was an essential element in that revolt."[74]

[70] Key and Munger, *op. cit.*, pp. 294–295.
[71] Angus Campbell, "Surge and Decline: A Study of Electoral Change," *Public Opinion Quarterly*, 24 (1960), 397–418.
[72] For a description of the campaign see Edmund Moore, *A Catholic Runs for President: The 1928 Campaign* (New York: Ronald, 1956).
[73] Key, *op. cit.*, pp. 4–6, 11–12, 13; Lubell, *op. cit.*, pp. 36, 37, 41, 42.
[74] *Ibid.*, pp. 37, 41.

. The election of 1928 played a major role in structuring the subsequent alignment of American voters. It clearly brought back to the national Democratic party all of the immigrant, Catholic, and Jewish vote which it had lost after World War I —and even added some.[75] Although many contemporaries blamed Smith's defeat on the success of a bitterly anti-Catholic campaign waged by the Ku Klux Klan and by many Protestant churchmen, the evidence does not sustain this thesis.[76] In fact, Smith secured 41 per cent of the national vote, more than any previous Democratic candidate in the twentieth century, except for Wilson running for re-election in 1916. It is likely that, as in the case of John F. Kennedy, thirty-two years later, Smith's religion won him many votes among co-religionists and other opponents of the Protestant Yankee Establishment. Given the fact that the country was still in the midst of its greatest prosperity in history, Smith's ability to increase Democratic strength in the cities and much of the North may be perceived as an indicator of the decline both of Prohibitionist and anti-Catholic sentiment.

In 1932, Roosevelt retained the Catholic-Jewish and recent immigrant vote which had supported Smith, and, of course, secured a considerable body of votes from other groups as a result of the reaction to the Great Depression. V. O. Key, Jr., reports data from the various New England states which indicate that, in comparing the 1932 with the 1928 vote by varying types of communities, "the proportion of new Democrats did not differ significantly among the groups of towns

[75] A number of studies indicate that the most consistent correlate of Democratic vote over the long term, and of the Smith gain over the past two elections in particular, was the proportion of foreign-born in the population. This has been found for Illinois, MacRae and Meldrum, *op. cit.,* p. 675; for New Haven, Dahl, *op. cit.,* pp. 49–50; and in a detailed national ecological study for the country as a whole. See Ruth C. Silva, *Rum, Religion, and Votes* (University Park: Pennsylvania State University Press, 1962).

[76] S. M. Lipset, "Some Statistics on Bigotry in Voting," *Commentary,* 30 (1960), pp. 286–290; William F. Ogburn and Neil S. Talbot, "A Measurement of the Factors in the Presidential Election of 1928," *Social Forces,* 8 (1929), 176; Peter Odegard, *Religion and Politics* (New Brunswick: Oceana Publications, 1960), pp. 165–167; Edward J. Richter and Berton Dulce, *Religion and the Presidency* (New York: The Macmillan Co., 1962), pp. 96–97; MacRae and Meldrum, *op. cit.,* p. 675; Silva, *op. cit., passim.*

examined."[77] That is, the Smith campaign had restored more
intensively than before the correlations which had previously
existed between presidential party voting and religious affiliation before the reactions to World War I had upset them.
The correlations continued under Roosevelt, as Samuel Lubell has pointed out, for regions such as New England where
a sizable Catholic population faced a previously dominant
Yankee Protestant one: "Between 1932 and 1944, New England's Democratic vote did not shift by more than 2 per cent
in any election; in the main, the bedrock cleavage in the East
remains a Catholic-Protestant one."[78]

Analysis of the various elections discussed thus far has had
to rest on ecological considerations. The only method used
to infer the relationship between social characteristics such
as ethnic origin or religious affiliation and voting habits was
to compare the social characteristics of different voting areas.
This approach has many methodological weaknesses; the in-
ference that one may deduce the behavior of individuals from
the correlates of areas or communities may not be valid in
any given case.[79] From 1936 on, however, a more reliable
measure of the correlates of vote decision exists, the data from
public-opinion surveys. Using such materials, it is possible to
analyze the relative contribution of class as distinct from religious factors, the variations among different denominations,
and so forth. Time and space do not permit the detailed types
of analyses which available data make feasible.

For purposes of this discussion, however, I have reanalyzed
public-opinion materials for each presidential election from
1936 to 1964, plus the congressional races from 1954 to 1962.
Unfortunately, most of the available surveys do not contain
detailed denominational information for Protestants, or if they
do, the size of the sample interviewed is too small to permit
any reliable interpretation of the differences among denomi-

[77] *Op. cit.,* p. 9; for Illinois see MacRae and Meldrum, *op. cit.,* p.
678.

[78] *Op. cit.,* p. 43. "After 1932, the presidential vote [in Illinois] continues to reflect the same cleavage of the electorate through 1956, even
while the proportions obtained by Democrats and Republicans fluctu-
ate." MacRae and Meldrum, *op. cit.,* p. 678.

[79] William S. Robinson, "Ecological Correlations and Behavior of Individuals," *American Sociological Review,* 15 (1950), 351–357.

nations. A denominational analysis must involve holding some measure of class position constant, since the Protestant denominations vary greatly with respect to the average socioeconomic level of their adherents.

To compare the effects of class and religion, I have followed a method, first used by Robert Alford, in which urban voters are divided between those in manual and non-manual occupations, and these groups plus rural voters are divided between Protestants and Catholics.[80] These measures of religious and class voting presented in Table 8–2 are only rough and relative measures of underlying social forces. Of all the forces affecting voting, only two are here analyzed (albeit two of the most important ones). Obviously different kinds of social circumstances might affect the operation of these forces. For example, if a depression (which would ordinarily increase class voting) and a Catholic candidate for President (which would increase religious voting) occurred simultaneously, the two indices would not increase as much as they would if either event were to take place without the other. Thus, there is no absolute standard; the effects of religion and class should be compared over time and in light of auxiliary knowledge, and a certain margin of error is to be expected.

Southerners and Negroes have been excluded from the tables because some of the relations dealt with here are different among them. Negroes, though predominantly Protestant, have voted overwhelmingly Democratic since 1936. White Southerners, ironically, continue their post-Civil War pattern of voting Democratic in state and local elections though this traditional loyalty has disappeared in presidential contests.

Comparing the internal variations within the Protestant and Catholic groups, it seems evident that the pattern described for much of the nineteenth century has continued during the past thirty years. Class factors consistently differentiate among Protestants. That is, the middle-class Protestants have always been much more likely to back the Republicans than manual workers with similar religious loyalties. Among Catholics, however, class differences in party support, while present, are

[80] See Robert Alford, *Party and Society. The Anglo-American Democracies* (Chicago: Rand McNally and Co., 1963).

somewhat less powerful. Alford, who reported similar findings in his analysis of survey data from 1944 to 1960 (including Negroes and Southerners), commented that the lesser strength of the class-party relationship among Catholics is "consistent with the presumed ethnic and minority sentiments among Catholics which override class sentiments as a basis for political loyalties."[81] As "out-group" minorities, Catholics, Jews, and Negroes are much more likely to respond politically in terms of their ethnic-religious group identification than are the majority white Protestant population. Other bases of diversity, of which class is historically the most significant, should affect white Protestant reactions more than they do the others.

Examining trends within both major religious groupings confirms the thesis elaborated by Lubell, from his examination of the votes of different geographical areas, that the Smith-Roosevelt effect on voting patterns reached a climax in 1936. Working people and Catholics completed the swing to the Democrats which had been triggered off in 1928. Both class and religious voting were extremely high in 1936. There was a difference of 52 percentage points between the Democratic vote of Catholic manual workers (86) and middle-class Protestants (34). Four years later, the differences were practically as great, although the Democrats lost part of their national majority. Various writers have suggested that this drop was a result of "isolationist" ethnic groups turning away from the interventionist anti-German and anti-Italian foreign policy of Roosevelt as they had once moved away from Wilson. This change did not affect the relation between religion and party support since presumably it included the Catholic Italians and the predominantly Lutheran Germans. The index of religious voting dropped considerably from 1940 to 1944, from a difference of 31 per cent in 1936 and 1940 to 23 per cent in 1944, a figure which then remained fairly steady for both presidential and congressional elections until the election of 1960. The change from 1940 to 1944 suggests that the issue of America's policy toward communism may have affected Catholics even before the war ended. Class differences, as

[81] *Op. cit.,* pp. 243–244.

measured by the gross indicator of manual vs. nonmanual divisions, also declined during this period, although the drop was smaller and less consistent than that of religion.

Table 8–2.

PER CENT VOTING DEMOCRATIC AMONG PROTESTANTS AND CATHOLICS WITHIN FARM, MANUAL, AND NONMANUAL OCCUPATIONS (NON-SOUTHERN WHITES ONLY)

Occupations	Total		Catholics		Protestants		Religious Voting (Difference between Catholics and Protestants)
				1936			
Farm	53	(330)	56	(32)	46	(190)	plus 10
Manual	71	(556)	86	(138)	63	(243)	plus 23
Nonmanual	47	(732)	71	(122)	34	(401)	plus 37
Class Voting (Difference between manual and nonmanual)	plus 24		plus 15		plus 29		
Total			76	(292)	45	(834)	plus 31
				1940			
Farm	47	(363)	56	(34)	47	(213)	plus 9
Manual	67	(692)	85	(178)	53	(295)	plus 32
Nonmanual	44	(990)	62	(174)	32	(523)	plus 30
Class Voting	plus 23		plus 23		plus 21		
Total			72	(386)	41	(1031)	plus 31
				1944			
Farm	39	(158)	61	(18)	36	(95)	plus 25
Manual	63	(458)	74	(111)	55	(178)	plus 19
Nonmanual	43	(398)	60	(70)	31	(217)	plus 29
Class Voting	plus 20		plus 14		plus 24		
Total			68	(199)	41	(490)	plus 27
				1948			
Farm	48	(138)	62	(13)	47	(123)	plus 15
Manual	64	(306)	75	(77)	57	(205)	plus 18
Nonmanual	46	(448)	59	(107)	35	(291)	plus 24
Class Voting	plus 18		plus 16		plus 22		
Total			65	(197)	45	(619)	plus 20
				1952			
Farm	32	(90)	36	(14)	31	(75)	plus 5
Manual	52	(370)	63	(150)	43	(202)	plus 20
Nonmanual	28	(336)	35	(85)	18	(211)	plus 17
Class Voting	plus 24		plus 28		plus 25		
Total			52	(249)	30	(488)	plus 22

Occupations	Total		Catholics		Protestants		Religious Voting (Difference between Catholics and Protestants)
			1954				
Farm	38	(69)	33	(12)	38	(56)	less 5
Manual	62	(265)	74	(89)	54	(167)	plus 20
Nonmanual	45	(236)	57	(65)	36	(148)	plus 21
Class Voting	plus 17		plus 17		plus 18		
Total			64	(166)	44	(371)	plus 20
			1956				
Farm	45	(62)	78	(9)	39	(52)	plus 39
Manual	50	(294)	60	(101)	44	(185)	plus 16
Nonmanual	33	(210)	49	(61)	21	(124)	plus 28
Class Voting	plus 17		plus 11		plus 23		
Total			57	(171)	35	(361)	plus 22
			1958				
Farm	55	(53)	67	(6)	53	(45)	plus 14
Manual	66	(282)	81	(95)	57	(178)	plus 24
Nonmanual	48	(271)	59	(81)	35	(156)	plus 24
Class Voting	plus 18		plus 22		plus 22		
Total			71	(182)	47	(379)	plus 24
			1960				
Farm	36	(120)	69	(13)	32	(106)	plus 37
Manual	58	(719)	84	(240)	43	(438)	plus 41
Nonmanual	40	(565)	78	(159)	19	(336)	plus 59
Class Voting	plus 18		plus 6		plus 24		
Total			81	(412)	33	(880)	plus 48
			1962				
Farm	75	(12)	*		*		
Manual	62	(180)	80	(66)	48	(106)	plus 32
Nonmanual	44	(186)	65	(51)	29	(110)	plus 36
Class Voting	plus 18		plus 25		plus 19		
Total			73	(122)	40	(222)	plus 33
			1964				
Farm	66	(33)	*		*		
Manual	77	(279)	85	(98)	71	(169)	plus 14
Nonmanual	59	(206)	75	(96)	45	(173)	plus 30
Class Voting	plus 18		plus 10		plus 26		
Total			80	(200)	58	(369)	plus 22
			1966				
Farm	36	(34)	75	(4)*	31	(29)	*
Manual	68	(194)	78	(55)	50	(115)	plus 28
Nonmanual	44	(241)	57	(67)	34	(142)	plus 23
Class Voting	plus 24		plus 21		plus 16		
Total			61	(132)	36	(337)	plus 25
					67	(126)	40	(281)	plus 27

Occupations	Total	Catholics	Protestants	Religious Voting (Difference between Catholics and Protestants)
1968 Presidential (Three-party)				
Farm	21 (56)	* (5)	20 (51)	*
Manual	51 (325)	60 (126)	44 (187)	plus 16
Nonmanual	43 (328)	47 (108)	31 (124)	plus 16
Class Voting	plus 8	plus 13	plus 13	
Total		54 (239)	35 (412)	plus 19
1968 Congressional Vote (Two-party)				
Farm	33 (52)	* (5)	32 (47)	*
Manual	58 (320)	64 (122)	52 (184)	plus 12
Nonmanual	44 (316)	45 (103)	34 (170)	plus 11
Class Voting	plus 14	plus 19	plus 18	
Total		55 (230)	42 (401)	plus 13

Sources: 1936–A.I.P.O. (Gallup Poll) #141; 1940–A.I.P.O. #248; 1944–A.I.P.O. #323K; 1948–A.I.P.O. #454K; 1952–Michigan (Survey Research Center) Election Study, 1952; 1954–A.I.P.O. #539K; 1956–A.I.P.O. #573K; 1958–A.I.P.O. #608K; 1960–A.I.P.O. #638K; 1962–University of Michigan (Survey Research Center) Fall Omnibus Survey; 1964–University of Michigan (Survey Research Center) 1964 Election Study; 1966–University of Michigan (Survey Research Center) Election Survey; 1968–A.I.P.O. #771.

In using the 1936 sample, it was necessary to define farmers as persons living on farms but not possessing manual or nonmanual jobs. In using the 1952 sample, it was necessary to define farmers as farm owners. Four states on the North-South border had to be excluded from this sample, but were included in the others.

* Too few cases.

The gross character of the indicators of class and religious voting makes it impossible to reach any definite conclusion concerning the relative weight of "class" as contrasted with "religion" as a determinant of party choice. An examination of the Presidential vote data presented in Table 8–2 does suggest that the Catholic-Protestant difference has been somewhat more important than the manual vs. nonmanual cleavage from 1936 to 1968. However, this result is in some part a consequence of the fact that the two factors have been dichotomized. When the impact of class is estimated by dividing the population into more classes, e.g., upper, upper-middle, middle, upper-lower, and lower, or in terms of a number of occupational classes, e.g., large business, free professionals, down to unskilled workers, the variations linked to class become much greater. Well-to-do businessmen often vote from 80 to 90 per cent Republican, while semi-skilled and unskilled workers who are union members will vote 75 per cent Democratic. In 1968, a national survey conducted by an affiliate of the Gallup Poll of the presidents of all the companies whose shares are listed on the New York Stock Exchange, conducted by the anonymous questionnaire technique, reported that less than half of one per cent (three men) were for George Wallace (who drew relatively well among workers), while 85 per cent endorsed the Republican candidate, Richard Nixon, and only 13 per cent backed Hubert Humphrey. Outside of the South, Humphrey continued the traditional pattern of Democratic presidential candidates running especially strongly among manual workers, especially union members.[82] Such differences are clearly larger than the variations between Catholic and Protestants. Similarly, the impact of religious affiliations on voting varies with degree of involvement in religious activities. Although the relationship differs with degree of commitment—the more religious members of a group are more likely to follow the dominant tendency of the group than the less religious or the irreligious—a correlation between voting and religion is not intensified as consistently or to the degree that occurs with the increased specification of class.

Some estimate of the effect of these factors may be seen in the statistics reported in Table 8–3, which were drawn from an analysis of a large opinion survey. Completed in 1954, it is based on a sample of 9,852 interviews in eleven states outside of the South. With a sample of this magnitude, it is possible to examine the variation among a large number of classes within each major religious grouping.

An examination of Table 8–3 suggests that there is some-

[82] S. M. Lipset, *Political Man, op. cit.,* pp. 303–306; and Harold Sheppard, Arthur Kornhauser, and Arthur Mayer, *When Labor Votes* (New York: University Books, 1956), pp. 42–45. The 1968 executive data are from Terry Robards, "Poll of Executives Puts Nixon Ahead," the New York *Times* (October 27, 1968), pp. 1, 72. For a detailed analysis of the Wallace campaign, see S. M. Lipset and Earl Raab, *The Politics of Unreason* (New York: Harper and Row, 1970), Chapters 9 and 10.

Table 8–3.

RELATIONSHIP BETWEEN SOCIOECONOMIC STATUS AND TRADITIONAL PARTY
PREFERENCE FOR THE THREE MAJOR RELIGIOUS GROUPINGS
PER CENT DEMOCRATIC AND REPUBLICAN—1954 (WHITE RESPONDENTS
ONLY)

Stratum	PROTESTANT Dem. Rep.			CATHOLIC Dem. Rep.			JEWS Dem. Rep.		
Nonmanual									
Upper	14	61	(169)	36	39	(39)	31	0	(13)
Upper Middle	24	49	(714)	36	27	(232)	55	10	(58)
Lower Middle	25	44	(910)	50	18	(406)	63	5	(79)
Lower	45	40	(62)	64	7	(28)	X	X	
Manual									
Upper Middle	36	37	(300)	49	10	(144)	X	X	
Lower Middle	40	30	(1696)	63	11	(945)	66	2	(44)
Lower	50	24	(361)	69	10	(267)	X	X	
Farm									
Upper	24	41	(34)	X	X		X	X	
Upper Middle	29	44	(168)	38	44	(16)	X	X	
Lower Middle	32	43	(402)	58	20	(96)	X	X	
Lower	34	41	(129)	44	12	(25)	X	X	

Source: Computed from the data of a survey conducted in eleven states
by International Research Associates in 1954. The states are California, Michigan, Minnesota, Massachusetts, Iowa, New Mexico,
Illinois, Ohio, Oregon, Pennsylvania, and New Jersey. Independents
are included in the base. They are the difference between the two
party totals and 100 per cent. "X" means too few cases for a reliable estimate.

what more variation within each religious group between the
highest and lowest class than between Protestants and Catholics in the same class. Thus Catholics vary between 36 per
cent Democratic in sympathies among "upper class" nonmanuals to 69 per cent within the lower manual stratum, or
a difference of 33 per cent. The corresponding difference
among Protestants between the highest and the lowest group
is 36 per cent. Within any one stratum, the largest variation
in per cent Democratic between Catholics and Protestants is
25 per cent, but most intraclass differences are less. A comparable analysis (not reported here) for actual vote in the
1952 election resulted in differences of comparable magnitude.

The usual concentration on the Protestant-Catholic-Jewish
trichotomy serves to conceal variations among the Protestant
denominations. When these are separated, the available sur-

vey evidence would suggest that the average socioeconomic status of the members of a given denomination is an important determinant of the relative position of the denomination with respect to support of the two major parties. However, there is some evidence that Protestant denominational differences do exist which are independent of class position. A large national sample of the electorate interviewed in the spring of 1952 was asked which party the respondents have most often favored between 1936 and 1952. When this sample was differentiated between those in manual and nonmanual occupations, the data indicated that the two "lowest status" and most fundamentalist groups of Protestants, Baptists, and those classified under the heading "other Protestants," contained the smaller proportion of Republicans within the manual and the nonmanual strata. Conversely, the denominations of the more well to do, the Episcopalians, the Presbyterians, and the Congregationalists, contributed heavily to Republican support. A substantial majority of the manual workers who adhered to the latter groups indicated they had voted Republican most of the time. Lutherans seemed more Republican than one might have predicted from knowledge of their socioeconomic position, while Methodists fell in a middle position with respect to Republican propensities.

To a considerable extent the data reported in Table 8–4 be-

Table 8–4.

PREDOMINANT PAST VOTING BEHAVIOR, RELIGION AND OCCUPATION—1952 (NON-SOUTHERN WHITES) PER CENT TWO-PARTY VOTE

Denomination	BLUE COLLAR Dem.	Rep.		WHITE COLLAR Dem.	Rep.	
Baptist	61	39	(31)	35	65	(23)
Lutheran	51	49	(29)	18	82	(45)
Methodist	48	52	(52)	32	68	(62)
Episcopal	40	60	(15)	24	76	(41)
Presbyterian	33	67	(28)	28	72	(39)
Congregational	27	73	(11)	21	79	(28)
Other Protestant	65	35	(39)	27	73	(56)
Total Protestant	50	50	(215)	26	73	(294)
Catholic	81	19	(170)	53	47	(106)
Jewish	83	17	(6)	74	26	(43)

Source: Data for analysis are from a 1952 survey by Elmo Roper Associates.

low would seem to confirm the generally accepted assumptions concerning intra-Protestant political variation, that the general political set of a Protestant denomination is determined largely by the average socioeconomic status of its adherents. When segregated by denomination and occupational status, it is clear that every Protestant group is more disposed to back the Republicans than Catholics or Jews are. The differences between all of the Protestant denominations and the Catholic and Jewish group are greatest among the white-collar strata. However, intra-Protestant variation is greater within the manual groups than in the middle classes. A substantial majority of workers adhering to the three highest-status churches, as determined by data concerning the average socioeconomic level of their adherents (the Episcopalians, the Presbyterians, and the Congregationalists), had cast most of their votes for Republican candidates.

These findings would suggest that worker members of predominantly high-status churches are greatly affected by the modal opinion of the group, or perhaps that the workers who adhere to such denominations do so in part because they are "upward mobile," that they seek to identify with the more privileged classes. Conversely, working-class members of the three lowest-status (in terms of average socioeconomic position) churches (the Baptists, the Methodists, and the Lutherans) are much more likely to be Democrats. The poorest denomination, the Baptist, is the most Democratic of all the major sects. Two groups, the Lutherans and "other Protestants," behave in a puzzling way. Workers so classified tend toward the Democrats, white-collar adherents are overwhelmingly Republicans. The behavior of the "others" may be a result of the conglomerate nature of the classification. "Other Protestant" workers are most probably members of low-status, small fundamentalist sects whose membership is almost entirely composed of relatively poor people. Such groups rank below the Baptists in social status. On the other hand, middle-class adherents of small Protestant groups are disproportionately members of high-status denominations such as the Unitarians, the Christian Scientists, or the Quakers. If these assumptions are valid, then there is in fact no discrepancy between the Democratic predisposition of manual workers and the Republican orientation of white-collar ones. The former belong with the Baptists, the latter with the Episcopalians. The variation between the voting behavior of Lutheran workers and middle-class persons is more difficult to explain. It may be that part of the answer lies in the different synods of the Lutheran church. As far as interaction is concerned, these are, in effect, separate groups. The members of the more fundamentalist ones, principally the Missouri Synod, are less well to do on the average than are those who adhere to the more liberal synods. It is possible, therefore, that the sources of the class variation among Lutherans are similar to those which explain the differences among the "others."

There clearly are significant differences among Protestants in comparable class positions which are associated with denominational affiliations. It would appear, however, that such differences are not a function of variation in theological beliefs, of the difference between ascetic and nonascetic, or religious liberal and conservative doctrines. Groups such as the Baptists or Fundamentalists who have stressed ascetic morality and anti-Catholicism—doctrines which should dispose them to favor Republicans—are, in fact, seemingly more inclined to support the Democrats.

Benton Johnson offers an explanation of the apparent paradox that the more fundamentalist and ascetic Protestant groups are disproportionately Democratic. He first points to another paradox, that the churches of the more well to do have also been more liberal not only in their theology but in their social and economic pronouncements. The liberal National Council of Churches, although representing the wealthier Protestant denominations, has given considerable support to the Social Gospel movement.[83] An analysis of the highest-status church in the United States, the Episcopal church, based on questionnaire data from clergy and laymen, demonstrates convincingly that the clergy of this predominantly well-to-do denomination are very liberal in their political views.[84] On the other hand, the churches of the poorer Prot-

---

[83] Benton Johnson, "Ascetic Protestantism and Political Preference," *Public Opinion Quarterly*, 26 (1962), 38–40.

[84] Benjamin Ringer and Charles Glock, "The Political Role of the Church as Defined by Its Parishioners," *Public Opinion Quarterly*, 18 (1954–1955), 337–347.

estants, predominantly the Baptists and the smaller but numerous fundamentalist groups, have on the whole opposed the social gospel, and have taken conservative positions on economic and political issues.

Johnson argues that the political positions of these groups are congruent with historic theological elements in ascetic Protestantism. The liberalism of the churches of the more well to do derives from the fact that their ministers are often men "who have received their training from the more influential and prestigeful seminaries . . . , many of which are close to large universities [and] have participated in the trend toward liberal humanitarianism that has been going on in intellectual circles for many years."[85] The churches of the poor, on the other hand, prefer a simple unintellectual theology which defines Christianity in traditional terms, and preaches good versus evil, God against Satan. Both parishioners and clergy tend to be low in educational attainments, and the seminaries of these groups are often deliberately removed from contact with secular university life.

The fact that there is a general correlation between the average socioeconomic status of the members of different denominations and the religious and political liberalism of their clergy and official church bodies suggests the hypothesis that the more integrated an individual is in the religious life of the liberal high-status churches, the more liberal he should be in his outlook, holding other factors constant; conversely the opposite pattern should occur among the adherents of the low-status and more fundamentalist sects.

An analysis of interviews drawn from one city, Eugene, Oregon, sustains these assumptions. As in the national data presented above, members of low-status Eugene churches are more likely to be Democrats than those adhering to the high-status ones. These tendencies hold up within classes as well. Manual workers and those in nonmanual occupations belonging to fundamentalist groups are more Democratic than those in the same class adhering to the liberal denominations. However, when the supporters of the liberal churches are divided

---

[85] Johnson, *op. cit.*, p. 39; for an analysis of the sources of the liberalism of American academics and other intellectuals, see Lipset, *Political Man*, pp. 332–371.

on the basis of church attendance, frequent churchgoers show a lower Republican propensity than do those who go rarely. Among the fundamentalist groups, the exact opposite occurs: frequent attenders are more likely to vote Republican, while those who are rarely seen in church retain a strong Democratic allegiance. This relationship holds up even when class position is held constant.

The data presented in Table 8–5 clearly suggest that re-

Table 8–5.

PERCENTAGE OF TWO-PARTY VOTE OF LIBERAL AND FUNDAMENTALIST BY FREQUENCY OF CHURCH ATTENDANCE AND CLASS POSITION

Occupational Class and Frequency of Attendance	Party Identification (Per cent Republican)		Voting Behavior (Per cent Republican)	
Liberal:				
White Collar				
Attend Frequently	54	(29)	62	(26)
Attend Seldom	63	(16)	93	(14)
Blue Collar				
Attend Frequently	44	(9)	38	(8)
Attend Seldom	56	(9)	63	(8)
Total Liberal:				
Attend Frequently	51	(37)	56	(34)
Attend Seldom	60	(25)	82	(22)
Fundamentalist:				
White Collar				
Attend Frequently	65	(17)	71	(17)
Attend Seldom	44	(16)	55	(11)
Blue Collar				
Attend Frequently	48	(27)	53	(17)
Attend Seldom	27	(11)	33	(6)
Total Fundamentalist:				
Attend Frequently	55	(44)	62	(34)
Attend Seldom	37	(27)	47	(17)

Source: Benton Johnson, "Ascetic Protestantism and Political Preference," *Public Opinion Quarterly*, 26 (1962), 43–44. Voting behavior is based on a scale derived from reported votes in four elections between 1952 and 1958.

ligious practice and class position operate independently to affect partisan choice. As Johnson points out, the varying Protestant religious beliefs serve to reduce the relation between class and party among church attenders. Low-status fundamentalist churchgoers vote less Democratic than their class position calls for, while high-status Protestants who attend religiously liberal churches are less Republican than one might anticipate, given their social position.

The finding presented earlier that adherents of different denominations are disposed to follow the predominant political choice of the denomination may be shaped mainly by those who identify with, but are not involved in, the religious life of a given church. To be a nonpracticing Episcopalian or Congregationalist means to have a public high-status attribute; nominal church affiliation affects one's self-conception and public image, but apparently it does not much affect one's values. Hence nonpracticing supporters of such churches are among the most Republican of individuals with comparable socioeconomic traits. Conversely, to remain identified with a low-status church means to retain a status-ascribing characteristic that lowers one's general social status. An individual who so defines himself is presumably less oriented toward upward mobility, toward the values of the higher-status groups. Consequently such people are among the most prone to vote Democratic within their stratum.

Religion, therefore, would seem to affect political choice in two independent ways, as a source of beliefs and as a determinant of status. And the two variables operate at cross-purposes among Protestants. Active membership in a liberal high-status church pulls one toward political liberalism; nominal adherence primarily serves as a source of status and hence strengthens the political conservatism associated with high position. And the opposite pattern operates among the inactive and active adherents of the more fundamentalist low-status groupings.

Since differences in ethnic background have been stressed by some commentators as being of greater significance than variations in religious affiliation in determining party choice, it is relevant to examine their contribution to party vote here. In fact, some have argued that correlations between religious affiliation and party choice are actually a consequence of ethnic background. Those belonging to low-status, more recently immigrant ethnic groups, presumably more Catholic than Protestant, are more likely to be Democratic. An analy-

sis of the variations by ethnic background within the two
major Christian groupings, however, does not confirm this
suggestion.

The data summarized in Table 8–6 do indicate some variation within strata and religious groupings which is linked to
ethnic background (as measured by responses to the question:

Table 8–6.

RELATIONSHIP BETWEEN PARTY AFFILIATION AND ETHNICITY AMONG RE-
LIGIOUS AND CLASS GROUPINGS—1954—PER CENT (WHITES ONLY)

Classification	Democrat	Republican	N
Nonmanual Catholics			
Ireland	47	19	(189)
Italy	44	17	(87)
Great Britain	49	17	(75)
Germany and Austria	33	36	(127)
Poland	44	13	(32)
Other East Europe	48	21	(42)
No answer on origins	43	21	(85)
Totals	45%	21%	(707)
Nonmanual Protestants			
Ireland	29	38	(138)
Great Britain	22	52	(637)
Germany and Austria	21	46	(390)
Scandinavia and Holland	26	50	(254)
East Europe	26	39	(38)
Other West Europe	19	53	(77)
No answer on origins	30	39	(314)
Totals	24%	47%	(1,860)
Manual Catholics			
Ireland	61	10	(244)
Italy	62	11	(251)
Great Britain	65	10	(152)
Germany and Austria	58	11	(192)
Poland	69	8	(167)
Other East Europe	68	10	(101)
Other West Europe	61	11	(113)
No answer on origins	60	13	(118)
Totals	63%	10%	(1,373)
Manual Protestants			
Ireland	44	23	(219)
Great Britain	37	32	(699)
Germany and Austria	35	36	(491)
Scandinavia and Holland	40	34	(362)
East Europe	49	26	(61)
Other West Europe	49	24	(113)
No answer on origins	48	24	(438)
Totals	40%	30%	(2,386)

Classification	Democrat	Republican	N
Farm Catholics			
Ireland	67	8	(24)
Germany and Austria	46	16	(50)
East Europe	55	30	(20)
Other West Europe	45	34	(38)
Totals	52%	21%	(147)
Farm Protestants			
Ireland	28	42	(57)
Great Britain	26	49	(201)
Germany and Austria	39	40	(200)
Scandinavia and Holland	29	37	(123)
Other Europe	25	53	(28)
No answer on origins	33	45	(132)
Totals	32%	43%	(744)

Source: Calculated from INRA 1954 Eleven States Study. Independents not reported but included in calculations.

"From what country did your ancestors come?"). However, it seems clear that there is no consistent pattern, and that in any case the variations are not large. Although studies of some cities have indicated relatively strong Republican support among Italian Catholics as compared to Irish, this finding does not hold up for the eleven states dealt with here.[86] The one group of Catholics who show any special Republican tendency is from Germany and Austria, a fact which may reflect the persistence of antagonism to the Democrats for having led two wars against Germany. Manual worker Catholics from eastern Europe show a greater Democratic propensity than do other Catholics in their stratum, but the difference is not very great. Among Protestants, curiously enough, those of Irish background, historically most opposed to the Irish Catholics of any group, give the Democrats somewhat more backing than Protestants of British, German, and Scandinavian origin, a phenomenon for which I cannot even suggest a slightly plausible *ex post facto* reason. And German urban Protestants, like Catholics of the same national background, are somewhat lower in support of Democrats than others of their religious group; farmers with the same ethnic religious background, however, do not seem to share this antagonism.

The findings from the eleven states survey are reiterated by the results of the analysis of data from the 1952 Roper

[86] Dahl, *op. cit.*, p. 60.

survey which secured information concerning ethnic origin
by asking for birthplace of father and grandfather. This study,
however, does not permit an intensive analysis of many national backgrounds since the sample size was much smaller,
and the largest single group was composed of those of fourth-
generation background. But a comparison of those of fourth-
generation American (and British) ancestry with those of
Irish and continental European background suggested little
difference between those of old American or Anglo-Saxon
background and those with other forebears within class and
religious groupings.

The slightly greater propensity of Catholic workers of recent immigrant background to vote Democratic is contributed
largely by twenty respondents of Irish background who are
almost all Democratic. The Republican discrepancy among
nonmanual recent immigrant Protestants is largely a product
of the behavior of fourteen Scandinavians who are equally
heavily Republican. Whatever the sources of the remaining
relatively small variations among different ethnic groups, it
seems obvious that the differences in party support which are

Table 8–7.

RELATIONSHIP OF ANCESTRY, RELIGION, CLASS, AND PAST VOTING RECORD
(WHITES—NON-SOUTHERN) PERCENTAGE—1952

	Democratic	*Republican*	
Catholics			
Nonmanual			
Fourth-generation American or			
British	51	49	(41)
All others	49	51	(47)
Manual			
Fourth-generation American or			
British	76	24	(54)
All others	82	18	(85)
Protestants			
Nonmanual			
Fourth-generation American or			
British	29	71	(205)
All others	22	78	(69)
Manual			
Fourth-generation American or			
British	49	51	(147)
All others	51	49	(47)

Source: 1952 Study by Elmo Roper Associates.

linked to ethnicity are much less significant than those tied to class and religion. Although national ancestry may continue to affect political reactions, particularly with regard to foreign-policy issues, this is one source of party diversity which time seems to be eliminating. It is significant to note that the largest remaining differences are among the farm population, a pattern which may reflect the maintenance of ethnic cultural communities in rural areas. The assumptions of those who contend that Americans no longer divide among themselves in national origin terms, that the country has blended into three melting pots—Protestant, Catholic, and Jewish—would seem to be borne out by these data.

Class and religious differences then remain as the two most significant correlates of party support. An examination of the survey data from 1936 to 1958 reported in Table 8–2 suggests that there was little change in the relationship of these two variables and party support during this period, although the parties varied in strength from election to election. Thus in the 1950's, Eisenhower gained among all groups—Catholics and Protestants *and* those in manual and white-collar occupations. With the exception of the small number of Protestant farmers, each class and religious category increased its Republican vote when Eisenhower was running (1952 and 1956) and decreased when he was not (1954 and 1958). As Philip Converse concludes from a national survey of a panel of voters conducted by the University of Michigan's Survey Research Center in 1956, 1958, and 1960:

> Of those citizens considering themselves to be Democrats and thereby voting Democratic unless they perceived compelling reasons to do otherwise, over one-quarter had defected to vote for Eisenhower in 1952 and 1956. Two facts stand out about this massive defection. First, it was a defection and in no sense a conversion. Democrats voting for Eisenhower continued to think of themselves as Democrats, and continued to vote Democratic at other levels of office, particularly when Eisenhower was not on the ticket. Our subsequent data since 1956 have made it clear that Eisenhower's appeal was rather completely dissociated from the Republican Party: even among Democrats most attracted to him, it is hard to find evidence of any change induced in personal loyalties.
> Second, and most important for our purposes here, the

Democratic defections of the Eisenhower interlude seem to have occurred quite independent of religious background. That is, rates of defection were essentially the same for Protestant and Catholic Democrats alike. By sample estimates, Catholic defections were slightly less frequent than Protestant defections in 1952, and slightly more frequent in 1956. However, neither difference exceeds sampling error. More generally, it may be shown that the Democratic rates of defection to Eisenhower were remarkably similar across all the commonly studied social groupings: he enjoyed an "across-the-board" appeal which paid no visible respect to the major social boundaries.[87]

However, the data presented in Table 8–2 do suggest that among Catholics there was a somewhat greater return to the Democrats in 1958 than there had been in 1954. Since this return was concentrated among Catholic manual workers it is tempting to suggest that the eclipse of McCarthyism, which had considerable support from the poorer Catholics, may have accounted for the return of this group to its normal pattern.

The 1960 election produced a major convulsion in the previously stable level of religious voting. The measures of religious differences in voting in Table 8–2 among both manual and nonmanual workers are far higher than in any other of the elections recorded. If the 1956 results are contrasted with those of 1960, one might be tempted to conclude that the shift in religious voting was entirely owing to changes among Catholics. If, however, the 1954 and 1958 elections, in which Eisenhower was not running, are regarded as the

[87] Philip Converse, "Religion and Politics: The 1960 Election" (unpublished dittoed paper: Survey Research Center, University of Michigan, 1962), pp. 4–5. A shortened version of this paper has been published in Angus Campbell, *et al., Elections and the Political Order* (New York: John Wiley, 1966), pp. 96–124. An analysis of the effects of moving to the suburbs by Catholics based on a survey in metropolitan St. Louis in 1956 reports that even in this Eisenhower year: "In voting, both central city and suburban Catholics remain heavily Democratic. When we control country of origin, generation since migration, and education, only in the suburbs and in the most extreme classes do we find small Republican pluralities among Catholics—those with northern and western European backgrounds, those who are third generation, those with college educations. And these are far less Republican than their counterparts among the non-Catholics." Scott Greer, "Catholic Voters and the Democratic Party," *Public Opinion Quarterly,* 25 (1961), 623.

"normal" pattern, we can see that both Catholic groups moved toward the Democrats (although the shift among manual workers was a small one), and that both Protestant groups moved toward the Republicans. Using results of a panel study interviewed in 1956, 1958, and 1960, Converse reaches a similar verdict:

> Instead of concluding that political choices of Catholics were profoundly affected by the candidacy of a Catholic while Protestants were left unaffected, we must conclude that the impact on the two religious groupings was rather more equal, although opposite in direction.[88]

At the end of the Eisenhower years, Catholics returned to and went far beyond their normal Democratic vote, while Protestants moved in the opposite direction.

Let us attempt to account for the Catholic shift toward the Democrats. Kennedy was a member not only of a minority religion, but also a minority ethnic group, albeit a highly acculturated one. He was our first Catholic President and our first President with Irish ancestry. Perhaps his national origin gained him support independent of his religion. Converse reports, however, that there is only a "mild sign that Irish Catholics were more affected by the Kennedy candidacy than were non-Irish Catholics." Italians and other non-Irish Catholics voted overwhelmingly for him, as thirty-two years earlier they did for Al Smith. Converse concludes therefore:

> While it is plausible to suppose from these data, then, that the ethnic factor contributed some extra "push" to Catholics in 1960, there is of course no question but that its role was entirely eclipsed, like an eddy in a torrent, by movement along broader religious lines.[89]

Given the unique pattern of Catholic voting in 1960, which is apparently not explicable in terms of class differences (which, of course, are controlled in the table) or ethnic loyalties, the reaction presumably can be accounted for only in terms of some more narrowly religious linked factors. In

---

[88] Converse, *op. cit.,* p. 9.
[89] *Ibid.,* p. 29.

1958, Converse found no consistent relationship between political party preference and church attendance, or between party preference and "identification with the Catholic community." The latter variable was tapped by two questions intended to measure "the sense of proximity and common interest which individual members feel *vis-à-vis* the group." However, in examining the *deviation* of the 1960 vote from the 1958 party preferences, Converse reports that both church attendance and community involvement were related to Kennedy voting.[90] He accounts for this result by suggesting that when the direct relevance of an election to the interests or values of a group is high, then conformity to its political norms will be related to involvement in the group, but if direct political relevance is low, this relationship is reduced. Thus in 1960, the nomination of a Catholic gave the group tie increased relevance, and the relationship between conformity to political norms and involvement in the group was intensified.

Since Protestants are much more diverse in their values than are Catholics, the intensity of their reaction against Kennedy was striking. In spite of the long-term decline in anti-Catholic feeling in America, the rapid rise of Catholics into a position of social prominence and power seems to have set off a new wave of uneasiness. Writing before Kennedy was nominated (the index of his book does not list his name) Will Herberg perceived this trend:

> Protestantism in America today presents the anomaly of a strong majority group with a growing minority consciousness. "The psychological basis of much of American Protestantism," *Social Action* (Congregational) somewhat ruefully pointed out in 1952, "lies in a negative rejection of Roman Catholicism. . . . The one emotional loyalty that of a certainty binds us Protestants together . . . is the battle against Rome." The fear of "Rome" is indeed the most powerful cement of Protestant community consciousness, and it seems to loom larger today than it has for some time. Discussion of Protestant communal affairs moves increasingly under the shadow of the "Catholic problem," and Protestant attitudes tend

[90] *Ibid.*, pp. 32–33.

more and more to be defined in terms of confrontation with a self-assured and aggressive Catholicism. The tension has become really acute.[91]

In a survey administered during the 1960 campaign direct references to Kennedy's religion were avoided, yet almost half of the white Protestant respondents spontaneously mentioned the matter. More than three-quarters of those who did mention it were coded as "unequivocally negative."[92]

The data which have been presented on voting trends suggest that deviations of Protestant manual and nonmanual workers caused by the candidacy of a Catholic were of about equal size. But the crude division into only two occupational groups seems to conceal a more complex relationship between status and voting deviation. Negative references to Kennedy's religion were given most frequently by unskilled workers, but least often from persons in the middle of the occupational scale, clerical and sales workers. The anti-Catholic reaction of the upper-middle-class occupations is at first glance surprising. In rural areas, and especially in the South, the expected relationship of low status and religious involvement to anti-Catholicism could be seen, but

> where Catholics reside in large numbers and have come to compete for some of the forms of secular power, the anti-Catholic's reaction fell much less clearly along lines of religious involvement in the narrow sense. This was particularly true of the upper middle class in the non-Southern metropolis, where the Catholic encroachment has been most notable. Here, despite the highest education level, the Protestant business and professional community responded in a manner which suggests a threat along a broad front, not simply a challenge to religious orthodoxy.[93]

The evidence strongly suggests that there were two types of anti-Catholicism in 1960. The lower-class nonurban kind is the religious anti-Catholicism of American history, tied to a lack of education, strong commitment to one's own Protestant

[91] Will Herberg, *Protestant, Catholic, Jew* (New York: Doubleday-Anchor Books, 1960), p. 234. Herberg's foreword is dated October 1959. The passage he quotes is from "Christian Faith and the Protestant Churches," *Social Action*, 18 (May 1952), 1.

[92] Converse, *op. cit.*, p. 39.

[93] *Ibid.*, pp. 50–51.

church, and little direct contact with the targets of one's feelings. Presumably, this attitude has been declining in importance in recent years and, with the spread of education and urbanization, will continue to decline.

Anti-Catholic sentiment among higher-status persons may be a different matter. Probably this is the response of Protestants to their "growing minority consciousness." The same forces which caused the old nativist anti-Catholicism to decline help the new form to flourish: the outdated stereotype of the Catholic immigrant as a drunk and a bum fades away, but a new picture emerges of a community which is fully American, yet not Protestant, in which the Catholic and the Jew continue to increase their visible importance.

Perhaps the most interesting result to be derived from the survey results bearing on elections from 1936 to 1964, reported in Table 8–2, is the rather astonishing consistency in class and religious differences, the Kennedy years apart. Thus the range of difference in class voting in this thirty-year period has been from 17 to 24 per cent, that is, the relative difference in favor of the Democrats among manual workers as compared to nonmanuals has remained fairly constant. In the eight elections, presidential and congressional, reported on between 1948 and 1964, the difference *was either 17 or 18 per cent in seven of them.* The variation in the difference in the proportion of Catholics voting Democratic as compared to the Protestant percentage has been equally steady. With the exception of the two Kennedy elections, 1960 and 1962, the differences between the two major religious groupings *varied between 20 and 22 per cent in all except one election, 1958,* and in the latter it was 24 per cent. The 1960 election saw the religious difference rise to 48 per cent, and in 1962, with Kennedy in the White House, the magnitude of the difference declined to 33 per cent, still considerably above the "normal."

Although the election of 1964 differed from most in twentieth-century history in that it presented clear-cut ideological alternatives, and Lyndon Johnson won it with the largest majority in many decades (61 per cent), the magnitude of the class and religious variations as reflected in the Protestant-Catholic and manual-nonmanual differences *re-*

turned to the typical post-World War II pattern, 18 per cent between the two class groups, and 22 per cent between the religions. The congressional elections of 1966 followed the same pattern. In effect, the relative variation in support for the two parties was the same as before Kennedy, the absolute magnitudes for the Democrats simply increased, much as during the Eisenhower landslides, the reverse pattern occurred. The Democrats retained their advantage among manual workers and Catholics; the Republicans continued strong among nonmanuals and Protestants. The nomination of a Catholic on the Democratic ticket in 1960 brought the party an increase in Catholic support, and a loss among Protestants. These changes, however, did not outlive John Kennedy's tragically short stay in the White House.

The 1968 elections, of course, introduced a very new element, a major third-party candidate in the form of George Wallace. Wallace, as I have documented elsewhere, secured his support outside the South more heavily from manual workers (9 per cent) than nonmanuals (5 per cent), and slightly more from Catholics (8 per cent) than from Protestants (6 per cent). Nevertheless, Hubert Humphrey also polled more strongly among manual workers and Catholics, indicating that Wallace had cut into, but not overwhelmed the traditional Democratic allegiances of these groups.

What is perhaps more significant than the Catholic-Protestant variation in the support of George Wallace is the differences among the Protestant denominations. Wallace's greatest backing, North and South, came from Baptists, followed by those classified as "other Protestants," presumably largely adherents of fundamentalist sects. These denominations are the most traditional of the Protestant groups, and contain the core of the religious resistance to modernism and cosmopolitanism. Their main strength has been in small towns and rural areas, and many who adhere to these denominations in the cities are migrants from more provincial areas.[94]

The comprehensive results from the various survey studies completed since the opinion poll became a permanent insti-

[94] For a detailed analysis of the Wallace movement see Lipset and Raab, *op. cit.,* chapters 9 and 10.

tution in the mid-1930's clearly demonstrate that the link between the American two-party system and class and religion which appeared long before the Civil War maintains itself as strongly as ever, in spite of all the intervening changes in American life. Major historical events, different issues and candidates, may enhance the over-all backing of one of the parties for a given period of time, but they have not been able to modify the generalization established well over one hundred years ago, that the Democratic party draws sustenance from the less well to do and the Catholics.

THE INFLUENCE OF RELIGION ON POLITICS

▪ *Social and group factors.*   It is obviously impossible to discuss the history of political life in America without paying special attention to the influence of religious groups and values. This relationship has in fact hardly been investigated by historians. There is much to be done before we can iron out the interrelated effects of religion, class, ethnicity, sectionalism, and the variety of other elements which shape American political behavior. But just as it is possible to construct a class or economic interpretation of political conflict and consensus in America, it would also be practical to do the same for religion; this, however, remains to be done.

At the moment we can say that, broadly speaking, there have been two main sets of facts relating religious influences to politics. The first may be described as *social or group factors,* and the second are *theological or value elements.* A number of processes affect the way in which the first set of factors operate.

1. The social situation of the dominant group within a given religion may lead to an identification between the denomination and given political tendencies. Thus, the needs of immigrants and workers have been identified with the politics of the Democratic party. Churches primarily composed of such groups have tended to back the Democrats in this country, and the more left party in other nations.

2. One party or ideological tendency may give more support than others to explicit needs of religious groups. Northern

Democrats have been prone to give more support to government aid to religious schools than have Whigs or Republicans. The latter have begun to change in recent years.

3. Direct links to a given political party may become a conventional method of mobility for aspiring members of different religious or ethnic groups.

A link between parties and religious groups may reflect a conscious identification by the members of a religious group with issues directly involving the group as such. It may, however, also result unwittingly from the common life experiences of members of the same group. That is, individuals belonging to a given religious group tend to have similar experiences and to react in the same way, without necessarily feeling that they are reacting as members of a religious community. In large measure, the indirect impact of a religious group on its members rests in the fact that membership in a church helps determine the social interaction of members of the group. Church members are more likely to interact with members of their own church than with others. Thus, the fact that a man is a Catholic generally means that he belongs to a Catholic family, most of whose members are Democrats, and that he is more likely to associate with other Catholics, the majority of whom are Democrats. In large measure the traditional identification of a religious group with a political tendency is mediated through primary groups without individuals being aware of the fact that religious factors motivate their political behavior.

This process will be accentuated if the link between the religious group and its modal pattern of political behavior becomes manifest. For much of American history, as we have seen, various ethnic groups associated with the Catholic church have dealt primarily with the Democratic party, and the party, in turn, has sought ways of retaining their loyalty. Catholics, historically, have been much more likely to gain office through the Democratic party. As Peter Odegard pointed out in 1960, before Kennedy was nominated:

> It is no accident that over 80 per cent of the Catholic members of Congress are Democrats. Nor is it surprising that under Democratic Presidents Franklin Roosevelt and Harry

Truman one out of every four judicial appointments went to a Catholic as against one out of every 25 under Harding, Coolidge and Hoover.[95]

The relationship between religion and composition of party representation in Congress makes manifest the sharp difference between the parties in this respect.

Clearly, involvement in the support for Democratic urban machines played a considerable role in facilitating social mobility among Irish and other Catholic groups. This process has been described and documented in detail for what has been, perhaps, the most extreme example of a state in which politics and social mobility have been intimately tied to ethnicity and religion, Massachusetts.[96]

Table 8–8.

RELATIONSHIP BETWEEN RELIGION AND PARTY AMONG MEMBERS OF BOTH HOUSES OF CONGRESS FROM DIFFERENT SECTIONS AS OF JANUARY 1960

Section	Per Cent Catholics of Democratic Members	Per Cent Catholics of Republican Members
East	56	12
West	13	3
South	5	0
Midwest	38	7
Total	26	7

Source: John H. Fenton, *The Catholic Vote* (New Orleans: The Hauser Press, 1960), p. 89.

The creation of a visible identification between one party and various ethnic-religious groups, however, may create a negative reference image for others, which presses them to support the other party. Thus, a study of British immigrants

[95] Peter Odegard, *op. cit.,* p. 121. The same tendency has been documented in detail for the New England states. See Duane Lockard, *New England State Politics* (Princeton: Princeton University Press, 1959), pp. 32, 66–67, 98, 134, 198–199, 241. See also Samuel Lubell, *op. cit.,* pp. 83–84.

[96] See Oscar Handlin, *op. cit.,* Earl Lathem and George Goodwin, *Massachusetts Politics* (Medford: Tufts Civic Education Center, 1960); Joseph Huthmacher, *Massachusetts People and Politics, 1919–1933* (Cambridge: The Belknap Press of Harvard University Press, 1959); and Murray B. Levin, *The Complete Politician. Political Strategy in Massachusetts* (Indianapolis: Bobbs-Merrill, 1962).

in nineteenth-century America reports that many of them joined the Republican party because they saw the Democrats in the hands of the Irish Catholics.[97] More recently, Adam Clayton Powell, then congressman from Harlem and minister of Harlem's largest church, the Abyssinian Baptist, appealed to the Protestants of New York to unite to gain political influence since almost no major judgeships or other major New York appointive offices were in the hands of Protestants.

■ *Variant religious values.*   In addition to the various social and historical factors that have shaped the political identity of religious groups, there are very direct relationships between different religious beliefs and value systems and different political tendencies. Such relationships may take two forms: (1) explicit religious formulations which carry with them political directives; and (2) the indirect effect of religious systems in creating the dispositional base for the acceptance of certain secular political ideologies.

The most obvious example of the first type are the encyclicals of the Roman Catholic pontiffs as was noted in Chapter 6. A number of them, especially in the late nineteenth and twentieth centuries, have dealt with political matters. For example, the papacy has condemned socialism and communism as materialistic and antireligious movements which no Catholic may support. The condemnation of socialism has, of course, been redefined so as to include only materialistic or atheistic socialism, and the bishops of the British Commonwealth have explicitly stated that their social-democratic or Labour parties do not fall under this ban since they are not Marxist or materialistic. Nevertheless, there can be little doubt that the encyclical denunciations of socialism have affected the political behavior of Catholics in many countries. They have made it difficult for socialists to make inroads among Catholics on the European continent, and within the British Commonwealth Labour parties Catholics have generally played a conservative role, resisting efforts to define these parties as socialist in a Marxist sense.

[97] Rowland T. Berthoff, *British Immigrants in Industrial America, 1790–1950* (Cambridge: Harvard University Press, 1953), pp. 196–198.

Conversely, the economic ideology expressed in many encyclicals, while anti-socialist, has tended to favor what has come to be known as the welfare state. Since Pope Leo XIII, the Catholic church has condemned the exploitation of labor by business, and has urged state protection against the insecurities of old age, unemployment, and the like. The Popes have also favored trade unions. In large measure, the theology of the Catholic church, stemming from precapitalist feudal and aristocratic origins, has been against what it calls "materialistic socialism *and* capitalism." It is difficult to describe the best state envisaged by the pontiffs, but in general it would appear to be a Christian state with church control of education and of the young, and with economic legislation which protected the lower classes against economic exploitation. A link between papal social encyclicals and American Catholic was provided in the statements of the American bishops which called for the adoption of "welfare state" measures long before they had a serious chance of enactment. Thus the yearly statement of the American Catholic bishops in 1917 advocated liberal economic measures which were not put into effect until the party of the Protestant majority was finally defeated in the 1930's. The bishops suggested a heavier graduated income tax, social security, unemployment insurance, and minimum wage legislation.

It should be recognized, however, that there has been considerable diversity of opinion among the Catholic clergy, even on church-related matters. For decades they have recognized a divergence between "conservative" and "liberal" persuasions on such questions as the wisdom of continuing the Index of Prohibited Books, the moral propriety of state-run schools, and participation in interfaith activities.[98]

Among the laity, too, striking evidence of diversity can be found. Efforts by the church have kept laws on the books forbidding private physicians from dispensing contraceptive information in two states, Massachusetts and Connecticut. Yet, when Gallup interviewers asked a national sample as long ago as 1943, "Would you like to see government health clin-

[98] Robert D. Cross, *The Emergence of Liberal Catholicism in America* (Cambridge: Harvard University Press, 1958), pp. 75, 105–108, 212.

ics furnish birth-control information to married people who wish it?" fully 45 per cent of the Catholics questioned responded in the affirmative.[99]

It is impossible to know how much effect official church positions have had on the political behavior of Catholics in different countries. Practicing Catholics have covered the range of the political spectrum from left-wing socialism to fascism. Local bishops have interpreted official church dogma to justify support of almost every political ideology except communism. There can, however, be little doubt that these church pronouncements have had some effect, given the authoritative aura of the Church. For example, the sympathy which Catholic doctrine has had for trade-union objectives, as contrasted with the greater emphasis on individualism inherent in Protestantism, may in some part explain why even nonunion middle-class Catholics are more supportive of union rights in this country.

A detailed study of the relationship between religious affiliation and vote in an Ohio referendum on anti-union "right-to-work" legislation held in 1958 found that regardless of what other factors also influenced the vote, the "religious factor" invariably emerges as an important determinant of voting behavior on the right-to-work issue. Ohio's counties were segregated (for analytic purposes) into twenty different levels of urbanism, income, and rural farm, and in all twenty of these groups the more Catholic counties exceeded the least Catholic in their opposition to right to work.[100]

Perhaps more important in their effect on politics and other areas of life than the directly political manifestoes of religious leaders are the ways in which religious doctrines operate to predispose adherents to favor one secular pattern rather than another. Many observers, for example, have called attention to the processes through which Protestantism has contributed to individualism, self-reliance, feelings of personal responsibility for success and failure, and interpretation of social evils in terms of moral turpitude. Catholicism, on the other hand, has tended to stress community responsibility,

---

[99] Source: A.I.P.O. Study No. 308KT, 1943.
[100] John H. Fenton, *The Catholic Vote* (New Orleans: The Hauser Press, 1960), pp. 37–38.

and does not emphasize individual morality. Émile Durkheim has pointed out the link between the differing stresses inherent in Protestantism and Catholicism in relation to variation in suicide rates. Durkheim's thesis is that Protestants are more prone than Catholics to commit suicide, for, among other reasons, Protestantism places greater responsibility on individuals for the consequences of their actions.

Similarly, it may be suggested that the differences among American Protestants and Catholics in their reaction to the welfare state may flow from a more or less conscious rejection of reliance on organized social action and the welfare state among Protestants. Studies of the 1948 and 1952 presidential elections indicated that Protestant Republicans were more opposed to social-welfare measures than Catholic Republicans.[101] Even when moral matters rather than welfare measures are at issue, white Protestants are less likely to support state action than are Catholics. In a study of the influence of religion on behavior Gerhard Lenski found that Protestants who thought that certain kinds of behavior, i.e., gambling, moderate drinking. Sunday business, were "always or usually wrong" were less likely than Catholics to favor legal suppression of the immoral practice.[102] Similarly, white Protestants in this survey were more liberal than Catholics with respect to matters of civil liberties, including issues such as attacks on religion, criticism of the President, and rights of free speech for Fascists and Communists.

Further evidence for the thesis that religious background may indirectly affect secular behavior may be found in a study of productivity among workers. Melville Dalton notes that Protestant workers have higher rates of productivity than Catholic workers, and suggests that this is a consequence of greater individualism among the Protestants. The same survey also reports that Republican workers (most of whom are probably Protestants) are higher in productivity

[101] A. Campbell *et al.*, "Political Issues and the Vote, November 1952," *American Political Science Review*, 47 (1953), 374–375.
[102] Gerhard Lenski, *The Religious Factor* (New York: Doubleday, 1961), pp. 177–178. However, Protestants as a group were much more likely than Catholics to think that gambling and moderate drinking were wrong.

than Democratic ones.[103] Similar differences in economic orientation are suggested in Lenski's study. He finds, when comparing Protestants to Catholics, holding class background and length of family immigrant history constant, that Protestants are more likely to have positive attitudes toward work, to be less active in unions, to expect to agree with businessmen rather than with unions on various issues, and to be critical of installment buying. After considering the various environmental factors which might create such differences between the two major religious groups, Lenski concludes that the traditional differences in religious ethos continue to play an important role in affecting attitudes such as these.[104]

Historically, as we have seen, the moralistic values of ascetic Protestantism have been fostered by the conservative parties—Federalists, Whigs, and Republicans. All of the major Protestant crusades, against drink, against slavery, and against the increase in Catholic and nonevangelical segments of the population through immigration, have found much greater support from these parties, and have most often been opposed by the Democrats. The varying attitudes toward work, success, individual responsibility, and public morality between Catholics and Protestants, especially Protestants adhering to the ascetic sects, may dispose the Catholic more than the Protestant to accept or support the welfare state. Consequently, the allegiance to the Democratic party may be facilitated by Catholic values, while ascetic Protestant values may contribute to the continuing disproportionate support which Republicans draw in the North from white Protestants, even among manual workers who belong to unions.[105]

An indirect relationship between politics and religion may be found in the role of new sects which split off from the Anglican church. The name given them in Britain is an insightful one, "nonconformists," or "Dissenters." Most new or dissenting religions tend to appeal to those groups in society who are in an underprivileged position. While religious protest may be couched in purely theological terms, it may

---

[103] See Melville Dalton, "Worker Response and Social Background," *Journal of Political Economy*, 55 (1947), 323–332.

[104] Lenski, *op. cit.*, pp. 75–119.

[105] See the data of A.I.P.O. Survey No. 622K, 1959.

give expression to feelings of resentment against various aspects of the social or economic structure as noted in Chapter 5.[106] Protestants are true protesters, not only against traditional religion, but against aspects of the social structure as well. It is important to note, however, that the relationship between theological and secular protest is rarely manifest. The Methodists, who contributed much to the growth of British labor, for example, were both conservative and apathetic toward politics, and in large measure most sectarian movements are hostile to worldly matters. The connection to politics seems to lie in these religions providing the first break with a portion of the established order, and in their giving lower-class individuals the opportunity for self-expression in organizations of their own.[107]

On the other hand, as I indicated earlier, discontent which expresses itself in religious terms is often contained by religion. That is, religions which promulgate transcendental doctrines, such as only the poor but honest will be rewarded, may reduce the pressures for social reform by enabling the discontented to project a future equitable situation in heaven. In effect, they constitute a functional equivalent for protest for many of their members.

An examination of history suggests that American Protestant sects have more often served to draw off antagonism from the social arena to the religious order, rather than forming the beginning of a breakthrough against the secular order. New sects have developed more readily here than anywhere else in the world. For the most part, these are drawn from economically and socially depressed strata, and their theology reflects transvaluational beliefs, such as the belief that wealth or ornate living is sinful or part of a corrupting process. During the 1930's, when efforts to form significant protest parties failed totally, the sectarians grew while other religions declined or showed no change.[108] Such movements have played

---

[106] For further discussion and references, see S. M. Lipset, *Political Man, op. cit.,* pp. 106–108.

[107] See William Kornhauser, *The Politics of Mass Society* (Glencoe: The Free Press, 1959), pp. 137 ff.

[108] W. W. Sweet, *The American Churches* (New York: Abingdon-Cokesbury, 1947), p. 73; A. T. Boisen, *Religion in Crisis and Custom* (New York: Harper, 1955); also Argyle, *op. cit.,* pp. 138–140.

a role as a "transmission belt" not for the left, but for the radical or extremist right wing. The differences between the American and European reactions reflect many factors, but two which seem important are the relationship of the dominant religion to the state, and the class composition of the sects. In much of Europe, the dominant religion, Anglican, Lutheran, Catholic, or Orthodox, has been a state church closely identified with the traditional ruling strata. Hence, the new sects were necessarily rejecting an institution which was part of the old social order, and their fight against established religion was also a fight against the conservative parties allied with established religion. In America, this issue did not arise after the early nineteenth century. Second, much of the support of fundamentalist Protestantism as well as of new sects has come from the lower nonmetropolitan middle and lower classes. The urban working class has been disproportionately Catholic. And the more dissatisfied, possible downwardly mobile or aging members of the lower middle class have politically identified with traditional old values rather than with new ones. Hence, perhaps, the propensity for sectarianism and right-wing politics to join forces.

The one important exception to these generalizations has been the Negro churches. Negroes have been even more inclined than whites to find the need to back transvaluational new churches. But such forms of religious innovation have often played a role in facilitating secular political or race protest movements. In a sense, these have played a role comparable to lower-class based new Protestant groups in Europe. The Southern Bible Belt has, in fact, thrown up two forms of religiously linked protest, a rightist white one, and a leftist Negro one. And since one group seeks to return to the old status quo, while the other seeks a new world, the reasons for the difference are not hard to comprehend.

■ *Some implications.*   In concluding the discussion of the influence of religion on politics, it may be important to point out that its important effect may not rest with its influence in determining the basis of party division. Many further avenues of exploration are suggested, e.g., the extent to which the unique character of pluralistic American Protestantism has contributed to exacerbating the nature of controversy. The emphasis on making politics an arena in which men seek to enforce the moral has been distinctly American, and over time has come to influence many groups which have no historic ties to Puritanism. A distinguished French Dominican student of American religion has criticized American Catholics for having absorbed this American Protestant view of religion and morality. He worries that they are becoming more like American Baptists and Presbyterians than like European or Latin American Catholics, that they have accepted Puritanism:

> What is Puritanism? A French Jacobin, Saint-Just, gave the most perfect definition of it that I know: "Either virtue or a reign of terror." . . . Sin must be repressed by all possible means of force and of civil and social legislation. One must force people to be virtuous. Virtue and sin are identified with human law.
> . . . [The] Puritan influence is very deep in America. Many non-Catholics suffer from it and would like to free themselves from it. Now, you would think that they should be able to count on the Catholics in this endeavor. But such is not the case and one often has the impression that American Catholics are more Puritan than anybody else and that they are close to setting themselves up as the champions of Puritanism. . . .
> . . . [An] instance of the same thing was the enthusiasm whipped up by McCarthy among certain American Catholics: "Either virtue or a reign of terror."[109]

This tendency to enforce virtue by law runs like a red letter throughout American history. Insofar as an issue has been linked to the moral sense of religious people it has given rise to movements designed to eradicate evil, whether the cause be abolition, white supremacy, temperance, or antipopery. Such behavior suggests an identity between religious commitment and intolerance of ambiguity. The more committed an individual is to a religious belief the less likely will he be to

[109] R. L. Bruckberger, "The American Catholics as a Minority," in Thomas T. McAvoy (ed.), *Roman Catholicism and the American Way of Life* (Notre Dame: University of Notre Dame Press, 1960), pp. 45–47.

appreciate the rights of "error," whether in the religious or secular arena. Lenski in his analysis of the impact of religion suggests that *"tolerance* and *secularism"* are closely interrelated, that both are fostered by modern urban society.[110] There is considerable evidence which attests to the validity of this thesis with respect to the behavior of individuals today. In a comprehensive examination of the attitudes of the American people and their civic leaders toward civil liberties for unpopular views made in 1954, Samuel Stouffer found "that more churchgoers are intolerant of . . . nonconformity . . . than are nonchurchgoers," and that this relationship holds "when education, age, region, and type of community are taken into account."[111] The same relationship between church attendance and intolerance occurred among community leaders as well. There was no consistent variation between Catholics and Protestants in this survey.

It has often been pointed out that moralist fervor linked to religion has typically marked the emergence of new American social movements, from temperance to the contemporary radical right. These social movements have also been marked by leadership from "displaced" groups in America, groups which have for one reason or another lost an earlier status.[112] At certain times religious groups, as such, have felt a sharp loss of status. Perhaps Protestantism as a whole is feeling such a loss today. In addition, as has been noted, the conservative in America has historically allied himself with religious and moralistic causes even more than with class issues—out of a necessity flowing from the nature of American society. These implications for American political life have to be explored further against the specific background of America's persistent religious-political design.

The discussion in this chapter of the various political behaviors which are related to religion may be subjected to the criticism that I am not properly speaking of "religious factors" at all. In large measure, the "religious" attitudes which affect

[110] Lenski, *op. cit.,* p. 9.
[111] Samuel Stouffer, *Communism, Conformity, and Civil Liberties* (New York: Doubleday, 1955), p. 147.
[112] See Lipset and Raab, *op. cit.,* for a detailed discussion of the role of elements in Protestantism in sustaining certain right-wing extremist movements.

political choice have been determined by special historical circumstances which affect many members of particular denominations because they were predominantly immigrants, workers, or businessmen, or lived in a certain part of the country. As Gibson Winter has noted: "If Protestant attitudes were really grounded in a religious factor, the positions of White and Negro Protestants would not be diametrically opposed on all issues."[113]

Clearly from the point of view of the theologian, of the "true believer," much of what has been discussed here, or in other writings of social scientists on religion, is not really dealing with religion as the area of man's experience in which he deals with God. However, if we recognize that the sociologist cannot deal with this subject as such, that in fact he must deal with religious groupings as one of the sources of men's subgroup identifications, an identification which involves the special way in which different groups see their relationship to the transcendental, then much of sociological analysis of religion becomes a specification of the way in which different religious communities have absorbed their various experiences, and the consequent effect of such absorption on their behavior in other "nonreligious" arenas.

Religion is of obvious particular interest to the sociologist since it is the one institution which is primarily concerned with values, with stating and teaching proper modes of thinking and acting. And whether the religion of the privileged or deprived, it translates experiences into value terms, into concepts of right and wrong. Since religious groups must define the right as divinely inspired, their structure serves to institutionalize reactions to historical experiences as norms which are passed on to subsequent generations.

The United States as a nation was in some part formed out of the historic experiences of the English dissenting Protestant sects. The very emphasis on morality in politics which so distinguishes much of our domestic and foreign politics is a consequence of our being a Protestant nation without an established church. And elements in the Protestant tradition

---

[113] Gibson Winter, "Methodological Reflection on 'The Religious Factor,'" *Journal for the Scientific Study of Religion*, 2 (1962), 56.

together with the focus on the voluntary principle have meant
that Americans have come to define reactions to new experiences in religious terms, often through creating or joining a
new religion. Thus even when the reasons men support a
given political party may be explained almost totally with respect to their economic or status position, the fact that their
position in the stratification hierarchy is in part mediated
through a religious affiliation affects the quality of the secular
political response. In this way the "religious factor" has affected the character of American politics. To attempt to explain American political history without a discussion of the
relationship of politics and religion is wrong: the fact that
men have done so only serves to demonstrate that to study a
subject does not necessarily mean that one understands it.

There is obviously no simple solution to the study of the
"religious factor" in American politics. Much of its influence
must be perceived as part of the total value system affecting
everyone. As we have seen, membership in the same denominations stimulated feeling for and against slavery before the
Civil War. Today, Southern Negroes and whites adhere to the
same denominations, both are largely Baptist and Methodist.
Foreign Catholic observers have noted to their dissatisfaction
that many American Catholics have taken over Protestant
puritanical attitudes, that the American Catholic's tastes, reactions, and ideas on moral issues are colored by people around
him, and thus he is more like an American Baptist than, let us
say, a Latin American or European Catholic. The problem
which covariation of diverse elements with religion poses for
analysis was explicitly recognized by Alexis de Tocqueville
when he attempted to make sense out of American political
life in the 1830's:

> There is in each religion a political doctrine which, by affinity,
> is joined to it. This point is controvertible in the sense that
> where nothing interferes with this tendency, it surely shows
> itself. But it doesn't follow that it is impossible to separate
> religious doctrines from their political effects. On the con-
> trary, in all the countries of the world, material interests have
> been seen to operate this separation. The Catholics in . . . the
> United States are the invariable supporters of the "democratic"
> party. Does it follow that Catholicism leads to the "demo-

cratic" spirit? No, but that the Catholics are poor, and come almost all from a country where the aristocracy is Protestant.[114]

The combination of the "political doctrine," which, as Tocqueville suggests, is inherent in every religion, with the fact that denominations in pluralistic America are variously located in the social and economic structure, and the continuing strong sense of commitment to an identification with religion, means that religion remains, today, as in Tocqueville's time, one of the main sources of party cleavage and of political tone.[115] And I would venture the prediction that analysts of American political life will continue to find evidence of its impact for generations to come.

The discussion of the relationship of religious affiliation to political orientation has dealt almost exclusively with different Christian groups in the United States. The Jews have been left out of this analysis, since their role has been tied up to many other factors not present in the specific experience of American Christian denominations. The following chapter turns to an effort to understand the changing relationships of Jews with the larger community which have affected their contribution to politics.

[114] Citation from Tocqueville's American diary as quoted in George W. Pierson, *Tocqueville in America* (New York: Doubleday-Anchor Books, 1959), p. 289. He makes the same point with less stress on the problem of methodology in the *Democracy* itself. "Most of the Catholics are poor, and they have no chance of taking part in the government unless it is open to all the citizens. They constitute a minority, and all rights must be respected in order to ensure to them the free exercise of their own privileges. These two causes induce them, even unconsciously, to adopt political doctrines which they would perhaps support with less zeal if they were rich and preponderant." Alexis de Tocqueville, *op. cit.*, p. 312.

[115] For a detailed analysis of the evidence which suggests that Americans have been among the most religiously active and committed people in Christendom, see S. M. Lipset, *The First New Nation* (New York: Basic Books, 1963), Chapter 4, "Religion and American Values," pp. 140–169.

CHAPTER 10

The Left, the Jews and Israel

The analysis of the politics of the Jews must in large part deal with Jews as leftists.[1] The history of the relationship between the left and the Jews indicates that the Jews have been intimately associated with the liberal-left side of the political spectrum. The Jews were an issue in the French Revolution, and have continued to concern political men ever since. For a century and a half, the left supported Jewish political and social rights against the existing establishments which tried to deny them. In Catholic feudal Europe, Jews had had few rights, and the universalistic egalitarian ideology stemming from the French Revolution served to break down particularistic restrictions on all groups, and helped thereby also to secure the emancipation of the Jews.

But leftist support for the liberation of the Jews, which

[1] For studies of Jewish politics see L. H. Fuchs, *The Political Behavior of American Jews* (New York: The Free Press, 1956); Werner Cohn, "The Politics of American Jews," in M. Sklare, ed., *The Jews* (New York: The Free Press, 1958), pp. 614–626; Nathaniel Weyl, *The Jew in American Politics* (New Rochelle: Arlington House, 1968); Nathan Glazer, "The Jewish Role in Student Activism," *Fortune*, 79 (January 1969), pp. 112–113, 126–129; Louis Ruchames, "Jewish Radicalism in the United States," in Peter Rose, ed., *Essays on Jewish Life in America* (New York: Random House, 1969), pp. 228–252.

helped gain them the right to take their part as citizens, was not an unmixed blessing. Historically the left has assumed (sometimes explicitly, more often implicitly) that one of the payments the Jews would make to the left for having liberated them would be to disappear. Liberal-left ideology of all varieties has assumed that within a free nation (and nationalism was historically a leftist revolutionary ideology in the nineteenth century), Jewish identity—like all other forms of parochial tribal loyalties—would be assimilated into the free, universalistic community. Jews would become members of the nation no different from anyone else: which meant that they would cease being Jews. The maintenance of Jewish particularistic customs—religious, ethnic, or any other—was not welcomed by the left. The feeling that Jewish particularism is somehow reactionary, tribal, traditional, unmodern, has continued down to the present.

There is another element in the ambivalent relationship between contemporary left ideologies and movements and the Jews. The Socialist and Communist movements have opposed anti-Semitism and various restrictions on Jews participating as free citizens sharing with other parts of the left the assumption that Judaism (*i.e.,* the Jews) would disappear in the forthcoming universalistic (socialistic) Utopia. Unlike liberalism, however, the Socialist left has had another special problem, namely, an association of Jews with capitalism encouraged by the disproportionate number of businessmen, bankers, traders, and merchants among Jews.[2]

FROM BEBEL TO HENRY FORD

Anti-Semitism, as August Bebel once pointed out, is "the socialism of fools." In fact, it was perceived as a form of socialism by many in the nineteenth century. Anti-Semitism (some Socialists thought or hoped) was a naïve, stupid beginning of a recognition that capitalism was evil. Therefore, anti-Semitism in itself was not morally bad, it was simply ignorant and incomplete. Some Socialists, including Marx him-

---

[2] For an excellent historical discussion of anti-Semitism among socialists and the Left, with a useful bibliography, see George Lichtheim, "Socialism and the Jews," *Dissent,* 25 (July–August 1968), pp. 314–342.

self, used the symbol of Jewish capitalism (of the Jews as merchants and "Shylocks") in their propaganda. Without going into the whole question of Marx's curious relationship with Judaism—it is certainly not a simple one—there can be little doubt Marx's belief system included some components which must be described as anti-Semitism.[3]

But the major aspect of Marxist nineteenth-century thinking on the subject—and this becomes relevant to some current developments in the American-Negro black community and to the reactions of leftist intellectuals toward those developments—was to see lower-class anti-Semitism as a form of embryonic class-consciousness among workers. To talk about "oppressive Jewish businessmen" and "Jewish bankers" was considered a step in the right direction, it was part of the masses learning that all bankers and businessmen—all capitalists—were bad. In Czarist Russia, some young Jewish revolutionaries hailed the emergence of the anti-Semitic anti-Czarist *Narodnaya Volya* as evidence that the revolution was really under way. According to J. L. Talmon in an article on "Jews and Revolution" published in the *Maariv* of 21 September 1969, three of the 28 members of the executive committee of this organization which called in 1881 for a pogrom directed against the Czar, the nobility, and the Jews, were themselves Jewish (as were many rank-and-file members).

This confused attitude toward anti-Semitism almost prevented the French Socialist party from taking a stand in the major Jewish *cause célèbre* of the Third Republic, the Dreyfus Case. While French radicals (liberals) like Zola and Clemenceau jumped to Dreyfus' defense, recognizing that a major principle was at stake in the persecution of a Jew, no matter who he was, a debate emerged among the Socialists. A number of them, particularly those on the revolutionary left, argued that Socialists should not be concerned about Dreyfus since he was a professional soldier, a captain in the army, that whether Gentile militarists (or capitalists) persecuted Jewish militarists (or capitalists) was of no concern to revolutionary Socialists.

[3] See Solomon Bloom, "Karl Marx and the Jews," *Jewish Social Studies* (January 1942), pp. 3–16; Edmund Silberner, "Was Marx an anti-Semite?" *Historia Judaica*, 11 (April 1949), pp. 1–52.

Jean Jaurès, the famous French revisionist Socialist leader, saved the glory of the Socialist movement by insisting that whenever injustice was done, Socialists and radicals had to be in the forefront of the battle, that it made no difference whether injustice was done to a capitalist, a general, a Jew, or anybody else. He argued the case for Socialist involvement in the defense of Dreyfus on a broad idealistic basis that had nothing to do with historical materialism or class struggle. Jaurès laid down the principle that the left must always oppose religious and racial discrimination regardless of the social or economic status of the victim.[4]

In general, between the French Revolution and the end of World War II, the political history of continental Europe has suggested that most of the tendencies classified on the right have been somewhat anti-Semitic, while those on the left have been more defensive of Jewish rights. The traditional religious-linked right groups regarded the Jews as outside of Christendom, and hence not properly qualified to be full citizens. Some more populist-oriented rightist movements used anti-Semitism as an anti-elitist tactic to win mass support against the blandishments of the Socialists. There were, of course, some major exceptions to these generalizations, particularly among monarchical and aristocratic elements concerned with protecting "their" Jews against the vulgar prejudices of the masses or the materialistic middle classes. The Socialists also tolerated some overt anti-Semites in their ranks, particularly in central Europe.

This historic link between position on matters of Jewish rights and the broader political spectrum helps to explain the presence of large numbers of Jews in the various leftist movements, particularly of many wealthy Jews, who have supported radical left causes. For much of European history, Jews had no alternative but to support a variety of left tendencies. This was especially true within the Czarist Empire before World War I. This limitation on political alternatives was paralleled socially. The German political sociologist, Robert Michels, accounted for the left propensities of many af-

[4] Edmund Silberner, "French Socialism and the Jewish Question, 1865–1914," *Historia Judaica*, 19 (April 1957), pp. 13–14.

fluent Jews as a reaction to this phenomenon in his justly famed study of the structure of Socialist parties, *Political Parties* (1911):

> The origin of this predominant position [of the Jews in the European socialist movement] is to be found, as far at least as concerns Germany and the countries of Eastern Europe, in the peculiar position which the Jews have occupied and in many respects still occupy. The legal emancipation of the Jews has not been followed by their social and moral emancipation. In large sections of the German people a hatred of the Jews and the spirit of the Jew-baiter still prevail, and contempt for the Jew is a permanent thing. The Jew's chances in public life are adversely affected; he is practically excluded from the judicial profession, from a military career, and from official employment. . . .
>
> Even when they are rich, the Jews constitute, at least in eastern Europe, a category of persons who are excluded from the social advantages which the prevailing political, economic, and intellectual system ensures for the corresponding portion of the Gentile population: Society in the narrower sense of the term is distrustful of them, and public opinion is unfavourable to them.[5]

The links of Jews to the left in Europe affected the political behavior of those who emigrated to America. Although the issue of Jewish emancipation, civil and social rights, did not concern American politics (and in any case, it was difficult to assign left-right labels to the two major U.S. parties in the second half of the nineteenth century which corresponded to the European divisions), the general ideological commitment of many Jews led them to support efforts to form leftist Socialist and Anarchist movements.

The small Socialist-Anarchist groups apart, Jews found it extremely difficult to respond in group self-interest or value terms to the American party system. Those attracted to the Abolitionist and civil-rights causes were faced with the fact that the Republican party, both before and after the Civil War, had strong ties to anti-immigrant nativism, that most Know-Nothings of the 1850's had become Republicans, including many top leaders of the party. The appeal to Jews by various agrarian elements and social reformers who sought

[5] Robert Michels, *Political Parties* (New York: Hearst's International Library, 1915), pp. 260–261.

to create anti-System "left-wing" third parties was limited, since many of these (from the Independent parties of the 1870's to the Populists of the 1890's) included among their spokesmen, leaders and writers who emphasized the exploitative role of the Rothschilds and other international Jewish bankers. Although some serious students of Populism report little or no anti-Semitism in the local publications of the movement in the Midwest, there can be no doubt that the party welcomed into its ranks many who focused on the Jews, who produced an American version of "the socialism of fools."

The nomination of William Jennings Bryan for President in 1896 by both the Democratic and Populist parties in opposition to William McKinley, the pro-industry candidate of the Republicans, seemingly gave a left-right dimension to the two-party system, one which might have affected the political orientation of left-disposed Jewish recent immigrants. Yet Edward Flower, who has studied that election, reports strong streaks of anti-Semitism in the Populist and Free Silver elements who provided a considerable part of Bryan's campaign organization. An Associated Press dispatch from St. Louis at a time when both the Populist and Free Silver conventions were meeting is particularly noteworthy on this point:

> One of the striking things about the Populist Convention, or rather the two conventions here and those attending them, is the extraordinary hatred of the Jewish race. It is not possible to go into any hotel in the city without hearing the most bitter denunciation of the Jews as a class and of the particular Jews who happen to have prospered in the world.[6]

Flower's examination of American Jewish publications of the day indicates considerable concern about the presence of anti-Semitism in the Bryan 1896 campaign generally, and among the Populists in particular. There were a number of references in these papers to anti-Semitic speeches by Populist and Democratic leaders. Mrs. Mary Lease, a prominent spokesman of Kansas Populism, toured the country speaking

[6] Edward Flower, "Anti-Semitism in the Free Silver and Populist Movements and the Election of 1896" (Columbia University History Department Master's Thesis, 1952), p. 27. The original quote is from the *New York Sun,* 23 July 1896, p. 2.

for Bryan in a manifestly anti-Semitic vein. After the election, Jewish Democratic politicians complained that Bryan had lost many Jewish votes because of the gibes of Populist orators.

The peculiar appeal of anti-Semitic beliefs which emphasized the negative role of Jewish wealth and banking among "left-wing" agrarians continued through the 1920's. Thus Tom Watson, the most prominent leader of southern Populism, who had opposed the coalition with the Democrats in 1896, and who tried to revive the party by running for President in 1904 and 1908, had become a flaming bigot by the second decade of the century. *Watson's Magazine* strongly attacked Negroes, Catholics, Jews, and Wall Street, and supported revolutionary left-wing movements abroad. He practically organized the lynching of Leo Frank, a wealthy Atlanta Jew, who had been accused of murdering "a working-class Gentile" girl; and he supported the Czarist government's charges that Mendel Beiliss had engaged in a ritual murder of a small Christian boy. The revived Ku Klux Klan was formed in 1915 by members of the Knights of Mary Phagen, an organization formed under Tom Watson's sponsorship to make sure that Leo Frank died for Mary Phagen's murder.

Yet Watson opposed America's participation in World War I as subservience to "our Blood-gorged Capitalists." He strongly defended Eugene V. Debs, the Socialist leader, for his opposition to the war. Elected to the Senate in 1920, he attacked the oil companies and the U.S. Steel Corporation, praised the Soviet Union and demanded that the U.S. recognize it. Professor C. Vann Woodward's description of reactions to his death in 1922, illustrates the confusion that attends any effort to line up a consistent appeal of a rational democratic left:

> Eugene Debs, recently released from the penitentiary, wrote in a letter to Mrs. Watson: "He was a great man, a heroic soul who fought the power of evil his whole life long in the interest of the common people, and they loved and honored him. . . ."
> Most conspicuous among the floral tributes [at his funeral] was a cross of roses eight feet high, sent by the Ku Klux Klan.[7]

[7] C. Vann Woodward, *Tom Watson: Agrarian Rebel* (New York: Oxford University Press, 1963), p. 486.

During the 1920's the most prominent advocate of anti-Semitic sentiments in America was Henry Ford. His weekly newspaper, *The Dearborn Independent,* distributed by the hundreds of thousands, denounced the Jews for everything evil under the sun, from Communism to short skirts, from bootlegging liquor to fomenting strikes, from control of Wall Street to control of the labor movement, from corrupting baseball to deliberate murder. But Ford and his paper also attacked non-Jewish international bankers, Wall Street, and the monopolies. And when dissatisfaction with conservative control of both major parties resulted in a movement in the early 1920's to create a third Progressive party, Henry Ford was boomed for the nomination. A poll conducted by *Collier's* magazine, in 1923, reported that over a third of those queried were for Ford. Senator Robert La Follette, who was himself to be the presidential nominee of the Progressive and Socialist parties in the 1924 election, declared in the summer of 1923 that "Ford had great strength among the Progressives." A student of the Progressive campaign, Gordon Davidson, reports that

> a group of Progressives, Farmer-Laborites, Independents, and Liberals from fifteen states met in Omaha on November 21 [1923] at the request of Roy M. Harrop, national temporary chairman of the Progressive Party. They passed a resolution endorsing Ford for President on a ticket to be known as the People's Progressive Party. . . .[8]

Ford, fortunately, was unwilling to run. The willingness of many of the leaders of what was then the largest left tendency in the United States to support Ford in spite of his vitriolic anti-Semitism illustrates again the extent to which segments of the left have been willing to accept anti-Semitism as a foolish but potentially progressive version of anti-elitism or anti-capitalism.

[8] Gordon W. Davidson, "Henry Ford: The Formation and Course of a Public Figure" (Columbia University History Department, Ph.D. Thesis, 1966), p. 286. For a detailed discussion of the Ford campaign and his anti-Semitic activities, see Lipset and Raab, *op. cit.,* chapter 4.

LIBERALS AND RADICALS

It is hard to generalize about the predominant political location of the mass of American Jews before 1928, although it appears true that East European Jews contributed heavily to the membership and support of the small Socialist and Communist parties. The identification of Jews with progressive and underdog causes as well as their opposition to Prohibition probably led the vast majority of them to back Al Smith for President in 1928. And from the 1930's on, American Jews not only were linked disproportionately to the radical left, they also in the large increasingly identified with Franklin Roosevelt and his New Deal.

The events of the years 1930–1945 clearly served to intensify the ties in many countries between Jews and the parties of the left, both moderate like the Democrats or Social Democrats, or extreme like the Communists. For portions of this period (especially 1936–1939 and 1941–1945), the Communists and the Soviet Union had a special appeal as seemingly the boldest and most prominent organizers of the anti-Nazi struggle.

This success of the Communists among American Jews occurred in spite of the fact that the most flagrant examples of "leftist" willingness to collaborate with anti-Semites who also espoused a version of "socialism" were the relations between Communists and Nazis in 1931–1932, and again in 1939–1941. During the first period, the German Communist party joined on occasion with the German National Socialist Workers Party (*N.S.D.A.P.*) in sponsoring strikes and a referendum which brought down the Social Democratic government in Prussia. This latter event ended the police action against the street terrorism of both extremist parties. During the second period, Molotov actually sent official fraternal greetings from the Soviet Communist Party to the German Nazis saluting their mutual interests. The French Communist Party applied to the Nazi occupation authorities for permission to publish the party organ *L'Humanité* (and to function in the occupied zone) on the grounds that the C.P.'s main concern was the defeat of the Allied imperialist forces. Although many quit the party in Western countries, these events (including co-operation of Stalin's Russia with Hitler's Germany in invading Poland in 1939) did not destroy the hard core of the party, nor did it prevent many Jews from remaining members or fellow-travelers in the U.S., Britain, Canada, and elsewhere.

Co-operation with the worst anti-Semites in history did not prove sufficient to alienate revolutionary leftists, Jews and Gentiles, from the Communist movement.

The heavy dependence of many liberal and leftist parties on Jews as leaders, financial backers, and as a mass base has concomitantly pressed such groups to react to Zionism more strongly than might have been anticipated given its limited size and scope. The moderate liberal-left in America and Europe, the Democrats, Liberals, and Social Democrats, have tended to be strong supporters of Zionism, accepting it as an appropriate response to the plight of Jews in "other" countries who suffered from persecution. Jewish moderates who adhered to such parties have tended on the whole to be less alienated from a Jewish identification than those supporting the extreme left, and, therefore, more likely to be willing to identify openly with Jewish causes.

The Marxist left also reacted to Zionism more strongly than its status as a movement would appear to have warranted. Its reaction tended to be one of total opposition. From its general ideological position, the Marxist left considered Zionism a "bourgeois philosophy," an outmoded expression of nationalism which had to be opposed by socialist internationalists. The East European left had opposed Zionism in part because in the Czarist Empire (in Poland, the Ukraine, Russia and Rumania, where there were very large, impoverished Jewish populations who were denied legal, political and social rights), Jews were an important source of mass support for the various left-wing oppositionist movements. For the East European left, therefore, Zionism became a major rival political tendency competing for the support of the Jewish masses. The Jewish radicals, Socialists, Anarchists, and Bolsheviks, saw Zionism, quite naturally, as a political opponent, and strongly opposed it. Much of the opposition of the Soviet

Communist Party to Zionism, after 1917, flowed from the earlier antagonism of the Jewish-Socialist *Bund* and other Jewish radical leftists to Zionism. Another source of the Jewish radicals' bitterness to Zionism derived from the fact that participation in the Socialist and Communist world meant, for many Jews, a way of escaping their Judaism, a way of *assimilating* into a universalistic non-Jewish world.

The extent to which Jewish radicals, left-wing Socialists and Communists, turn out to be much more anti-Zionist than the non-Jewish radicals has been striking, and it is worthy of special comment. The non-Jewish radicals could look upon Zionism as simply another movement, another opposition tendency, but one among the many movements to which they were opposed. The Jewish radicals, both European and American, had to resist Zionism much more strongly since many of them felt both tied to it in some ways, and also experienced the need to disassociate themselves from anything which smacked of their hated inferiority status as Jews. They argued in classic left terms that the solution to anti-Semitism lay in Jewish assimilation in a Socialist society, where presumably all forms of nationalistic particularism would disappear.

THE STATE OF ISRAEL

Whatever divisions existed about alternatives to European anti-Semitism faded during World War II, under the impact of the holocaust. Six million Jews were murdered. By 1948 and the creation of the State of Israel, there was, for a very short, very unique period, almost complete unanimity about the value of creating a Jewish state. The justifications which produced this unanimity varied greatly, but clearly the holocaust settled the argument advanced by many Socialists, that Jews should not emigrate to Palestine, that they should "remain and fight to create socialism at home." No one could really argue any longer that Jews should stay on in lands in which almost all of their brethren had been decimated.

The Soviet Union found it in its interest to support the creation of the State of Israel, which meant that the international Communist movement also gave enthusiastic support to the emergence of the State. This period, of course, lasted for only a moment as far as world history is concerned; shortly thereafter, Stalin's paranoia focusing on the Jews as "foreign agents," gave birth to a new wave of Soviet anti-Semitism, in the Doctor's Plot in the U.S.S.R., in the various treason trials in Rumania and Czechoslovakia, and in the trials of economic speculators, as well as in the repression of various Jewish rights in the Soviet Union. It has been suggested that the creation of Israel, itself, contributed to the revival of anti-Semitism in the Soviet Union—because of the clear evidence that the Jews of the Soviet Union (and other Eastern European countries) were as positively and enthusiastically impressed and gratified by the creation of the State of Israel as Jews in the West or anywhere else. Russian Jews exhibited their strong support for Israel publicly in many ways. When Golda Meir went to Moscow as the first Israeli ambassador, she was greeted by tens of thousands of Moscow Jews. There were scores of comparable incidents which showed the passion of Russian Jews for Israel. Such behavior was viewed as evidence of disloyalty by Stalin, for it suggested that the Jews did not have a total commitment to the Soviet Union. Some Russian experts have pointed to Stalin's long-time personal history of anti-Semitic sentiments and behavior. But whatever the source of Stalin's revival of anti-Semitism, the fact is that the Soviet Union quickly turned from a supporter to an enemy of Israel, a role which it has maintained under all of Stalin's successors. Governmental support for anti-Semitism within the Soviet Union and the rest of Eastern Europe had had its ups and downs, its ebbs and flows, but it has never been totally repudiated, and has continued to exist.[9]

The persistent Russian opposition to Israel, of course, has affected a part of the left, that still considerable section which sympathizes with the Soviet Union. China and its followers

[9] See William Korey, "The Legal Position at the Jewish Community of the Soviet Union," in Erich Goldhagen, ed., *Ethnic Minorities in the Soviet Union* (New York: Praeger, 1968), pp. 316–350; Moshe Decter, "Soviet Jewry: A Current Survey," *Congress* (December 5, 1966), pp. 6–40; Zygmunt Bauman, "The End of Polish Jewry—a Sociological Review," *Bulletin on Soviet and East European Jewish Affairs*, No. 3 (January 1969), pp. 3–8.

in the Communist world have been even more vitriolically anti-Israeli, although Israel was one of the first countries to recognize Communist China. Technically Israel still recognizes it, although Communist China has never "recognized" Israel. (In the United States, those organizations which by their own description are pro-Maoist Communists include both wings of SDS, the "right-wing" Revolutionary Youth Movement and the "left-wing" Worker-Student Alliance, the Progressive Labor party, and the Black Panther party. Most recently, however, the latter has shifted somewhat, identifying with the North Korean wing of Communism.) The emergence of the anti-imperialist Third World bloc, a non-aligned group of countries mainly in Asia and Africa, also has affected the relations of the left to Israel, since much of the Arab world joined with various other new nations, to form this non-aligned group.

The Arabs successfully demanded that Israel be excluded from this camp, even though Israel made some initial gestures to establish its role as "an Asian state" that was part of the Afro-Asian world. The Arabs, however, had a lot more votes in the UN, more political power, and that part of the Afro-Asian world which though not directly a part of the Communist world had strong ideological links to it (*e.g.* Indonesia, Guinée, Mali, and Tanzania) pressed for the rejection of Israel. Israel has never been able to become part of the Afro-Asian world, although it has succeeded in establishing strong links with many countries in black Africa. The leaders of the Afro-Asian group of nonaligned countries have defined themselves as strongly in opposition to the Western imperialist countries, among whom they place Israel. The Arabs have continued, with greater or lesser success (depending on the part of the world they address), to argue that their conflict with Israel is essentially a continuation of the anti-colonial struggle with imperialist powers, that Israel is essentially a satellite of the United States—of the European-American World—thrust into the Afro-Asian border areas, and therefore, that it has to be eliminated.

This image of Israel inevitably has had a great deal of influence. Its acceptance is, of course, not just a propaganda success, but reflects a degree of validity. Clearly in the context of having been rejected by the Soviet Union and China, of not being welcomed by the Afro-Asian alliance-countries, and of being strongly dependent on financial support from American Jewry and political support from Washington, Israel has had no alternative but to maintain strong links with the United States and Western Europe. Realistically, whatever the sources of its original international position, Israel had to become part of "the American alliance"—of the grouping of states which emerged around the United States.

In spite of the opposition of China, the Soviet Union, and many Afro-Asian states to Israel, much of the left retained a strong sense of identification with Israel until the Six-Day War. The existence of a large viable co-operative movement and economy in the form of the Histadruth and the *kibbutzim* . . . the fact that all Israeli governments have been dominated by Socialist parties—the strong enthusiasms for Israel and its institutions voiced by the highly influential group of left-oriented Jewish intellectuals, and the strong sense of guilt felt by many for their ineffective response to the Nazi holocaust . . . all served to maintain Israel's credit within the liberal-left movement (including almost all Socialist parties in developed countries, and many Communist ones as well).

The Six-Day War, however, had a decisive effect in changing the reaction of the left to Israel because (and I think this is also true with respect to much of the Christian world) Israel by its quick victory ceased being an underdog nation. Leftist values, as well as religious sentiments (particularly Christian ones), tend to make common cause with underdogs against the more powerful. Many seem to believe that anybody who looks underprivileged and poor must be right, and should receive moral support. Jews and Israel were long regarded as the underdog, as victims . . . an image reinforced by their treatment by the Germans in the last war, by the Communist world's massive opposition to Israel, by its being surrounded by a hundred million Arabs. But from this perspective, the Israeli victory in June of 1967 was much too good, much too quick, to maintain sympathies and solidarities. The Arabs became the underdog for many on the left as well as throughout Christendom. Israel is now held to be a strong and rich nation, while the Arabs are weak, underdeveloped, poor. Anybody defined as an underdog is good, anybody seen as powerful is bad. This sentiment has affected and continues to affect the images of Israel and the Arab world. The only way Israel can change it is to lose.

THE NEW LEFT

The most important political event affecting Israel in Western politics in recent years has been the rise of the New Left. Without going into the reasons for its emergence, there is no question that the New Left movement has been significant. Though it arose mainly as a campus phenomenon, it has also affected the older world of left intellectuals. New Left ideology originally was new or different from that of the Old Left in the sense that it opposed *all* powers, by announcing its hostility to "all Establishments" including some of the Communist world, particularly that of the Russians, and to some extent (it varies from country to country) that of the Chinese as well. Unlike earlier Western student groups, the movement was unaffiliated to the major adult left-wing parties. Basically it lacked a clear-cut, positive program as to what it wanted, how to achieve power, how to change society "fundamentally." Increasingly, however, its need to find a defensible ideological position led it into an association with dissident forms of communism, mainly Maoist. At the 1969 convention of SDS, the most important New Left group in the United States, all major factional tendencies proclaimed themselves as Marxist-Leninist pro-Maoist Communists. They even used quotes from Stalin (who is still viewed positively by the Maoists) against each other in debate. The weekly New Left newspaper, *The Guardian,* concluded in its editorial on the convention:

> The new left as it has been known during this decade disappeared during the Chicago SDS convention. It is being replaced by Marxism-Leninism. (July 15, 1969, p. 12).

The New Left, particularly since June 1967, has identified Israel with the American Establishment. This view has been affected by the relationship of Jews and Negroes in the

United States, the growth of black nationalism, and the links of certain radical Negro groups with the Arab world. This Negro view of the Arab-Israeli conflict is related to the growing tension between a section of the black militant leadership and some Jews. The conflict is largely a result of American events, and there is not very much Israel can do about it. Even though various black leaders in this country (*viz.,* Stokely Carmichael, Eldridge Cleaver, and others) have become overtly pro-Arab, I do not think this derives from a serious view of the Arabs as "oppressed peoples," or even a conception of *Black* (Arabs) *v. White* (Jews), which sometimes seems to be implied in black nationalist literature.

The split between the Jews and the Negroes, which has affected attitudes toward Israel, stems much more from the American situation than the Middle East conflict. Ironically enough, part of the tension stems from the fact that Jews have been so involved in civil rights. The integrationist movement was largely an alliance between Negroes and Jews (who, to a considerable extent, actually dominated it). Many of the inter-racial civil rights organizations have been led and financed by whites, and the majority of their white members have been Jews. Insofar as a Negro effort emerged to break loose from involvement with whites, from domination of the civil rights struggle by white liberals, this meant concretely a break with Jews, for they were the whites who were active in these movements. The black nationalist leadership had to push whites (Jews) "out of the way," and to stop white (Jewish) "interference" in order to get whites (Jews) "off their backs."

Perhaps more important than the struggle within the civil-rights movement has been the conflict inherent in the historical fact that most Negro ghettos in the North were formerly Jewish ghettos. Negroes moved into Jewish areas such as Harlem, Bedford-Stuyvesant, Roxbury, Watts, as well as Jewish districts in Washington, Chicago, Philadelphia and many other cities. The reasons for this pattern of ethnic succession attest to positive aspects in Jewish racial attitudes—they were less resistant to Negroes moving into their neighborhoods, they reacted much less violently, than other white communities. This process meant, however, that though Jews eventually moved out as residents, some of them remained as land-lords and store-owners. Hence many Negroes came to see Jews not as neighbors, but in the role of economic oppressors. Reinforcing these consequences of ecological succession has been the effects of the fact that during the 1930's, large numbers of able Jews found that the only place they could secure employment was in government service, as teachers, social workers, or other professionals. Thirty years later, many of these same Jews (now in their fifties and sixties) are at the summits of the civil service hierarchy as school princi-pals, division heads, etc. And as Negroes follow the Jews into the civil service, they find that the directors of units operating in Negro areas are often Jews. The request that "blacks be given top jobs" in such organizations often has become a demand that Jews be removed from positions which they obtained through merit and seniority.

These economic relationships which have helped produce the tension between Negroes and Jews have had their obvious effect on the white New Left (which is itself disproportion-ately Jewish). It is told by the black nationalists: "We don't want whites, but we particularly don't want Jews, and we are expressing antagonism to Jews in the form of opposition to Israel." They attack Israel and Zionism as an expedient way of voicing their anti-Semitism. In essence, therefore, the at-tack on Israel on the part of some sections of the Negro com-munity reflects tensions in the local American scene, not in the Middle East.[10]

I should stress, however, that the large majority of the Negro community, even the majority of those active in vari-ous black militant organizations, are *not* anti-Semitic or anti-Israel. The data available from various public-opinion polls

[10] It is particularly ironic that much of black Africa has a strong antipathy to the Arab world. The Arabs are the historic slavers of Af-rica; a small African slave trade which arranges the shipment of blacks to portions of Arabia to serve white masters *still* exists. In addition, there are two "hot wars" between Arabs and African blacks in the Sudan and the Chad. In the Sudan, the dominant Arabs in the north are fighting black Christian and animist rebels who seek equal political rights. In the Chad, the formerly dominant and more advantaged Arabs of the north are the rebels seeking to overthrow the government of the animist and Christian Africans who are the majority of the country. I have seen no evidence that any American black organization has de-voted the slightest attention to the civil wars in the Sudan and the Chad.

show that the level of anti-Semitic feeling in the Negro community is no greater than it is in the white community, that it remains relatively low in both. The existence of "black anti-Semitism" is being highlighted because of the expression of anti-Semitic sentiments by the most militant and radical leaders and organizations; and it is they who get the most publicity from the white-controlled mass media. These sentiments should not be ignored, however, since they are growing among younger black spokesmen, who are unaware of the close ties between Jews and Negroes in the past. They also have an impact far exceeding their importance within Negro public opinion among those sections of the white population, whose guilt feelings about being white, or desire to use the Negro to build a mass radical movement, lead them to follow the political path of the most militant black leaders. As one SDS leader has described the process: "S.D.S. has consistently supported the political viewpoints and actions of the most militant segments of the black movement and has consciously shaped its own analysis and program in response to those elements as they have evolved during the sixties from Malcolm X to SNCC to the Black Panther Party."[11] Thus, the anti-Semitism, "the socialism of fools," occasionally voiced by groups such as the Black Panthers, SNCC (now the Student National Coordinating Committee) and other black militant ones have had a considerable impact on their white fellow-travelers inside SDS and other sections of the Left.[12] The earlier Marxist attacks on anti-Jewish appeals have been forgotten, and the contemporary New Left has been condemned to repeat the foolishness.

[11] Michael Kazin, "Some Notes on S.D.S.," *The American Scholar* (Autumn 1969), p. 650.

[12] For example, *Black Panther,* the weekly organ of the *Black Panther* party, published an article by Field Marshall, D.C., "Zionism (Kosher Nationalism) + Imperialism = Fascism" in its issue of August 30, 1969, in which Zionism is described several times as "Kosher nationalism" and as a variety of "fascism." The article refers to the "Fascist Zionist pigs." The *SNCC Newsletter* of June–July 1967 contained a two-page center spread on "The Palestine Problem," which among other statements asked its readers whether they knew, "THAT the famous European Jews, the Rothschilds, who have long controlled the wealth of many European nations, were involved in the original conspiracy with the British to create the 'State of Israel' and are still among Israel's chief supporters? THAT THE ROTHSCHILDS ALSO CONTROL MUCH OF AFRICA'S MINERAL WEALTH?" (emphasis in original).

The task of analyzing the impact of the New Left on Israel's position is further complicated by the fact that Jews play a very great role in the student-based New Left, considerably disproportionate to the number of Jewish students on campus. This is not only true of students; it is also characteristic of the older left community as well. Many of these Jewish leftists exhibit familiar forms of Jewish self-hatred, of so-called "Jewish anti-Semitism," of the sort which were widespread within the left before the Nazi holocaust and the creation of the State of Israel. Self-hatred is becoming a major problem for the American Jewish community. There is a real need for some serious analysis of the sources of Jewish anti-Semitism. It is not an inconsiderable phenomenon, and one of the forms it takes among Jewish youth is the denunciation of their parents as "hypocrites" (a criticism which attests to the fact that their values are not terribly different from those of their families, otherwise why accuse them of hypocrisy?).

Various studies of American student militants in the late 1960's indicated that the left activists tend to come from liberal-left families, disproportionately Jewish. Basically there is continuity in family ideology, rather than a break. To see the New Leftist students (in Kenneth Keniston's phrase) as "Red Diaper Babies" is not an exaggerated image. Many of them come from families which around the breakfast table, day after day, in Scarsdale, Newton, Great Neck, and Beverly Hills have discussed what an awful, corrupt, immoral undemocratic, racist society the United States is. Many Jewish parents live in the lily-white suburbs, go to Miami Beach in the winter, belong to expensive country clubs, arrange Bar Mitzvahs costing thousands of dollars—all the while espousing a left-liberal ideology. This is their hypocrisy, and it is indeed the contradiction which their children are rebelling against. Many Jewish parents, unlike Gentile parents of equivalent high economic class background, live a schizophrenic existence. They sustain a high degree of tension between their ideology and their life style.

Some years ago, Nathan Glazer, Herbert Hyman, and I did a study of Jewish behavior and attitudes, through secondary analyses of various public opinion studies that had been gathered in New York and other places. We isolated large samples of Jews and discovered, among other things, that at the same middle-class income-level, 40 to 60 per cent of the Jews had part-time servants, as against 5–10 per cent of the Protestants. People outside the South who had a full-time servant were preponderantly Jewish.[13] Relatively fewer Christians had one. We found a pattern, a style of social life, of relative asceticism among middle- and upper-middle-class Protestants which did not exist among Jews on an equivalent income level. But, though affluent Jews lived well, spent considerable sums on housing, vacations, servants, costly cars, they also as a group continued to maintain a relatively liberal-left view of the world. This "left-wing" outlook and "right-wing" style has created grievous tension between parents and children.

Young Jews take seriously the leftist ideologies they imbibed at home, particularly when they move to the liberal campus environment. They see American Jewish life as essentially immoral and hypocritical, and not a few of them extend this view to Israel's relations with Arabs. Israel, in effect, seems to be behaving like their parents. Israel itself does not really interest them. They are essentially reacting to American Jewish conditions and to the American way of life. But the very significance and the quantitative importance of the Jews within the American left—and even within parts of the European left—mean that Jews are beginning to take the lead in an attack on Israel and on Jewish customs. This fact serves to alleviate any senses of guilt or tension about anti-Semitism which non-Jewish leftists might have.

THE BREAKING POINT

What is being done about this? One thing which presumably might have some positive effect on the left's attitude toward Israel is a revival of the image of Israel as a center of social experimentation. The *kibbutz* still remains the only

---

[13] Since these servants are almost invariably Negro, this fact reinforces the image in the black community of the Jew as an economic exploiter.

viable example of a decentralized anarchist-socialist society. Those who want to see "participatory democracy" in action, the workers actually running their institutions, can point to nothing as successful as the *kibbutz*. Here it must be acknowledged that Israel and its public relations may be more at fault than the New Left youth for their ignorance on these matters. In the past decade, Israel has done little to establish itself as an example of social reform, of institutional experimentation. In its efforts to secure investments and contributions from wealthy Americans, it has placed more emphasis on creating an image of Israel as a successful, free-enterprise "boot-strap" operation, a sort of small mini-scale Japan. But in selling itself thus to the business community, it may well have contributed to weakening a major portion of its political base.

Yet in this connection it may be useful to examine the contents of a recent book, *Obsolete Communism,* by Daniel and Gabriel Cohn-Bendit. "Danny the Red" was one of the major leaders of the French student revolt of May 1968, and the Cohn-Bendit brothers emerge in this book as Anarchists. As a positive example of anarchism in action, they point to the Makhno movement in Russia of 1918 to 1921, which dominated a large area of the Ukraine. Yet though they discuss politics in many countries they do not say a word about Israel or the *kibbutzim.* Evidently they are not "relevant" to the proposals for new anarchist forms of society. This, surely, is not a result of ignorance, since some years ago Danny Cohn-Bendit spent several months in Israel, mainly on a *kibbutz,* and even considered settling there. He tries to make a case for anarchist institutions, but does not even mention the one country where concrete examples of such institutions exist. He also fails to mention the fact that there were Al Fatah Arab terrorist booths in the Sorbonne during the 1968 student sit-ins, and that the New Left anarchist as well as the Marxist Leninist groups supported them. Danny Cohn-Bendit, who admires the anarchist Makhno but does not know the Israeli *kibbutzim,* is not an atypical Jewish boy. We will be seeing many more like him.

Older left-wing critics of Israel such as I. F. Stone and Professor Noam Chomsky also cannot be accused of ignorance concerning the Israeli Socialist movement or its radical institutions. Both men who now write harshly about Israel have visited the country on a number of occasions, and are personally well acquainted with the Israeli left, the Histadruth and the *kibbutzim*. Like Daniel Cohn-Bendit, Chomsky considered settling in Israel, and also appears to have strong anti-Communist anarchist sympathies. But Stone, Chomsky, and Cohn-Bendit are today committed supporters of the international revolutionary left. And that left currently defines the Al Fatah terrorists as "left-wing guerrillas," and Israel as "a collaborator with imperialism," if not worse. One doubts whether even the most sophisticated presentation of Israel's case could ever regain their support.

The moderate left, of course, can still find a basis for strongly supporting Israel, since it is concerned with the preservation and extension of political democracy. The case for Israel in these terms has been strongly put by a new group, the Youth Committee for Peace and Democracy in the Middle East, organized by members of the Young People's Socialist League, but including a wide range of youth leaders, such as James Blake, the Vice-President for Youth Affairs of the NAACP, Spencer Oliver, president of the Young Democrats, Joe Burke, the Civic Action Director of the Catholic Youth Organization, and others. Their statement points out:

> Whatever its shortcomings, Israel is a democratic country. The governments of her Arab opponents, by contrast, are all to one degree or another staunchly authoritarian. Iraq, Syria, and Egypt are one-party states, in which all political rights have been suppressed. The same is true of the Kingdom of Jordan and the anachronistic sultanate of Saudi Arabia. The press in these countries is rigorously controlled. So are the courts. . . .[14]

In fairness, I should note that the various wings of the far left, while all anti-Israel, are not united in their estimate of Al Fatah, or the positive worth of Arab terrorism. The Russians and their followers in the Communist movement exhibit some opposition to terroristic and guerrilla tactics by Arab groups. In the March 1969 issue of *Dokumentation der Zeit*,

[14] See "Student Group Formed on Middle East," and "Youth on Middle East," *New America* (September 29, 1969), p. 12.

a magazine published by the East German Institute for Contemporary History, the Al Fatah was described as a group whose student founders were inspired by "the reactionary terrorists of the Moslem Brethren," and who now secure most of their funds and supplies from "the Arab oil states of Kuweit and Saudi Arabia." The article argues:

> The slogans and general tendency of *Al Fatah* represent the most extreme elements of the resistance movement. By strictly prohibiting any political and ideological activity of its members, *Al Fatah* is preventing the necessary process of ideological clarification among the resistance organisations and trying to pin the movement down to a rigid extremist line, which in the last resort, amounts to nothing but a reinforcement of imperialism through a policy of Left adventures.

The considerable support which the intellectual left once gave to Israel is gone, and it is not likely to be revived, certainly not on the same basis.[15] Israel must expect to be criticized by the extreme left for the foreseeable future. Since left intellectuals have been, and continue to be important in forming public opinion, this is obviously a major loss to Israel's public position. It is also important to recognize that, short of another war, the almost unanimous support that Israel has received from the Jewish community will not continue. The division (partly age-linked and partly ideological) between younger and older Jews, and between left-groups and Jewish-identified groups, will continue to affect attitudes to Israel. The Jewish community in America, particularly, is likely to become much more polarized politically than it has been for a long time. We are going to see an upsurge of large numbers of overtly conservative Jews. A kind of backlash is occurring among Jews who remain more identified with Israel and Zionism—or with the Synagogue—as a reaction to the attacks on Jews and Israel coming from the left and the black nationalists.

[15] Ironically, the reverse process appears to have occurred in the Communist countries of Eastern Europe. There, Israel has become a symbol among protesting students and intellectuals of a free small power which has stood up to powerful bullies (backed by the Soviet Union). To support Israel in Poland, Russia, etc., is a way of voicing opposition to the anti-Semitic policies of their Communist governments.

But if Israel has lost support on the left, it has gained among groups not previously known for their sympathy for Jewish causes. Those aspects of Israel's foreign and military policies which alienate left-wing sympathy attract rightist support. Many non-Jewish conservatives see in Israel's successful military resistance to the Arab world, and its defiance of United Nations resolutions, an example of the way in which a nation which has self-pride—and which is not "corrupted by the virus of internationalism and pacifism"—can defend its national self-interests. Some see in the Israeli defeat of the Arabs, the one example of an American ally which has decisively defeated Communist allies in battle. Thus, Israel and its supporters find themselves with friends on the right, and enemies on the left.

Although many archconservatives (*e.g.,* Barry Goldwater and some of the contributors to William Buckley's magazine, *The National Review*) are now strongly pro-Israel, the extremist right, like the extremist left, remains very hostile, an attitude linked to their continued anti-Semitism. Thus, *The Thunderbolt,* the organ of the racist National States Rights party, stated in April that it supports "a strong Arab stand against the brutal aggression of Israel." Gerald L. K. Smith's *Cross and the Flag,* repeatedly condemns Israel for crimes against the Arabs. The Italian neo-Fascists strongly back the Al Fatah and (like the New Left), reprint much of its propaganda. The fascist magazine *La Nation Européenne* also supports Al Fatah and advertises its publications. The German National Democrats, in their paper, *Deutsche National Zeitung,* take a similar pro-Arab terrorist line. I do not think it would be unfair to say that the revolutionary fascist right and the revolutionary communist left have similar positions with respect to Middle East conflict and the role of Al Fatah. But it should be stressed the opposition of the left extremists is by far more powerful than that of the fascists, who have little influence.

The pattern of increased support for Israel among the democratic conservative or rightist groups has been paralleled on the American home front with respect to domestic issues. Those Jews who are concerned with the adverse consequences of Negro militancy on areas of Jewish concern (*e.g.,* the preservation of the merit system in civil service employment and standards of admission to university, the rights of Jewish businessmen in the ghetto) find more support from conservatives than from liberals. Conservatives eager to gain Jewish support have made overtures to the Jewish groups. Recent local elections indicate that the vaunted "near unanimous" commitment of Jews to liberal and Negro causes is breaking down.[16]

The separation of the Jewish population into the same constituent parts that divide the American electorate as a whole, may be testimony to the end of the almost two-century period in which the politics of Jewry has been a subtheme to the politics of the Revolution. The identification of Jewish causes with those of the left reached an all-time high point between 1930 and 1950, periods dominated internationally by the anti-Nazi struggle and the fight to create the state of Israel. Within the United States, this link was reinforced by the strong involvement of Jews with the civil-rights cause which lasted through most of the 1960's.

The rise of the New Left, the shift in the international position of Israel, and the tensions between sections of the Jewish and Negro communities, have all contributed to breaking the relations between the left and Jewry. Jews will, of course,

[16] In the 1966 referendum on the retention of a civilian police review board in New York City, Jews divided in this way: 40 per cent for keeping the board, 55 per cent for abolishing it. In the 1965 mayoralty election the Tammany candidate Beame secured 56 per cent of the Jewish vote as compared to 41 per cent for the Republican-Liberal Lindsay. In 1969, Sam Yorty running against a moderate Negro candidate, Tom Bradley, for Mayor of Los Angeles, did much better than anticipated in Jewish districts in the final election, securing 35–40 per cent of the vote. In the New York City Democratic mayoralty primary in June 1969, the Jewish Democratic vote split into three parts. Slightly less than a third went to the more conservative "law and order" candidate, Mario Procaccino; another third backed the centrist candidate, former mayor Robert Wagner; and somewhat more than a third divided among the three more "liberal" candidates, Badillo, Scheuer, and Norman Mailer.

In the November election, according to an NBC computer precinct analysis, John Lindsay, the victorious Liberal party nominee who defeated the more conservative Democratic and Republican candidates, secured 42 per cent of the Jewish vote, exactly the percentage he received among the electorate as a whole. The more affluent, younger, and irreligious Jews tended to vote for Lindsay, while the less privileged, older and more religious ones opted for his more conservative rivals.

continue to contribute in heavily disproportionate numbers to the activist left, particularly to that section which derives its main strength from the university and intellectual worlds. But they will also increasingly sustain moderate liberal and conservative politics. Israel will probably find its greatest supporters among American Jews and non-Jews in the ranks of such center groupings, and this may well make life difficult for those who seek to remain both Socialist and Zionist.

ACKNOWLEDGMENTS

Previous versions of various chapters in this book have appeared in different publications. I would like gratefully to acknowledge the permission of the original publishers to reprint these here. The chapters have appeared in the following form:

"History and Sociology: Some Methodological Considerations," in S. M. Lipset and Richard Hofstadter (eds.), *Sociology and History: Methods* (New York: Basic Books, 1968), pp. 20–58.

"Revolution and Counter-Revolution—The United States and Canada," in Thomas Ford (ed.), *The Revolutionary Theme in Contemporary America* (Lexington: University of Kentucky Press, 1965), pp. 21–64.

"Values, Education, and Entrepreneurship," in S. M. Lipset and Aldo Solari (eds.), *Elites in Latin America* (New York: Oxford University Press, 1967), pp. 3–60. Copyright © 1967 by Oxford University Press, Inc.

"The American Jewish Community in a Comparative Context," *The Jewish Journal of Sociology*, 5 (December 1963), pp. 157–166.

"Social Class," in David Sills (ed.), *International Encyclopedia of the Social Sciences* (New York: The Macmillan Company & The Free Press, 1968), XV, 296–316. Copyright © 1968 by Crowell Collier and Macmillan, Inc. Reprinted by permission of the Publisher.

"Political Sociology," in Neil Smelser (ed.), *Sociology* (New York: John Wiley, 1967), pp. 463–470.

"Political Cleavages in 'Developed' and 'Emerging' Polities," in Erik Allardt and Yrjo Littunen (eds.), *Cleavages, Ideologies and Party Systems* (Helsinki: The Westermarck Society, 1964), pp. 21–55.

"The Changing Class Structure and Contemporary European Politics," *Daedalus*, 93 (Cambridge, Mass.: American Academy of Arts and Sciences, Winter 1964), 271–303.

"Religion and Politics in American History," in Robert Lee and Martin E. Marty (eds.), *Religion and Social Conflict* (New York: Oxford University Press, 1964), pp. 69–126. Copyright © 1964 by Oxford University Press, Inc.

" 'The Socialism of Fools' The Left, the Jews and Israel," *Encounter*, 33 (December 1969), pp. 24–35.

INDEX